Pic
Naturalist
on the
Plains

The Diary of Elam Bartholomew
——————1871 to 1934——————

PIONEER
NATURALIST
ON THE
PLAINS

The Diary of Elam Bartholomew
───────── *1871 to 1934* ─────────

David M. Bartholomew

Sunflower University Press®

1531 Yuma • P. O. Box 1009 • Manhattan, Kansas 66505-1009 USA

Cover: Photo, Kansas sunflower and thistle, by Robin Higham

Mushroom illustrations courtesy of Charles L. Kramer, professor of Biology and Experiment Station Mycologist, Division of Biology, Kansas State University, Manhattan

ISBN 0-89745-221-6

Technical Editor, Ruth Ann Warren

Layout, Lori L. Daniel

Sunflower University Press is a wholly-owned subsidiary of the non-profit 501(c)3 Journal of the West, Inc.

To my grandparents — Elam and Rachel Bartholomew;

    Their children and spouses, who were my parents and uncles and aunts;

        Their grandchildren, who are my brother and cousins;

            Our children, who share the legacy.

Our heritage — their love for and devotion to

    Spiritual values

        Nature

            Farming.

Contents

Acknowledgments   ix

Preface   xi

Introduction   xv

Chapter 1   Farming in Illinois   1

Chapter 2   Homesteading   10

Chapter 3   Farming in Kansas   34

Chapter 4   Weather and Other Acts of Nature   68

Chapter 5   Personal Aspects: Earlier Life   94

Chapter 6   Personal Aspects: Later Life   134

Chapter 7   Debates   189

Chapter 8   Politics and Government Affairs   194

Chapter 9   Botanical Interests   230

Chapter 10   Religion   274

Afterword   312

Bibliography   318

Index   321

Acknowledgments

Joe Snell, Assistant State Archivist at the Kansas State Historical
    Society, now retired, who has given gracious guidance and en-
    couragement
Other personnel at the Kansas State Historical Society for cordial
    and efficient responses for archival material, especially Patricia A.
    Michaelis, Director, Library and Archives Division
Rooks County Historical Society, especially Lora Belle Sander and
    Vada Hazen
Fern H. Taylor, of the Fulton County, Illinois, Historical Society,
    who so generously provided authentic documentation of genea-
    logical data pertaining to Elam and Rachel's kinfolk in that area
Mrs. J. Sandy Tracy of Canton, Illinois, for sharing her insights of
    the area and its people
State Library of Kansas for archival material

Dundee Township Public Library of Dundee, Illinois, and Algonquin Pub-
    lic Library of Algonquin, Illinois, for so diligently securing materials
    through inter-library loan and making available a microfilm reader
Numerous current botany professionals who provided great inspiration for
    the writing of this book
Relatives, especially those still living in the area, who supplied useful doc-
    umentation
My wife, Martha, for editorial guidance, and many friends for expressions
    of encouragement in the development of this project
Dr. Charles L. "Bud" Kramer, professor of biology, *emeritus*, Kansas State
    University, for his mushroom illustrations
Dr. Robin Higham, Carol A. Williams, and Ruth Ann Warren of Sun-
    flower University Press, for their enthusiasm and professional guidance
    in making this book a reality

Preface

I N A VERY REAL SENSE, this is the *autobiography* of one man: Elam Bartholomew. He never found time to write his own because he was too busy living life to the fullest. But he did keep a diary. Relying heavily on that work, I can now tell my grandfather's story. The direct quotes from Elam's diary should help to keep the reader's attention focused on the realities of life at that time without getting caught up in the romance of nostalgia. It has been said, "The good old days used to be 'these trying times,'" a statement verified by Elam's writings.

This account tells of the way things were in the last 30 years of the 19th century and the first 34 years of the 20th century, as experienced by a man of the soil, from his 18th year until his 82nd. Chronicling the latter stages of the Industrial Revolution, the diary moves through the years when inventions now common were put into use for the

Elam Bartholomew, 1852-1934.

first time: telephone, phonograph, electricity, radio, automobile, farm tractor, airplane.

In 1871, from well-established west-central Illinois, the scene soon shifts to the frontier of western Kansas, where buffalo had roamed in huge herds just a few years earlier. Trips taken to the four corners of the nation and points in between provide much color beyond life confined strictly to the prairie.

Of course it has been necessary to condense the 5,600-page diary to a manageable size. With an entry for every day, there were many redundancies. An attempt has been made to balance those things that are exciting, stimulating, thought-provoking, and intriguing, along with the more ordinary, because that's the way life really was, and is. Taken as a whole, the diary weaves a fabric with a most interesting design. Quotations from Elam's diary have been printed in italics so that they are easily identifiable, and they appear exactly the way Elam wrote them.

Elam's diary style is typical for that late 19th-century era — prosaic, almost stoic much of the time, for men were not supposed to be too sentimental. But his emotion does come through, oftentimes emphatically, when it comes to politics and religion. When there is personal grief, journaling in his diary is a wonderfully healing outlet. Sorely lacking, though, is a show of affection for those he loves, truly a product of that late-Victorian era. After keeping a diary just a few years, Elam realized that it would not be forever private, thus he could not bring himself to display much affection where others could read it. Nevertheless, it is obvious that he was a sensitive, caring, loving person.

During the editing of this story it was decided that the most interesting style would be the identification of major themes that dominated the fabric of Elam's life. To provide continuity, each theme is followed from its beginning to its end, enabling the reader to concentrate on topics one at a time without distracting clutter from crosscurrents of other themes. What is hampered in so doing is full appreciation for the complexity of this man's life, which was lived with many themes intertwined — but even that can be comprehended, at least in part.

The original diary is preserved in the archives of the Kansas State Historical Society at Topeka, along with other documents and some photographs. In its pages researchers will find a wealth of information on diverse topics. It is especially useful because of the thorough manner in which all aspects of life are documented.

The diary has been transferred to microfilm, making it available via inter-library loan. Also available on microfilm are most of the newspapers of that era that were published in Rooks County and many other Kansas counties.

An unabridged copy of the research done in the preparation of this book has also been placed in the Kansas State Historical Society archives.

Introduction

*T*HE EARLIEST RECORD OF THE NAME *Bartholomew* appears in the gospels of Matthew, Mark, and Luke, and in the book of Acts* — Bartholomew was one of the 12 apostles. (In the gospel of John the name *Nathanael* is used.) The biblical references guaranteed not only that the name would be preserved for all time as people through the ages sought out Christian names, but also that its use would proliferate as an act of veneration of saints.

Use of the name multiplied near the end of the 16th century. On August 24, 1572, St. Bartholomew's feast day, King Charles IX of France ordered the killing of all Huguenots, the Protestant followers of John Calvin. This was not so much a religious persecution as a political one, because the king's mother, Catherine de Médicis,

---

* *Matthew 10:3; Mark 3:18; Luke 6:14; Acts 1:13*

convinced him that Huguenot leaders were going to try to overthrow him. Many thousands were massacred, but some escaped to other countries. Quite naturally refugees from persecution tend to cluster together in their new settlements. And as usually happens, the indigenous people refer to those immigrants by a common name that somehow denotes their reason for being there. In this case they were simply referred to as "the Bartholomews."

Many went to Holland, where Roman Catholics were a distinct minority. The newly arrived Protestants found a safe haven there — and also in Switzerland, England, and Germany. Their descendants eventually came to America, lured by prospects of even greater opportunities for individual expression.

Henry Bartholomew, one of these descendants, had been born in Holland (date unknown), settled in Philadelphia, and died there in 1743. Obviously he was one of those referred to as "Pennsylvania Dutch." Three generations later George E. Bartholomew was born — on November 23, 1814, in Lancaster County. He was a millwright, building and repairing mills. In 1843 he married Fanny Bowman, ten years younger. They had nine children (eight boys) who lived to maturity; the middle one was Elam.

It is interesting to notice the birth dates of these children; they are all about two years apart, except for the last one:

Amos	June 1, 1844
David	August 7, 1846; died 1864
Elias	February 17, 1848
Ann	July 27, 1850; died at seven months
Elam	June 9, 1852
John	December 11, 1854
George	February 20, 1857
Emma	July 20, 1859
Edmund	September 30, 1861
Franklin	August 9, 1866

The Civil War began in 1861 and ended in 1865. Evidently George and Fanny did not want a pregnancy when it might be necessary for him to get involved in a war in which he could be killed. When the war ended, they had one more child.

To supplement his earnings as a millwright, George also farmed, but as

George and Fanny (Bowman) Bartholomew, the parents of Elam, in 1880, just months before George died at age 66 on their new homestead in Kansas.

a renter, not a landowner. Renting allowed him to move to better opportunities. Thus in 1854 the family — which by that time included four children — moved to Licking County, Ohio, near Granville, just east of Columbus, where four more children were born. Then in 1865, at the end of the war, they moved again to Farmington, Illinois, near Peoria. There the last child was born.

Fourteen years later, after most of the children had migrated to Kansas to become landowners under the Homestead Act of 1862, George and Fanny followed, and for the first time they were no longer renters. He was

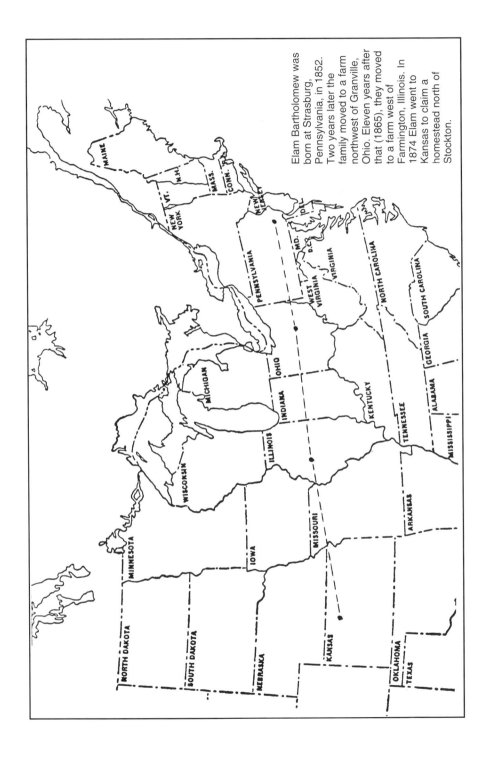

Elam Bartholomew was born at Strasburg, Pennsylvania, in 1852. Two years later the family moved to a farm northwest of Granville, Ohio. Eleven years after that (1865), they moved to a farm west of Farmington, Illinois. In 1874 Elam went to Kansas to claim a homestead north of Stockton.

65 and she 55. In fact, all the children went to Kansas except David, who died in military service in 1864, and Amos, who, after being discharged from duty in the Civil War, went back to live in Pennsylvania.

Having no property to call their own, this family of the land into which Elam was born was constantly watching for that opportunity which seemed always to exceed their grasp, until they found it in Kansas. Appropriately, the motto on the Kansas state flag and seal is *Ad Astra per Aspera*: to the stars through difficulty.

Pennsylvania . . . Ohio . . . Illinois. The climate was much the same. Soil and other agronomic factors were not that much different. One tried to avoid major shock in such moves, for adjustment was always difficult, even in the best of times.

This was the worst of times. The United States were in some instances "disuniting." The Union was splitting. Who could know where it would all end or how it would be resolved? When there is political upset of such magnitude, economic chaos is inevitable. Families were polarized. The entire social fabric was being torn apart. It was easy to become cynical about the entire scene.

What does one do who has just brought into existence a family? Maybe it is best not to be tied down by ownership of land. Renters are permitted flexibility to move out of trouble's way, and hope — yes, hope with no guarantee — that things will not be so bad in the new choice of location. But renters can seldom be choosers. They often have to make concessions. Never is this truer than in a situation of political and economic crisis, of major upheaval of the worst kind: civil war!

Elam was nine years old when the Civil War broke out. But it had been brewing for a long time — a very long time for a nine-year-old lad — all his life. He had heard plenty from conversations in his family. Two older brothers had gone off to join the Union Army. How traumatic it must have been to know there would be fighting against fellow Americans, just across the border in the next state! Or that it could go poorly for the North, with hostilities moving into the same state where you live, and maybe even into your own community — on your farm!

Life was tenuous enough without getting involved in a war of any kind, but especially with one's fellow countrymen. War was too close for comfort when one's brothers were in it and when it was raging so near. Elam would turn 13 before it was over.

His brother David had died during Sherman's march across Georgia and was buried in Georgia. He died not in battle, but of diphtheria, as did a large number of soldiers.

How does one discern vocation in such tumultuous times? The war had ended, but could peace be achieved? Anger and bitterness permeated all of life. There was still a place called "America," but how long would it be before the country could truly be described as "The United States"?

President Lincoln had been assassinated! He had been the glue that held things together, albeit ever so tenuously. So yet another major uncertainty had been added to the list that clouded a young man's future.

Despite all these issues of major consequence, and probably because of them, there was a'birthing a vibrant new era farther west in the Plains states, notably Kansas. It was the decision to admit Kansas into the Union as a slave-free state in 1861 — the 34th state — that had precipitated the declaration of war between South and North. With that issue resolved, migration commenced in much greater volume, and it increased even more rapidly when the shooting stopped in 1865.

The U.S. Cavalry began in earnest clearing out remaining Indians to make way for settlers, as is well depicted in Michael Blake's book *Dances with Wolves* and the subsequent movie. That story took place in 1863, from Fort Hays, Kansas, and northwest. Elam's older brother, Elias, went in 1868, and Elam himself in 1874, both going to Fort Hays and then north to the next county. Even then there were still some remnant buffalo and Indians.

Some contemporaries of Eli and Elam are worthy of mention. "Wild Bill" Hickok (1837-1876) had been born at Troy Grove, Illinois, 72 miles northeast of Farmington. He was a scout for the Union Army, an Indian fighter, and later a scout for Colonel George Custer. He was the U.S. marshal of Hays, Kansas, from 1869 to 1871, then the marshal of Abilene from early to mid-1871. He returned to Hays as U. S. marshal to 1872.

Wyatt Earp (1848-1929), another contemporary, had been born at Monmouth, Illinois, 36 miles west of Farmington. He, too, became a U.S. marshal, riding stagecoaches as a guard when valuable cargo was hauled. In 1869 he was a buffalo hunter on the Kansas plains with government survey teams. He was a deputy marshal in Wichita and at Dodge City, a post Bat Masterson also held.

"Buffalo Bill" Cody (1846-1917) born in Iowa, spent six years of his adolescence near Leavenworth, Kansas. In 1860 he rode for the Pony Express for several months; its origination point was St. Joseph, Missouri, just across the river. Then in 1861 he became part of the anti-slavery organization known as Jayhawks. By 1863 he was a cavalry scout in raids against the Kiowa and Commanche Indian tribes. In 1868 he was hired to kill buffalo to supply food for railroad crews aggressively building lines across Kansas; hence, he was designated "Buffalo Bill."

Carry A. Nation (1846-1911), the celebrated prohibitionist, had been born in Kentucky. Her first marriage, in 1867, soon ended when her husband died from alcoholism. Ten years later she married David Nation, a lawyer and minister, and settled in Medicine Lodge, Kansas.

Kansas had a poorly enforced prohibition law from 1880. Mrs. Nation had good reason to feel strongly about the issue. In 1890 she began a nonviolent campaign by praying in front of saloons. Obviously facing ridicule, and being unable to observe any positive results, she resorted to more active methods, wrecking saloons with stones and finally using a hatchet. After cleaning up her own town, she moved on to other Kansas locations and then to other states.

Also contemporaneous with Elam was the familiar song "Home on the Range." Dr. Brewster Higley of Smith County, Kansas, wrote the words in 1873, just one year before Elam went to make his home there, one county farther west. Dan Kelley, also of Smith County, wrote the tune. The song was originally called "Western Home":

> Oh, give me a home where the buffalo roam,
> Where the deer and the antelope play;
> Where seldom is heard a discouraging word
> And the sky is not clouded all day.
>
> Chorus:
> Home, home on the range,
> Where the deer and the antelope play,
> Where seldom is heard a discouraging word,
> And the sky is not clouded all day.
> (*Kirwin Chief* newspaper, March 21, 1874)

Though a man of the soil, Elam Bartholomew was equally at home at his desk in botanical research.

Chapter 1

Farming in Illinois

*W*HEN ELAM BARTHOLOMEW WAS 12, in March 1865, he and his family moved from a farm 5 miles northwest of Granville, Ohio, to a farm owned by John S. Green 3½ miles west and 1 mile north of Farmington, Illinois, in Fulton County, near Peoria. Five years later they moved to the Burbridge farm 2½ miles west of Farmington on the Burlington road on Littler's Creek.

1871

As the diary begins, in 1871, Elam, now 18, is engaged in digging coal from an outcropping on the farm and hauling it for sale to the plow factory in Farmington. Obviously selling coal was an economic benefit to farmers of the area, because they could turn a natural resource other than agricultural produce into cash. Moreover, the coal was useful for heating their homes and for cooking without using wood. It should be no surprise, however, that eventually that farm and many others in the area went out of existence after one or more coal mining companies strip-mined large expanses there.

After digging out and hauling numerous loads of coal from the out-cropping, it became necessary to build some supports to retain access to the coal. Regarding January 19 and 20 Elam wrote: *Worked both of these days at the coal bank in making repairs and in cutting entry and room props.*

The economic depression that followed the Civil War hit hard on farm prices. On January 9, 1871, Elam wrote: *Hauled 3 loads, 101 bu., of corn on the cob to Farmington for which we got 35¢ per bushel.*

With such low prices, expanding production became imperative. Thus in late February they began clearing a nine-acre piece of land that had a considerable growth of brushy hazel plants. First there was cutting of top-growth, followed by pulling out the stumps and roots. Then came plowing, of course with a horse-drawn walking plow. This was described on March 7: *Began today to plow the land previously cleared working thereat all day. It is a tough job as the hazel roots throw the plow out so often.* Again on the 9th and 10th: *Spent both of these days in holding the handles of the breaking plow.*

Just how primitive things were in 1871 compared with current times was illustrated again on March 25: *Worked in the a.m. in helping to haul in a load of shock corn that had been husked and thrown on the ground and several shocks of corn fodder. In the p.m. went to Farmington to mill a grist of wheat and corn.* Also on April 4 and 5: *Worked these two days at harrowing in oats which father had sown broadcast,* by hand, of course.

April 15 provides another illustration: *Worked at making rails and fixing fence,* a frequent chore, taking a lot of time in repair and replacement. Barbed wire for fencing had not yet been invented. However, not long after this date, in 1873, Joseph F. Glidden, of DeKalb County, invented barbed wire. Some years passed, though, before it was widely accepted where wood or stone was readily available without cost. Woven wire was also too expensive for many farmers when it became available.

Corn was planted by hand in check-rows: each planting (hill) was equidistant from the next in all directions, making it possible to cultivate in three directions for optimum weed control. Spacing was 42 inches, allowing horses or mules to move between rows without trampling the corn. To assure accuracy in spacing, a device called a "marker" was used.

On May 1: *Worked at plowing corn ground until 10 a.m. and the remainder of the day at running a 3-row marker, laying the ground off for planting.* It was not until later that a horse-drawn corn planter was invented that accurately dropped seeds at proper spacing.

There was no riding cultivator, at least not on this farm. On May 25 and 26: *Worked both of these days at cultivating corn with a 2-horse walking cultivator.* Harvest was also a tedious affair. On June 17: *Our crop of rye being ripe worked in the p.m. at cradling rye.* The cradle was a scythe that cut and gathered small grains in one operation, with heads still on the stalk. These were then gathered into bundles and tied. The next operation was to collect bundles and stand them into shocks or stack them while waiting for threshing. The first "Self-Binder" was not made until 1876.

Next came wheat, with neighbors helping each other. On June 26, for example: *Bound wheat in the a.m. for neighbor John Abbott and in the p.m. for neighbor Henry Hunter.*

Each farm, of course, had to be as self-sufficient as possible, having its own garden and preserving its produce for use in the months ahead. Nevertheless, some ingredients, such as vinegar, had to be purchased. On July 25: *Made a trip out 3 miles east of Farmington to the Harkness cider mill where I got 10 gallons of vinegar and came home at noon.*

The final phase of harvesting began when the threshing machine and crew arrived. There may have been only one in a neighborhood, owned by a farmer who moved it from one farm to the next until all had been serviced. On August 14: *The threshing machine having pulled in last evening worked all day at assisting in the work — my job being the carrying of grain into the granary from the nearby machine.*

On subsequent days Elam assisted several neighbors as the threshing machine and crew progressed around the area: George Day, Thomas Montgomery, and the Bumpers brothers. All three were especially close friends, and their names come up frequently in many business and social relationships.

Then came potato digging (150 bushels that year) followed by sorghum harvest, from which molasses was made. On August 24: *In the morning made an errand over to neighbor James Armstrong's and on returning worked the rest of the day at stripping, topping and cutting sorghum for the cane mill.* On the next day: *Hauled four loads of sorghum to Herron's cane mill, one mile east.* More loads followed on subsequent days.

Buckwheat was another staple of the diet, so a buckwheat crop was part of a farmer's enterprise. On September 23: *Cradled buckwheat in the a.m. and helped husk a load of corn in the p.m. In the evening went to Farmington after the mail.* Then on October 3: *Worked all day at threshing out with a flail the buckwheat and running it through a fanning mill finishing the season's crop.*

Hauling grain to market was another time-consuming project when done with a team and wagon. On September 28: *With father started to Peoria with a load of rye at 2:30 oclock a.m. and got there at 10. After selling our rye and looking over the city awhile we left for home at 2:30 p.m. and got here at 8 oclock. Distance 26 miles.*

With autumn came other tasks. On October 6: *Worked in the a.m. at husking pop corn and in the afternoon at making fence rails over north a mile on the Nelson Oldfield farm, from some timber we had recently bought.* Younger brothers provided help on October 13: *Began the fall husking and cribbing of our field corn crop working thereat all day with the help of brothers John (age 17) and George (age 14).*

1872

Getting hogs to market was no easy task when the only mode of transportation was a team and wagon, so they were driven on foot, as on January 3, 1872: *In the forenoon we drove a good bunch of our fat hogs to market at Farmington and returned at 1 p.m. spending the remainder of the day knocking about at not much of anything.* The next day he helped neighbor Andy Ferguson drive his hogs to market. Then came the butchering of hogs for home use.

Other winter-time activities included many days of hauling corn fodder from the field, storing coal at home, and taking coal to town for sale. The coal came from both the Ferguson coal bank and Hunters.

Then on January 12 Elam tried his hand at salesmanship: *Having on hand a number of the D. W. Hughes hand corn planters, on father's suggestion, I made a buggy trip east and south of Farmington several miles selling to various farmers along the route. Reached home about 5 p.m. having driven 20 miles.* On the 15th he canvassed the area north and northwest of Farmington.

A wagonload of ear corn was about 40 bushels. Occasional trips to market were made when weather and time permitted, and when some cash was needed. There were also times when a concerted effort was made, with numerous consecutive trips. February 7 was one of those times: *Took two*

Elam Bartholomew in 1873 at age 21, the year he became engaged to Rachel. One year later he went to claim a homestead in Kansas. Two years after that they were married.

Rachel Montgomery in 1872 at age 17. One year later she was engaged to Elam Bartholomew. In 1876 they were married and homesteaded in Kansas.

loads (79 bushels) of ear corn to Farmington to market. Then on the 8th to the 10th: *Brother John and I hauled, with one team, 4 loads of ear corn to Farmington to market each of these three days:*

> *On the 8th we took 165 bu.*
> *On the 9th we took 167 bu.*
> *On the 10th we took 157 bu. Total 489 Bu.*

Another winter-time chore was cutting and splitting fire wood for the cook stove — a project that consumed nearly all of two weeks in March. They would have enough to last through the summer and to get the job done before spring field work began.

As corn planting season commenced, additional sales of planters were made. On April 16: *In the p.m. made business trips to neighbors Isaac and John Leeper's. Took them each a hand corn planter.* Some were not paid for until after harvest. For example, on October 10: *Made a trip out*

Thomas (left)
and Elizabeth
(below)
(Knouse)
Montgomery,
parents of
Rachel, who
remained
on their
Farmington,
Illinois, farm
while so many
others went
West to
homestead.

Rachel Montgomery Bartholomew, 1855-1941.

Children and Grandchildren
of Elam and Rachel Bartholomew

George Edgar — Born May 1, 1877; died September 11, 1900

Elbert Thomas — Born October 18, 1878; died October 2, 1967
    Wife — Mary Lucille Keene (1888-1982)
    Martha Lucille — Born September 30, 1921
    Lois Jeanne — Born June 15, 1924

Elizabeth Fanny — Born January 3, 1881; died February 6, 1966
    Husband — Chester Ingle (died 1949)
    Chester — Born January 30, 1911

Jesse Elam — Born March 21, 1882; died December 12, 1976
    Wife — Florence Cook (1890-1975)
    Robert Daniel — Born August 16, 1926
    David Morris — Born October 12, 1928

Earl Robert — Born August 17, 1884; died December 5, 1964
    Wife — Alice Fern Hale (1894-1992)
    Elizabeth Alice — Born May 13, 1914
    Earl Robert — Born February 5, 1918; died November 15, 1924
    Marie Fern — Born December 22, 1920
    Ethel Roberta — Born December 5, 1925

Hubert David — Born June 7, 1886; died January 15, 1887

Lee Montgomery — Born March 8, 1889; died February 13, 1975
    Wife — Emma Lillian White (1890-1984)
    Rachel Caroline — Born March 31, 1914; died December 28, 1994
    Margaret May — Born February 6, 1917
    Elam Albert — Born December 25, 1919; died September 4, 1931

northwest about 10 miles collecting money for hand corn planters we sold last spring.

After oats, corn, clover, and timothy were planted, the late spring of 1872 turned very wet. Things came to a head on Thursday, June 6: *Rained nearly all forenoon and was so wet during the day that no work of any kind was done. Went to Farmington in the evening after the mail and while I was there a most terrific thunderstorm broke over the country which made raging torrents of every gulch, branch and creek in the community. Came home about 10 oclock.*

On the next day it was possible to view the damage. *The freshet in Littler's Creek last night washed out for us 6 or 7 acres of corn and potatoes and swept off about 100 rods of rail fence! In the afternoon worked with the rest of the farm force at hauling up scattered rails to re-build the fences washed away.* The following week was consumed in putting things back together. *Worked each of these four days (10th to 13th) with little variation with the whole farm force and some hired help at hauling rails and re-building our "washed-away" fences!*

That year farmers began to experiment with fall-sown wheat varieties — called "winter wheat" — instead of traditional spring-sown wheat. On October 1: *Father having gotten some seed wheat yesterday at "Uncle" Henry Merrill's he sowed it the same day, broadcast, and I worked all day at harrowing it in on our newly broken hazel ground.*

1873

Not all the wheat planted that season was of the experimental "winter wheat," either because of fear that it might not turn out well, or because the seed was expensive — or both. So on April 2: *Continued plowing in the a.m. and in the p.m. went over to neighbor John Abbott's after some seed wheat and came home with it at 6 oclock.* The next two days: *Worked at harrowing in wheat after father's broadcast sowing.*

No details are given for the results of the "winter wheat" experiment. It was not a good year for wheat of any kind. On August 15: *Helped to do our small job of grain threshing in the a.m. and studied in the p.m.*

Elam turned 21 years of age in June, and with that event he began studying to qualify for a teacher's certificate. Thus in the summer he had little time for farming, and in the following months even less, because he got a job teaching elementary school some miles away.

1874

Then in March of 1874 Elam went west to homestead in Kansas, bringing to a close the "Farming in Illinois" part of his life.

Chapter 2

Homesteading

*E*LAM'S OLDER BROTHER ELIAS — later known as Eli — went to Kansas when Elam was only 16 years old. He stayed in the northeastern section of the state until the western section was more subdued and amenable to settlement. It is obvious that letters from him prompted Elam to follow in his footsteps, but there is no written account confirming the idea.

Shortly before Elias died (June 20, 1943), he made this entry in his own journal: *In the spring of 1868 I came to Kansas with my cousin W. D. Sharp, in the proverbial covered wagon, between Holton and Circleville where my cousin had two brothers living who had come out from Ohio the fall before. In the spring of 1873 I got the western fever and took a Homestead in 1874.*

1874

Both brothers went to Bow Creek, north of Stockton (in Rooks

County*) and south of Phillipsburg, in northwestern Kansas. Conditions were primitive in every sense, sharply contrasting with Illinois farm country, where rainfall was more reliable and more plentiful. Soil fertility in Fulton County, Illinois, though, was nothing to be proud of — at least not in the locality where Elias and Elam had grown up, so the soil was similar to Kansas soil. In fact, Kansas soils were in a way more fertile, because they had been in grass since the beginning of time. And there was no problem with removal of trees and stumps before crops could be sown, for there weren't any except along creeks and gullies where moisture collected. The paucity of native timber was actually a problem when it came to constructing buildings and fences, and needing firewood. Certainly there would be no split-rail fences, which the Midwesterners had at the same time depended on and cursed.

People had lived closer together back East, making practical the establishment of schools, churches, Sunday schools, and other fixtures of society. And those people were most likely to be the kind that had appreciation for moral values and decency. They came to Kansas for just one reason: to acquire land ownership.

For this very reason Elias and Elam and other family members moved. They had been renters before, putting down shallow roots. Because of economic forces, land ownership would never have been possible for them if they had stayed back East. So with the opening up of the West and the government offer of free land under the Homestead Act, they moved. They would endure whatever nature and society dealt out, no matter how hostile.

Elam had heard about the hardships of severe weather changes, of grasshopper plagues, of prairie fires, of marauding bands of remnant Indians, of gunfights among lawless renegades. But he had to give homesteading a try, even though it meant being away from his beloved Rachel

---

* *Rooks County was named in honor of John Calvin Rooks, who gave his life in the Civil War as a private in the 11th Kansas Volunteer Cavalry. He was born in 1835 in Potter County in northwest Pennsylvania near Bingham Center. Three years later the family moved to Kansas, acquiring a farm near Burlingame, Osage County, in the eastern part of the state. He was killed in late 1862 in northwest Arkansas in a successful battle that some say prevented Confederate troops from invading Kansas.*

   Lieutenant J. B. McAfee, who attended Rooks at his death, later became Adjutant General of Kansas and in 1867 selected the names of war heroes for identification of new counties being formed on the frontier, Rooks being one of them.

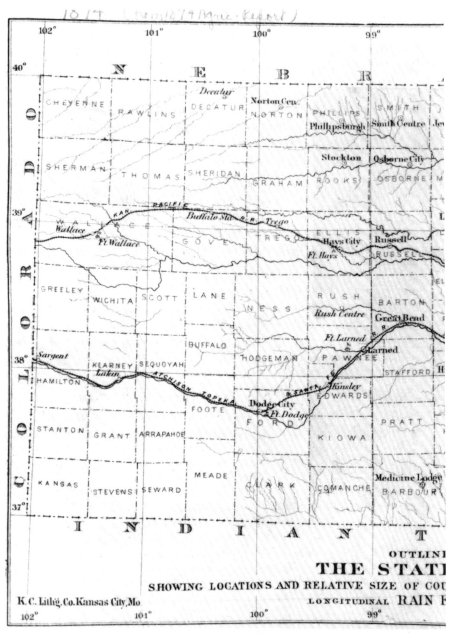

Above and opposite: Kansas as it appeared in the 1874 State Board of Agriculture Report, "County Maps." Outline map of the state of Kansas showing locations and relative size of counties, R.R. connections, principal towns, and longitudinal rainfall belts.

Kansas State Historical Society

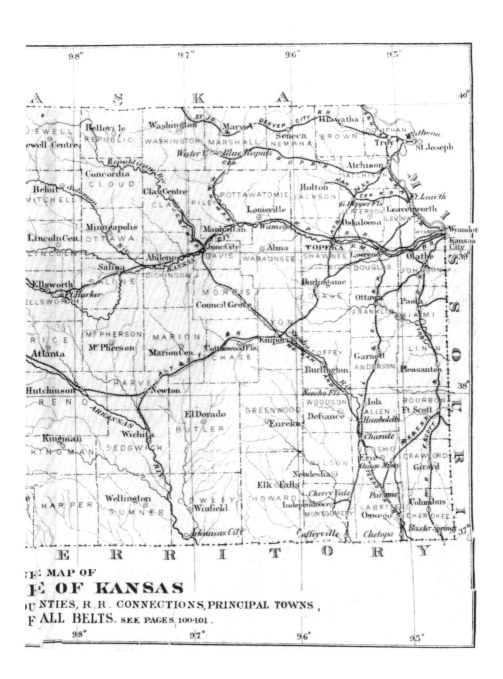

E MAP OF
E OF KANSAS
NTIES, R.R. CONNECTIONS, PRINCIPAL TOWNS,
ALL BELTS. SEE PAGES 100-101.

for a time. Thus on March 16 began the quest. He decided to go to Stockton, Kansas, to live. Elam packed his personal effects and went to see Rachel. Then he spent the night in Farmington with Charlie Day, who was boarding at Dr. M. T. Harrington's.

March 17: *Got aboard the 6:30 a.m. train and going by way of Galesburg arrived at Quincy at 2 oclock p.m. where I remained, looking about the city somewhat and visiting the large cemetery on the Mississippi river bluff, until 10 oclock at night when I took the west bound train over the old Hannibal and St. Joe road for Kansas City Mo.*

March 18: *Reached Kansas City at 10 a.m. where I changed cars, and after a short stop headed again toward the west over the Kansas Pacific for Hays City Kansas where I am to leave the train for a wagon trip 40 miles north.*

March 19: *Arrived at Hays City at 2 oclock this morning and put up for the rest of the night at the Gibson house. In the early morning I met my brother Elias who had come over from Stockton to meet me. He and I in company with H. M. Hill a merchant of Stockton left Hays in a wagon about 9 oclock a.m. and drove through to Stockton at 7:30 p.m. and put up for the night at G. W. Patterson's.*

March 20: *With Elias in the wagon, left Stockton about 9 a.m. and drove out nine miles north to Bow Creek to the home of Mr. Chas. C. Foote where we arrived shortly before noon. Mr. Foote's family consists of himself, wife and daughter Kitty about 16 years of age. My brother is living with the family. They all came here together from Louisville, Pottawatomie Co. Kans. last summer, Mr. Foote and my brother each homesteading a quarter section of land (160 acres). Spent the p.m. with Elias, or as everyone calls him, Eli, in looking over the land along the creek with a view to selecting a piece suitable for homesteading. Put up for the night at Mr. Foote's.*

March 21: *Continued viewing the landscape for much of today and finally decided to homestead the N.W. quarter of Sec. 10, Town 6, Range 18 about two miles up the creek west of Mr. Foote's. Spent the night as last night and will probably make this my headquarters for some time to come if I can get work here.*

Many days were spent plowing sod on his new homestead and on Eli's, and planting and cultivating spring crops on their land and Mr. Foote's. In the middle of summer, when it was too dry to plow sod, there was time to begin work on a house for Elam and his bride-to-be. On July 10: *With brother Eli's help worked on my homestead at commencing the excavation for a dwelling house, working thereat all day.*

On the first day of August there was a break from other work to go hunting: *With Mr. Foote, D. A. Duff and Eli went buffalo hunting out south-west several miles and while we saw a few buffaloes and a good many antelopes we got none whatever.*

August 11 provided Elam with his first encounter with a prairie fire: *With Mr. Foote and several of the neighbors worked from morning until 2 p.m. at fighting a prairie fire that was coming in on the north side of Bow Creek from the northwest.*

The new house was constructed of wood because sod houses took longer to build. (Some years later Elam would build a sod house, which was easier to heat in the winter and cooler in the summer, and was fire proof.) Lumber was scarce and, therefore, expensive, so the only solution was to cut down some cottonwood trees along the creek. On September 7: *Worked at cutting cottonwood saw logs to be hauled to Stockton and made into lumber for use in my new house.* There followed numerous days of hauling them, one log at a time, into town to the mill. Then on the 28th: *Went to Stockton and brought home a load of lumber made from my logs.* And the very next day: *With the help of Mr. Foote, John Kling and Chas. Steward (Mr. Foote's nephew) put up the frame work of my house today.*

The house was insulated, thus on November 5 to 7: *Worked each of these three days in placing stone and mortar concrete between the studding in my house.*

Life was tough on the Western frontier, especially for a new settler who had minimal income and no produce yet for sale. So on December 10: *Went to Stockton where I got a blanket, an overcoat and a pair of shoes on the Government aid deal.*

1875

Again in early 1875 people in need received donated goods to help them through rough times on the frontier, only this time the aid came from charitable sources. On January 7: *Mr. Foote having brought out from Stockton a load of aid goods of one sort and another for the destitute settlers of this region, I took a good part of it up west 6 miles to John Marshall's for distribution up in that community which occupied nearly all day. The aid was stuff that had been shipped in from the east somewhere.*

Many historians have told about the wanton slaughter of buffalo around the middle of the 19th century in western Kansas (mostly from 1850 to 1860). It was considered high sport and was done mostly by renegades who had no interest in any other kind of gainful labor. Part of their motivation was economic. There was a market back East for the hides, and this was a way to make some ready cash while "having a good time."

There was also political motivation. If the buffalo were annihilated the Indians would likewise be exterminated, for they were dependent on buffalo as a source for tepee covers, bedding, clothing, meat, and ceremonial motifs. The U.S. Cavalry sanctioned the slaughter with the rationale that if there were no buffalo there would be no more problem with Indians — they would die off or at least they would move out of the way of white settlers. And the Cavalry was right on both counts. This manner of depleting the Indian population seemed more "civilized" and had more thorough results than had been possible from running battles between Indians and Cavalry. Moreover, the method minimized the casualties inflicted on the Cavalry. It mattered not if some renegade hunters were lost in skirmishes with Indians trying to protect their buffalo herds. Society considered the rebels expendable anyway, because they had already removed themselves from the norm.

Some buffalo roamed the area where Elam had settled, but not as many as in earlier times. Estimates run as high as 60 million head prior to 1830 in North America. By 1873 Colonel Richard Dodge, from his Army post in Kansas, reported: "Where there were myriads of buffalo the year before, there are now myriads of carcasses. The vast plain, which only a short twelvemonth before teemed with animal life, was a dead, solitary, putrid desert."**

Many of these carcasses littered the grasslands near where Elam settled. On December 6, 1875: *Helped Mr. Foote at gathering for the market at Hays City a load of buffalo bones!* These were shipped by rail to the East for processing into fertilizer and other chemical and medicinal uses. The supply at one time was so large that entire trainloads were shipped from Hays.

1876

There were still some Indians in the area in 1876. Those Elam encoun-

---

**From Greg Breining's article "Back Home on the Range," in *Nature Conservancy Magazine*, Nov./Dec. 1992, 13.

There is no photo of Elam's original house, built in 1874, but this artist's drawing by Pearl McMillen shows its appearance and location. The picture depicts the home's relation to a dugout cave, the well, and trees planted for orchard and wood supply. Bow Creek is on the extreme right. This dwelling, built into the side of a hill, served as home for 25 years. All the children were born and raised here. It measured 14 x 22 feet.

tered on the way to his school teaching job were friendly. On February 25: *In the morning when on my way to school stopped at the encampment of a band of about 60 Omaha Indians who were located on the creek a half mile east of Samuel Hebrew's. They were returning from a buffalo hunt to the southwest to their reservation in Nebraska. They were loaded down with spoils of the chase.*

When Elam returned to Illinois during the spring and summer of 1876, he had not finished the house begun months before. He had become discouraged in his loneliness. Life was hard — really hard. Farming was not as reliable in Kansas as in Illinois. There had been prairie fires, a gunfight in Stockton involving horse thieves, and remnant Indians battling the Cavalry. (Custer's Last Stand occurred in late June of that year, not terribly far away in South Dakota.) He was not certain that his fiancée would make the adjustment.

But the wedding did take place, and Elam's bride did make the trip to

Kansas. He regained self-assurance when they arrived in early September of 1876. She began to like the place, and he vigorously set about to finish the house. On the 13th: *Went up to work on our house to complete it for residence soon as possible.* On the 14th: *Went to Stockton after a load of lumber* [cottonwood] *and getting home at noon spent the p.m. at work on the house.* And the next day: *Continued work on the house all day.*

Women of the neighborhood seemed to want to get to know the new bride and help her feel welcome. On the 16th: *Mrs. J. A. Southard and son Summer came along in the morning and taking Mrs. Foote and Rachel and I in the wagon we drove over N.W. about 12 miles onto the North Fork of the Solomon where we spent the day picking plums of which we got about 7 bushels and came home at 6 p.m.*

The next day, being Sunday: *At home until 3:30 p.m. at which time Rachel and I with Kittie Foote went down to H. E. William's where we spent a couple of hours in social chat and singing and came home about 6:30 oclock.*

Most of the next three weeks were spent finishing the house, with time out to go to Hays to get the goods shipped by rail. On October 9: *Started in the morning to Hays City after our household goods which have been a long time on the road, and passing through Stockton at 10 a.m. continued my journey on over to the Saline river where I put up for the night at the Martin post office.*

October 10: *Continuing my journey reached Hays at 10 a.m. where I loaded my goods and started on the return trip at 2 oclock p.m. and crossing the Saline river I camped on the Paradise, about 8 miles north, for the night.*

October 11: *Resuming my journey a half hour before sunrise I reached Stockton at 10 a.m. where I stopped for dinner and came on over home at 3 p.m. which wound up the work of the day.*

Finally on the 14th: *Spent the day moving our household goods from Mr. Foote's to our own house and establishing the same therein. Our <u>home</u> is now established permanently and the night was spent within its hallowed precincts!*

Just one week later Rachel began to learn something about the wild animals in the vicinity of their new home. Elam wrote: *Husked corn until*

3 p.m. when I started home along the creek and treed a wild cat with which I had a battle royal for about an hour fighting the animal with stones and clubs and finally after knocking one of its eyes out he came down the tree when I attacked him with a club and killed him, and brought him home. And on the 22nd: *Spent the day at home in reading and rest being sore and stiff from head to foot from my wild cat "scrap" of last evening.*

1877

The Homestead Act of 1862 allowed settlers to claim, from public domain, 160 acres of land (¼-mile square) by occupying it and making improvements on it within six months of filing a claim. They were required to live on that land for five years, after which clear title was granted. Forfeiture occurred if the homesteader was absent from the property for any six-month period during that time. Thus, on January 4, 1877: *Brother Elias of Louisville, Ks. made us a call and staid all night with us on the 5th. He is here to comply with the homestead law so that his claim near here may not be contested for abandonment.*

Finally there was time to dig a well for the homestead, after hauling water from the neighbor's homestead for seven months. On March 30: *Worked at quarrying rock to wall a well.* And on the 9th of April: *Went down to H. E. Williams after a windlass to do well digging and getting home at noon spent the p.m. at work in the well. Sam Shell assisted.* By the 21st it was finished: *Worked at the well today — finishing the walling thereof.*

1878

Things got really scary on October 7, 1878: *A grand stampede of settlers today and last night from the frontier counties caused by a reported Indian raid from the Indian Territory. All reports lacked positive confirmation. However, a militia company was formed and sworn in with Co. Clerk L. C. Smith for captain. It fell my lot to be one of the volunteers.* On the 18th more of the gory details were learned: *Confirmatory reports of the Indian raid which was done by a large band of the northern Cheyenne's who had been removed to the Indian Territory, have been received and show that in the last days of Sept. and first days of October much damage to property and the killing of many settlers was the result especially in the counties of Sheridan, Decatur and Rawlins. In Decatur the murders and scalpings are said to aggregate about 18.*

This was the very same day the second baby of Elam and Rachel was born (Elbert). There they were, only two counties away from where this carnage had taken place, with a newborn and another not yet two years old! There must have been thoughts of returning to the East, if not to Illinois at least some place where life could be more serene.

1879

On March 15, 1879: *Went to the post office and received a letter from brother George of Farmington, Ill. informing us of the fact that father, mother, himself* [age 22] *Emma* [19], *Ed* [17] *and Frank* [12], *which constitutes the whole family* [except Amos and John] *would start for this place on Monday the 17th to make it their future residence and desired me to meet them at Hays City on their arrival.*

March 18: *Went up to the postoffice at 9 a.m. to see if any other intelligence had arrived in regard to our folks starting for Kansas, and got home again at half past ten and at 11 started for Hays City, getting to Stockton at 1 p.m. and stopping an hour again resumed my journey passing through Plainville at about half past four oclock and got to the Saline river at sunset, putting up for the night at the Davis ranch.*

March 19: *Started at half past 6 oclock this morning and met father, mother, Em and Frank about 5 miles on this side of Hays coming over with a livery team and I then took them in charge and let the livery team return again to Hays and we turned and started for home getting to Plainville at noon and stopping for dinner about an hour again resumed our journey, passing through Stockton about three oclock and got home shortly before sunset. Geo. and Ed. coming with a chartered railroad box car had not arrived and will not for several days.*

March 20: *Went over S.E. about a mile to Mr. John Allen's with father to look over the country and seek a location. From there we went down to Mr. Foote's and remaining there about an hour came home about two oclock p.m. having come to the conclusion to contest the Homestead now held by F. M. Rowland who has abandoned said homestead for a period of over 6 months, said claim being the N.W. ¼ of sec. 11, Town 6, Range 18.*

March 21: *Went to Kirwin and securing the services of Clift and Lewis as attorneys, proceeded to get out contest papers on the land mentioned yesterday, said contest to come off on the 25th day of April.*

March 22: *Went over onto sec. 11 in the morning with father to assist him in establishing a residence on the land which he is contesting, by laying a foundation for a house upon the same.*

March 23: *Father, in company with J. M. Mellon, started to Hays City this morning for the purpose of meeting George and Ed and to bring over two loads of their goods — Mr. Mellon to bring one load and father having shipped a team and wagon with his other goods, calculates to bring over another load.*

March 31: *George and I started to Hays City this morning after another load of Father's household goods, passing through Stockton about 10 oclock a.m., arriving at Plainville shortly after noon, where we stopped for dinner, and to feed our horses. Resumed our journey at about 1 oclock, crossing the Saline river about 3, and arriving in Hays at sunset, where as a matter of course we put up for the night, having driven 50 miles during the day.*

April 1: *Loaded our wagon up this morning and after looking about a short time started for home at 11 oclock a.m. recrossing the Saline about 4 oclock and arriving at Plainville about dark where we put up for the night.*

April 2: *Resumed our homeward journey quite early in the morning, arriving in Stockton about noon, where we stopped about an hour getting home at 3 oclock p.m., spending the remainder of the day in knocking about at a little of everything.*

On April 25 the legal process was completed on the homestead application of Elam's father: *Went to Kirwin in company with George and James Hebrew and Hiram Shell to attend the contest commenced on the 21st of last month and it being an ex parte case its continuance did not exceed five minutes.*

A new sod school house was constructed by neighborhood men, who completed it on May 2, 1879.

Prior to July 2 Elam spent many days helping dig a well on his father's place, but without success: *Worked for father at his well and we having dug 38 feet and bored nearly 30 more and then finding no signs of water he has about come to the conclusion to start another well at some other point on his farm.* There followed numerous attempts, boring before digging, but nothing positive until July 30: *Spent the day in working over at father's boring for water, he having struck rock in the well in which he was digging yesterday. Late in the p.m. we found water beyond a doubt on the east side of the farm at a depth of about 16 feet.* That effort was successful. On August 6: *Worked for father at helping to finish digging and beginning to wall his well, he having obtained an abundance of water.*

Work began on a sod house for Elam's parents on September 4. It was completed two months later. On November 3 they moved in: *Father's folks having completed their house and having gotten all things in readiness for moving will leave us tomorrow and begin life once more in their own house.* Just about two weeks before his 65th birthday, Elam's father, for the first time in his life, was no longer a renter. Now he had a farm and a home that were his own — a most significant occasion indeed! (He died exactly 14 months later, on January 3, 1881.)

1880

The last remnant of the Bartholomew clan arrived on the scene from Illinois on February 19, 1880: *Split wood until 10 a.m., then went to Rockport after the mail and got home at 11:30. Until 1 p.m. was spent in reading, when we were very much surprised to see brother John and his wife Mary and little boy who had just arrived from Illinois; getting to Kirwin last night they were brought out here by a livery team. We knew they were coming out but supposed they would not come until tomorrow and Geo. was going down after them.* (The railroad had reached Kirwin on February 2, 1880.)

1883

Other kin were attracted to the lure of free homesteads in Kansas. On October 11, 1883: *In the evening Rachel's brother Robt. of Bedford, Iowa accompanied by three other men from the same location came unexpectedly on us on a tour of pleasure and exploration visiting the country for the purpose of locating if suited. They came through by wagon.*

1886

Another homesteader prospecting visit occurred on August 17, 1886: *In the evening two of Rachel's brothers, Will of Cawker City and Tommy of Farmington, Ill. accompanied by Will Fleming of Glen Elder, Mitchell county, came in upon us for a visit and a look over the country with a view to securing a location. Will paid us a visit last year in July and was not much of a stranger but Tommy had grown entirely out of my recollection as I had not seen him since Sept. 6, 1876, a period of ten years.*

The next day a tentative decision was made: *In company with Rob went*

Important to Homesteaders.

DEPARTMENT OF THE INTERIOR,
GENERAL LAND OFFICE,
Washington, D. C., Jan. 17, 1880.

Registers and Receivers U. S. L. O.:

GENTLEMEN:—Referring to circular of April 15th, 1879, under act of March 3d, 1879, requiring published notice of intention to make final proof in homestead and pre-emption cases, you are now instructed to require claimants in all cases hereafter to specify, in form No. 1, the DAY and DATE on which they will appear with witnesses for the purpose of making proof, and, in homestead cases, they must give the official name and residence of the officer before whom the proof is to be made. You will also request each claimant to name FOUR of his neighbors who may be able to testify as to his compliance with the law, any two of whom will be competent witnesses when proof is made. Such a course will prevent much inconvenience and delay.

The post-office address of the witnesses should be given in all cases. It is not sufficient to give the county only.

You will see that the foregoing requirements are incorporated in form No. 2, (Notice of Publication,) so that such notices will hereafter be substantially in the following form, viz: "Notice is hereby given that the following named settler has filed notice of his intention to make final proof in support of his claim and secure final entry thereof, and that said proof will be made before the clerk of the court of Reed county, at the county seat, on Thursday the 22d day April, 1880, viz: John Doe, homestead entry No. 3784, for ne ¼, sec. 30, township 46 w, range 20 w, and he names the following witnesses to prove his continuous residence upon and cultivation of said tract, viz: John Smith, Thane Bundy, Peter Pinder, all of Jay, Reed county, and Samuel Small, of Roscoe, Reed county." ——Register.

The object of the law requiring such notice is to give to parties having adverse claims or filings, or to those having knowledge that the claimant has not complied with the requirements of the statutes, full notice of the time and place of presenting proof in order that opportunity may be given them to be heard prior to the perfection of an entry.

You will use the blanks on hand, making the necessary alterations, until you receive new and revised blanks from this office. Very Respectfully,

J. M. ARMSTRONG,
Acting Com.

From *The Stockton Record*, January 31, 1880.

over N.W. about three miles to look at a piece of land that Will and Tom had been looking at last week and as Rob was not suited with it we returned home. The other boys when out also looked at the C. H. Dewey farm of 320 acres in Sugar Loaf township which place Rob also visited in company with Mr. Dewey yesterday before coming to our place and being better pleased with it than anything else yet seen, a partial bargain was made for its purchase at $3500. When Rob goes home, if everything is all satisfactory with the boys Will and Tom, the bargain will be closed next week.

Finally on November 5: *By a card received last evening learned that the Montgomery boys were in transit from Cawker City to their recently purchased farm in this county and that Rob's wife and two children and her*

Elam Bartholomew's Homestead Certificate for the 160 acres at Kirwin, Kansas.

aunt would be at the Commercial house in Stockton this morning, having come up by rail, while the boys were on the road bringing up the wagons, cattle and horses, and requesting me to meet the women folks in town and bring them out to our place; so I went to town, got the folks and returned home by 11:30 a.m. After dinner went down to Jim Hebrew's to return the iron kettle borrowed Monday and returning at 3 p.m. worked the remainder of the day at fixing up our cattle corral for winter use.

In the evening Rob and Will Montgomery put in an appearance and put up with us for the night while Tom and Will Fleming kept the cattle and part of the horses over at mothers. They now have all their goods and chattels in Rooks county and will proceed tomorrow morning to occupy their new home in Sugar Loaf township.

1887

Another relative arrived on February 4, 1887: *About one oclock we found Rob Montgomery here and with him Rachel's sister Lizzie and her husband Millard McComb of Macon, Ill. who have come out to locate here.* A place was selected on March 19: *In the evening about 6 oclock brother-in-law Millard McComb and wife came down from Sugar Loaf to stay with us over Sabbath. They have bought a farm out near the S.W. corner of Bow Creek township, (Section 30) to which they expect to go to housekeeping next week. It is about 17 miles from our place.*

1888

After a terribly hot summer in 1888 and consequent corn crop failure, Millard and family headed back to Illinois on October 14: *At 2 p.m. in company with wife and Elbert, Lizzie and Earl started out to brother-in-law Millard McComb's in Bow Creek township, wishing to see them and bid them good bye as they expect to pack up and leave for Illinois tomorrow, they having sold their farm and most of their stock a short time ago.*

On the next day: *Helped the folks do most of their packing of household and other goods and at 9 oclock a.m. Millard and Lizzie with one team, Wm. Collins with another and Rob Montgomery and I with another pulled out for Logan at which place the folks are to take the train for the east. Wife and the children, with Rob's wife took our team and returned to Montgomery's. We got to Logan at 1 p.m. and after getting dinner worked the remainder of the day at packing goods and implements into the car and fixing stalls for the horses. Lizzie took the evening train for Kansas City while Millard will wait until tomorrow morning and go on the freight.*

1890

More kinfolk decided to move back East in 1890, and it is obvious that Elam was opening up to the possibility himself. Beginning on October 3: *Went up to brother-in-law Wm. Hebrew's* [Elam's sister Em had recently married] *in company with wife where we spent the day in helping them at making preparation to move next week down to Pottawatomie county in this state.*

Then on the 6th: *Spent the entire day at Wm. Hebrew's place working at making further preparations to get him off to his new location, bringing a load of his goods home with me in the evening to be taken to Phillips-burg tomorrow. From present expectations I will accompany them to visit several days at Louisville and Manhattan.*

The next day: *In company with Mother, who will accompany Hebrew's to their new locating, started with Will's load of goods to Phillipsburg at 8:30 a.m., arriving there at 1 p.m. Spent the afternoon in helping to load one of the cars with household goods, farming implements, lumber, etc. Bro. Ed, Sum Southard, Jim Hebrew, Evan Hebrew, and old Mr. Hebrew, all having taken loads over helped also at loading the car. Geo. and Elbert who helped to drive the hogs over took our team and started home about 4 oclock, and Ed, Jim and Sum went home after dark while the rest of us passed the night in town.*

And on the day following: *Mother, Em and the baby started east on the 7 a.m. express while Will, Evan and old Mr. Hebrew and I spent the a.m. in completing the loading of the two cars. We put into one car 170 hogs and pigs & besides the other goods in the car loaded yesterday p.m. we put in 5 horses and three cows.*

At 2 p.m., everything being in readiness, Will and I boarded the caboose attached to the stock train and proceeded on our journey. We continued the rest of the day and until midnight without incident worthy of mention, when we arrived at the little station of Wabaunsee in the county of the same name, where we had the cars set off and we proceeded to a hotel where we spent the rest of the night.

Then on the 9th began the unloading process: *At an early hour Em came over from Louisville where she and Mother had arrived at 2 p.m. yester-day, and with two hired teams and one that we brought along we soon had three loads of goods and the car load of hogs on the road for Louisville where we arrived at 5 p.m. where we proceeded to unload the wagons and fix up pens on a town property Will had previously rented.*

At supper time called at the residence of brother Elias whom I had not seen for ten years. As he was away at Topeka attending the state G.A.R. reunion I did not meet him but made the acquaintance of his wife and little daughter whom I had never previously met. Passed the night at Will's.

On the 10th: *Will and I each took one of his teams and went to Wabaunsee after a load of goods and returned at 4 p.m.*

Then the next day: *Very early in the morning I went to brother Elias' house and disguising myself and my voice somewhat I succeeded in playing it on him very successfully by intimating that I had a sick horse down the street which I desired him to go and see. He was completely sold and did not recognize me until I made myself known when he was ready to boot me out of the yard.*

Missing baggage is not just a modern day phenomenon: *Em and Mother's baggage not having followed them to Wamego, but having remained at Manhattan, it was necessary that it be seen to so Em, Bessie, Etheleen and I secured a buggy and taking one of Will's teams we proceeded to make a trip to Manhattan to see about the baggage delay. We went by way of Wamego and thence up the Kansas river 15 miles. It was a very pleasant drive indeed. We took dinner in Manhattan and then hitching up after transacting our business we drove out to the State Agricultural College grounds and thence homeward.*

During the next week there were trips of about two miles each on four days in various directions out from Louisville. The following week more trips were made, each seven or eight miles in distance. On one of those days Elam writes: *We were looking at lands with a view to renting.* Possibly that statement referred only to Will, but it probably indicates that Elam could have been persuaded to relocate there also if the right situation had been presented to him. He would not have stayed there so long if he were not interested.

Besides the fact that the weather would be more favorable for farming and stock raising, and that several kinfolk now resided there, the most powerful magnet that attracted Elam was the close proximity to Manhattan and the state college with its offerings in agriculture and botany. His work on fungi had already attracted academic recognition. He felt a need

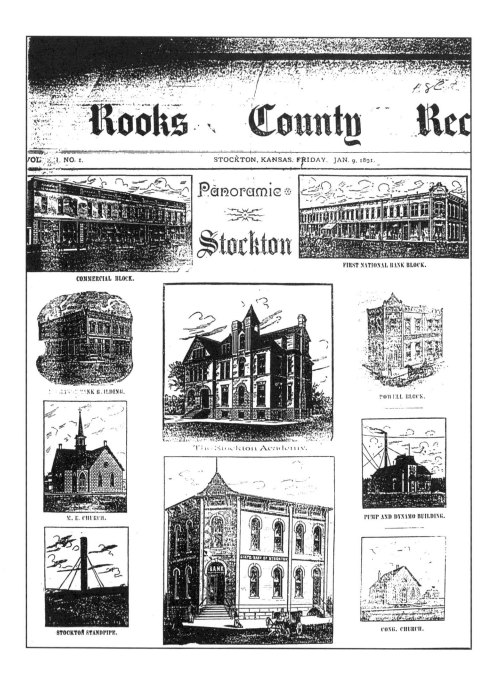

Rooks County Rec

VOL. 1. NO. 1.   STOCKTON, KANSAS. FRIDAY. JAN. 9, 1891.

Panoramic Stockton

COMMERCIAL BLOCK.

FIRST NATIONAL BANK BLOCK.

BANK BUILDING.

The Stockton Academy.

POWELL BLOCK.

M. E. CHURCH.

PUMP AND DYNAMO BUILDING.

STOCKTON STANDPIPE.

STATE BANK OF STOCKTON

CONG. CHURCH.

for more scientific study, and the possibility of actually becoming a member of the college staff had presented itself.

But all these seductive impulses were shrugged off. He returned to western Kansas where he felt an even more powerful sense of belonging. His roots there were deeper than he had realized until he actually considered pulling them up.

Rooks County and Stockton Population					
Year	Rooks County	Stockton	Year	Rooks County	Stockton
1875	567	NA	1899	7,593	948
1876-1879	NA	NA	1900	7,641	846
1880	8,113	411	1901	7,788	952
1881	NA	NA	1902	8,295	867
1882	7,249	301	1903	8,274	949
1883	7,270	437	1904	8,667	1,117
1884	6,579	427	1905	9,482	1,037
1885	7,796	534	1906	10,483	1,318
1886	9,535	937	1907	10,540	1,340
1887	10,884	1,346	1908	10,511	1,217
1888	10,007	1,506	1909	10,884	1,420
1889	8,598	1,133	1910	11,425	1,470
1890	7,796	858	1911	10,961	1,279
1891	6,245	730	1912	10,465	1,402
1892	6,694	826	1913	10,625	1,371
1893	7,144	922	1914	10,167	1,283
1894	7,179	721	1915	10,596	1,291
1895	7,440	789	1916	11,010	1,384
1896	7,270	736	1917	11,010	1,417
1897	7,290	731	1918	10,127	1,194
1898	7,440	851	1919	10,026	1,116

1891

Still that decision was sorely tested just four months later when on February 16, 1891: *With wife and George went up to Montgomery's to help them at making further preparations toward moving to their new location at Bedford, Iowa. Will M. and George each brought down a load of straw for cattle feed while I brought a load of miscellaneous stuff of all sorts which will be useful to us but which would not pay to ship to Iowa. Rachel remained all night to help Addie at performing her part of the preparations; such as baking, packing goods, etc.*

On the next day: *Went to Montgomery's early in the morning and spent the entire day in packing goods, loading wagons and all sorts of work preparatory to moving. Staid all night as I expect to take a load of their goods to Stockton tomorrow. In the evening about sunset Rachel, Addie and their children, Lizzie and Fanny, went down to our house to pass the night calculating to go from there to Stockton tomorrow p.m.*

The move actually got underway the following day: *Yesterday, John Robinson and Will Montgomery each took a load of goods to Stockton and this morning six additional loads were taken in by the following persons: J. W. Baldwin, John Robinson, Rob Montgomery, Will Montgomery, our Elbert and myself. I. C. Smith drove down 18 cows. In all we had 12 head of horses including colts. We got to town shortly after noon and after getting dinner at a restaurant worked the remainder of the day at packing the wagons, machinery and household goods into half of a 34 foot car. Rachel, Addie and the children came over at 4 p.m. in the buggy and put up for the night.*

Farewells were said on February 19, 1891: *Mr. Robinson, Rob, Will and I spent the greater part of last night in completing arrangements for loading the stock early this morning. We did not go to bed at all. At 6 a.m. we saw Addie and the children aboard the east bound train, after which we proceeded to load the stock and everything being completed we bade the boys farewell and at 8:30 oclock saw them pull out on the east bound freight for their new location at Bedford, Iowa where they lived during the years 1882, '83 & '84.*

Then in a reflective, maybe remorseful, mood Elam recounted the parade of kinfolk that had come and gone during the previous 15 years: *By reference to this diary it will be seen that its author came to Rooks Co. Kansas and settled in this community in March 1874. At that time he had a brother, Elias, living here who was a homesteader and came here in July 1873. In Aug 1874 on account of crop failure this brother, then unmarried,*

abandoned this part of the country and located at Louisville, Pottawatomie county Kans where he now resides. I was then without relatives in this part of Kansas until March 1879 when it will be seen Father's family moved here from Farmington, Ill. The family then consisted of Father, Mother, George, Em, Ed and Frank. In Feb. 1880 brother John and family came here also from Ill. and settled. In Nov. 1880 brother George thought he had enough of the country so he went to the east part of the state and finally settled at Wichita where he married and now resides. Father died in Jan. 1881. In Nov. 1882 brother John also thought he had enough of Western Kansas so he removed with his family to McDonough county Ill., his former residence, where he now resides. In June 1886 brother Frank thinking that he could better his condition left Rooks county and located at Wichita with brother George, where he now resides. In Nov. 1886 the advent of wife's folks in the way of three of her brothers, Robt., Will & Tom Montgomery, of Jewell Co. Kansas, formerly of Ill. located here and bought land. Rob's family consisted of himself, wife and two children, Will & Tom being single. Today has witnessed their departure. In Feb. 1887 wife's sister Lizzie and husband M. M. McComb also located here and bought land, but the two disastrous crop years of 1887 and 1888 were too much for them so in Oct. 1888 Mr. McComb and wife changed their location to McLean county Ill. where they now live. In March 1890 Tom Montgomery who came here with Rob and Will in Nov. 1886, took up his departure for the east and is now at home with his parents at Farmington, Ill.

In Oct. 1890, Mother, sister Em and her husband W. J. Hebrew, concluded that they had sufficient experience with western Kan. and they too set their faces toward the rising sun, locating in the eastern part of Kan. in Pottawatomie county.

And thus have come and gone one after another of our relatives until we are now situated as we were in Oct. 1876, with the exception of our children, and brother Ed's family who are still here. [Ed remained and so did his family to the second and third generation.]

When our turn will come I do not know but I do know that it makes us feel sad to think so many of those who are near and dear to us have tried in vain to build up for themselves a home in this region.

There were many other friends and neighbors who gave up and moved away. Elam attended numerous auctions when those folks had to dispose of goods or raise cash to move elsewhere. From these sales he got some good bargains, but then, as now, it was saddening to go through the experience of liquidation.

Often a sign was seen on the rear end of wagons leaving Kansas in the last half of the 19th century, expressing the feelings of the occupants:

> In God We Trusted;
> In Kansas We Busted.

Elam and probably his kinfolk would never have been so cynical as to show such a "bumper sign," for they had a keen respect for nature and for "what God doth provide." They recognized their limitations and the limitations of western Kansas, its soils, and its weather. Those who left simply did not care to adjust.

Elam and Ed chose to adapt, and they did better than just survive. They did not become wealthy in the worldly sense from the produce of the farm. However, they did find a spiritual wealth that enriched their souls, and those of wife and family.

With a desire for synchronization with nature, Elam came to the frontier seeking what it could provide, instead of demanding that it perform in the same way as land in Illinois or elsewhere. He proved that it could be productive in its own way, and sought to learn about that way. He was happy in a diversified agriculture, raising cherries and sweet potatoes and other fruits and vegetables, in addition to the traditional grain and hay and livestock.

With every issue of local newspapers in the late 1880s and the next decade there was an increase of listings of land for sale through normal channels, from government resale of claims forfeited, or from sheriff's sale due to non-payment of taxes.

1904

In spite of everyday problems, Elam perceived beauty in his surroundings and satisfaction in the struggles of life on the prairie. On March 20,

1904, he indulged in rare eloquence: *Just 30 years ago today I landed in this part of Kansas and looked over this piece of raw government land which on the following week I entered us a homestead and it has constituted my residence continuously from that day to this!*

What sowings in a life history and what changes have been wrought by the hand of man in redeeming the desert and making it to blossom as the rose! A land teeming with a rapidly growing population, a land filled with peace and plenty, a land flowing with milk and honey!

Kathleen Norris has written in *Dakota: A Spiritual Geography*: "To be a good citizen of the Plains one must choose the life consciously, as one chooses the monastery. One must make an informed rejection of any other way of life and also undergo a period of formation" (147).*

Chapter 3

Farming in Kansas

I MMEDIATELY AFTER SELECTING and securing a homestead site in March of 1874, Elam found it expedient to do some work for those who had put forth the effort to bring him from the train and provide shelter and meals while he was getting established — Mr. Foote and brother Elias (or Eli, as he was known locally). All three of them were starting fresh in this new land, the latter two having come from eastern Kansas just a few months earlier.

The first chore was to cut, rake, and burn "gigantic" sunflowers that had grown on their pieces of land. Elam was definitely not impressed with the fertility of some of the land, calling it "very foul land." The soil on his father's farm in Illinois was not the best in the state, but it must certainly have been better than this. At least it looked better, for it was black while this was sandier, and lighter in color.

On March 31: *In the p.m. went down the creek 6 or 7 miles to a Mr. Patterson's after some seed potatoes with Eli. He paid $2.50 per bu.*

Next came plowing, followed by planting corn. A hand planter was used, just as in Illinois.

It became obvious that Elam would be having no crops of his own for cash income the first year, so on May 18 he found employment with his friend: *Commenced work today for C. C. Foote at $20 per month!* That work was primarily breaking prairie sod, and it went on intermittently for several weeks until late June when the soil became too dry. This employment continued in 1875.

1876

After Elam was married in 1876, he began preparations for planting crops on his own land. What a thrill that must have been, having land of his own — something his father had not yet experienced! On May 9: *With one of Mr. Foote's teams began breaking prairie on my claim and worked thereat all day.* Then on the 15th and 16th: *Worked at planting corn and sorghum on some of the land plowed last week.*

It was imperative that some kind of shelter be provided for the farm tools and implements that Elam expected to acquire. Least expensive, of course, would be to use what nature provided. Since wood was relatively scarce, Elam decided to dig into the side of a hill. The terrain of his homestead included a stream of water (Bow Creek), with an embankment rising about 30 to 40 feet along the edge of the flood plain.

The house had been built at the bottom of this incline, so Elam decided to dig into the side of the hill for a sort of barn. The location had the added advantage of protection against out-of-control prairie fire. Thus on November 4: *Commenced work on a dugout to be used as a storehouse for various articles in the way of tools and implements.*

Certainly Elam knew how to dig into an embankment and shore up the walls and ceiling. He had gained this experience in Illinois digging out coal from embankments at the home place and for the neighbors. Now he wished it were fuel he was digging out instead of dirt and shale rock so that he didn't have to be dependent on wood for heating his new home.

1877

A late winter storm developed April 26 and 27 of 1877 so that on the 28th it was reported: *Many cattle perished from the severe storm of yesterday and day before.* But none were Elam's — he had none yet.

Harvest in 1877 began on June 27: *Worked for two days for neighbor N. Jerby at cradling, raking and binding rye. Mr. Jerby, J. A. Bailey, John Hastings and I expect to exchange work through harvest, running three cradles and sufficient additional force to rake, bind and shock the grain.*

Other structures were needed on the new farm. First there was a milk house. Then: *Worked at cutting and hauling poles from which to construct a pig pen.* Next, on July 26 to 28: *Worked these three days at excavating and hauling up timber from which to build a stable.*

The days after Christmas of 1877 were spent *butchering two of [their] fat hogs* from their own farm, which had to be very satisfying for the young couple.

1878

Bow Creek provided a source of wood for cooking food and heating the home, as well as for timber and poles for construction. Elam looked at all those seedling trees and realized they were too close together to all grow into useful timber. Moreover, shade was needed elsewhere. So on March 6: *Went down the creek about a mile and a half in the forenoon where I pulled up several hundred seedling cottonwood trees and returning at noon spent the p.m. in setting them out in various places about the farm.* And again on the 11th: *Got about 500 more cottonwood trees on the nearby sandbars and came home at 6 p.m.*

Already the well dug the previous year had gone dry, so on May 26 he began digging a new one, also walled with cut stone, and finished it eight days later.

Surveyors relied on local help, so on May 18: *Worked in the p.m. with the County surveyor and several others in laying out a county road on the section line on the north of our farm. I acted as chain carrier.*

1879

Elam still did not have a team of draft horses after nearly three years in Kansas, as noted on January 28, 1879: *Went down to Jas. Hebrew's in the morning after a team to commence plowing with, calculating to begin to plow for spring seeding.* Breaking sod (plowing it under) was a slow, tedious job. During the week ending May 10 a total of 8 acres was completed. The next week was just 6½ and the following week only 6 acres.

On June 22, 1879: *Large numbers of grasshoppers flying in a northerly and northwesterly direction.* No other mention is made of any specific consequences. Not many miles east and south there had been serious infestations of grasshoppers in 1874 and subsequent years, but since Elam makes no mention of them it may be assumed that they were not serious in his area.

Harvesting of small grains (wheat, oats, and rye) was still done with cradles, making bundles and stacks. Threshing took place on August 18 in 1879: *Spent the a.m. in making preparations to do our threshing and in the p.m. the machine having arrived we went to work and completed the job about sunset, my part of the job being to carry the grain from the machine to the bin which was an exceedingly hard row to hoe. Yield from 13½ acres: Wheat 124 bu, rye 32 bu. the small grain crop being considerably lighter than usual throughout the county.*

In his new environment, farming virgin land in climatic conditions where there was no experience or tradition, Elam's inquisitive mind led him to do some experimentation. One of the first experiments involved a different kind of corn, described on October 13, 1879: *Having about 3½ acres of Egyptian or Rice corn to gather commenced work on it this morning by cutting the heads or ears off and throwing them in piles on the ground. Spent the entire day thereat having Rachel help me in the afternoon.* Finally on the 17th the harvest was completed: *George and Ed helped haul in the remaining load of corn just before dinner which made 6 large loads, making of the corn in the ear about 300 bushels from 3½ acres of ground.*

Next began an experiment in orcharding. First were 50 apple trees, five of each: red Astracan, Wine Sap, Marden's Blush, Early Harvest, Ben Davis, Ramboy, English Russett, Willow Twig, Jonathan, and Famuse.

1880

Just as soon as Elam could secure title to his homestead he decided to borrow against his collateral. On January 30, 1880, he applied for a $300 mortgage contingent on completion of the homestead documentation.

Finally, six years after establishing a homestead and four years after beginning to farm it, Elam had enough money available to purchase his own horsepower. On March 6: *Brother Ed and I went to Stockton on various business and while there I purchased a span of light draft horses of Ballentine and Buchman for the sum of $105 in cash.* Already by the first of April one of the horses had gotten sick, requiring medication, but it recovered.

The purchase of a team meant it was also time to go shopping for a wagon, so on March 18: *Went to Stockton to buy a wagon and not seeing any that suited me, I returned without making a purchase.* Even though the wagon deal did not go through, it still was exciting to try out the new team on the following day: *Went over to Theodore Allen's in the morning about 10 oclock and borrowing his wagon, hitched our new team up for the first time, and taking Rachel and the children we went over to father's where we remained until past dinner when we went down to Sam'l Hebrew's, where we spent the afternoon.*

When a horse cannot be worked for one reason or another, a lot of time can be wasted seeking an alternative, as on June 3: *One of our horses having quite a sore shoulder and not wishing to work her for several days I went out in quest of one to take her place, going to Theo. Allen's, O. P. Coy's, J. A. Hebrew's and father's but did not succeed in getting a horse so returned home about noon, and did not do much of anything the remainder of the day owing to the high winds and threatening rain.* Then on August 8 death strikes: *Attended Sab. School alone at 10 a.m. getting home about noon, none of the rest of the folks going on account of one of our horses being sick which prevented us from taking the team. Said sick horse died shortly after sunset which fact leaves us without a team until another horse can be obtained.*

A new labor-saving implement began to make its appearance in western Kansas by 1880. Called a "header," it simplified grain harvest immensely. Instead of cutting stems close to the ground, necessitating tying bundles and building shocks, the header cut higher up on the stem, near the head, thus the name "header." The heads were then elevated by moving a canvas apron to a "header box" or "header barge" trailing along behind or to the side. This "header box" was simply a wagon with sides made out of slats, one side higher than the other. When full, it was pulled to a location where a stack was built. When a thresher came by, the grain was threshed.

Thus on June 21: *In the morning went down to J. A. Hebrew's to see about getting the Hebrew boys to cut our wheat crop, which I expect will be ripe sometime next week, but they being up at Rockport I returned home and went over northwest about two miles to Mack Marshall's to buy some pigs, but he was not at home so I went from there to Rockport where I saw the Hebrew boys who agreed to cut my 27 acres of wheat for 75 cts per acre with the header.*

Harvest began on July 6: *Our wheat crop of 27 acres being ripe and having engaged the Hebrew boys to cut it with their header, Bill and Sam came along in the morning and we got to work thereat. Had Mr. Mellon and brother John each run a header box while I did the stacking. Cut during the day 18 acres.* And on the 8th: *D. A. Duff and Bill Hebrew came along this morning and we went at it to cut the remainder of our wheat. Had brothers John and George run the wagons while I stacked. On account of several machine delays did not get through until about 3 p.m.*

Then it became necessary to protect the wheat stacks — or ricks, as they were sometimes called — from rain, so on July 10: *Had brother George help me and spent nearly all day in covering our four wheat ricks (each 30 feet in length, 8 foot base and 10 feet high) with willows 6 to 8 feet long which we cut at the creek and weighting the same down with heavy stones and wires.*

Threshing took place on August 23: *Having made all due preparations and the Cummings Bros. as threshers having arrived last night, calculated to go to threshing early this morning but on account of the rain last night we were unable to do anything until after dinner so the a.m. was spent at not much of anything. After dinner we went to work, threshing out our entire crop of 240 bushels.*

This, of course, was a very poor yield, which was seriously affected by the drought in late 1879 and early 1880. Even before threshing began Elam knew it was a poor crop, so on July 19 it was decided that more land must be devoted to grain production: *Commenced plowing on a 36 acre piece of ground on which I hope to sow fall wheat.* This was planted on October 7.

Payment for the costs of threshing was customarily made after the grain was sold. Thus on December 16: *Went to Stockton to take over some wheat*

Harvesting wheat with a header. To the right is the beginning of a stack, beside which is another load brought by a specially-designed wagon called a "header barge." Later a threshing machine and crew were hired to thresh out the stack.

to sell and attend to other business. Then on the 17th: *Owing to the inclemency of the weather did not do anything until 11 a.m. at which time I started on a horseback ride of 7 miles down the creek to Den. Cummings' to pay our threshing bill of $8.33 contracted last August.*

1881

In 1881 numerous days were spent plowing sod to enlarge crop acreage, and five acres were plowed to plant trees on. Wheat harvest was again a major disappointment. On August 30: *Finished threshing begun the day before, getting only 151 bushels from 31½ acres.* That is less than five bushels per acre!

On October 26 Elam planted two acres of ash tree seeds and half an acre of hackberry seeds. In the spring the other 2½ acres of dedicated timberland were planted with cottonwood seedlings.

On November 15 Elam applied for another mortgage, this time $450. Nine days later the new mortgage was paid out: $450 less commission of $27. Most of this was used to pay off the previous mortgage of $300 plus $26.20 interest.

A major expedition was conducted on November 29 preparatory to establishing more timber in the area: *Sam Hebrew, T. J. Allen and I went over to the South fork* [of the Solomon River] *3 miles west of Stockton after young cottonwood trees and getting several thousand we then went down to town and after staying about half an hour, came home where we arrived about 5 oclock.*

1882

In early April of 1882 over 1,600 cottonwood trees were planted. But shortly after that, on the 17th, the new plantings were ravished by vandalism: *Three rascally reckless boys, Jimmy Noonan and Ed and John Richards having broken down, pulled up and destroyed a large number of my young cottonwood, box elder and other trees, last Saturday while I was in town, I went up the first thing after breakfast this morning to hold interviews with their guardians, Jas. Hebrew, Sr. and Mrs. Privett whom I had come down (Mrs. P. sending her son W. C.) and view the mischief. Settled everything up satisfactorily by 10 a.m. and from then till noon harrowed 7 acres for planting corn.*

The wheat crop of 1882 was exceptionally good, as confirmed by the results of threshing on September 25: *The threshers having arrived last night about 10:30 oclock and everything being in order this morning, we went to threshing occupying the whole day thereat, finishing the job of 280 bu. of wheat from 14½ acres of ground.* Yield was just over 19 bushels per acre. The state average that year was 20 — the best recorded since records began in 1866, which would not happen again until 1914. It was not that good again until 1952!

1883

A second attempt at establishing a hardwood grove of trees was made on April 12, 1883: *Worked in the a.m. at plowing and harrowing a portion of the hillside NW of the house and in the p.m. worked at planting the same to walnut and ash trees, the trees, seeds and cuttings planted on the same ground having proved almost a failure.*

When it came time to thresh grain, and the threshing machine and crew came, other obligations were set aside, as on September 10: *Spent the a.m. in making preparations to do our threshing tomorrow and in the p.m. went to Stockton in company with Sam Hebrew on business and got home about 8 oclock in the evening. While in town was "snapped up" by the Sheriff on a special venire of the petit jury (court being in session) but by hard pleading and informing the judge that I expected to go to threshing in the morning I was finally excused from attendance.*

The huge steam engine that pulled the threshing machine along the road and supplied belt-driven power lumbered from farm to farm in direct succession. It was much too cumbersome to do any differently, so if a farmer missed his turn in sequence, it could be a long time before crew and equipment would return. In fact, they might not return at all for one small acreage such as Elam's.

Despite the poor harvest locally, it must have been better elsewhere, because the price was disappointing. On October 1: *Had brother Ed go with me and we each took a load of wheat over to Marvin. Found the place a dull trading point and the wheat market weak at 60¢ per bu.* But when money was required to pay some bills there was no alternative.

1884

Some of the wheat money went for a more modern binder so that grain bundles did not need to be tied by hand. On June 25, 1884: *Ed and I each took a team and went to Stockton and brought out a Buckeye twine Binder with which to cut our 150 acres of wheat and rye. Bought of Callender and Dewey and we are to pay $225 for the machine.* They tried it out the next day: *Went over to Mother's in the morning and worked until noon at helping to set the harvester up, which we left there last night. Mr. Fred Still of Stockton and also Ed and Frank worked at helping. In the p.m. worked at helping to get the machine to run properly and from 4 oclock until evening shocked rye.*

This was a very timely acquisition, as noted on the 30th: *Had Ed and Frank help me and worked at cutting and shocking wheat, said wheat being the heaviest in straw that I have ever seen grow.* Harvest went extremely well as the 150 acres were completed by July 17 with one day out for rain.

With no coal nearby and the petroleum industry not yet developed, wood was the fuel of choice in those early years. But it definitely was not plentiful on the western prairie, where annual rainfall averaged no more than 18 inches, and some areas as low as 12. Moreover, some of it had to be reserved for building material, corral fences, and so on. In just a few years Elam had cleaned out most of the wood available on his place, especially along the creek. Then in a couple years he purchased and hauled home wood that was available from widow Foote. After another two years he did the same from Lovells' place, and after that from Southards' place. It required a lot of work just to keep the house warm in winter and the cook stove supplied year round. Much time and energy was expended. The wood had to be cut to stove length with a two-man cross-cut saw six feet long. Then it had to be split with an ax or with wedges and a sledge hammer. Fortunately Elam had brothers nearby, but he had to return the favor to supply wood for their houses. Later he had sons who could help.

1885

By the winter of 1884-1885, those wood sources had been pretty well depleted. Luckily by then there was railroad service as nearby as Kirwin and Marvin, and the trains brought coal from eastern Kansas or elsewhere. That was a pleasant development, because Elam had had lots of experience burning coal in Illinois. Thus many days were spent like January 26, 1885: *Took a load of rye to Marvin and brought home a load of coal.*

Fence posts also had to be bought, since native timber had become more scarce or was too soft to have a long life. On February 12, 1885: *Had J. M. Mellon, Stephen Wilkin and brother Frank each take a load of rye to Marvin for me. I also took a load and we each brought back a load of posts for our proposed pasture fence.*

Barbed wire had come to the Western prairie! It had been invented 12 years earlier at DeKalb, Illinois, inspired by the efficient way thorned shrubs such as Osage Orange confined livestock within its bounds. Thus on April 4: *Took a load of wheat to Marvin and brought home a half ton of barbed wire to stretch on the posts set last month.*

Serious rainfall and flooding damaged the new fence just a few weeks after it was completed, as seen on May 28: *The high waters of Sat. night having taken out our wire fence at both crossings on the creek the a.m. was spent in repairing the same.* What a disappointment!

1886

In early 1886 Elam planted another three acres of cottonwood sapplings plus 200 catalpas. But on May 6: *Hail storm did a vast amount of damage to all kinds of vegetation, especially to small grain and young forest and orchard trees.*

A major sweet potato project commenced on the 29th: *With George and Elbert's help I set out 330 sweet potato plants.* The success was encouraging, so in subsequent years this project was greatly enlarged.

1887

On January 29, 1887, an informational meeting was held, the forerunner of Extension Service meetings that came later: *Went to Stockton to attend a farmer's institute which commenced yesterday at 2 oclock p.m. and to continue through today. The meeting was held in the court house and much interest was manifested in the several subjects up for discussion in the line of stock raising and agricultural topics. I read a four page foolscap* [legal sized] *paper on "Tame Grasses" which brought up much friendly discussion and comment.*

A new record was set on June 27: *Cultivated 10 acres of corn in a period of 12 hours which is the biggest day's work in that line that I have ever done.*

1888

A load of hogs was sold in Stockton on March 15, 1888, at $4.50 per hundredweight.

Eldest son George (age 11) had a serious accident on June 7, but Elam recorded it on the 13th: *Under date of the 7th it should have been mentioned that while George was using the horses to do a small patch of harrowing they became frightened and ran off, tangling themselves in the harrow and falling thereon. One of them, a fine $140 mare received a bad wound over the left kidney from the effects of which she died about 9 a.m. today, which proves a serious loss and inconvenience hard to overcome just at this period.* It was early in the growing season, and the team was needed nearly every day.

Acting as agent for a New York company, Elam tried his hand at selling nursery stock throughout the county, mostly fruit trees. His enthusiasm and personal success in growing trees made him a natural promoter, so he made many sales. When the shipment arrived he spent numerous days delivering the orders. In some cases he had to go back more than once to get payment. One instance turned out to be a barter deal. On December 12: *Went up N.W. about 5 miles to Thos. Cunningham's to bring home a cow as payment on one of the nursery stock notes.*

1889

A cattle drive was organized on February 6, 1889: *Went to Marvin to take over some steers sold last week. John Elliott, "Doc" Woods, Luther Marshall and I each went over on the same business so we drove our cattle together.*

Hog prices fell because feed price was high and farmers liquidated as soon as possible, as on February 15: *Took a load of 6 hogs to Marvin averaging 269 lbs per head for which I received $3.90 per cwt.*

Being on the lookout for a replacement for the dead horse as a result of George's accident, Elam was quick to pick up a good deal when it appeared: *Went over to Lee McMillans and brought home two young mares that I bought of him yesterday. One is a three year old and the other two years. They are good animals and I got them very cheap; $135 for the two.*

Hog prices continued to plunge. On December 7: *Took a load of 6 hogs averaging 295 lbs to Stockton for which I received $3.10 per cwt.* In March of the previous year the price had been $4.50.

Two days before Christmas: *To Stockton with a 41½ bu load of corn for which I got 13½¢ per bu. When about four miles on the road home the team became frightened and shying suddenly out of the road threw me out violently head first. They then made a couple of circles around where I was thrown out, turned the wagon over, threw the bed off, broke the wagon considerably and the harness very badly. With the help of several persons who were near at hand I got things fixed up so I could travel again and although pretty badly shaken up myself arrived home without further accident.*

Another load sold the next day brought 13¢, and then the day after Christmas: *Took a combined load of hogs (2) and corn (15 bu) to Marvin, getting $3.00 per cwt for the hogs and 12½¢ per bu for the corn.* Individually those prices seem terribly low, but when calculating the relationship it's not so bad after all. That is a hog:corn ratio of 24 to 1, which is really pretty good. (The bottom of the local corn market came on January 10, 1890, at 12¢).

1890

The annual meeting of farmers and professors reached new status on February 6, 1890: *Went to Stockton accompanied by W. F. Miller to attend the Farmer's Institute to be held today and tomorrow. By invitation took dinner in company with Hon. Eli Sherman at the residence of Clerk of the Dist. Court Geo. Farr after which I went with Mr. Sherman to the Hotel Hicks where I had the pleasure of meeting Hon. Geo. T. Fairchild, President of the State Ag. College at Manhattan, Prof. C. C. Georgeson the new professor of Agriculture in the same institution and S. C. Mason, foreman in the Horticultural Department.* (These introductions would be of great significance later when Elam began serious involvement in botanical studies.) *At 2 p.m. the Institute met in the opera hall and after singing by a select choir we listened to a well prepared opening address by Eli Sherman, President of the Institute. This was followed by a few well chosen remarks by President Fairchild congratulating the people on the establishment of the Institute and ended by saying that the faculty of the college were not there so much to* <u>teach</u> *as to* <u>learn</u> *and hoped we might all go away at the close of the institute mutually benefitted.*

A big surprise awaited Elam on the next day: *The opening address at the institute this morning was by D. H. Budd on "Is Horse Breeding a Profitable Industry in Rooks Co?" Mr. Budd's paper was historical as well as practical and showed that much labor had been performed in its preparation. Much discussion followed the reading of this paper. "Market Gardening" came next on the program and was well handled by Ralph Wood of Stockton followed by free discussion. Institute then adjourned until 1:30 p.m.*

At the adjournment I found brother-in-law Will Montgomery of Sugar Loaf in the hall who introduced me to a young "Mr. Snyder" of Armourdale with whom I chatted awhile, as to a stranger, only to be let down hard shortly after by it being made known to me that the supposed Mr. Snyder was none other than my own brother-in-law Geo. Montgomery of Farmington, Ill., who had just arrived on today's train from the east whom I had not seen since he was 7 years old, he now being 21. They immediately started for Sugar Loaf while I went with Mr. Toepffer to dinner. At 1:30 Prof. Georgeson gave us an illustrated address on "Scientific Stock Feeding in the Light of Practical Farming", which was quite lengthy and resulted in bringing out many questions for the Professor to answer. This address was a good one and threw much light on many important matters in its line.

"Are we making a Success of Hog-Raising in the County?" was practically treated of by N. R. McNutt in an extemporaneous address followed by much general discussion.

The last matter on the program was "What is the cause of the corn stalk disease in cattle"? by Elam Bartholomew which was treated of in quite a lengthy paper advocating the "germ theory". After considerable discussion of this important subject the hour of final adjournment being near an election for officers for the ensuing year was had resulting in the choice of Elam Bartholomew for president, & W. R. McNutt, Secy.

This meeting of the Farmer's Institute was more significant in the evolving life and career of Elam than he realized, or than seems evident at first reading. It brought him in personal and professional contact with the president and some professors at the state agricultural college, and they became aware of his fertile scientific mind when they heard his speech and conversed with him.

Hogs brought only $3.00 per hundredweight on June 20, weighing 246 pounds, but they recovered before long, no doubt because the 1890 corn crop was so poor. On September 9 some 260 pounders brought $3.70 per hundredweight.

On November 24 to 27 it was time to thin out the cottonwood grove: *Worked these four days at chopping down, trimming out and cutting up into stove wood young cottonwood trees, most of which we planted ten years ago.*

A closing comment on the last day of 1890 mentions only despair for the corn crop: *And thus has ended another year without a corn harvest which is in striking contrast with the fall of 1889.*

1891

After such a bad year, and several others before that, interest in irrigation grew. On January 7, 1891: *In company with wife went up to Montgomery's in Sugar Loaf and from there Rob and I went up to the Adamson postoffice in the N. W. part of the county to attend a sort of irrigation meeting but under the direction of C. P. Judd, the noted blatherskite, it was a flat fizzle.* A much better presentation was heard on the 13th: *Went to Stockton in company with A. B. Wilson to attend the county irrigation meeting which was held in the opera hall at 2 p.m. and was well attended. The principal speech was by W. S. Tilton of Osborne. It was a very interesting meeting.*

More consideration was given to irrigation at the Institute on February 5 and 6, along with many other timely topics: *Today and tomorrow being the days set for the holding of the annual meeting of the Rooks County Farmers Institute, and being president of the association, I went to Stockton where I arrived at 11 oclock a.m. By invitation took dinner with the family of W. R. McNutt who is secretary of the institute.*

At 2 oclock p.m. the Institute met in the opera hall. Several short talks were made by various parties after which the regular program was taken up and "Can Agriculture be made a Success in Western Kansas?" was treated of in a fairly well written paper by Eli Sherman. This was followed by a half hour's discussion, when "How shall we secure self-sufficient moisture for Agricultural Purposes in Western Kansas?" being next on the program was treated of in a short paper by J. B. Kelley. This all important matter elicited much discussion and the idea of building dams, reservoirs and catch basins to prevent the rainfall from passing into the streams and thence out of the county seemed to be the most feasible plan and the prevailing idea in the meeting.

Part of the program on the second day included additional thoughts from Elam concerning his presentation the previous year: *Presented my paper, "Supplemental Notes on the Corn Stalk Disease". Considerable rather animated discussions followed.*

Elam found he could enlarge his farming activities temporarily, because now there were sons old enough to be of significant help, so on October 17: *Having rented the old Mellon farm, adjoining us on the east, for the next year, worked until 9:30 a.m. at sowing wheat on said place on corn ground, George working at cultivating it in.*

It was a good year for corn, too, with a crop of 1,600 bushels in 1891. Hog prices dropped back to $3.25 per hundredweight on December 12 for 277 pounders, but they improved a little by January 16, 1892, to $3.50 per hundredweight for five hogs averaging 293 pounds.

1892

Farmer's Institute met on the 5th and 6th of February 1892. The first presentation reflected polarization between farmers and ranchers: *"Cattle or Wheat; Which?" was presented in a very well written paper by W. W. Aldrich who favored the wheat side of the question. A number of speeches were made on the subject and were about all on the side of Mr. Aldrich.* Elam mentions another interesting topic: *"The Ideal Farm Horse and How to Care for Him". This was opened in a well written paper by C. H. Babbit who held that among other things the horse for this county should weigh not less than 1400 lbs. This part of the paper elicited much discussion and resulted in almost a unanimous verdict for a horse from 1100 to 1200 lbs!*

Elam prepared a display for the Institute: *I had exhibited on the curtains of the house 47 species of the "Native and Naturalized Grasses of Rooks County". This seemed to prove of much interest to many of the persons present.* A major snowstorm had come up during the event. Speakers failed to show up, and attendees began leaving for home, so the Institute adjourned to reconvene two weeks later. Routine matters were taken up at that time, except: *A resolution was passed voicing the sense of the Institute that Rooks county should be represented by her material products at the World's Fair next year at Chicago.*

Seed oats treatment is described on March 31: *Worked nearly the whole day at treating seed oats for the prevention of smut, using both the Jansen hot water treatment and the sulphide of potassium solution.*

For several years Elam had had good results growing sweet potatoes, so on the 1st of June 1892 he set out 1,300 plants that he had started in a hotbed.

1893

An invitation to visit one of the leading ranches in the area was accepted on March 18, 1893: *At noon George and I went to Stockton in the cart and shortly after getting there drove out southwest of town about four miles to Box Elder Creek to visit the stock ranch of H. V. Toepffer. Was accompanied by Mr. Toepffer who kindly showed me everything pertaining to the whole business. I found among other things that he had 35 head of very fine thoroughbred Holstein cattle which presents an attraction worth going a long way to see.*

On May 6, hogs brought $6.30 per hundredweight, more than double what they had been three years before. Inflationary factors were at work as a result of national debate on gold and silver coinage, among other things. (But a major depression developed not long after this.)

The sweet potato enterprise continued to expand, with 2,100 plants set out in June of 1893. Meanwhile dry conditions ruined the small grain crop. On August 7: *Today, with the Elliott and Potter machine, did our <u>immense</u> job of threshing, having 140 bu of wheat and 20 of rye! Finished* *at 3 p.m.* This notwithstanding, the wheat price declined by December 5 to 46¢ per bushel even though it graded #2 and had a good test weight of 61 pounds. Hog values also had dropped by that date to $4.25 per hundredweight.

1894

By early March 1894 the timber grove near the house included ash, walnut, ailanthus, locust, poplar, and cottonwood. Later the same month a cherry orchard was planted.

An irrigation ditch was constructed five miles up Bow Creek, so on May 15 Elam and George went to see it. There was some trepidation that it would provide no benefit to his farm and would siphon off water that would otherwise have flowed through his property, but no action was taken to interfere. Two more visits to see what was going on were made in the early and late summer, with another the following year.

1895

Extreme heat and blowing dust and sand in late May 1895 did extensive damage to all vegetation. Especially painful was the loss of 4,000 young sweet potato plants that had just been set out. Then rains came, so right away on the 31st Elam and his boys quickly set out 2,000 more.

Despite the series of dust storms of April and May, Elam proceeded to plow up more sod in early June. There was a natural inclination to conclude that the dust that blew in came from origins far beyond his own farm, which was true, and that his aggressive planting of trees would protect his own soil from blowing, probably at least partly true.

In spite of the drought, corn brought only 15¢ per bushel on December 15 during the economic depression. Because of the drought, hogs were liquidated, forcing their value down to $2.85 per hundredweight on the next day.

1896

More cherry and plum trees were planted in the spring of 1896, plus 600 box elder trees.

While in Oakley at a political convention on April 29, Elam got further exposure to operation of an irrigation system: *Visited the state irrigation plant a half mile west of town where I met Prof. C. C. Georgeson of Manhattan, "Judge" W. B. Sutton of Russell, member of the state board of irrigation and Mr. Isaac Jones of Lincoln county who has charge of the plant.*

Hog prices slipped to $2.60 per hundredweight on May 18, 1896.

Only 50 bushels of rye were secured in the small grain harvest, because of unfavorable weather — just one wagonload.

By early October, when it appeared that William Jennings Bryan and the "Free Silverites" would win the election, hogs fetched just $2.50 per hundredweight. But after the election, won by William McKinley, who favored the gold standard, things started to improve. On April 5, 1897, hogs brought $3.40 per hundredweight. Most of the remainder of that year the price hung around $3.00 per hundredweight.

1897

Elam began growing alfalfa in 1897. Results were mediocre because of less-than-favorable weather, but he was convinced of the merits of this crop to supplement prairie hay and pasture. That contributed to his decision in early December of 1897 to become more active in the cattle business. *With Elbert and Jesse went to Stockton and while there made a deal by which we purchased 50 head of 2-year old steers for the sum of $1100 from H. LaRue. Brought home also a half ton of fence wire and 65 posts.* Then on the 6th to 8th of December: *With the boys help worked each of these three days at setting posts and putting up wire fence on the 160 acres joining us on the east.*

One week later he was honored to be named a delegate to a state-wide meeting: *Went to Stockton to attend a meeting of the stockholders of the Rooks County fair association of which I am a member and was elected a delegate to the meeting of the State Board of Agriculture at Topeka next month.*

1898

Orchard harvests began to attain impressive proportions. On July 11, 1898: *In the p.m. helped wife and Lizzie at canning fruit. We put up 44 quarts of cherries and 21 of currants.* Three days later: *We canned 24 quarts of cherries, 8 of gooseberries and 6 of currants.* Finally the totals of various days' efforts: *Completed the canning of our small fruit crop for the year which now consists of 154 quarts of cherries, 85 of gooseberries, 54 of currants and 7 of Juneberries, making a total of an even 300 quarts — 75 gallons!*

Selling cattle to feedlots became a tedious process for Elam. First he tried in eastern Kansas at Blue Rapids on November 12: *With one Ora Ritchie as driver went out with one of Sharp's livery teams 7 miles northeast of town to a Mr. Holt's to see him on business connected with the sale of some cattle which I desire to sell. Meeting no success we returned to town at a little after noon.*

Then he made a special trip to the west, commencing on November 30: *Left home at 9 oclock a.m. for a trip up northwest some 40 miles into Norton and Phillips counties to try to sell some cattle to the feeders on the Prairie Dog Creek. Stopped at Logan with our minister, Rev. R. Arthur for dinner, after which I drove on up to Calvert in Norton county where I arrived about sunset and put up for the night with my old friend elder C. D. Bieber.*

On the next day: *Left friend Bieber's at 8:30 a.m. and drove east to Almena and thence on to Long Island by noon. Took dinner at the hotel where I met my friend elder G. Culbertson. Spent part of the p.m. at the Culbertson bank and part of the time with him at driving about town and the near vicinity visiting cattle feed lots. Passed the night at Mr. Culbertson's hospitable home.*

Finally on December 2: *Left Long Island about 8:45 a.m. and drove to Phillipsburg shortly after noon, taking dinner with my friend elder Phil Townsley. Left Phillipsburg about 3 oclock and came home at 6 having made no sales but being well paid for the experience and things seen on the trip.* He had hoped to be rid of the job of maintaining the cattle through the winter, with potential loss of weight — or worse, the loss of life.

(Meanwhile hog prices slumped again on December 5 to $2.90 per hundredweight on two loads.)

1899

Finally Elam, in a somewhat desperate mood, decided to get rid of those cattle. On January 20, 1899: *In the p.m. beginning at 1:30 oclock we had a public sale of cattle but soon called the sale off as prices at which the cattle were going were not satisfactory.*

Since that did not work out, he kept the cattle through another pasture season until August 14, when he sold them to a friend, thinking that if he could not get a desirable price elsewhere, he might as well do a favor for

someone he knew: *Went to Marvin in the morning on business and sold
our steers — 48 head — to Chas. A. Bracken. Came home at 1 oclock p.m.
and at three oclock with Jesse, Earl and Lee [on] horseback and wife and
I in the buggy we started to drive the cattle to Marvin where we arrived at
sunset but not being able to get them weighed this evening we all came
home at 10 oclock.* Then the next day: *I drove back to Marvin in the morning and we had to take the cattle over N. E. of there about 6 miles to Harry
Simms to weigh them, so I did not get home until 4 oclock p.m.*

In December 1899 wheat brought only 47¢ per bushel. Elam decided
that it was necessary to enlarge the area farmed, with such frequent low
prices. Thus on October 1, 1900: *Went to Stockton on business and while
in town bought the quarter section (160 acres) of land adjoining our
homestead on the east for $1,000.* That is $6.25 per acre.

Hog prices advanced significantly by November 5 to $3.80 per hun-
dredweight.

1901

The year 1901 was not a good one for most crops, but wheat was har-
vested before the worst heat came in late June and all of July, so results
were fairly good by comparison at 1,280 bushels from 100 acres rented
west of the homestead. *The corn crop, hay crop, potato crop, oats, barley
and gardens have all proven to be almost entire failures.*

Despite the heat and drought, it was a good year for some fruit. On September 27 Elam wrote: *We canned today 90 quarts of plums and 4 of
peaches.* Sweet potatoes did well also with results reported on October 19:
*Finished the taking up of our sweet potatoes, there being about 100
bushels on ⅝ of an acre, 77 bushels of which we sold for $127.00.*

1902

So successful were plum trees that it was decided to expand production
of that crop. On March 3, 1902: *With Jesse went down the creek toward
Kirwin about 13 miles to John Zollers where we got about 225 plum trees
and returned home shortly before five oclock.* Of these 180 were planted
at Elam's place on the 27th and the remainder given to neighbors.

From this time forward there were fewer diary entries describing farming activities. Elam's days were largely spent on botanical matters. It was a very convenient time for a career shift. He was 50 years old and had sons who could run the farm. Farming was still his first love, and always would be, but it was time to let the boys do the work for which he had trained them so well.

1903

On January 14, 1903, Elam went to Topeka as a delegate to the annual meeting of the state Board of Agriculture. This unique Kansas organization had always been strictly non-political, guarding this precept religiously through the years. The delegates represented officially recognized county farm organizations such as Farm Bureau, Farmer's Union, Fair Associations, and so on. From the delegates a 12-person board was selected that, in turn, chose best-qualified employees to run its affairs. In most other states the Department of Agriculture was controlled by the legislature or the governor and was staffed by political patronage.

On May 23 Elam bought a New Champion grain binder for $133.

Spring rains in 1903 were ample and provided uncommonly good crops for Elam and much of western Kansas. While they became excessively heavy farther east, resulting in devastating floods whose records were not broken until 1951, the financial benefit to Elam enabled him to build a modern house and barn in the next few years. When grain threshing was completed on September 18, the results were recorded: *Wheat 2,062 bus. Rye 260 and Barley 260.*

1904

By 1904 the cherry orchard had matured sufficiently to produce impressive fruit. On June 25 Elam *took several bushels to Stockton to market.* But the 27th was more significant: *A day of unusual activity in our cherry orchard! Many persons here either picking or buying, so I was in the midst of the hubbub all day. About 14 bushels of cherries were picked in all!*

1907

Another horticultural enterprise was conducted on March 7, 1907: *Assisted R. M. Garber of Stockton, who came out with me last evening, at preparing material for grafting about 1000 Laire plum scions onto seedling peach plants.*

More experimental work began on May 6: *With Lee's help worked in the a.m. at preparing the ground on which to plant some Central American corn on experimental work for the U.S. Department of Agriculture. In the afternoon, with wife's help, we did the planting.* The work was inspected and additional projects were arranged on June 7: *At 10:20 a.m. met the train with Prof. G. N. Collins on it, of Washington D.C., special agent of the U.S. Department of Agriculture, reaching home at 12:30 oclock. The p.m. was spent in social chat with Mr. Collins and in inspecting the experiments which we are carrying on here.*

Five days later: *Spent most of the day with Earl and Lee in putting out 24 plats of alfalfa 9x200 feet in size in conducting some experimental work for the U.S. Department of Agriculture.*

On September 7 another inspection finds things favorable: *At 10:30 a.m. Profs C. J. Brand and Edgar Brown of Washington D.C., special agents of the U.S. Department of Agriculture, came in by way of Phillipsburg to examine the experimental work we have been doing here this season in Central American corn and some 24 varietal forms of alfalfa. Expressing themselves as well pleased with the work accomplished and arranging for a widening of the scope for next year, they remained with us until 5:30 oclock p.m. at which time they returned to Phillipsburg on their way to investigate work in Nebraska.*

1908

On April 29, 1908, 38 varieties of Central American corn were planted in the experimental program. Then on May 25 the other work was done: *In the p.m. worked with Earl and Lee at marking out the ground and at commencing the planting of 113 plots of various strains and well-marked varieties of alfalfa for the U.S. Department of Agr., the same to be planted in hills 3x3:10 feet each way.*

Professor Brand stopped by on July 9 on his way to California. Upon inspecting the experimental work he *seemed to be much pleased.* Then a new venture is explored on September 7: *At 10 a.m. Prof. S. C. Mason of Washington D.C. came in by way of Phillipsburg to arrange for the culture here of various fruits not grown in this region, so the time was spent with him until 4 p.m. at which time he left us to continue his journey to Arizona and California.*

1909

On March 13, 1909, Elam received an attractive offer: *At the close of the Rooks Co. Farmers Institute Prof. J. H. Miller of Manhattan, Supt. of Institute work for the State Agr. College made me an offer of $1500 per annum to take up the work of "Dry Farming" demonstrator for the State Institute Association to work throughout the western one-third of the state, but at present I cannot see my way clear to accept the position.*

A new experiment was begun on May 10: *From 10 a.m. until 4 p.m. with brother Elias* [who was visiting] *and the boys, spent the time at planting a small tract of experimental cotton for the U.S. Department of Agriculture.* Even though Elam had good success with growing cotton for a few years, the idea was abandoned. It was decided that this area was too marginal for results to be reliable as a general rule. Moreover, it is a labor-intensive crop — unattractive to western Kansas farmers at a time when grain farming was becoming mechanized and cotton farming was not.

Meanwhile, a more interesting experiment was continued on May 17: *With the assistance of Earl and Lee worked all day at preparing the ground and laying it out into suitable plots and planting the seed of 90 different strains of alfalfa in our government experimental work for the Department of Agriculture at Washington.*

On October 18 Professor J. H. Kinsley of Washington came to inspect results of the cotton experiment.

1910

The price of hogs was up significantly on February 19, 1910: *With Lee and two of our neighbors Thos. McCue and Howard White, took 4 loads of hogs — 30 — to Glade where we delivered them at $8.15 per cwt. receiving for them the neat little sum of $471.50. We all took dinner at the Taylor hotel and came home shortly before 4 oclock p.m.*

Work began on the new barn on September 1, 1910: *With Jesse worked*

The Bartholomews' new barn, 1910.

Picking cherries in 1914. Elam noted that 35 people picked 38 bushels in one day.

all day with plow and scraper at excavating for our new barn which is to be 38x44 feet on cement foundation.

Carpenters arrived on September 12: *With boys worked at taking down the forms to our cement barn foundation and nearly completed the grading and fills, in and about the structure. In the p.m. at 4 oclock Kay and Snyder of Stockton came over and began active operations on the carpenter work.*

Elam prepared the shingles on the 19th: *Worked all day at dipping barn shingles in a mixture consisting of 1 part linseed oil and 2 parts coal oil with Venetian red for pigment.*

On October 13 the barn was nearly finished: *As the work is nearly finished we paid the carpenters off — $155 — and will do ourselves what little inside work is yet needed to complete the building.*

Almost immediately, on October 25: *Helped Earl and Lee at putting stacked hay into the barn with slings.* A track along the ridge of the roof, on the inside, was equipped with pulleys and ropes. A team on the other end of the barn would pull the load of hay up from the hayrack into the mow and dump it inside the barn.

Just as work was commencing on the new barn, Elam took time out for a visitor. On September 2, 1910: *Prof. W. F. Wight of the Dept. of Agr. Washington, D.C. having come in last evening about 7 oclock and remained for the night, the time until 10 a.m. today was spent in social and scientific chat with the professor and in superintending the laying out of the barn foundation.*

At 10 oclock the professor and I in the buggy made a trip down N.E. about 15 miles to the residence of Abram Laire to establish the origin of the well-known "Laire plum" of this region establishing the fact of its apparent origin and first cultivation from wild stock planted by Mr. Laire on his Bow creek farm in 1878.

1911

Then on April 11, 1911: *Assisted Earl and Lee at setting out several hundred Laire plum grafts.* One has to wonder if these Laire plum grafts are the same as what was previously called "Layer" plums.

1913

The year 1913 was a good one for cherries. On June 16: *Busy as a "cranberry merchant" all day with about 40 people who were here either picking or buying cherries. Over 23 bushels went out of the orchard which is the biggest cherry day we have ever had.*

The Stockton folks had a big picnic dinner in the grove and later many of them went fishing in the creek near by and caught several fine messes of fish. Taking it all in all it was quite a gala day and one long to be remembered. The next day a crowd picked 17½ bushels.

1915

Another fine crop of cherries was realized in 1915. Elam recorded on June 16: *Spent a very busy day in the orchard with the cherry pickers. Over 70 persons were here today, including children, after cherries and we got out 38 bushels of remarkably fine fruit! This is a record breaker as to the number of persons calling in one day and the amount of cherries picked.* The final tally was 75 bushels!

Elam had to look for outside help around the farm, so on November 2, 1915, he wrote: *With Lee made a trip to Stockton in the auto where we met a hired man and wife of Clinton, Kans. who are here to look the matter over as to working for us next season as Lee expects to move to Burns, Wyo., in the early spring, where he has bought a half section of land.* An agreement was reached for the hired help to begin March 1.

A new road in the area was agreed upon on December 8, 1915: *At 10 a.m. County Commissioners Hulse, Thomas and Wallace with County Surveyor Carl Cooper and the Farmington Tp. Board, met here to lay out a new public road through our creek pasture and we worked thereat until 3 p.m. at which time the work was completed.*

1916

Wheat brought a good price in early 1916, on February 19: *While in town sold 630 bushels of previously delivered wheat at $1.05 per bu.* Then, while in town: *Hired man and wife and little 7 year old girl came to town on the morning train and we brought them out home with us and will be with us as man and woman of all work for the next year, at least, beginning Mch. 1st.*

Cherry harvest was good again in 1916. On June 19: *This was "Cherry Day at Bartholomew's" and with a large force of pickers 40 bushels of fine*

Picking cherries at the Bartholomews, June 16, 1916 — 106 bushels were picked that year.

fruit was carted away from the ranch! Yes, I am tired thoroughly, having had to superintend the whole business, do the measuring and keep the accounts!

The price of wheat continued to climb as the war in Europe was obviously going to eventually expand to include the U.S. On October 27, 1916: *Took a load of wheat to Stockton today for which I received $1.70 per bushel which is the highest price at which I have ever marketed wheat.*

The hired man did not work out well at all. On October 16: *Early this morning the hired man and wife left us by team for Palco, this county, where they expect to make some sort of attempt to do farm work for H. T. Sutor. With us they have been the rottenest and most unsatisfactory individuals with which we have had to do in all our 40 years' work on this farm!*

Both man and woman are petty sneak thieves and socially and religiously are below the zero mark! Their gall and disposition to lay hands on things not their own was simply astonishing so they had to be kicked out in simple justice to ourselves.

We paid them a cash salary of $35.00 per month from March 1, 1916 to Oct. 1, 1916 and perquisites convertible into cash or its equivalent to the amount of $35.00 per month additional making a total of $70.00 per month, or better! Yet they were the most grasping, ungrateful and abusive outfit that I have ever known and that's going some!

We now have Jas. O'Connor, a 17½ year old boy working for us who took his position last evening.

Elam soon came to the realization that it was not practical to expect a hired man to do the work the way he wanted it done, and that he really needed to have someone take charge. He was 64 years old and getting rapidly deeper into botanical involvement. He was ready to accept the fact that Lee was the right person for the job, and that he should become more involved in the total farm management responsibility, and not be just a "hired man."

Thus, on November 24, 1916: *Busy all day in knocking about at odd jobs and ridding the yards about the two dwelling houses and thus making things look "spic and span" and neat and clean about the place. At 5:30 p.m. with Earl, we went over to Phillipsburg with the auto to meet*

Lee, Lily and little Rachel who came in on their return to Kansas from Wyoming.

Our effort to conduct the farm with hired help was a most dismal failure. Lee's have rented their 320-acre farm in Wyoming and will now assume control of the home farm and live in the new house built last spring.

1918

The watermelon harvest in 1918 was a good one. On August 22: *In the morning with Jesse in his auto drove to Stockton with a load of 32 watermelons, weighing 640 lbs for which I received $14.40.* More were picked on the 30th: *At 7 a.m. with Jesse in his auto took 40 watermelons to Stockton for which I received $13.90.* An additional sale on September 9 of 35 melons weighing 713 pounds brought $14.

Formation of another farm organization attracted Elam on September 14, 1918: *In the p.m. with neighbor Frank Ives drove to Stockton with him in his car and while in town attended a preliminary county "Farm Bureau" meeting at the library building. The meeting was conducted by Profs. Scott and Tinker.*

A major windmill installation took place on December 6: *Had a 42 ft. tower windmill put up at the barn today, by Robinson and Smith of Stockton.*

1919

While in Manhattan to attend the meeting of the Kansas Academy of Science on April 18, 1919, Elam heard a speech on a topic that is still of popular concern: *Heard a good address by Dr. H. B. Ward of the University of Illinois on "The Rapid Growth of Stream Pollution".*

As time passed some orchard trees died and had to be replaced. One such time was on April 26: *In the p.m. with Lee worked at grubbing out old stumps in our peach orchard.* And this comment on June 28: *Trimming out old cherry trees. Our once famous cherry orchard is fast approaching the vanishing point, principally due to old age.*

1920

Wheat produced a very good crop in 1920. On July 19: *Earl and Lee finished their big 430 acre wheat harvest late this evening, having been at it since June 28. The crop was most excellent and it promises the great-*

est yield we have ever known in this region. Yield was 26 bushels per acre.

Plums also did well that year. On August 30 Elam wrote: *Our annual plum harvest beginning today, the whole time from "early morn till dewey eve" was spent in picking plums and waiting on and serving customers of whom there were 22 and they took out 32 bushels at $1.50 per bu.* Another 14 bushels were picked the next day.

1921

Wheat price on April 18, 1921, was not so high but still reasonably good: *Lee and I sold 3300 bu. of wheat at $1.05 per bu.*

Elam decided to give Lee a partial interest in the family farming operation on May 14: *Transferred our east 160 acres to Lee for a consideration of $7000.*

There was trouble with incompetent farm help on June 30: *Made a trip to Stockton to take over two harvest hands who had become too tired to work any longer and to bring out two new Chicago hands to take the place of the tired ones!*

1924

Exploration for petroleum had been going on for years in the area, finally reaching Elam's place in 1924. He received a message while in California on August 18: *Gave today an oil lease on our homestead — 160 acres. Check for $80 as royalty or rent was also received today. Boring on premises to ensue within one year from date of lease.* Nothing ever came of it.

1926

Because of Elam's involvement in things other than farming by this time, there are very few comments providing details on the subject. Nevertheless, a summary statement on the last day of 1926 reveals what kind of year it was: *Agriculturally the year was the slimmest that I have ever seen here in my 52 years residence! The total rainfall, including melted snow, was only 14.31 inches which is nearly 10 inches below our annual average!*

1929

Because Elam made the decision in 1929 to leave the farm and go to a position at the college in Hays, a farm sale was held on July 25: *Had our public sale of live stock, farm machinery and household goods today. A very large crowd was present. Sale amounted to nearly $2000 and prices were very satisfactory.* Of course it was an emotional event as it is for every farmer, regardless of circumstances. In his case, he had been the first owner, starting out from "scratch." But he was too old now to carry on, so that made the situation easier. He refrained from expressing any emotion in the diary.

A deal for sale of land and buildings was made on August 6: *With Lee in the car drove up west 4½ miles to B. D. Stephen's where we talked farm sale until 10:30 oclock and came home to Lee's at 11:00. In the p.m. banker Kirkpatrick of Bogue drove down to examine our farm to see if he thought it would be a profitable investment for his friend Stephen, and he decided that it would be.*

It was concluded the next day: *Mr. Stephen drove down to Lee's, in the morning, to see us and with him in the Stephen car we drove to Bogue where we consummated a deal for the sale of the north half of Sec. 10, Town 6, Range 18 for the sum of $15,000; $2000 cash in hand; $2000 Oct. 1st and $4000 March 1st 1930 when a deed is to be exchanged for a 5-year 6-per cent mortgage. In the $15,000 deal made today I am to get $10,000 and Lee $5,000.*

1930

Another step was taken in settlement of the sale of the farm on February 17, 1930: *At 5:45 p.m. with Lee and his daughter Rachel in the car, left for Stockton where we arrived at 7 oclock and met Mr. & Mrs. B. D. Stephen, by appointment, relative to setting up and giving a deed to our homestead. We set Friday of this week to close the deal.*

That phase was concluded on the 21st: *At 7:30 a.m. with Lee in the car left for Stockton and got there at 8:45 where shortly after we met Mr. & Mrs. B. D. Stephen and Banker Kirkpatrick of Bogue with whom we went into conference in the Stockton National Bank where we proceeded to close the deal of transferring our old original homestead to Mr. Stephen for the sum of $10,000. 5500 dollars has been paid to date and $4500 is yet standing on a 5-year 6 per cent mortgage.*

1932

The new owner ran into financial problems. Elam wrote on October 27,

1932: *While in the area on other business drove over to Bow Creek to our old farmstead to interview the present owner, B. D. Stephen, who is falling down badly on defaulted interest payments and taxes.*

The matter was pursued on November 9: *At 9:30 a.m. with Lily in the car, made a business trip to Bogue, Graham Co., relative to the man, B. D. Stephen who bought our farm in June 1929. No good news.*

1933

An attempt to resolve the situation was made on July 4, 1933: *With sister-in-law Celia Fink, Lee & Lilly and Jesse's boy, Robt. left Hays at 8 a.m. and drove to Stockton where we dropped Robert at son Earl's and the rest of us drove out to the old homestead on Bow Creek and thence back to Stockton where we all took dinner at Earl's. Later B. D. Stephen, who occupies our old home place, drove in to confer with us on the payment of the $4500 mortgage we have on the place. With him we drove to Webster to confer with I. Gilliland about getting a loan through the Federal Land Bank Corporation at Wichita, Kans. Made very little headway.*

Finally a deal was made on December 22: *At 9 a.m. with Lily in our car drove to Stockton where we arrived shortly after 10 and remained there until about 1 p.m., having met B. D. Stephen, our tenant-owner of our old farm, we drove with him over to the home of I. Gillen at Webster where I did business with both Stephen and Gillen on settlement of the farm mortgage, by the Land Bank Corporation, of the $4500 due us.*

Signed up all the necessary papers and thence back to Stockton with Mr. Stephen where we dropped him off and then came on to Hays at 6 oclock. While we hope not, yet, we fear there will be much <u>red tape</u> to be unwound before complete settlement is attained.

Chapter 4

Weather and
Other Acts of Nature

*T*HE YEAR 1871 APPARENTLY PROVIDED an abundance of moisture in the area of Farmington, Illinois, for on many days work was interrupted by rain. No mention is made of specific details for 1871, but in subsequent years there is meticulous and methodical notation of moisture amounts, temperatures, and other natural phenomena.

One of the most significant of these other events was the great Chicago fire. On October 11, 1871: *A great fire is raging in Chicago which has burned over hundreds of acres of buildings!* Spoken just like you might expect from a farmer's point of view. But there was no other mention of this catastrophe, even when details became known in subsequent days. (It raged for over 24 hours, destroying 17,450 buildings in an area of 3¼ square miles, over 2,000 acres. At least 300 persons died, 90,000 were homeless, and damage was estimated at $200 million.)

1872

Ample rains fell again in 1872. Then came a heavy snow on December 19, but that did not stop Elam from going 2½ miles to Farmington the next day on his weekly trip to get the mail.

1873

An extreme cold spell hit on January 29, 1873: *The weather being 34 degrees below zero this morning the day was spent closely within doors mostly in reading.*

1874

Nothing very specific was reported about weather conditions when Elam went to western Kansas to take up residence in early 1874. There were, however, observations about extreme heat and bitter cold that first summer and winter, with seemingly ample rain for 1875 crops.

1875

There was a notation, without comment, of a celestial event on August 5, 1875: *Occultation of Spica by the moon.* The moon passes in front of Spica about every 18 years. Spica, the brightest star in the constellation Virgo, is a blue star of the first magnitude.

1877

Prairie fires occurred frequently until years later when most of the sod had been plowed under to plant crops. On April 22, 1877: *A prairie fire from the south being the order of the day until 1 p.m. the time until then was spent in fighting the same, with many others, about 2 miles east of here.* More fires broke out on November 9: *Spent the entire day, with many others, at fighting prairie fires and burning fire guards north of Bow creek and over in the south edge of Phillips Co.*

1878

Sometimes all the neighbors from miles around pitched in to fight the fires. On April 23, 1878: *In the evening with a company of the neighbors went over south three or four miles to fight prairie fires and having succeeded in our work returned home at one oclock!* One would not dare go to bed until the job was done, because a wind-driven fire can go many miles in a short time.

A grain crop about to be threshed can be threatened by a prairie fire that could race through the stubble. On October 14: *Got ready this morning to commence our small grain threshing when a rather fierce prairie fire came in from the northwest, so we were compelled to let the threshing stand and go fight fire which we did until noon when we got it under control. In the p.m. started the threshing machine but broke a tumbling shaft knuckle about 3 oclock which put us out of business for the rest of the day.*

1879

A rather severe earthquake hit on April 27, 1879, something unusual for that region: *In the evening attended church meeting at Mr. Jacob Shell's and almost exactly at the hour of 9 oclock, just about the closing of the sermon, a rolling, shaking sensation was experienced by all and it seemed as though the roof of the house was about to fall in when a great rush was made for the door and a portion of the people got out, very much frightened, while the remainder stayed within. The cause of alarm was a rather severe though not disasterous shock of earthquake which seemed to go to the southwestward.*

1880

A prairie fire got frighteningly close on March 29, 1880: *In the p.m. directly after dinner a prairie fire having got out over south east about 1½ miles and a brisk S.E. wind being the order of the day, I started for the scene of action. The fire came to the creek and crossed as though no creek was there and went on away to the northward with a horrible speed. Worked until about 5 p.m. when the 30 or 40 persons engaged in the fight had whipped the fire out of the country.*

A drought-breaking rain was received on May 4, 1880: *About 5:30 p.m. a heavy soaking thundershower came up from the N.W. drenching the earth completely. As no moisture of any importance had been precipitated either in the form of rain or snow since Nov. 11, 1879, the rain of this evening was a godsend indeed as thousands of acres of wheat in western Kansas have already been destroyed by the extremely prolonged drought. As a consequence of the continued dry weather many people were getting the blues badly and the chronic croakers were all proclaiming the droughtiest drought that ever struck Kansas. People west of us on the extreme frontier were commencing to turn their faces toward the land of the rising sun.*

The rain seemed to be quite general and not merely local and it is to be hoped that it was universal, at least throughout western Kan. that, if for no other reason, the tongues of the croakers, grumblers and fretters may be enabled to take a rest. A stagnation of the mercantile interests of the county had also set in which it is also to be hoped has been completely averted by today's refreshing rainfall and the succeeding precipitations which we hope to see follow. (It was not until 1882 that weather provided a good crop.)

1881

Temperature extremes of significant magnitude in 1881 made life

FROM BOW CREEK.

Rockport, Jan. 6th, 1879.

Ed. News:—I herewith hand you a summary report of the transaction of "Old Probabilities" for the past twelve months, as viewed from northern Rooks county, and taken from my Meteorological Report for 1878 Some of the statements will undoubtedly seem very improbable to many of your readers, yet, they are nevertheless true and perfect in every particular, as I have taken the greatest possible pains to have the state of the weather for each day of the past year recorded correctly.

The number of days on which rain fell are as follows: January, 1; Feb., 3; March, 3; April, 8; May, 10; June, 13; July, 9; Aug., 4; Sept., 3; Oct., 1; Nov., 3; Dec., 0; total, 58. Days on which snow fell—Jan , 2; Feb, 4; Oct., 1; Dec , 6; total, 13.

Number of days that were calm: Jan , 10; Feb., 5; Mar., 3; April, 5; May, 3; June, 6; July 4; Aug., 8; Sept., 3; Oct., 5; Nov , 11; Dec , 6. The number of days that were windy —297, divided as follows: high wind, 35; brisk wind, 49; fresh wind, 86; light wind, 127.

Number of days that were totally clear: Jan. 17; Feb. 7; March 9; April 14; May 4, June 10, July 16 Aug 23, Sept. 20. Oct. 22, Nov 18.

Dec, 12 total 172. Number of days that were heavily clouded during the year, 65. Number that were hazzy or partially cloudy, 123.

The prevailing directions of the wind for the year are as follows: North 42 days. South 41 days. East 7 days. West 6 days. N. E 18 days S. E, 30 days. N. W 50 days. S. W 22 days. From different or various directions during the day, 81 days.

Those who have heretofore been disposed to croak about the extreme drouth ness of this country need have no fears hereafter that they will be compelled to wither completely away as long as we have 58 days of rain per annum.

For high and "uproarious" winds. March carries off the palm to the tune of 9 days, while for calm weather Nov. takes the lead with 11 days, and for clear weather Aug. stands first with 23 days, while "bemirred blossoming May" only gives us 4. It will be seen that the North and South winds are almost equal, as are also the East and West, and N. E. and S. W , while the opposing currents from the N. W. and S. E. come far short of producing an equilibrium, standing 50 to 30 respectively.

Having made this report more exhaustive than I at first calculated I will not trespass on your time, space and patience any further.

ELAM BARTHOLOMEW.

Elam enjoyed things scientific, including keeping meticulous records of the events of weather to the best of his ability with limited measurement devices. Because there was no government weather station in the vicinity, and no one else to do the job, the local paper was pleased to print his records. His handwritten account is from his weather log (see next page).

Meteorology for 1885

May 22 10 per cent cloudy at 62-88 with brisk S. wind
" 23 80 per cent cloudy at 60-80 with fresh S.E. wind
" " Series of moderate thunder showers set in as
" " 7:30 a.m. continuing until 11:30 when they ceas
" " At 7 P.m. one of the most terrific and
" " drenching thunder storms I have ever seen
" " broke from th. N. and N.E. continuing with
" " the greatest violence for about two hours
" " when it abated somewhat but continued
" " showery until long after midnight
" " Streams very high, Bow creek 6 feet. A great
" " deal of damage done by washing of plowed
" " lands where somewhat rolling.
" 24 30 per cent cloudy at 60-74 with fresh N. wind
" 25 25 per cent cloudy at 38-80 with light easterly winds
" 26 80 per cent cloudy at 48-82 with fresh S.E. & E. winds
" 27 75 per cent cloudy at 58-76 with light shifting winds
" " Moderate rain fall from 4 a.m. until 8.
" 28 75 per cent cloudy at 52-72 with fresh N.W. wind
" " Occasional light rainfalls in th. afternoon.
" 29 90 per cent cloudy at 52-62 with fresh N.W. & N. wind
" " Showery from 6 a.m. until afternoon
" 30 Clear at 48-82 with very light N.W. wind.
" 31 Clear at 48-89 with brisk S. wind
" " Moderate thunder shower at 10:30 P.m.

June 1st 10 per cent cloudy at 58-90. Calm & very oppressive
" " Brisk thunder shower at 1:30 a.m. accompanied
" " by much vivid lightning and heavy thunder
" 2 40 per cent cloudy at 60-99 with light shifting breeze
" " Threatening rain nearly all day with mod.

An example of Elam's weather log.

nearly intolerable. The 9th of January saw 22 degrees below zero. Then on July 19: *The afternoon was spent in trying to keep cool, it being one of the hottest days I ever saw, the mercury getting up to 106, averaging fully 100 from sunrise to sunset.* It was even worse on the 20th: *Today was, I believe, the hottest day that I ever saw, the mercury standing at 111 in the shade and 122 in the sunshine, and as a brisk S.W. wind was blowing the greater part of the day, the consequence was that the corn crop was almost anni-hilated, being scorched badly.*

Significant relief was received on the 29th: *A heavy soaking rain fell this morning about sunrise which was one of the greatest blessings imag-inable to western Kansas as a few days more of dry weather would have completely ruined the corn crop.*

1882

It is of utmost significance to note the observation of March 17, 1882: *A very high wind being the order of the day and it being exceedingly dusty and disagreeable, the time was spent almost exclusively within doors, reading, writing, etc., etc.* Precisely eight years before, Elam had laid out his homestead claim in Kansas, but not until this date in 1882 was there even one word mentioning blowing dust. A vast amount of prairie sod had been turned to plant crops in those eight years as the flood of settlers moved in and began to farm rather than leave the grass for pasture. Much more sod was turned in the next few years, some of it on Elam's farm. From this date forward Elam mentioned fewer and fewer prairie fires, and more and more dust storms.

Elam, being of a keen and observant mind, could imagine the hazardous potential of soil erosion by wind. This was one reason he so assiduously planted trees about the place. (One concentration was on the northwest corner of the farm.) He was probably one of the very first to conceive of the idea that 50 years later would become known as "shelterbelts" — rows of trees or shrubs planted to protect the soil, buildings, or animals from the wind — widely promoted by various governmental agencies. Of course, his other reason for planting trees was simply that he needed the wood for lumber, fence posts, fuel for heating and cooking, and so on. Thus not only was he trying to fight wind erosion, he wanted a marketable timber crop.

The government had taken steps in 1873 to encourage tree planting as well as crop production, by passing The Timber-Culture Act, in which

Elam participated. Under the subheading "An act to encourage the growth of timber on the Western prairies," the act stated:

> Be it enacted by the Senate and House of Representatives of the United States of America in Congress assembled, That any person who shall plant, protect, and keep in healthy growing condition for ten years, forty acres of timber, the trees thereon not being more than twelve feet apart each way, on any quarter-section [160 acres] of any of the public lands of the United States, shall be entitled to a patent for the whole of said quarter-section at the expiration of said ten years, on making proof of such fact by not less than two credible witnesses: Provided, That only one quarter in any section shall be thus granted.

More dust blew a few days later, on the 20th and 21st of March.

A most unusual celestial event took place on December 6, 1882: *Between the hours of one and two oclock the clouds broke away partially and we got a moderately good view of the transit of Venus across the sun's disc and as another transit will not occur until the year 2004 it is probably the last one we will witness.* Since this happens only once in 122 years, it is not seen at all by a good many people.

1883

Another prairie fire needed attention on March 19, 1883: *Went down to Lovell's after a load of wood in the morning and a prairie fire coming in from the north worked with a number of others at extinguishing the same, not getting home until toward evening.*

More trees were planted on April 18: *Worked in the a.m. at plowing on our timber claim, calculating to plow 5 acres thereon, which must be done previous to June 17, in compliance with the law regulating timber culture entries.*

1884

Dust blew again on March 15, 1884: *Spent the day mostly in reading and writing, owing to the disagreeableness of the weather without, it being very dusty with high S. & S.W. wind.*

Fires occurred nearby on May 9: *Plowed in the a.m. and either fought or watched prairie fires at home and over on our timber claim in the p.m.*

Then the spring of 1884 turned very wet with frequent rains. The south fork of the Solomon River flooded at Stockton, causing problems for grist mills, which, of course, were dependent on water wheels for power. On May 23: *Went to Stockton with a grist of wheat, but not being able to cross the river at the mill, on account of high water, went on down to French's mill which is on this side of the river, but on arriving there found the dam washed out so returned to town where I left my grist to await the fall of the river.*

1885

Heavy rains were also experienced in the spring of 1885. Elam wrote on May 23: *After dinner went to Stockton to mill and to attend to other business. Started for home about 6 oclock and when about three miles from home one of the heaviest thunderstorms that has ever been known here broke upon us (brother Frank being with me) and we took refuge in John Sheibley's stable which was little better than no shelter at all. We finally went to the house where we stayed until after 10 oclock and then started on a mud and water trip for home and before arriving discovered that a large straw stack at mother's place had been struck by lightning, so Frank got out of the wagon and struck straight for home while I continued on and arrived here at 11 oclock pretty thoroughly soaked.*

Damage was slight, as viewed the next day: *Went over to Mother's in the morning and found that the fire of last night did but little damage as with the assistance of the neighbors the machinery and implements in a shed connected with the stack were saved.* But other areas suffered heavily. On the 26th: *Took two loads of wheat to Kirwin and got home at 7:30 oclock p.m. Stephen Wilkin accompanied me. The whole distance of 18 miles we saw continual evidences of the terrible water deluge and hail storm of last Sat. evening. Damage great.*

A very wet summer followed. On July 31: *Knocking about at not much of anything, the heavy rains of last night and this morning preventing any work. Bow creek was higher than I have ever seen it before during an eleven years' residence in this locality. The water took away or tore down about 100 rods of our wire fence.*

Winter began with a vengeance on December 4: *Took a load of rye to Marvin and returned home at 1 oclock p.m. I must say that the trip was one of the most disagreeable that I have ever made anywhere as an exceedingly high N.W. wind was blowing which filled the air with dust and flying debris of all sorts, rendering progress toward the north almost impossible.*

1886

It remained abnormally cold late that winter. Elam wrote on March 30, 1886: *Weather the coldest that I have ever experienced at this time of the year, the thermometer registering 6 degrees below zero at sunrise.*

1887

More dust blew on April 9, 1887: *A most uncomfortable dust storm being the order of the day the time was spent pretty closely within doors, reading and writing.*

1888

The summer of 1888 turned extremely hot. The 13th of July reached 108 degrees. The 29th got up to 112, and the corn crop was obviously in trouble. Next day, 111 degrees. Then on the 31st: *The weather being intolerably hot — 113 — the time was mostly passed in trying to keep cool, which trial proved a failure. The past three days, in point of heat, surpass anything heretofore recorded in this part of Kansas. Throughout western Kansas a very large area of corn was planted this year and as a result of the excessive heat and dry weather for the past 30 days, a very large per cent of the crop will prove an entire failure. A great deal of our 60 acres of corn is already in a bad plight with very little prospect of rain.* August began equally hot with the first two days at 107 and 106 degrees.

1890

A serious blow came up on March 23, 1890: *The day was very disagreeable with an exceedingly high south wind, filling the air with great clouds of dust and all manner of debris.*

Again a prairie fire had to be contained on April 5: *Worked in the a.m. at planting potatoes, and a big prairie fire coming in from the southwest* shortly *after noon the time until 4 oclock was spent with a large number of the neighbors in fighting the fire. We then got it extinguished. The losses were confined mostly to the burning of a number of haystacks.*

Just three days later another dust storm occurred: *Worked in the a.m. at plowing in a small patch of oats and a most horrible dust storm being the order of the day from 9 a.m. until after sunset the p.m. was spent in reading and writing.*

Summer of 1890 had some extreme heat as well, reaching 109 on July 9 and 113 on the 29th. Summer of 1891 was better, with good, timely rains in June and partly into July.

1891

A light earthquake shock was felt at 7 a.m. on November 29, 1891.

1892

Dust blew again on April 1, 1892: *Sowed oats until about 10 a.m. and then worked awhile at cultivating them in when a most violent windstorm prevented further field work for the day as the air was filled with clouds of dust and sand and flying rubbish of all sorts.* And again on the 19th: *A most terrible dust storm from the north.*

1893

And, on April 19, 1893: *A most terrible dust storm from the north.*

Then came a prairie fire on the 27th, coming very close to home: *Took a 38 bu. load of corn to Marvin and getting home at 1 p.m. went immediately to help fight a prairie fire which came in from the south and reached the creek 1½ miles west of us. Got it out and came home about 5 oclock, hungry and tired.*

1894

Dust blew on March 10, 1894: *A very disagreeable N.W. dust storm with very high wind prevailed all day.* Again on the 17th: *Spent the time until 3 p.m. at miscellaneous work and setting out cherry trees, but the remainder of the day was spent mostly in reading owing to the fact that a terrific south dust storm was in progress.* Also on the 19th of April: *Spent the day in reading and writing. A very disagreeable day with bad N.W. dust storm.*

An unusual late freeze occurred on May 19, 1894: *The thermometer registered only 26 degrees above zero at sunrise this morning and as a result we have had the most disastrous freeze that has ever been known in this part of Kansas. The damage will amount to thousands of dollars.*

1895

Extreme winter weather prevailed for five days in early February 1895, the 4th through the 8th: *The weather being very cold each of these five days the time was spent in reading, writing and botanical study. On the 6th occurred one of the most disagreeable snow and dust storms that was ever known in this or perhaps any other region. A very high N. wind prevailed.* March 30 was also *very dusty with a high south wind.* Again a week later *a most terrific dust storm.*

Temperatures turned *exceedingly hot; 100 in the shade!* on May 8, 1895. (Just a year before, on the 19th, there had been a killing freeze.) Then on the 27th it got up to 103 degrees, with *vegetation suffering greatly.* And on the 28th: *The wind continued almost a hurricane throughout all last night with some abatement this forenoon, but in the p.m. it came with renewed force as a blast from the infernal regions and continued into the night.*

It was a day to be long remembered by everyone. The weather was clear both days with the exception of the clouds of dust and sand that filled the air! A large amount of damage was done to vegetation of all sorts — trees as well as herbaceous plants.

And on the next day: *The terrible dust blizzard continued throughout all last night and ceased about sunrise this morning. For us, aside from the great damage to fruit, garden and field crops, it actually swept away ridges and all 4000 sweet potatoe plants previously set out! Light sprinkle of rain at 7 p.m.*

1896

The year 1896 also had its spring dust storms, beginning April 3: *Left Kirwin at 10 a.m. and getting to C. R. Robbins at noon stopped there for dinner and came home at 4 oclock p.m. in the midst of a severe south dust storm.* Again on the 11th: *Very dusty with high wind.*

1898

Dust became serious again in early 1898, on March 14: *A terrible dust storm from the S. & S.W. being the order after 9 a.m. the whole day was*

The Precipitation of Moisture at Rockport. Rooks Co. Kansas. has been as - shows for th time specified.

	1889	1890	1891	1892	1893	1894
January	1.75	2.25	2.85	75		
February	1.50	.50	.95	2.85		
March	3.35	.55	5.25	2.85		
April	2.65	2.40	2.85	1.15		
May	4.05	.90	4.80	5.35		
June	3.15	5.40	7.80	1.10		
July	10.40	1.10	6.55	4.05		
August	2.00	1.45	.85	3.70		
September	.30	.20	4.75	10		
October	.85	.65	2.45	1.25		
November	2.40	1.35	.20	55		
December	none	.40	2.05	1.70		
Totals	32.40	17.05	41.35	25.40		

Elam's handwritten records of precipitation in Rooks County, Kansas, 1889-1892.

spent strictly within doors in reading and social chat with Rev. Arthur who stopped here on his way home in the forenoon and staid the rest of the day and all night also. But rains came with unusual frequency in May.

1899

Early February of 1899 was extremely cold, being down to zero each day from the 7th to 11th, plunging to 26 below on the 12th.

Dust got really bad on April 30: *Came home at 12:30 p.m. in a most terrible S. & S.W. dust storm which during the whole afternoon was simply awful in its severity and did much damage to growing vegetation generally.* Rain on May 19 broke the drought: *A good rain having fallen last night, which is the first one in a period of six weeks, the day was busily spent at miscellaneous work and making garden.* Several heavy rains came in June with some flooding.

1901

A serious blizzard developed on Sunday, February 3, 1901: *A very severe snow storm having developed from the one of yesterday and having continued all night and until after noon today, depositing about 8 inches of badly drifted snow, the day was spent at home in reading.*

June ended with a full week of extremely hot weather, each day over 100, *averaging 107 degrees*, and July began with 111 degrees. Then came a refreshing rain followed by more heat at mid-month, peaking at 114 on the 16th with high south winds. Finally on the 28th: *The first heavy rain of the summer, amounting to 2 full inches, fell last night and the fearfully destructive drought of 1901 was brought to a close.*

The past five weeks, beginning June 23rd and ending last evening, has been the longest almost intollerably hot spell that was ever known in this region and as a result thereof the corn crop, hay crop, potato crop, oats, barley and gardens have all proven to be almost entire failures! The hot summer of 1901 will long remain a <u>scorched</u> <u>spot</u> in the memory of all our western Kansas people!

1902

When 1901 ended and 1902 began, the weather was so mild that the family played croquet several times during the holidays. Then on January 20: *A most awful dust storm from the north was in progress all day.* On the 25th came first a snow storm from the southeast, and a few hours later *a very fierce northwest blizzard set in continuing into the night and getting exceedingly cold.* On the 26th, Lizzie and Earl were *storm staid* in Stockton at Judge Smith's home. On the 27th: *Mercury down to 15 degrees below zero.*

More storms came on March 14: *A most awfully disagreeably dusty day with very high south wind which veered to the northwest about 6 p.m.* And again the next day: *A very bad west and northwest dust storm raged all afternoon, growing quite cold toward night.*

Because of recurrent problems with blowing dust, Elam decided to do something more for wind erosion control, so on April 1: *With Jesse and Earl's help worked in the a.m. at setting out osage hedge plants to make wind breaks.* These were planted along edges of fields. Not only did they break wind velocity, they provided shade for men and horses and cover for wildlife. They caused the deposit of snow on fields, and they were one of the hardest of woods, useful for fence posts, implement handles, and so on. But there were some disadvantages too. Snow drifts kept fields from being dry enough for early planting; the trees and associated plant growth sapped moisture from nearby soil, thereby diminishing crop yields nearby; and they harbored insects such as grasshoppers that could devastate crops.

Hot, dry weather came early in 1902. On April 20: *A very peculiar day and phenomenally hot! Mercury ranging from 100 to 104 in the shade from 1 till 4:30 oclock p.m. being mostly clear or light west to southwest breezes blowing. Have never seen such an April day.* Again on the 21st: *Still very hot; 100 at 2 p.m. and from then until night very dusty with high southwest wind.*

Then cooler but very dry the next da*y: This was a most disagreeably chilly day and outrageously dusty with high northwest wind.* Still it was bad on the 25th: *Today being another most outrageously disagreeable day with a violent northwest dust storm at play from "morn till night" the time was spent closely within doors at reading, writing and work with the microscope among my fungi.*

The summer of 1902 produced rains from time to time, and then on September 21, 4½ inches fell in four hours. More rain came on the next two days: *The rain continued all through last night and intermittently today until about 4 oclock p.m. when it ceased and the clouds broke away with a clear sunset, having again precipitated about 4½ inches of water making the phenomenal and unheard of fall of 9 inches in 48 hours! This of course made every stream in the country boom! Bow creek was higher than at any time since the great flood of July 31, 1885.*

1903

Other rains followed less ominously, but winter storms were bad, as during the last days of February 1903: *Weather very stormy and disagreeable with heavy falls of snow making the roads impassible! And thus endeth the month which for snow and bad roads has been the worst of my recollection in Kansas.*

The ensuing spring thaw only made conditions worse. On March 8: *Mud 2 feet deep in low places on the roads! Water, water everywhere! All draws and other water courses running with great floods of water!* And on the 12th: *In the early morning went up west a mile to Dan Shaw's to assist in rescuing with ropes a young man, Bert Forrey, from a rather perilous and uncomfortable position in a tree where he had lodged from a raft which he was trying to propel across the raging torrent of Bow creek which is very high and way out of its banks.*

A severe freeze and snow storm on April 30 was in sharp contrast to the extreme heat of just one year earlier: *This morning the ground was covered with a blanket of snow much drifted in places and the mercury was down to 20 above zero, completely ruining the entire fruit crop and killing all forms of tender vegetation!!!*

Beneficial rains were received in the spring of 1903, but they became excessively heavy elsewhere. On June 4: *Received the first news today of the terribly devastating floods in eastern Kansas and at Kansas City wherein millions of property was destroyed and hundreds of lives lost.*

1904

Winds of late winter and early spring can be very frightening on the western plains. On March 2, 1904: *A most fearfully terrific north dust storm set in with such acute violence as to cause me to get out of my buggy and hold it down to keep it from upsetting. After 10 to 15 minutes I resumed my journey.* Dry conditions had returned late in 1903, as mentioned on March 30, 1904: *A good soaking rain began at 7 p.m., the first precipitation of value since last November 1st.* But soon thereafter it was dry again, as on April 8: *A most terrific dust storm from the N.W. being the order of the day, the time was spent closely within doors.* Fortunately rains returned at frequent intervals during the spring.

Elam's reputation for having a keen scientific mind and meticulous accuracy had become known outside botanical circles. On June 18: *Drove to Marvin in the morning where I met Prof. Chas. P. Brand of the U.S. Dept. of Agr., Washington, D.C. who accompanied me home at noon to establish an observatory or station for the record of soil humidity and temperature. He remained until 3 p.m. and then had a liveryman who accompanied us over to take him back to Phillipsburg on his way toward the Pacific coast.*

On November 28 Elam encountered a prairie fire while traveling home from Hill City: *Driving in a somewhat round about way, through a raging prairie fire which swept down from the north, reached home at 6:30 p.m. having driven 46 miles in 5½ hours!*

1905
The first two months of 1905 were bitter cold, with many readings from 9 to 16 degrees below zero and one reaching 24 below. Snowfall was frequent and generous.

1906
A terribly destructive storm devastated the area on June 23, 1906: *Last night about 10:30 oclock one of the most violent and destructive thunder, wind and hail storms broke upon us that we have ever seen or passed through. The rainfall amounted to from 4 to 6 inches in various localities and the flood waters of the small streams and Bow creek destroyed much property in the flooding of plowed lands, the washing away of fences and the drowning of much livestock. The hail which remained until today, deposited in various localities, consisted of thousands of cubic feet of ice and of course beat into the ground all forms of growing crops, destroying them in toto!*

Every acre of small grains a complete loss! Peaches, apples, plums and all sorts of fruit entirely stripped from the trees, and many trees will die from the effects of the severe barking received.

1907
The next spring had its problems too. On April 29, 1907: *In a brisk N.E.*

snowstorm I left Hill city at 9 a.m. for home, driving 24 miles N.E. to Jas. McCroskey's where I stopped for dinner and to get warm. The storm having somewhat abated I started out again for home shortly after which it began to snow faster than ever! Continuing on I reached here at 6 p.m. thoroughly chilled, having made one of the most disagreeable drives in all my missionary work!! It ceased snowing at 7 oclock in the evening having deposited about 6 inches of snow.

Then on the next day: *This is my 34th April in Rooks county and for disagreeably cold and destructively freezing weather this exceeds them all.*

The destruction of the entire fruit crop, the freezing of the alfalfa and all other forms of tender vegetation has been calamitous in the extreme, and the "oldest inhabitant" wonders aloud when spring time will arrive!

Then, to make matters worse, on May 27: *Another severe freeze last night, freezing ice and doing considerable damage to tender vegetation. A circumstance never before known in this region as late as this!*

1908

It happened again in 1908, on April 29: *Very hard freeze last night almost totally destroying the fruit crop and doing incalculable damage to all sorts of tender vegetation including many species of trees and vines! Mercury down to 25 degrees at sunrise! April 29th seems to be a sort of hoodo for this region.* Another comment on May 2: *Every morning for the past 6 days ice has frozen at the stock well near the barn! Surely unprecedented weather!*

1909

Elam describes a repeat performance in 1909, on April 30: *Temperature below the freezing point with a most terrific N.W. dust storm.* And on May 1: *Very hard freeze last night. Mercury 25 at sunrise this morning. Great damage to fruit and other tender vegetation.*

1910

No mention is made of Halley's Comet in 1910, which may seem odd, but since Elam was not a superstitious person and there was so much superstition surrounding that event, even bordering on hysteria, he chose to ignore it.

1911

The summer of 1911 was exceedingly hot, reaching 100 degrees or more nearly every day in June and continuing into July, with a new record on the 5th: *Hottest day ever officially recorded in this region with a standard government thermometer, it being 114 at 3 p.m. with light south breeze.*

Finally generous rains came on the 11th: *Heavy thunder shower of 1.98 inches at 6-8 p.m. being the heaviest rain of the year. Bow Creek running again after being dry 17 days, no water having run in it since June 24th. First time in 37 years that it had ceased running across our farm!* Another two inches fell the next day. Two inches more came on the 22nd. The July total was eight inches.

1912

Extreme heat is often followed by extreme cold, and this was certainly true as 1912 began. The first 12 days all had lows of zero or mostly below zero, culminating with minus 22 degrees on January 12.

Heavy drifting snows fell in late February and early March so that on the 9th: *While I have been a resident of this community for the past 38 years I am sure that there is more snow on the ground now than at any other time in all these years that I have taken a trip to Stockton. The amount of snow now on the ground is perhaps about the same as it was 21 years ago — March 1891.*

But then more came five days later: *Most terrific snow blizzard set in about 3 a.m. continuing until 5 p.m. with wind veering to the north and later to the northwest resulting in a very heavy fall of snow and producing the deepest and most wonderful drifts ever seen in this part of Kansas, rendering all railroad and vehicle traffic most emphatically impossible. Snow drift on south side of house, against the building, 8 feet deep!*

However, four days after that — March 18 — a trip was attempted by team: *With Lee made a general business trip to Stockton, especially to do proof reading on labels for Cent. 37 Fungi Columbiani. Roads the worst I have ever traveled over in this country. When about a mile from home we got stuck in a snow drift and broke a doubletree and singletree to the buggy which we had to leave in the drift, and carrying as much of our purchases as possible, walked the rest of the way home.*

Finally by March 30: *Roads getting fairly good. On account of illness and bad weather this was wife's first trip to Stockton since last fall. And* the next day: *This was the first Sunday School service we have been able to hold since Feb. 18th.*

But things dry out in a hurry in the high plains of the West. Just two weeks later, on April 14: *The weather exceedingly disagreeable with a most terrific west wind and dense clouds of dust filling the air.* It was so bad that dedication of the new Mt. Nebo church building had to be delayed.

1913

A hot, dry spell in the summer of 1913 seriously affected crops and waterways. On November 30: *Heavy rain last night of 1¼ inches. About July 10th Bow Creek, through our pasture, ceased to be a running stream and continued thus until last night when a good load of water found its way down the valley. In 1911 the creek was dry during a period of 17 days in June and July. These two instances are the only ones during the past 40 years that Bow Creek ceased its flow at this point.*

The drought was definitely broken. On Saturday, December 6: *Since Friday, Nov 28th, we have had the phenomenal rainfall for this time of the year of 5.22 inches of water! And thus ended a period of the severest and most devastating drouth this region has experienced in the 43 years of its settlement!*

1914

But then it turned dry again. Dust blew in April 1914. Finally on April 27: *Rainfall of the past 24 hours has been 2.40 inches, which is the first rain of any consequence since early last December.*

1915

Snowfall in early 1915 was heavy. Elam wrote on March 5: *The deposit now amounts to fully 20 inches and with the drifts the roads are entirely impassable.* The subsequent thaw made travel in the new auto impossible for a while. On April 3: *First time we have had the car out for about 6 weeks on account of the awfulness of the roads, which now are getting quite good again.*

Heavy rains followed. On June 3: *The rain of last evening (4.15 inches) was a "gully-washer" of unusual proportions. Much damage was done by flood waters in all the streams, large and small, taking out many rods of fence, injuring crops, roads and bridges, and floating off much cut alfalfa on low lands. Bow Creek way out of its banks at about 10-foot stage above low water mark.*

1916

The summer of 1916 was excessively hot, reaching 106 degrees on August 2 and 109 on the 3rd. *Corn crop about totally ruined.*

1917

Dry conditions set in again for the next eight months, as Elam reviewed on April 18, 1917: *We had a brisk S.W. thunder storm and the precipitation was .76 of an inch which is the greatest rainfall in one day since the 20th of last June! This evening again at 8-9 oclock we had another thunderstorm and got .48 of an inch of water!*

The rainfall for last season, and thus far through this, has been the lightest recorded here in the past 43 years! As a natural consequence of these conditions, including an almost snowless winter, the winter wheat crop will be almost, if not altogether, a complete failure. This was especially critical, because the U.S. was about to become directly involved in the World War.

1918

A violent storm on February 8, 1918, caused some damage: *A most terrific N. wind arose about 5 a.m. which continued all day, ceasing after nightfall. At 8 a.m. it rained a little and later turned into a fierce snow blizzard which ceased at 4 p.m. with an estimated snowfall of 3 inches. The violent blow broke our windmill all to flinders and broke down our dinner bell post! An unusual gale.*

A special treat was visible in the skies on March 7: *Fine aurora borealis from 8 to 12 p.m. Finest in many years!*

As in several past years, there was a killing freeze in late April 1918, this one on the 28th. Another violent storm was experienced on May 30, similar to one almost exactly two years before: *A very heavy rain with considerable hail having fallen last night between 8 and 9 oclock and Bow Creek and all tributaries being exceedingly high and much damage to fencing — at least 100 rods taken out — and many limbs blown from the orchard and forest trees, the day was spent in trying to restore order where chaos reigned supreme in the early morning.*

Much damage done to fruit trees and gardens by the hail. Bow Creek 10 feet above low water mark. Several acres of freshly cut alfalfa was swept down the creek and that uncut on the bottom land much damaged by mud and lodged debris!

A celestial event occurred on June 8: *Eclipse of the sun at 5 p.m. which was total in S.W. Kansas but only about 90% of the sun covered at this point.*

Most days in June 1918 and part of early July were above 100 degrees. Finally, on July 14: *Hottest day of the season — 107 at 4 p.m. At 5:30 a series of brisk thunder showers set in which continued into the night. The long drouth extending from May 31st to July 14th now broken. In this time of awfully hot weather most of the days the total precipitation has been only .89 of an inch of water.* The next day: *The total rainfall of last evening and night was 1.54 inches. A truly blessed relief from the scorching drouth through which we have passed in the past six weeks!* Yet from the end of the month into early August there again were numerous readings of over 100 degrees, reaching 110 and 111 on the 3rd and 4th.

1919

Weather extremes were frequent in late 1918 and early 1919. On April 7: *A beastly day with high S.W. to N.W. winds with a superabundance of dust in the air nearly all day.* Then on the 9th: *A most unusual day! So unlike the past three weeks of fine spring weather.*

Sometime last night, perhaps about midnight, a full fledged N.E. blizzard broke loose and veering to the north continued with much violence throughout the day, but ceasing shortly after nightfall having precipitated about 7 inches of wet snow with quite heavy drifts in places. In my 45 years residence here this is the heaviest April snowfall that we have ever had. Mercury 27 and much damage done to early and tender vegetation. Moisture amounted to 1.74 inches.

Drifts were still bad two days later despite some melting: *With Lee in the surrey made a very difficult trip through the snow drifts to Stockton, being nearly 3½ hours going over and just even 3 hours making the return trip.*

On August 7, 1919, Elam recalled an event that predated the beginning of his diary: *How well do I remember this day 50 years ago! I was then a 17-year old boy living at home with my parents near Farmington, Ill. After dinner that day I rode our old saddle horse, Charley, into town after the mail and about 4 oclock, if I remember correctly, the much expected total eclipse of the sun occurred.*

It was the first time I had ever seen a total eclipse of the sun and I have never been in the direct path of one since that memorable 7th day of August 1869.

Birds, chickens and all sorts of animals were in consternation at the unusual phenomenon! My old horse pranced about at the hitch-rack acting as tho he wanted to lie down but in a few seconds the sun flashed out from behind the moon's disc and the great show soon lost interest to the hundreds of interested spectators!

1920

Balmy weather began 1920: *The month just closed has been a most remarkable one for this region with only one or two unpleasant days with no zero weather, snow not to exceed ¼ inch and many clear, calm sunshiny days!*

A serious wind storm developed on March 15: *A very disagreeable dusty day with high west wind which set in motion tens of thousands of Russian thistles!* These are also called tumble-weeds. They were not known while the area was still in grass. The seed was thought to have been introduced from Eurasia in flaxseed. A common pest in fields under cultivation, this plant has, during years of drought, been used as emergency cattle feed while still young and green, either in grazing or by making hay and silage. When the mature ones blow, as they did on this date, they can become impacted against fences, causing them to break down, especially if there is drifting snow.

Then on the 21st: *Went over to Mt. Nebo to attend S.S. at 10:30 a.m. but on account of the terrific dust storm of three days before the church was so full of dirt from the adjoining corn field that it would take several people several hours to clean it out. We came home at 11:30.*

It got worse the next day: *A most terrific dust and Russian thistle storm from the south, too awfully awful to describe!* And again on the 28th: *And still another terrific northwest dust and Russian thistle storm being the order of nearly the whole day, the time was spent at home in reading.*

1921, 1922

The last part of 1921 and early 1922 were mostly dry, until March 19: *The precipitation of moisture yesterday including melted snow and ice was 1.36 inches while the total from last Sept. 19th up to, but not including yesterday was only 1.32 inches for the 6 months. An astonishing record indeed, never duplicated in the past 48 years!* More rains followed through the spring.

1925

Foul weather developed on March 28, 1925: *Yes, for weather, this was a clinker indeed with a furious S.E. gale which filled the air with dust and debris! The worst we have had for a number of years.*

1926

Dust began to blow again in May 1926, especially on the 5th: *It being too windy to work we took the painters to Stockton this forenoon and came home at noon. A most frightful south dust storm being the order of the p.m. no outside work could be done.*

Summer of that year was exceedingly hot, with most days above 100 degrees from late June, through July, to the first half of August, after which some rains came, but Elam wrote: *Corn crop 95 per cent failure for 1926!*

1927

Dust blew several days in February 1927, especially on the 17th: *A most wretchedly disagreeable day with high northeast to north wind with a little snow and dust galore!*

Heavy rains fell on several days in mid-April. Then came unseasonably cold temperatures on the 21st: *This morning we were greeted with a temperature at 6 oclock of 25 degrees with frozen ground and a heavy scale of ice over tanks, pools and ponds! Damage? Yes!*

Dust blew again on May 8: *A very awfully dusty day with high south wind.* And the next day: *Another fearfully dusty day with high west to northwest winds!*

1928

April 1928 was exceptionally dry, with only 0.25 of an inch of rain. But May and June turned wet. Then came heat in July, with a serious storm on the 9th: *A most terrific north northeast wind storm struck us about 6:30 oclock p.m. which broke off and blew down wagon loads and wagon loads of limbs, both large and small, from our large trees of all sorts, uprooting one very large cottonwood.*

No damage to our buildings but very much to our neighbor, W. F. Miller, 80 or 90 rods north, by completely wrecking his large barn and cattleshed and hogshed and killing two cows and two large hogs. The storm also carried away his barn windmill and practically ruined many of his shade trees! Only 0.22 of an inch of rain fell.

The next day: *Spent most of the day with others of the family at clearing up part of the debris and wreckage of yesterday's storm. Late in the p.m. went over to Miller's to view the wreckage of their barn and other buildings. Wonderful damage by a "freak tornado", one that came from the northeast instead of the southwest. Yes, it was a veritable "twister"!* Later that month, on the 29th, 4.80 inches of rain fell.

1929

Another heavy rain, measuring 4.45 inches, fell on July 22, 1929, right in the middle of the time when Elam was moving to Hays. Roads became muddy. The farm sale was three days later, and a good crowd was present because they could not work in the fields.

1930

The summer of 1930 was very hot, most days in July above 100 degrees. Scattered showers followed, plus some dust storms. Then on October 5: *Rainfall the past two days was 4.07 inches!*

1931

The winter of 1930-1931 was unusual: *The last two weeks of December have been unusual weather — very moderate, almost clear and little or no wind!* January was a continuation: *The whole month almost a perfect dream! No wind, nearly clear with unusually high temperatures. One night nearly down to zero for a short time. Snow flurry of about two inches.* Again in February: *A good counterpart of January only much warmer. Early trees and flowers in bloom the latter part of the month.*

A typical late March storm arrived on the 26th: *Light rain at 6 last night turning to snow at 1:30 p.m. today. Continuing wet fall turning from N.E.*

to N.W. at 5:30 and a veritable blizzard into and through the night. Blizzard ceased on the 27th about 4 p.m. with 6 inches of badly drifted snow. Precipitation 1.60 inches.

A severe dust storm blew up on April 7 and then a soaking rain. *Unusually warm or hot weather toward month's end.* May of 1931 was far from typical: *A most peculiar month! Frosts and occasional snowfalls through and close to the end of the month. Many rainy days!*

June turned hot again: *The last 12 days were scorching hot thruout the middle west causing the death of more than 500 by excessive heat. 95-105 degrees! 99 the highest at Hays!* July continued the series: *A dry month — 102 on the 11th, 106 on the 22nd and 109 on the 27th.*

Precipitation began to improve by mid-August, until in November things were much more moist but there were problems on the 24th: *About an inch of solid ice covering the entire landscape. Many posts broken and wires down demoralizing telephone service throughout the region. Many serious accidents from persons falling on ice.*

These occasional interruptions to the drought pattern did little to change the basic pattern of heat and blowing dust, for the "Dirty Thirties" had begun.

1932

The year 1932 began with numerous periods of snow, some drifting badly. Good rains were spread throughout the spring. July turned hot, with ten consecutive days over 100 degrees. Good rains followed from late July through August.

There was more rain in early September, especially on the 10th when 5.62 inches fell. That sent Big Creek out of its banks, flooding parts of Hays.

The first half of December turned unusually cold, with the mercury down to 15 degrees below zero on the 12th. Then the last half turned abruptly milder. With the change came dust, as Elam noted on the 21st: *Bad dust storm rolled up from the S.W. in the late afternoon, high in the air but with almost no wind.* The next day: *Everything out of doors covered with a heavy coat of dust this morning.*

Later, on the 26th, came this comment: *Dust storm of the 21st drifted on toward the N.E. as far as Chicago where light rainfalls made a positive rain of mud!*

1933

Early February of 1933 brought more blowing dust. Then during the second week frigid temperatures set in with lows from 5 to 23 degrees below zero. Dust blew on scattered days in March and April, with good rains coming in the latter days of that period. But on April 29: *High south wind in the p.m. with heavy <u>yellow</u> dust storm.* This denotes dust from the southwestern states instead of closer Kansas fields.

Heat returned in June with numerous days over 100 degrees, reaching 113 on July 1.

1934

The winter of 1933-1934 was mild, precipitation light and scattered. There was blowing dust on some days. It is interesting to note that in western Kansas dust can blow in a very short time after a shower or rain. The moisture makes a crust on the sandy-loam soils that predominate there, inviting wind erosion. One of the preferred conservation tillage practices has been to cultivate lightly following a rain just to break up the crust.

Heat returned early in 1934 with the last days of May all reaching 100 degrees or more. June brought thundershowers until the last 10 days, which were again 100 degrees plus. Bad dust storms came again on numerous days. Nearly all of July registered 100 degrees or more, reaching 117 on July 13, and the barometer was unusually low, at 26.87 inches.

Dust mobility was enhanced by economic factors. Two things were involved. Wheat prices were abysmally low so farmers felt compelled to plant more acres. They were able to do just that as mechanization of farming was going full speed ahead as tractors replaced horses. The industrial revolution had encompassed agriculture to a degree never before thought possible.

Chapter 5

Personal Aspects:
Earlier Life

*E*LAM HAD SEVERAL FRIENDS among the other farm boys of the neighborhood near Farmington, Illinois. Frequently they went to town together — especially in the winter — or spent the night at each other's homes.

1871

The very first entry in the diary, written January 1, 1871, when Elam was 18, tells about a time he and *some young folks of the vicinity* spent most of the day at George Day's. Then on Saturday, January 7: *Went to Farmington where I spent the whole day knocking about with some of the boys. In the evening was accompanied home by my friend Howard Day who staid all night with me.*

Despite the fact that life on the farm was primitive by today's standards, and that there was no labor-saving equipment, boys sometimes found extra time on their hands, especially in the winter. On the 17th:

Went to Farmington in the morning and spent the whole day there knocking about and visiting with the boys, not returning home until evening.

Of course, there was no such thing as rural mail delivery, so people had to go to town to see if they had received any mail — or send someone else to check on it. Most people made the trip at least once a week, usually on the same day every week so that friends could see each other and get caught up on visiting. With Elam, the favored time was Saturday afternoon. On February 4: *Spent the a.m. working on the new coal bank and in the p.m. made my usual Saturday trip to Farmington after the mail, etc., etc.*

Sometimes trips to town were made to relieve boredom. On February 15: *Went to town "just to be going,"* and on Monday, March 20: *In the p.m. made a trip to town just to be going somewhere!* The balance of the week was spent mostly in hauling manure from the barn or transporting ear corn and corn fodder from the field, except Thursday: *Not much work and not much play.*

Not all trips were made on horseback, even by teenagers. On Sunday, May 14: *Spent the a.m. at home in reading and after dinner* [the noon meal] *went over to Mr. Day's and with Charlie made a trip to Farmington in his buggy and came home in the evening.*

Some social events had a religious orientation. Tuesday, the Fourth of July, 1871: *Attended a Sunday School picnic about 3 miles north and east of Farmington gotten up by the schools of Yates City, Elmwood and Farmington. A large crowd and a good time. Came home about sunset.*

1872

Elam spent increasing amounts of time with his boy friends as he approached his 20th birthday in 1872, realizing that soon they would all have to take on adult responsibilities, which could mean moving to another location. He would not be needed so much at home, because his three younger brothers were growing up.

The farm on which the family lived was only rented. Elam's older brother, Elias, had already gone to Kansas to see about taking up a homestead. That was in 1868, and there was an attraction to this offer of land ownership that could not be denied. Thus Elam was always eager to be the

The boyhood home of Elam Bartholomew on a rented farm near Farmington, Illinois.

The Presbyterian Church in Farmington, Illinois, built in 1865 and still in use today. It was here that Elam was baptized in 1873 and became a church member. His fiancée, Rachel Montgomery, and her parents were active members.

one to make the trip to town each week to get the mail. On March 16, 1872: *Worked at hauling up firewood until 3 p.m. and then went to town after the mail and after getting home went with Howard Day over to his uncles the Bumpers brothers* [Silas and Irvin] *where I staid all night.*

1873

One of the few times that Elam's siblings are mentioned by specific name during this phase of his life occurred January 13, 1873: *The weather and roads being bad I took the children, brothers John, George, Ed and sister Emma to school in the morning and brought them home in the evening.*

As romance bloomed between Elam and Rachel, he began to spend more time at the Montgomery home, and also at working for her father. When they went some place, it was often to church services, but sometimes they went out simply for pleasure. On May 6: *In the evening with Miss Rachel Montgomery attended a concert and exhibition entertainment at the town hall in Farmington. Got home at 1 oclock.*

Then came a very special day, on June 9, 1873: *Birthday! Age 21 years! Worked all day at cultivating and harrowing corn alternately. In the evening called at Thos. Montgomery's where I spent several hours very pleasantly and received from the eldest daughter of the household, Miss Rachel, a fine copy of the New Testament with copious notes.*

Independence Day that year was a special time of celebration because a recently split nation had come together again and had survived another year despite the economic and political chaos that followed the war. It was also an occasion for young lovers to do something together. *Went to Farmington to participate in the celebration of the 97th anniversary of American independence. Was in company of Miss Rachel Montgomery all day. At 5:30 p.m. we went to the station and getting aboard the train went to Yates City for a ride and returned an hour later. We staid in town for the fireworks at night and came home at 10 oclock.*

Now that he was 21, Elam decided to seek employment beyond farming activities, not only to improve his financial status, but also to more fully utilize his mental capabilities. Thus on July 29 he wrote: *Having decided to prepare myself for school teaching this fall and the law now being such that one must pass an examination in the elements of the natural sciences this and probably many succeeding days will be spent in reading and study.* It was not uncommon for a teacher of elementary grades to have no more formal education than eighth grade.

The examination would not be given until October, so the next ten weeks were spent mostly in study for that event. Subjects of concentration were *grammar, botany, natural philosophy and physiology*, because Elam felt sufficiently prepared in other areas. In the midst of his studies he secured a job, to begin after certification was completed. On September 11: *Took a horseback ride out west and south 8 or 10 miles looking for a school to teach this fall and winter. Finally engaged with the board in the*

Mt. Pisgah district 7 miles west of here for a 5-months term at $45 per month. Took dinner with A. D. Wilson, one of the board, who lives one mile southeast of the school house, with whom I expect to lodge during the school term.

One month later, on October 11: *Went to Farmington in the morning where I met my friend Chas. N. Dunn and at 10 oclock we took the south-bound train to Lewistown, the county seat, where, before County Supt. Benton we took our examination for teachers certificates and being successful in our efforts returned to Farmington at 6 p.m. and thence home.* Just two days later, classes began: *Went over to the school house and opened my school promptly at nine oclock with a rather small attendance, there being only about 15 pupils in the district all told and they were not all present.*

Despite the ten weeks of intensive study preparatory to taking the examination, Elam's social life was not neglected. On August 20: *In company with Miss Rachel Montgomery took a buggy ride over northwest about 12 miles, near Maquon, by Spoon River where the day was pleasantly spent in picnicing, playing croquet and in fishing, there being 16 other young ladies and gentlemen in our company from near home. We started home late on account of it being very hot and dusty and did not get here until 10 oclock p.m.* And on September 3: *In the evening drove over to Thos. Montgomery's and getting Rachel and her sister Lizzie took a buggy ride over to J. T. Dunn's to attend a social party of young folks and a very heavy rain storm coming up we were compelled to stay all night, not going to bed!*

Sunday, September 7, 1873, was an especially significant day: *Stopped for an evening call at Thos. Montgomery's and while there I entered into a marriage engagement with Rachel the eldest daughter of the household with the understanding that the "happy event" should not occur until two or three years in the future. The pleasure of this alliance to me is supreme and if in the days to come my visits to this household should seem to be rather frequent, the reader will understand the cause and I trust spread the mantle of charity over my failings.*

On the 18th the engaged couple had some time together on a major excursion: *Went to Farmington in company with Miss Montgomery and getting aboard the 8:20 a.m. train made a trip to Peoria to visit the state fair. Arrived about 10 a.m. spending the time until 6 p.m. in seeing the sights and then left for home getting here at 9:30 oclock.*

Weekends during the school semester were spent at home — and, of course, with his fiancée as much as possible. Often the activity was attending "singing school" or the "literary society" at nearby Liberty school house. But on Saturday, November 22, Elam was feeling especially spritely: *Went to town in the morning and remained there nearly all day. Spent the evening at Mr. Montgomery's again! Isn't it awful?*

On Saturday, December 6: *In the evening attended singing school at Liberty with "that girl" again!* Then on Saturday, December 20, there is again a feeling of exhilaration: *In the evening attended singing school at Liberty with altogether the finest girl in these parts. I'll mention no names!*

1874

Every weekend for the next several weeks involved time with Rachel — at her home, at literary society, or at singing class. On February 28, 1874, the explanation is quaint: *Went to Farmington in the a.m. and remaining there attended preparatory communion services at the Presb. Church at 2 p.m. after which I returned home and spent the evening in making a presumptively very necessary call at the home of Thos. Montgomery.* But there is more here than meets the eye. School will soon be out, and Elam will depart for western Kansas, so the engaged couple has a lot of preparation to do for the great unknowns and separation that lie just ahead.

One week later, Saturday, March 7, finds him saying his good-byes to numerous friends: *Came home in the morning and made a quick trip to town and returned at 1 p.m. spending the rest of the day mostly in social chat and visiting with callers.* On the 13th, just one emphatic line: *Last Day of School!*

Then just three days later: *Having made up my mind to go to Stockton, Rooks Co. Kansas, as a place of future residence I spent the a.m. in packing my personal effects. After dinner I went over to Thos. Montgomery's where I spent the last afternoon that I expect to spend for many months in the company of the dear girl who has promised to become my wife on my return from the west. Bade her a sad good bye and returning home went at once to Farmington where I put up for the night at Dr. M. T. Harrington's with my boyhood school mate, Charlie Day, who is boarding at the doctor's.*

Upon arriving at Stockton, Elam lost little time securing certification to teach in Kansas. He passed the examination on April 25.

The Fourth of July, 1874, was somewhat different than the Fourth had been in Illinois: *In company with several other young folks of Bow Creek attended the national celebration at Stockton, which was held in the McNulty grove west of town. Stockton is a very small place containing not more than a dozen houses all told. Had a very good but rather <u>small</u> time and came home at 8 oclock.*

Elam found that in his new neighborhood there were others interested in singing, just as back home in Illinois. So on October 29: *In the evening attended a singing social at Mr. Kling's.* Another such event was recorded on November 12: *Attended singing school at Samuel Hebrew's Sr. in the evening.*

1875

Attending a spelling contest sounds like a mighty tame and innocent thing to do, but on one such occasion extenuating circumstances made it exciting. On April 16, 1875: *In the evening attended a spelling school match at D. H. Duff's and came pretty near getting "licked" because I went home with another fellow's girl. The other fellow was Thos. Watson and the girl was Mary Hebrew. Considerable blood shed but it wasn't mine!*

Some real excitement of another kind developed suddenly on May 27: *Cultivated corn until 11 a.m. when a heavy rain and hail storm came up preventing further work for the day. Just about noon as the storm was about over I went out and saw a team of black ponies hitched to a dilapidated buggy coming in from the west on the run! I caught and tied the team and then started on the back track on horseback to see whence the team came. After going a short distance west the track led to the southeast and I followed it, finding the dashboard* [a kind of carriage] *in the draw, about 3 miles S.E. to the Stockton and Kirwin road where I found a dead man lying by the roadside. It was Wm. Wetherilt the mail carrier between the two above-named points. I rode north to Bow Creek and notified several of the neighbors and a runner was sent to Kirwin, the home of the dead man and one also to Stockton to notify the coroner. I then rode back home, got some dinner and thence about 2 p.m. back to the scene of the calamity. On examination it was found that the man had come to his death by a stroke of lightning and it was so declared by the coroner's jury. The body was taken to the Hugh Williams house where it was to be kept for the night, the creek being so high that the friends from Kirwin could not cross to the south side and probably will not be able to do so before tomorrow morning.*

Less than two weeks later, Elam became involved in an episode that illustrates that tales of the "wild West" are not strictly fictional. On June 7: *Arrived at Stockton about 10:30 a.m. Shortly after getting into town and while in one of the stores I heard the rapid firing of several guns and on stepping out onto the street saw men running in all directions. The shooting occurred on the south side of Main St. out on some vacant lots. It seems that Sheriff Ramsey and his deputy, Shepard, had run down and located two horse thieves who had a bunch of ponies which they were selling at $20 per head. The battle was short but very decisive! Sheriff Ramsey was killed as was also one of the thieves. The other thief got away, riding through a shower of bullets, to the north. The deputy sheriff was unhurt. The sheriff was mortally wounded and died in a short time. An inquest was held over the remains of the dead thief and I acted as one of the coroners jury. The whole affair was surely a scene in wild western life.*

Years later, the *Rooks County Record* of November 24, 1911, carried Elam's three-column description of the June 7, 1875, episode, which he titled "A Day of Blood." Bartholomew wrote,

> The tragedy recorded in these narratives occurred more than a generation ago, yet they are fresh in the memory of the writer and he has given them to the reader as they transpired without allowing his imagination to mar the historic value of the account.

Eager for more quality social life in his neighborhood, Elam went to a nearby gathering on November 22, 1875: *In the evening attended the organization of a singing school at H. E. Williams two miles east, with Mrs. Williams as instructor.*

Christmas Eve of 1875: *In the evening attended a Christmas tree entertainment down the creek 7 or 8 miles at the next house east of Sayler. Home at midnight.*

1876

Finally he is able to put his teacher qualification to work and earn some much needed money. On January 3, 1876: *Commenced the teaching of a 3-months term of school in dist. 16 Phillips county, Sayler school house, at a salary of $85.00 for the term. The trip to and from school morning and evening will be made on horseback. The distance from Mr. Foote's, my boarding place, is about four miles almost straight across the country north east to the school house.*

The school semester ended on April 7: *Last day of school! All told I had 28 pupils enrolled for the term. Attended a singing social at J. A. South-ard's in the evening.* But not until the 15th of May was payment made for his services: *Went down to B. F. Sayler's in the morning to meet the school board and make settlement for my recently taught 3-months term of school and came home at noon.*

Later that month Elam began the trip he had desired for so many hard, lonely months. On May 26: *Having made up my mind to return to Illinois for the summer I made all due preparations and was taken to Stockton by Mrs. H. E. Williams and Kittie Foote where I arrived at noon and spent the p.m. about town and remained there all night.*

May 27: *Left Stockton at 7:30 a.m. for Hays City with the mail carrier. Took our lunch on the Saline river at 1 p.m. and reached Hays at 6 oclock. At nine oclock took the east bound train.* He stopped over a few days in eastern Kansas to visit his brother, Elias.

June 1: *Reached Quincy at 3 a.m. where I staid one hour and thence on over the C.B.&Q. to Galesburg at 8 and thence to my old boyhood town of Farmington at 10. Came home to Father's at noon where I remained 2 hours and then went over to Thos. Montgomery's where I spent the rest of the day and remained all night. Just 2 years, 2 months, 2 weeks and 2 days since I left home in March 1874.*

June 2: *Remained at Montgomery's all day in company most of the time with the dear little girl who has promised to soon become my wife. Came home in the evening at 7 oclock.*

June 3: *Made a trip to Farmington in the morning and came home at 1:30 p.m. and then attended a school picnic on the creek below the bridge a half mile northwest of home. Picknic was given by Miss Grace Snyder the teacher at Liberty — our district school. In the evening with the Mont-gomery young folks attended a singing social at John Leeper's and on our return I stopped at Montgomery's where I remained all night.*

With only two weeks remaining before the wedding date, a lot of time was spent with his fiancée, getting reacquainted after two years' absence and discerning if they still wanted to go ahead with their plans. One prime consideration was whether or not Elam could convince Rachel and her family of the suitability of life on the Western frontier.

Wednesday, June 14, 1876, was the BIG day: *Returned to Montgomery's at 10 oclock and remained until 4 p.m. and then came home to Father's and returned to Montgomery's at 6 oclock. Due preparations having been made and all things being in readiness I was united in marriage to Miss Rachel I. Montgomery by Rev. A. R. Mathes, the Presbyterian pastor at Farmington, at 8:30 oclock p.m. The wedding was a quiet affair participated in by only the several members of the Bartholomew and Montgomery families. The wedding supper and attendant festivities were kept up until midnight which closed the old and ushered in the new chapter in my hitherto uneventful life!*

June 15: *Remained at Mr. Montgomery's until after dinner and then in company with Rachel went over to Father's where we spent the p.m. and returned to Mr. Montgomery's where I will expect to make my home until our departure for Kansas sometime later in the season.*

Much of the summer was spent working on various farms in the neighborhood. There was a new vigor, not only because of the recent marriage, but also because Elam was now a man of his own standing who had proven himself in the hardships of the Western frontier. Everyone wanted to know what frontier life was like, and he had plenty to tell.

There were numerous post-nuptial parties and visits with old friends. On June 26: *In company with Rachel went over to the Bumpers brothers where we spent the afternoon in social visiting. In the evening we went from there to Alex McKeighan's where we spent the evening in social visiting and in singing.*

A really special event was the Independence Day celebration. The nation, 100 years old, was healing and knitting itself together again after the Civil War that had ended only 11 years before, and — at least for this 24-year-old — the future looked promising. The festivities began on July 3: *Went to Farmington in the morning to witness and take part in the grand centennial celebration which is to occupy today and tomorrow. The exercises were opened with a soldiers re-union and a couple of sham battles. Came home at noon and in the p.m. went back to town again in company with Rachel to attend further the celebration and came home at 8 oclock in the evening.*

July 4: *Centennial, Centennial, Centennial! 100th year of American Independence! Went to Farmington again with Rachel where we, with thousands of others, spent the day enjoying the festivities of the great occasion consisting of soldiers parades, the booming of cannons, speech making, music and fireworks. Returned home at 10 oclock p.m. greatly pleased with the great occasion.*

An outing with the boys was enjoyed on the 27th: *In the p.m. in company with Mr. Montgomery and 6 of the neighborhood boys went out west and north 12 or 14 miles to the Spoon river country where we arrived in the evening and camped for the night in the woods.* On the next day: *Spent the entire day in picking blackberries near our camp and in having a jolly good time all round. Left for home at 6 p.m. and arrived here 3 hours later.*

This was quickly followed by a quiet walk in the woods for the new couple. On the 31st: *At 5 oclock p.m. Rachel and I walked over to Father's and after a short stay at the house we took a stroll out into the woods south east of the house to revisit some of the old familiar haunts of by-gone days. After having spent a "sadly-pleasant" hour thus, we retraced our foot steps toward the house thinking that perhaps never again in this life would we enjoy the sweet privilege of being permitted to revisit the dear old spots we may soon be leaving behind us forever!*

Another good time took place on August 2: *In the evening the Montgomerys gave an ice cream social in honor of Rachel and I to which 30 guests were invited. It was a most beautiful night with bright moonlight and a grand good time was enjoyed by all. The party broke up shortly after midnight.*

Then on the 10th came another outing: *At 2 oclock p.m. a party of 12 young folks including Rachel and I started for the Spoon river and we arrived there all right at 6 oclock and after securing lodging at a neigh-*

boring house for our girl folks, we of the sterner sex bivouaced for the night in the woods. On the next day: *Spent most of the a.m. in picking blackberries and in the p.m. in amusements of various sorts including singing, playing croquet and in having a general good time! Started for home shortly after 5 p.m. and got here 4 hours later.*

Finally, with the coming of the 28th day of August begins the count-down toward the couple's day of departure for their new home: *Spent the whole day with Rachel in packing household goods for shipment to Kansas for which place we expect to embark on the 6th of next month.*

August 29: *Went to Farmington in the morning to take in some boxes of our household goods for shipment and returned at 11 oclock. Then in company with Rachel and her father and mother went on a visit over to J. T. Dunn's where we had a most enjoyable time and returning at 7 p.m. left in a few minutes for Farmington where we attended a sociable at the home of Rev. A. R. Mathes, the Presbyterian pastor.*

September 2: *In the evening 13 of our young friends, including Rachel and myself all piled into a big wagon, bountifully supplied with spring seats, to which was attached 4 horses and went out to the home of my old friend, A. D. Wilson, where we attended a singing social. The night being clear and the moon near its full we all enjoyed ourselves to the full and came home at 12:30 oclock.*

September 4: *The p.m. was spent in visiting with Rev. A. R. Mathes and family who were out to pay us a farewell call before our departure for Kansas.*

September 6: *Spent the a.m. in completing our journey preparations and at noon after bidding a portion of our nearest friends and relatives good bye, we were taken to Farmington accompanied by quite a number of other friends and after a short stay in town and a brief call on Rev. A. R. Mathes we went to the station and bidding the friends there present a sad and tearful farewell we boarded the 2 p.m. train for Galesburg where we arrived at 4:30 p.m. and purchased tickets for Hays City, Kans. Left for Quincy at 7:30 oclock and arrived there at midnight.*

September 7: *At 12:30 a.m. we left Quincy for Kansas City, Mo. But owing to the heavy rains in northern Mo. we did not reach Kansas City until 1:30 p.m. At 3 oclock we boarded a west bound train over the Kansas Pacific R.R. for Hays City, continuing the journey westward through Kansas the remainder of the day and throughout the entire night.*

September 8: *We arrived in Hays City at 6:30 a.m. where we remained in waiting until 3 oclock p.m. at which time we took one of C. C. Foote's teams with which he had been working at putting up hay at the military post south of town and placing our personal belongings into the wagon set out alone for our future home north of Stockton. We drove 16 miles north to the Saline river and put up for the night at the Martin postoffice.*

September 9: *Continuing our journey in the morning we reached Stockton at noon where we stopped to eat our lunch and feed the team, after which we came on over to Bow creek at 3 oclock p.m. and put up with my old friend and patron C. C. Foote where we expect to remain until we get our own house ready for occupancy which will take a number of days.*

Sunday, September 10: *In the a.m. Rachel and I took a 2-mile walk up to our place so that she might see her future home in the far west. Returned at 1:30 p.m. and at 3 we and the Footes drove over to D. H. Duff's and thence on to church services at Sayler. On the way home we made a pleasant call at H. E. Williams and reached here at 8 oclock.*

On December 11 Elam began another teaching job, but this time for less money: *Began the teaching of a 3-months term of school in Dist. 14, Rooks Co. 2 miles west and north of here for a salary (?) of $70 for the term! The school room is part of the residence of J. A. Bailey which consists of a dugout in the side of a hill built up in front and part of the sides with sod and for a roof covered with poles, willow brush with sod and dirt on top!*

One day was taken off for Christmas: *With wife went up to J. T. Stroup's at Rockport to a Christmas dinner where we remained until evening and then came home and with Willis Privett and some other young folks in the wagon went down to Samuel Hebrew's to attend a social party and oyster supper which continued until long after midnight and we did not reach home until 4 oclock. Extremely cold with deep snow but clear and calm.*

The year 1876 ended on a decidedly more positive note than the one before: *And thus has passed another year but of greater achievements and of more momentous character than any of the preceding five years,"* — a commentary on the five years covered so far by the diary.

1877

The year 1877 began on a most happy note indeed: *Having a holiday and not holding school, the day was spent in reading and writing. In the evening a genuine surprise party occurred at our house when about 30 of our neighbors came in unheralded with baskets and baskets filled with New Years' eatables, so we all enjoyed a good supper and a general good time all round in pleasant chat, games and amusements until one oclock at which time our guests departed to their several homes.*

Many years later Rachel told her grandchildren of times in the winter when Indians came to the windows of their home at night, peering in to see how things were in a white man's house. When she perceived that they were hungry, she put out food on a bench by the door and went back inside. Soon both the food and the Indians disappeared.

There was a sad event on January 24: *Went to the school house in the morning and on the way there learned of the death, yesterday, of our young friend and neighbor John Kling, so I dismissed school and returned home and in the afternoon at 2 oclock we attended the funeral at Samuel Hebrew's (where the young man was boarding) which was conducted by a Rev. Mr. Jerold of Kirwin. The interment was made in a newly proposed cemetery on the S.W. corner of Mr. Sam'l Hebrew's farm. Came home about 5:30 p.m. with a saddened heart as this was the first funeral of one of my young men friends that I have ever attended.*

On April 3 and 4, during his time of grieving, Elam worked on John's grave: *Went down to C. C. Foote's where I worked each of these two days at making railing and posts for an enclosure to the grave of our late lamented friend John Kling.* Again on the 7th: *Went down to Mr. Foote's in the morning and with him went down to the new cemetery where we put up the enclosure mentioned on the 3rd and 4th and getting back to Mr. Foote's at 2 p.m. worked the remainder of the day for him at repairing a wagon.*

Then on the first day of May 1877 came a blessed event: *With Mrs. Mary C. Jerby assisted by Mrs. Sarah Privett and Mrs. Mary Messinger I was presented with a 10 lb. son and heir at 5 oclock this morning and thus dawns another era in my life history. Spent the day at chore work in and about the house.* This first child was named George.

October 14 was a major milestone: *Spent the day in reading and rest. First anniversary of life in our own home! Our living expenses for the 12 months ending today have been as follows for the articles enumerated, viz:*

Flour	*630 lbs*	*$17.00*
Corn meal	*260 lbs*	*4.00*
Potatoes	*12 bu*	*4.00*
Pork	*70 lbs*	*4.70*
Dried fruit		*5.55*
Sugar	*30 lbs*	*4.00*
Lard	*10 lbs*	*1.25*
Coffee	*6 lbs*	*1.50*
Beans	*25 lbs*	*1.75*
Salt		*1.00*
Tea		*1.00*
Coal oil	*5 gal*	*2.25*
Sundries		*4.00*

making a total for the year of even $54.00, or about $1.04 per week!

Elam and Rachel took their turn entertaining guests. Thanksgiving Day ended with a social event: *In the evening a neighborhood social singing party was held at our house.* Then Christmas was spent at a neighbor's: *With wife and baby went up to J. A. Bailey's where we had dinner and spent the time in social visiting.*

1878

A big event occurred on March 14, 1878, when children of two best friends were married: *At 2 p.m. went down to Mr. Foote's and at 4:30 oclock witnessed the marriage of Jas. A. Hebrew to Kittie Foote. Staid for the wedding supper and other festivities and with wife and baby came home at 11:30. Ceremony performed by Rev. Baker of N. Solomon.*

On the next day: *At noon with wife went down to neighbor Sam'l Hebrew's to attend the wedding infair* [house warming] *dinner at 3 p.m. after which we spent the time in social visiting and singing and again came home at 11:30 oclock.*

On October 18, a second son, Elbert, was born: *A big day indeed, for both self and wife! At 8 a.m. became heir to an 11½ lb boy.*

1879

The year 1879 began with this eloquent essay: *A year with its toils and vexations, likewise its joys and comforts has passed into eternity, leaving a train of events behind that the traces of time cannot obliterate from our memories. Many things have transpired that we can rejoice over while others have occurred that cause us regret. And thus we ever find it — the gold and the dross are never perfectly separated.*

Another year has dawned upon us but what it has in store for us none but the Infinite and the Eternal can tell.

In January of 1879 Elam and Rachel decided to give a party in appreciation for all the support that had been given in helping to get established. So on the 21st: *Spent the day principally in getting ready for a grand social party which we are expecting to give to our neighbors tomorrow.* And on the next day: *According to previous calculations and expectation our company all arrived in accordance with invitations previously sent out, and a good social comingling and neighborly chat and gossip was indulged in until half past two oclock p.m. when dinner was served, lasting until half past four oclock, after which some singing was indulged in by the lovers of the Polyhymnian art* [Polyhymnia was the muse of the sacred lyric] *and shortly afterward the happy party came to a final close about dark and the guests repaired to their several homes, all having enjoyed themselves immensely so far as heard from.* The guests, all named, totaled 34 plus 8 children.

Then a surprise party occurred at their place on February 5: *In the evening 20 or more of the young folks of our neighborhood came in upon us and held a singing social which broke up about half past 10 oclock.*

On March 18 of 1879 Elam's family arrived from Illinois. In addition to his parents there were brothers George, Ed, and Frank, and sister Emma.

The 9th of June was again a special day: *Birthday. Age 27 years: Found under my plate at breakfast a pair of fine socks as a birthday present from Rachel!!!!!!!!*

On Sunday, July 27: *About the close of Sab. School took quite severe cramping pains in the chest, being scarcely able to navigate when we reached home, going directly to bed and remaining there the rest of the day without partaking of any dinner or supper, suffering considerably at times during the afternoon but being far better late in the evening, having taken two doses of spirits of camphor, one dose of ginger tea and about 10 grains of cayenne pepper in three tablespoonfulls of Port wine; the latter giving almost instantaneous relief.*

Selecting medications for ailments was an imprecise art that usually involved trying various products to find one that worked, if good fortune prevailed.

Brother Elias came for a surprise visit on August 9: *At noon we were happily surprised at receiving a visit from brother Elias of Louisville, Pottawatomie Co. this state — he having not visited us since Jan. 1877 and not having met any of the other folks for over eleven years as he left Illinois in the spring of 1868. He will perhaps remain with us about two weeks before returning to Louisville.*

On September 11, a neighborhood wedding started out pleasant, but then turned ugly: *In the p.m. at two oclock Rachel, George and I went down to Mr. Samuel Hebrew's Sr. to witness the marriage ceremony performed by Rev. Theo. Bracken on behalf of Elmer S. Stroup and Mary E. Hebrew. Got there a few minutes before the performance of the ceremony and about half an hour later had the pleasure of sitting down to a most bountiful and sumptuous repast to which I, at least for one, succeeded in doing ample justice. There were 65 or 70 persons present and all went away satisfied fully as far as the replenishing of the inner man was concerned. Jas. and Wm. Hebrew were very much opposed to their sister uniting in marriage with a member of the Stroup family owing principally to their dislike of his parents and as a consequence of former threats about 5 oclock p.m. after doing all manner of deviltry, including cursing their father and mother in the most indecent terms in presence of the assembled company (which state of things had continued since last evening, the minister and his wife being then present including several of the neighbor women) Wm. Hebrew (being upheld by his brother Jas.) went into the room where Mr. Stroup and his newly made bride were sitting and taking hold of him pulled him out into the yard and demanded in the most insolent and provoking language the immediate handing over of a "ten dollar bil". The excitement at this stage of the affair arose to fever heat on all*

quarters and much was the hurrying and running to and fro to see what would be the outcome of the fracas. Bill being a wild devil-may-care sort of a chap and Stroup being rather of a timid nature allowed himself to be bulldozed out of the above stated sum. Then he was let return into the house and molested no further. Shortly thereafter several of the boys started for Kirwin for the purpose of spending the extorted money in the way most gratifying to their tastes. All agree in saying that the action of Jas. and Wm. Hebrew in the above affair has been the most degrading and disgraceful occurrence that has ever transpired in this community, lowering their social standing to the lowest notch in the eyes of everybody, thereby grieving and wounding the hearts of their parents and sister to the very core. Got home shortly after sunset.

1880

Rachel's birthday was celebrated a day early, on February 21, 1880: *Tomorrow being Rachel's birthday and it being Sabbath and not suitable for the occasion and she being desirous of giving a dinner to the members of her Sab. School class as a birthday <u>fete</u>, all the members thereof found their way to our house, as did also several others of the little ones in the neighborhood. After indulging in some singing the children enjoyed themselves for some time at play and then came dinner at 1:30 oclock after which the children all amused themselves as best they knew how until time to go home, which was about 4 or 5 oclock p.m. There were 21 children present, ranging from 3 years to 13.* Elam listed all 21 by name.

Stockton was a growing town, as would seem natural, but that growth was not always to the liking of citizens such as Elam. On May 25: *Stockton has just become a city of the 3rd class and the town council has licensed two of the Devil's man traps to deal out liquid damnation to the base cravers of alcoholic beverages and the result was that at 2 oclock this afternoon I saw more drunken men on main street than I have ever seen before at one time.* And on the next day: *King Bacchus held another grand festival today, disgraceful in the extreme.*

On July 8: *Received a card from Father Montgomery of Farmington, Ill. dated the 5th informing us that himself and wife would make us a visit in the course of two or three weeks.* They arrived on the 29th: *Rachel, George*

and I started for Kirwin at 6 oclock a.m. arriving there at 10:30. About an hour later we went to the depot and in short time the western bound express brought in our visitors with whom we started for home shortly after noon and got here at 5 p.m. (Now there was rail service to Kirwin—much closer than Hays.)

The first day of the visit was spent amiably, because Father Montgomery was pleased with at least some of the accomplishments of his son-in-law: *Father Montgomery and I spent the a.m. in social chat and in walking about over the farm viewing its <u>many</u> <u>points</u> <u>of</u> <u>excellence</u>.* There is profound pride in that statement, with maybe a tinge of humility.

But that evening the conversation turned to politics, and differences of opinion grew intense, as was related the next day: *Having taken quite sick yesterday evening from an overdose of Greenbackism administered by father Montgomery, did not get about much until after dinner when he and I took a trip up to Rockport getting home at three oclock passing the remainder of the day in reading and social conversation.*

Elam's father became seriously ill on December 9: *At 2 p.m. Ed came over to inform us that father, who has been bedfast since the 1st of September with a complicated liver and kidney disease, had grown very suddenly worse and I went over at once and found him in excessive pain and agony. We sent at once for Dr. H. J. Fuller but he did not arrive until 6 p.m., pronouncing the cause of the pain the effect of taking cold which settled in the bowels.* By Sunday, the 12th, things looked worse: *Went again to see father (having also called a few minutes just before church) and found him in a very low condition, it seeming that the feeble, flickering light could burn but very few days at the most.* But on following days he showed some improvement.

With the children now old enough to appreciate Christmas, Elam began to get into the mood on the 23rd of December: *At 4 p.m. went up the creek about 2 miles to J. T. Stroup's cedar bluffs to get some cedar out of which to make a Christmas tree for our little boys.*

Christmas day was celebrated, but with apprehension about Elam's father: *Having prepared our Christmas tree for our little boys last night, and loaded it down with good things, previously procured, we were prepared to give them a good surprise and a good treat which they enjoyed greatly during the day. At 11 a.m. I went over to father's and found him worse again.*

The last day of the year was spent tabulating records: *Having kept a daily record of visitors, callers and sojourners entertained I find that the average number for each month during the year has been 90 making a grand total for the year of 1081.*

Having also kept a like record of the number of meals furnished to persons not of our own family I find the monthly average to be 65, footing up to 783 for the year.

Amount of produce raised on farm for the year has been as follows:

Wheat	*285 bu*	*$212*
Corn	*150 bu*	*38*
Rice corn	*12 bu*	*3*
Millet hay	*6 tons*	*24*
Corn fodder	*145 shcks*	*20*
Onions	*2 bu*	*3*

Making a total of $300, notwithstanding the report that crops in western Kansas for 1880 were an entire failure.

1881

The year 1881 began with extreme sorrow mixed with great joy. On January 2: *After Sab. school I went over to see father a short time and found him in a very feeble condition, he having been sinking and growing gradually weaker every day for the past three weeks, without any hope whatever of ultimate recovery. Got home at 2 oclock p.m. spending the remainder of the day principally in reading. During the afternoon and evening I experienced a dull and heavy depression of spirits; a singular and strange presentiment or foreboding of coming evil which I could not shake off or rid myself of, but which seemed to grow stronger as the evening passed.*

January 3: *After going to bed last night the feelings spoken of yesterday evening seemed to increase, every little noise startling me in a most singular manner, making the night pass in fitful dreaming; dreaming among other things that I was wading through much deep water which came up to my neck.*

Shortly before 5 oclock in the morning Rachel awoke me desiring that I should get up and make the fire, she having passed a sleepless night in anticipation of the near approach of a certain event whereby the probabilities were that another human being would be ushered into the world. A few moments later brother Ed came over in great haste telling us that father was much worse and not expected to live but a short time, and desired me to go over at once, but owing to the peculiar state of affairs I could not go.

After daylight I went after Mrs. J. M. Mellon and Mrs. Jacob Shell to come and see to matters, and at about 8:30 oclock brother Frank came over to let us know that our father had forever passed from this stage of action about an hour previous; desiring that I should return home with him; but still I could not go. At 9 oclock the announcement was made that a daughter [Elizabeth] *had been born to our household!*

A father's death at 7:30 oclock and the birth of a daughter at 9 oclock!! Is it a wonder that my spirit travailed and groaned within me yesterday and last night? Verily not. (Elam's father was 66 years old at the time of his death.)

About 10:30 oclock went over to father's where I met several of the neighbors with whom arrangements were made for the funeral to take place from the school house at one oclock tomorrow, the sermon to be preached by Mr. Bracken. Got home again about noon or shortly after, and spent the remainder of the day in and about the house, taking Mrs. Shell home about sunset and going from there over to father's to get mother and had her come and stay all night with us that she might have the rest and quiet which she so much needs.

January 4: *Spent the time until nearly noon in and about the house and then took mother and little George to the place which was once our father's dwelling place, to pay the last sad rites to the departed.*

Mr. Bracken was unable to be with us so Mr. Thomas was secured to conduct the services. Owing to unavoidable delays the funeral did not take place until three oclock when the sad <u>cortege</u> moved from the dwelling to the school house, a few rods away, and the services were opened by the singing of the hymn entitled "He Leadeth Me" followed by the reading of the 14th chapter of John. After a short prayer another hymn was sung and a short sermon preached from the 11th chap. of Ecclesiastes, and while the *singing of "Go bury thy Sorrow" was in progress, an opportunity was given all who desired, to take a last look at the inanimate form of our father lying at rest in the coffin before us. Gathered there as mourners around the bier were our widowed mother, sister Emma, brothers John, Ed and Frank, John's wife, little Georgie and myself. Brothers Elias and George were not with us, they being in the eastern part of the state.*

Unbidden tears filled my eyes and refused to be restrained when with heart-felt sorrow I gazed upon that emaciated face which was reposing in the cold embrace of death before me, when I thought of the four weary months of suffering which he had to endure, unsupported by the precious consolation and promises of God's word to bear him up and soothe his pathway to the tomb, making the journey across the dark river of death a pleasure and not a dark uncertainty.

And again, how my heart was moved with sorrow to think that never more in life would I behold that form whose image I bear, and who was the author of my being and physical nature.

As my memory reverts to the days of my childhood and a thousand incidents recur to my mind wherein "father" was the principal character the feelings of sympathetic sorrow and regret are deepened when I think that he who was the subject of these recollections has passed away to his eternal rest. Even the memories and recollections of maturer years cause the heart-strings to vibrate with pain and sadness when are called to mind many of his words, deeds and actions, especially those of the last year or two, as they are more vividly impressed upon us. His coming here to establish a home for himself in his old age and his incessant toil to that end, his desires and many plans for beautifying and making pleasant his home in the west; all these and many more painful and touching memories rise up before me and cause me to sorrow to think that all these things have forever passed from the shores of time!

Immediately after the last hymn was sung the procession made ready and started on its journey to the Hebrew graveyard about 2 miles down the creek and after arriving Mr. Thomas read the 53, 54 & 55 verses of the 15th chap. of 1st Cor. which was followed by prayer by Sam'l Hebrew, Sr., the coffin having previously been lowered to the depths of the grave just as the sun was sinking beneath the western horizon.

The grave was soon filled up, the earth closed over all that was mortal of our father, and he was sleeping his last, long sleep beneath the clods of the valley, there to remain until the Angel whose right it is, standing with one foot upon the sea and the other upon the land shall swear by Him that liveth forever and ever that time shall be no more. The day was pleasant and a large number of friends and neighbors were present to pay their last respects to him who had passed from time to eternity.

All being now over we wended our way in sadness home, getting back to father's place at 5 oclock, and I getting home about 15 minutes later, Mary, John's wife, coming home with me to stay all night with Rachel, Mrs. Mellon having staid with her during the day.

Many are the times Elam has spoken of days or partial days spent in reading, but seldom does he identify titles or topics. An exception appears on January 26: *Spent nearly all day in reading. Read "Ten Nights in a Bar room" and a portion of "Uncle Tom's Cabin."*

When the new baby became ill, fear and apprehension set in, beginning January 31: *Dr. H. J. Fuller stopped by taking dinner with us and our little girl being quite sick he left some medicine for her and gave other directions for her treatment.* The next day: *Our little one still worse and I being quite sick myself, Rachel sat up all night.*

There was no improvement on the following day, so more medicine was procured, and Elam's mother came to help take care of the baby. Finally on February 3: *Took mother home, our little one being considerably improved.*

Brother Elias, 33, sent word, received on September 10, that he had gotten married. Elam cannot conceal his wry sense of humor: *Received a letter from brother Elias of Louisville stating that he was married to a Miss Bessie Bains of that town on the 25th of August. Long may he wave! His third attempt to commit matrimony has proven successful and we all hope he will be happier as a married man than a dried up old batchelor.*

One of Elam's earliest friends on the Kansas frontier, Mr. Foote, was beyond medical help on October 5: *About 3 p.m. went down to see Mr.*

Foote again and found him very low and not expected to live through the night. As a consequence of which I remained with several other of the neighbors to watch by his bedside during the night. He had been unable to speak since about 10 a.m.; his disease is diabetes in its worst form, a cure of which is said to be impossible.

October 6: *Came home at 4 oclock this morning and after taking a short sleep and partaking of a light breakfast, Rachel and I went down to Mr. Foote's again, finding him growing rapidly weaker. We came home at noon. Spent the p.m. in plowing and at 7 oclock in the evening we returned again to Mr. Foote's and found him <u>dead</u>, he having passed away an hour previously. About 9:30 oclock S. R. Guthrie and I went to Stockton after a coffin and other necessary articles, getting there about 11 oclock, and remained in town several hours while things were being gotten in readiness for our return.*

October 7: *We got back at 4 a.m. and shortly after, I came home and about 8 a.m. went up to Rockport and from there up to Jerby's to inform them of Mr. Foote's death and getting home at 9:30 oclock went over to mother's after Rachel and the children and after partaking of dinner we came home and getting ready, all went down to Mr. Foote's to attend the funeral at 3 oclock.*

Thus has gone to his final rest a valued personal friend, a man of an eventful career and a checkered life, cut down in the prime of middle life in the 49th year of his age.

1882

A fourth child was born on March 21, 1882: *About half past 12 oclock last night I had to get up and "rack out" after old mother Shell, who performed her duties in a straight forward manner and presented us with a bran new boy shortly after 2 oclock a.m.* This one was Jesse Elam, the father of the present author.

In November Rachel took the two youngest children, Lizzie and Jesse, for a visit back home in Illinois. The two oldest, George and Elbert, stayed with Grandma. Accordingly, on November 13 Elam notes: *Spent the a.m. in doing housework as I am occupying the office of chief cook and bottle washer and chamber maid.*

Finally the family is reunited, on December 22: *Thus has ended our long and tedious six weeks of separation from "momma" and we are all thankful in the extreme for her safe return and the pleasure of again being united as a family. But, as is always the case, "those who go are happier than those who stay behind". The p.m. was spent very pleasantly and joyously in social converse with the returned ones.*

1883

The first child of Elam and Rachel started to school on April 9, 1883: *As today was the first day of our spring term of school, and it being the first day "at school" for George, I went around that way in the morning and took him over.*

A family outing on July 2 was both productive and pleasant: *In company with Rachel and the children went over south about 8 miles on a curranting expedition. Had good success, getting a bushel of excellent currants.*

1884

Another son, Earl, was born on August 17, 1884: *Last night between 12 and 1 oclock we were presented with heir number five in the shape of another fine boy, so the day was spent in and about the house with the exception of making a trip over to Mrs. Shell's and back about noon. "All's well that ends well".*

1885

Rachel's parents arrived for a ten-day visit on September 9, 1885. They never did move from Illinois.

It was a big day on October 23, when the two oldest boys, now ages 7 and 8, were old enough to be trusted with more mature responsibility: *Went to Stockton in company with George and Elbert where we arrived shortly before noon. The boys returned at once with the team while I met with my colleagues on the Webster townsite commission. Put up for the night at the Commercial house.*

1886

Just two days before Elam's birthday, on June 7, 1886: *Being heired again this morning about 6 oclock in the shape of an eleven pound boy* [Hubert], *the day was spent mostly in and about the house attending to household duties of various sorts.*

One week later a special event elicited considerable heart-felt eloquence: *This is the 10th anniversary of our wedded life. These ten years have passed rapidly away and have brought us much toil and care and also many vexations and heartburns. Yet the numberless rich blessings we have enjoyed have far outweighed these, for if we have had trials we have also had triumphs.*

The love we bore for each other ten years ago has not grown cold but burns with a brighter and purer flame as the real worth of each is made more apparent to the other, and the little ones that have been added to our household in this time have also acted as a tie binding us closer together, and we hope that as these anniversary days roll into the past from year to year that we may remember the date with a pleasant and joyful satisfaction and not with bitterness and heartaches.

Brother Frank grew dissatisfied with farming and with life in western Kansas. On June 23: *Went to Stockton accompanied by Sam Shell and brother Ed and Frank. Sam and Frank took the eastbound 11 a.m. train, the former to go down the country a ways to hunt work and the latter to Wichita where he expects to make his future home with brother George and engage in the real estate and loan business with him.*

And thus crumbles to pieces slowly but surely the old household — a piece broken off here, another there and so on until only a nucleus is left consisting of a mother and two children — Ed & Em. (And, of course, Elam.) Not long after this, his mother and Em moved to eastern Kansas.

What may seem like a minor incident can become a major event, for it is a long trip to the doctor's office on horseback or by horse-drawn wagon, and the rough ride causes irritation every step of the way. On August 25, 1886: *Worked in the a.m. for W. F. Miller at helping to do his threshing, and just as we were finishing up I had the misfortune to get a rye beard into my right eye which caused intense suffering rendering it impossible to see with either eye, so I was compelled to make a trip to Stockton to have it operated on. Mr. Miller took me over and going to Dr. W. A. Leigh's office the painful obstacle was soon removed and much relief was the result. The beard was imbedded in the eye lid big end first and the little*

end was cutting fantastic curves across the eye ball at every movement of the eye.

A good friend lost an infant son on November 16: *The 6-months old son of Summer Southard having died yesterday at 3 oclock a.m. I attended the funeral at 10 a.m. and listened to a most excellent sermon by Mr. Bracken at the house. Interment took place at the Hebrew cemetery and was very slimly attended as a most terrific snow storm raged throughout the whole day. No women folks were at the grave.*

Elam would go through the same grief just two months later.

1887

On January 7, 1887, it became obvious that Elam and Rachel's baby had more than a routine ailment: *Our little 7 months old boy, Hubert, having not been very well for the past two or three days and being worse in the evening, we sat up with him all night.*

January 8: *Passed the day in helping to take care of the little sick boy. Mrs. S. A. Hebrew and sister Em will sit up with him tonight.*

January 9: *Sat up through the night with the baby.*

January 10: *Passed the day in caring for the little sick one who was very poorly last night and no better today. Mother and Mrs. Miller will sit up tonight. We have sent for Dr. W. A. Leigh.*

The doctor came on the 11th but obviously did not know what was wrong: *Last night at 1:30 oclock the doctor came and left medicines for the little sufferer who, he says, is suffering from a complication of diseases resulting from teething. He says that he is not dangerously sick and has strong hopes for his speedy recovery. Mr. & Mrs. A. B. Wilson will sit up with him tonight.*

January 12: *Helping to take care of the little sick boy. S. T. Shell and I will sit up tonight.*

On January 13 the doctor experimented further: *In and about the house helping to care for our little sick one who has been worse than on any previous day. Sent for the doctor again and he came about 10:30 p.m. He left other medicines and remained some time and when going away said we need have no fear of the child's recovery. Rob Montgomery came at noon and remained to sit up tonight. Mr. & Mrs. A. B. Wilson also came to sit up.*

January 14: *Same as yesterday. Little Hubert very low and restless all day. The doctor called about sunset but spoke less hopefully of the little sufferer's recovery. Rachel's brother Tom came down this evening and he and Mrs. Wilson with myself will sit up tonight.*

Finally on the 15th: *Our dear little boy having failed very rapidly during the past two days and having obtained no rest last night nor relief from the medicine administered, the time was passed as on previous days until the middle of the afternoon, when it became evident that the hour of dissolution was near at hand and as the death dews began to gather on his pallid little brow, I took him from the arms of Mrs. O. P. Coy who had been holding him, and sitting down in the rocking chair held him tenderly until about half past three oclock when the dreaded summons came from the dark angel and with a light struggle his spirit, sinless from his birth, and made white in the blood of the Lamb, took its flight and went to mingle with the angelic hosts beyond the river, in the boundless ocean of God's love.*

A large number of sympathizing friends and neighbors came in during the day to offer their sympathy and assistance in our affliction and bereavement, some to remain for the night.

The next day: *Many of the neighbors came in during the a.m. to lend us their assistance, and at 2:30 oclock p.m. all things having been arranged and a number of people being present we all followed in sadness all that was mortal of our dear little boy, over to the school house where many others were awaiting our arrival and where the funeral services were to be held. Mr. Bracken preached the sermon and took for his text 2nd Sam. 12:22&23. A very large number of people were present.*

After the services we continued our way on down to the Bow Creek cemetery [previously known as the Hebrew cemetery] *and just as the sun sank beneath the horizon we laid our darling little one to rest, there to sleep beneath the clods of the valley until the trumpet of the arch-angel shall animate the slumbering dust on the resurrection morn.*

The last sad rites being over we returned home as soon as possible, but oh, how sad to see the empty crib! How sad to know that our family circle has been broken! That one link from the chain has been taken away! Yet we know that it is well with the child and that we should be able to say from our hearts "Thy will, oh God, not mine be Done", and "The Lord hath given, the Lord hath taken away; blessed be the name of the Lord".

Through all these days and nights of care and tearful anxiety Rachel has been almost a constant watcher over our little boy, and few times indeed has refreshing slumber been her portion. Robt. Montgomery and wife and two children will stay with us all night.

While Elam was in Stockton attending the county Sunday school convention, a momentous event happened: *Tonight witnessed my first sight of the electric light system.* The date was September 14, 1887. Elam was 35 years old. George was 10, Elbert 9, Beth 6, Jesse 5, and Earl 3 years old.

A disclosure of Elam's feelings about the year is given on the last day of December: *And thus endeth the year 1887! Although we have all enjoyed our usual health and strength and many blessings have fallen to our lot, yet sorrows and perplexities have also come. In the first month of the year we were called to mourn a broken family circle in the death of our dear little boy Hubert. Then came a season of great drought followed by very short crops and a consequent period of hard times and unusually perplexing circumstances. Still we know that the blessings, both spiritual and temporal, far outweigh these light afflictions which the apostle says are "but for a moment".*

1888
Rachel went to see the doctor on February 25, 1888: *Wife went to consult Dr. Leigh on a heart trouble which has troubled her for some time.*

It was a grievous task that Elam had to perform on April 11: *In the p.m. went up north about five miles and got a load of hard stone with which to build a foundation for a monument to be put up tomorrow at Father's grave at the Bow Creek cemetery.*

1889
Elam seemed a little vexed at being excluded from his brother's wedding on February 12, 1889: *Brother Ed was married today at Stockton to Myrtle Southard by Rev. A. B. Conwell. No friends or relatives present.*

On March 8, 1889, just a little over one year after baby Hubert died, another son was born to Elam and Rachel, their last child: *Miscellaneous work at and about the house, being presented with another big 12 pound boy* [Lee] *at 2:30 p.m. Mrs. A. B. Wilson and Mrs. W. F. Miller officiating. All doing well!* But just 2½ weeks later the three oldest children got the measles, which was of some concern.

Wild fruit was still available on August 15: *In the p.m. in company with Wm. Hebrew and wife and Rachel went south about eight miles to the south fork (of the Solomon river) after plums and grapes. Secured several bushels.* And again on the 27th: *Took wife and the children up S.W. about three miles on a graping expedition and came home at 3 p.m. having secured an abundance of very fine grapes.*

1890
When it was not possible to purchase toys, they were made at home. On January 7, 1890: *Spent the greater part of the day in making a good iron-shod hand sled for the boys.*

A good friend died on June 26, 1890: *Old Mrs. Shell, our near neighbor, having died last evening, I, in company with A. B. Wilson, made a trip to Stockton after a coffin and other things. Left home at 1:30 a.m. and returned home at 8:30 a.m. Passed the time from then till noon in reading and writing and at 2 p.m. attended the funeral services at the house. Listened to a good sermon by Rev. Bailey from John 11:25. A large concourse of people were present.*

1891
During the summer days of 1891 the family went to gather several bushels of grapes, plums, choke-cherries, and mulberries along the creek and the south fork of the Solomon River.

Eldest son George, 14, went away to attend high school on November 26: *Having made all due preparations started at 1:30 p.m. to Phillipsburg to take George over to take the train tomorrow morning for Louisville,*

Kan., where he expects to attend school until next spring. He will board with his aunt Emma Hebrew.

1892

By early 1892 Elam had acquired a horse-drawn sled, which was used for transporting the children to and from school on snowy days.

When Elam reached 40 years of age, on June 9, 1892, his reaction was much the same as reactions are today: *Birth-Day — Age Forty Years! At 20 this period seemed a long way in the future but tonight as I look back over the past 20 years it seems but a few months ago since the first score of years of my life had passed away. As I look forward the next score of years looks much shorter than the last one did at its beginning! Wife made me a present of a fine Oxford Teachers Bible today, and the children a cup and saucer.*

1893

Grave markers were made on April 4, 1893: *Having taken a contract to make 30 head and foot posts to mark that number of unmarked graves in the Bow creek cemetery, I worked all day at the matter of cutting and preparing the material which consists of 2x8 and 2x6 hard pine planks for head and foot respectively.* These were put in place on May 2: *In company with wife went down to the Bow creek cemetery where we met with several other of the neighbors and proceeded to put up 22 head and foot boards at the graves of that number of unmarked interments.*

On May 9 Elam began a train trip to Washington, D.C., with stops to see friends and relatives in Illinois, and a layover in Chicago to observe the Columbian Exposition (400 years after the coming of Columbus).

May 10: *Arrived at Quincy at 2 a.m. and continuing on toward Chicago arrived at Bushnell, Ill. at 5 oclock where I remained 2 hours and at 7 oclock, after having taken breakfast, desiring to go west 9 miles on the T.P.&W. R.R. to Good Hope, and no train being due in that direction until 11 a.m., I took passage out on a hand car with the section hands about 4½ miles and from there walked to Good Hope and not being able to secure a conveyance of any sort at the livery stable I proceeded to walk out*

1886

Postage and Stationery

Jan.	30	Stamps 10 Wrappers 5 Pencil 5	20
Feb	27	Paper 45, Stamps 20, Wrappers 10	75
Mar.	30	Pencils 5, Stamps 5	10
April	30	Pencils 20 Stps. 15 pens 5, Envelps 20 Ink 10	70
May	31	Day Book 20 Stamps 15-10-10	55
June	30	Stamps -5-10 pencils 5	20
July	31	Stamps 5-5	10
Aug.	31	Stamps 10-5	15
Sept.	30	Pen 5 Stamps 10	15
Oct.	31	Cards 5	5
Nov.	30	Stamps 15	15
Dec.	31	Stamps 10 -15 not book 15	

Books & Periodicals.

Jan.	13	Topeka Capital 10 Our Family Physician 50	1	50
"	13	Inter Ocean 100, Dict. of Synonyms 35	1	35
Apr.	15	Third Reader 65 + Speller 25		90
May	28	Stockton Record	1	25
"	28	Louisville Republican	1	75
"	28	Farmington Bugle	1	75
Nov.	26	Stockton Record	1	50
Dec.	1	Stockton Record	1	75
"	1	Kansas Farmer	1	00
"		St. Louis Evangelist	2	00
"	24	Watson Speller 25 U.B.6 20		45
			15	**20**

.1892

Taxes, Notes, Interest + Book Accounts.

Jan.	2	Hultman Miller + Co. Note	26	13
"	2	Levy + Smith on account	10	00
"	20	K.L. + J. Co. Int.	47	90
Feb.	20	Dewey + Smith 5.70 Coolbaugh Bros 7.00	12	70
March	24	Z. Baldwin Bros.	31	65
Apr.	30	Int. Z. Bks.	1	10
May	30	K.L. + J. Co.	47	45
June	8	Z. Baldwin Bros.	10	25
"	21	Taxes	6	60
Aug.	18	K.L. + J. Co.	47	10

Books + Periodicals

Feb.	20	Fungi, Mycetzoa + Bacteria	5	35
"	20	Cryptogamic Botany	8	15
"	20	Histology + th Microscope	1	35
"	20	Diseases of Plants		85
"	20	Stockton News three years	3	00
June	9	Oxford Teachers Bible	2	25
Aug.	27	Academician		50
"	29	Gospel Hymns		65
Sep.	17	Atchison Champion		50
Dec.	10	North Am. Pyrenomycetes	4	35
			22	15

Above and page opposite: These pages from Elam's personal expense accounts of 1886 and 1892 provide additional insight into what he was reading.

5 miles north west of town to visit with brother John and family who left Kansas for this place on Nov. 9, 1882.

Arrived at John's at 11:30 oclock where I spent the remainder of the day in social chat, being quite foot-sore from my walk, having on a new pair of shoes and the weather being unusually warm. In the evening participated in a social prayer meeting which was held at their house. Found John doing quite well — much better than when he was in Kansas — also that his family had increased from two in 1882 to seven now with additional prospects ahead.

May 11: *At 7 a.m. brother John hitched up to the buggy and took me to Good Hope where I boarded the east bound train shortly after getting to town and got a ticket to Cuba where I dropped off at 9 oclock to call on my old friend and school mate Howard Day of whom mention is often made in this diary during the years 1871 and 1872.*

I found him stationed at this place as ticket agent and telegraph operator for the Narrow Gauge R.R. which crosses the T.P.&W. here. I spent four hours very pleasantly with him in social chat and reminiscence. I took dinner at his pleasant home and formed the acquaintance of his wife and family.

At one oclock p.m. I again resumed my journey, arriving at Canton a half hour later where I remained two hours, calling for a half hour on Rev. A. R. Mathes, a former pastor of the Farmington, Ill. Presbyterian church, who performed a service in my behalf which is mentioned in full under date of June 14, 1876 [the marriage of Elam and Rachel]. *At 3:30 took the north bound train over the C.B.&Q. and arrived at Farmington 11 miles north in due time and once more stepped on the ground hallowed by many memories of my boyhood days.*

Nearly 17 years had gone by since I had left these once familiar scenes and many striking changes had occurred during that time. After looking about town sometime I came across several of my old time acquaintances with whom I passed a short time in conversation. The first I met was Steve Dikeman who is now a resident of the town but when I knew him years ago was a farmer. I also met farmer Jake Brimmer, Frank Montgomery (wife's cousin), Cap Merrill, Frank Whitaker and Will Dikeman.

No other way offering, and the roads being exceedingly muddy, I walked out 3 miles west on the Central Iowa R.R. which runs through father-in-law Montgomery's farm to which place I desired to go, arriving at 6 oclock where I found them all — Father & Mother M. and the three boys, Tom, Jim and George — all glad to see me. It is my purpose to remain here until next Monday morning.

May 12: *In company with George and Jim Montgomery went to Farmington and Geo. being engaged in carpenter work there remained for the day while Jim and I went out south of town about a mile to Wright's nursery where we got some fruit and shade trees and returning home to Mr. Montgomery's at noon Jim and I spent the whole of the p.m. in setting out the trees — making a new orchard. I met also today several more of my old time acquaintances, viz: Olney Morgan, John S. Green and Miss Addie Day.*

May 13: *Spent the a.m. in company with brother-in-law Geo. Montgomery, who came home again last night, botanizing on the woodland north and north east of the house about 100 rods, being very successful in finding many interesting flowering plants and fungi.* This had to be satisfying to Elam, who now had botanical skills that had not been developed the last time he was here.

In the p.m., in company with father Montgomery, went in to Farmington where I met quite a number more of my old friends and acquaintances, viz: Jas. Torrens, E. M. Rose, Emerson Clark, Jas. Tenley, J. Y. Dunn, Jas. H. Hunter, Mrs. Emma (Dunn) Rose and Mrs. Lanta (Dunn) Dikeman.

May 14 (Sunday): *In company with father Montgomery went to Farmington where we attended services at the old Presbyterian church with which I united 20 years ago.*

Of the old church war horses I met today and renewed the acquaintance of Matthew Jack, Sam'l Jack, John Marshall, John Simpson and Mr. Steck. I also met cousin Ed Montgomery. Spent the afternoon in social chat and reading.

May 15: *Arrived in Chicago at 6 oclock p.m. Went to 5734 Wabash Ave. to the boarding house of the Haskin sisters of Farmington who are here for the fair season.*

May 16: *Walked down to the World's Fair grounds at Jackson park early in the morning, the distance being about one mile, where I staid until 6 p.m. seeing the sights of the great Exposition which I found to be far from complete as the exhibits in many of the buildings are not yet in place and it seems to me that it will take yet a full month or more to make them complete.*

I made hasty visits during the day to the Agricultural Building, Machinery Hall, Manufacturers Building, Art Building, Horticultural Building,

U.S. Govt. Building, Fisheries Building and the Kansas and Washington state buildings. Got back to my boarding house at 6:30 oclock, very tired but well pleased with my first day and night in Chicago.

May 17: *After doing some writing early in the morning I took a State Street cable car and going north to Adams St. I walked over to the "Q" depot where I got my baggage and transferred it over to the B&O depot on the corner of Fifth Avenue and Harrison Street, and after loitering about for an hour or more I bought a ticket over the B&O for Washington D.C. and getting aboard of the 10:45 east bound train on that road resumed my journey eastward.*

Did not get dinner until 3 p.m. at which hour we stopped for that purpose at the little town of Garrett in northern Indiana 143 miles east of Chicago. At 5:30 oclock we passed North Baltimore where we came into and first saw the many derricks of the oil wells in the oil belt of northern Ohio. Continuing on without incident worthy of mention I went to my berth in the sleeper at 10 oclock at Newark, Ohio, a thriving city ten miles N.W. of which my boyhood days between two and 13 years were spent.

May 18: *Our train arrived at Wheeling, West Va. about 4 oclock a.m. and there being a freight car wreck on the main line a short distance ahead caused by a washout we were compelled to back up a distance of 77 miles on a branch line to Pittsburgh at which place we did not arrive until 8:30 oclock where we remained about an hour. We got a most excellent breakfast at the Monongahela House.*

Continuing on our journey we passed up the Monongahela river through the great iron region and coke oven country and on up the Yohoghany river up to the divide across the Alleghaney mountains and thence downward on the other side of the Potomac valley, arriving at Cumberland, Md. at 2:30 p.m. where we stopped twenty minutes for supper. The scenery between Pittsburgh and Cumberland is the grandest that I have ever seen.

At 4 oclock we passed the historic old town of Harper's Ferry rendered immortal by "Old John Brown". At 7:30 we arrived in Washington. While Elam was there, he attended the meetings of the General Assembly of the Presbyterian church and made contacts at the U.S. Department of Agriculture relating to his botanical interests. There was time on various days for visiting all the places of special appeal to visitors. Back in Kansas, the *Stockton Record* printed Elam's May 17, 1893, observations of "The Fair Through Kansas Eyes."

On the return trip in early June, Elam again stopped in Chicago for the sole purpose of an extensive tour of the World's Fair, which by now was in full operation. He visited the buildings seen previously plus many others. Without question the most rewarding was near the end of the day on June 6: *Evening having now come an hour was spent on the court of honor near the great fountain admiring the wonderfully astonishing electric displays and listening to the enchanting music from the various bands — Sousa's and the 7th Regt. Band of N.Y. especially!*

The remainder of the time until 10 oclock p.m. was spent in the great Electricity building where were on exhibition some of the most striking wonders that man has ever seen in electric display.

On August 5, 1893, Rachel had an unpleasant task: *With wife went to Stockton on miscellaneous business and she to get the remaining teeth extracted from her upper jaw preparatory to getting a new set. Dr F. S. Webster did the work.* She was not yet 40 years old.

Brother Ed's daughter Mabel died on September 7, 1893, at age seven months.

With Elam's family growing, it was time to secure improved transportation, so on October 2: *Early in the morning, with George, went to Stockton after a new two-seated buggy or spring wagon, buying the same of J. Q. Adams for the sum of $60.* Immediately the family set out on a trip to eastern Kansas to visit relatives and friends.

1895

Elam was thrilled when he saw his first aerial demonstration at the Rooks County Fair on October 4, 1895: *At 4 p.m. occurred a very fine balloon ascension and successful parachute descent. This was my first experience at seeing a sight of that sort and it was well worth seeing.*

On October 19, 1895, one of Elam's best friends died: *At 10 oclock p.m. went to the Bow Creek post office to assist in arranging the funeral*

services and attend to other matters connected with our dear old friend and neighbor elder Samuel Hebrew who died quite suddenly yesterday at 11 oclock a.m. Remained there through the night.

October 20: *Remained at Hebrew's until nearly noon when I came home spending the p.m. in reading and writing. At evening went down to Hebrew's again and remained there until 10 p.m. and then came home being accompanied by Mr. Bracken for whom we had telegraphed at Hays City to come and preach the funeral sermon.*

October 21: *The funeral having been set for 10:30 a.m. we all went down at that time to attend it. It was the largest funeral ever held in this part of the country. We all came home at 1 oclock p.m. accompanied by Mr. Bracken and brother-in-law Wm. Hebrew who had come up from Pottawatomie county. In the evening they both went back down to Mrs. Hebrew's to pass the night.*

1896

An explorer came to town bringing pictures on April 4, 1896: *With wife went to Stockton on business and to attend the lecture given by the famous hunter and arctic explorer, Prof. L. L. Dyche of Lawrence, which was grand indeed, it being illustrated throughout by several hundred fine stereopticon views.*

Rachel's mother came to visit on May 5: *At 6 p.m. with wife went to Stockton to meet Mother Montgomery of Farmington, Ill. who has come to make an extended visit with us.*

Even horse-drawn conveyances were not immune to having collisions. On September 16: *In company with George drove over near Stockton on Dibble creek where I stopped to do several hours botanizing while George drove on into town to do some business and while there met with a rather serious accident by being run into by a run-away team which completely demolished our spring wagon so that we had to borrow one to come home in.* It was only three years old.

Having completed his studies at Stockton Academy, George was ready to go to college on September 28: *In the p.m. with George went over to Phillipsburg where we met Newton Bracken with whom he will start for Emporia tomorrow by wagon to enter the freshman class in the College of Emporia as the commencement of his preparation for the ministry.*

Music had been a significant part of the lives of both Elam and Rachel from their youth. Finally on October 31 they managed to get an instrument: *With Elbert went to Stockton on business and to bring home a recently purchased cottage organ.*

Sad news came from Rachel's Iowa relatives on November 22: *About 2 oclock last night we got a telegram by carrier from Stockton from Rob Montgomery, wife's brother, of Bedford, Iowa, saying that his brother "Will is dying!"*

1898

The Stockton Academy passed from the Congregational church to a civic association on January 3, 1898: *At 3 p.m. attended a meeting of the stockholders of the Stockton Educational Association which now has control of the old Academy building. Was elected one of the trustees for the ensuing year and also vice-president of the Association with G. Farr as president. At 7:30 p.m. attended at Farr's office a meeting of the trustees of the Stockton Academy for the purpose of conveying the Academy to the Stockton Educational Association. Those present were Judge R. M. Pickle, R. R. Hays, Geo. Farr, S. N. Hawkes, W. L. Chambers, Rev. J. A. Nield and myself.*

Through the years Elam had experienced various ailments, and each time he must have pondered the possibility of not recovering. After all, numerous friends of similar age had already passed on for one reason or another. But on January 30, 1898, he really did have a nearly fatal confrontation: *At 7 oclock a.m. took a most violent cramping pain at the heart which continued to get worse until 8:30 when it seemed that the end was close at hand. At 11, from a sitting posture on the edge of the bed where I had been since 7 a.m. I was able to be placed in a chair where I remained until 9 p.m. and then went to bed.* The next day Elam remained in bed, but he was much better by evening, and the crisis passed.

Chapter 6

Personal Aspects:
Later Life

*A*FTER 25 YEARS the original house built of native cotton-wood timber had to be replaced, so on June 3, 1899: *Our old house built in the fall of 1874, having practically succumbed to the ravages of time we worked at taking it down today preparatory to building another with all possible speed.* Timing could have been better. There were frequent heavy rains, and then there was harvest of small grains and hay to put up. A temporary structure of sod would be used until a really good house could be built. By the third week of July it was nearly finished. A local plasterer refused the job, so Elam and boys did it themselves, just as they had done the doors and windows and the floor installation.

Elbert, having completed courses at Stockton Academy, took a teaching job to earn money to go to college. His first job was ten miles to the southeast, teaching school.

1900

Every year Elam made note of his own birthday, but considerately almost never mentioned Rachel's, because women did not care to have their age noted. But February 22, 1900, was different: *Took wife up to old Mrs. Privett's to spend the day and returning home at 11:30 oclock found a number of the neighbors here who had come in to surprise Rachel on her 45th birthday. So while Mr. Brodbeck drove over to Privett's after her, brother Ed and I made a flying trip to Stockton after oysters etc. and returned at 3 oclock p.m. The remainder of the day was spent pleasantly with our company.*

In the evening the real surprise party came in good shape and filled the whole house. A good oyster supper was served by the ladies after which the time until far past midnight was spent in social chat with games and musical entertainment. A light rain and snow storm came up late in the night and some half dozen of the guests remained until daylight before going home.

On June 9, Elam's birthday was especially gratifying: *Spent today at home in reading and writing and social visiting with George who has so successfully and with such high honors completed his collegiate education. So this, my 48th birthday, is one of unusual pleasure and gratification.* Elam was proud to have provided his firstborn son with a college education — something he had never had.

Any parent of children in their teens or just beyond knows how complicated life can become in accommodating their varied agendas. Elam provided details on August 24: *The events of the day are of such a varied character that they are difficult to record! The county normal institute closed yesterday at Plainville! Elbert, Lizzie and Jesse have been in attendance. Early this morning George took the wagon and drove over after them, and in the p.m. drove to Stockton in the buggy to attend to various items of business, where at 5:30 p.m. I met the young folks on their return from Plainville.*

Jesse taking the wagon proceeded homeward at once. Elbert having ridden his bicycle and going by a round-about way had not arrived in town yet. Lizzie took supper with some girl friend and George and I took supper at the Clark Hotel where he and Elbert will remain all night.

The sod house of Elam and Rachel Bartholomew on Bow Creek, north of Stockton, Kansas, which was in use from 1899 to 1905. Elam is on the left. There is no picture of their first home, a native cottonwood structure built in 1876.

Another view of the sod house, ca. 1899, showing the fine grove of trees planted by Elam.

This wide-angle view of the sod house, *ca.* 1899, conveys the reality of harshness of life on the prairie. There was no time or energy for landscaping when beginning life on the frontier.

George having been elected some time ago as Professor of Natural Sciences in the Hiawatha academy, having made all due preparations, will leave tomorrow morning to visit various places in the east part of the state and finally arrive at Hiawatha in due time to take up his work there on the 12th of next month; so, bidding him a kind farewell and a God speed in his approaching work at 6:30 oclock, Lizzie and I started at once for home and arrived here about 8 oclock while Elbert remained to see George off on the train tomorrow morning.

After finishing the equivalent of high school at 18, Jesse, like his older siblings, took a job teaching elementary school to earn money to attend college. Thus on September 4: *With Jesse went over east about eight miles, into Lanark township, to secure a school for him to teach this winter. We were successful and he got a contract for the Thrasher-Lambert school*

at $25.00 per month. While in the neighborhood we visited, as members of the board, B. G. Lambert, J. W. Manners and R. D. Thrasher, taking dinner with the latter.

Just 17 days after sending George on his way to his first job following college came this sad news: *At 11 a.m. we received a great shock in the form of a telegram from George at Hiawatha stating that he was sick and wanted his mother to come to him at once! At noon Elbert started on his bicycle to Marvin to see if an eastbound train could be caught this afternoon or evening. A slow rain set in immediately and soon increased to a steady downpour so that he did not get home until about 3 p.m. with*

satisfactory information. At 4 oclock in the face of a disagreeable north rain storm, wife and Jesse started to Marvin, where, at 6 oclock she took the train for Hiawatha.

Two days later, on September 12: *With Lee went to Stockton to attend the fair but on reaching town received a telegram from wife in Hiawatha containing the unutterably sorrowful news of the death of our dear George last evening and that she would be at Stockton with the body tomorrow night. We returned home at 11 oclock bringing the sad news to those here.*

To make some necessary arrangements made quick trips to neighbors W. F. Miller and Jack Shaw's and remained at home until 3 p.m. when, having sent for J. M. Mellon, went with him to Stockton to complete arrangements for the funeral at 10 oclock a.m. Friday. At noon Elbert went to Phillipsburg to secure the services of Rev. Dr. Theo Bracken, but as he was in Oklahoma they telegraphed him and received word in reply that he would be here Friday morning.

Many kind friends and neighbors called during the afternoon to express their heartfelt sympathy and offer their assistance in any way possible.

September 13: *Spent the day at home in the darkest sorrow that has ever come into my life, praying for comfort and finding none. Wondering why or for what purpose the dear Lord has sent this overshadowing sorrow and deep affliction upon us, not seeing clear how to say 'Thy will O God be done", or "The Lord hath given, the Lord hath taken away; blessed be the name of the Lord".*

At three oclock p.m. Elbert and I, in company with neighbor W. F. Miller, went to Stockton to meet poor stricken momma on her return with the inanimate clay of our dearly beloved and gifted first-born son!

At 8 oclock with many sympathizing friends, especially of the Woodman and Royal Neighbor camps, we went to the station to meet the heart broken mother and extend to her our tenderest sympathy and condolence in this darkest of all dark hours! She was accompanied from Glen Elder by Miss Mary Nash of that town, George's finacée. With wife and Miss Nash went to F. P. Hill's where we passed the night. Elbert staid at Chas. Mead's. The casket was taken to the undertaking establishment where it was cared for.

September 14: *At 8 oclock a.m. with many persons who desired to be in attendance we left Stockton and arrived at the Mt. Lebanon school house at 10 oclock at which time the funeral services were immediately conducted by Rev. Dr. Bracken. After the concluding service at the cemetery,*

An inside view of the sod house, featuring Elam's library, the pump organ, and a portrait of his father.

wife, Elbert, Miss Nash and I went to Evan Hebrew's where we took dinner and returned home at 4 oclock p.m.

Again our home circle has been broken and another dear one has gone to that higher eternal home beyond the skies!

Despite the grief of September, there was a proud moment on October 12: *It was a peculiarly pleasing sight about sun set to see our three school teachers, Elbert* [age 21], *Lizzie* [age 19] *and Jesse* [age 18] *all returning from their week's work at their respective schools; the former in Rush township and the two latter in Lanark township.* None of the three had yet been to college, but they were earning money to do so.

During 1900 it was obvious that more space was needed than the new sod house provided, especially with Elam's botanical activities and the space needed for the Rockport post office, so Elam and Rachel decided to add on a new kitchen. Improvements were squeezed in between other obligations, but finally the work was completed, on November 27: *Spent the time in rearranging our household goods and moving some of them, with the postoffice, into the new kitchen.*

An eloquent soliloquy finished the year: *Thus closes a 30-year period in the keeping of this diary! A faithful record of my life's doings has been carefully made for each and every day for the past 10,957 days!*

Oh the joys and sorrows, the sunshine and shadows of that long period covering the best part of my life! How the lights and shadows play along life's pathway! Today, the bright joyous sunlight and the sweet melody of the feathered songsters; tomorrow, the drooping head, the tear-stained cheek, the dark cloud and the blackness of ashes! Earth's contrasts indeed!

1901

Soon thereafter came some disquieting news. On January 25, 1901: *At 9:30 a.m. a telegram came announcing the dangerous illness of Father Montgomery, who with his wife, has been visiting several months with brothers-in-law Robt. and Thomas Montgomery at Bedford, Iowa.*

The day was spent in making the necessary preparations and in taking wife to Marvin to take the 6 p.m. east bound train for Iowa that she might attend the bedside of her sick father.

Things looked worse on the 31st: *Word received from wife at Bedford, Iowa says that both her father and mother are in a very critical condition.* But by February 23 things had improved enough that Rachel returned home.

Elbert got a teaching job in the community where his Uncle Eli lived, so on September 3: *Elbert bade us good bye this morning and mounting his bicycle turned his face toward the sunrising for a 200-mile jaunt to Louisville in Pottawatomie county where he is to enter the school room as teacher in the intermediate department next Monday.*

One year after son George's death, Elam still feels the anguish. On September 12, 1901: *Oh the sorrow, the heart aches and the blackness of ashes of this day one year ago! How intensely fresh in our minds, and how the heartfelt sorrow refuses to be banished from our memories!* And on the 14th: *One year ago today it was a household and a very large community wrapped in gloom! Today 80 millions of people mourn at the bier of the dead President!* (McKinley).

More sad news was received on November 11: *At 11 a.m. a telegram, that usual harbinger of ill to the countryside resident, came from Farmington, Ill. telling that Father Montgomery was sinking rapidly and could not last long! Rachel would like to have gone on to be at her dying father's bedside, but her enfeebled health and other causes prevented her going.* Death came later the same day as was revealed on Saturday, the 16th: *Word came by letter this evening from Ill. that Father Montgomery died at his home there last Monday evening at the age of 73 years.*

1902

Another moment of grieving is triggered on May 1, 1902: *Twenty five years ago today — one quarter of a century — witnessed the birth of our first-born baby boy in whom we centered our early love and the fondest pride of our maturer years! But alas! The dark day of Sept. 11, 1900!*

A stone was set at the grave of George on July 21, 1902: *At 10 oclock with wife drove down to the Bow creek cemetery where at noon we were joined by Earl, who had gone over for that purpose, and W. H. Sage, marble cutter of Stockton, who brought out a fine monument to mark the resting place of our dear boy, George. We came home at 3 oclock p.m.*

Finally Elbert had earned enough money from teaching school to go to college on August 29: *Elbert having made all due preparations for that purpose bade us all good bye and started to Stockton to take the early train tomorrow for Emporia where he expects to take a course in the State Normal school.* He would be 24 years old in October.

Jesse continued to earn money for college. On October 4: *Jesse having engaged to teach in the school district where Elbert taught two years ago, three miles S.E. of Webster, he went this afternoon over to his field of labor for a 6-months term of school.*

Elizabeth soon left for college also. Elam recorded on November 5: *Daughter Lizzie having made all due preparations therefor, Lee took her to Stockton at 2 oclock p.m. that she might take the early train out tomorrow morning for Emporia where she goes to attend the State Normal school until next June.*

1903

New neighbors moved into the house that had been originally built for Elam's parents, so on February 20, 1903, Elam wrote: *In the p.m. with wife made a call on our new neighbors, Albert White's.* Whites' daughter would one day become the wife of son Lee.

Serious flooding that year in eastern Kansas interfered with travel. On June 10: *At 9 a.m. Elbert and Lizzie came in from Emporia having been flood bound at Junction City since May 28th.* It also had some affect in the West when on the next day: *Left Plainville at 7 a.m. for Hays City. In crossing the Saline river the water was much deeper than I anticipated and I lost a number of things out of my buggy! After getting across the stream I stripped off most of my clothing and plunging in secured my floating chattels from their onward course toward the gulf of Mexico!*

Telephone service had reached towns in the area by 1903 but had not yet come to the rural localities. Elam first mentioned it on July 24. While in town on business he *phoned from Stockton to Logan for Rev. Arthur to attend the funeral tomorrow* of the 9-year-old son of a neighbor, W. H. Cadorett.

In the autumn, Earl entered high school at Stockton. He rented a room in town so that it would not be necessary to commute daily such a distance. Jesse departed to attend the College of Emporia, following the footsteps of deceased brother George. Elbert and Lizzie were also at Emporia at the state school. Thus only Lee, the youngest, was still living at home, though Earl returned on weekends.

1904

On June 7, 1904, Elam and Rachel went by train to Clay Center to the state Sunday school convention. They stayed at the home of former state senator F. P. Harkness, located at the corner of Fifth and Crawford Streets.

This bears intriguing significance — just six years later Elam's son Jesse became acquainted with Florence Cook, who lived at 530 Crawford. He married Florence in 1919. She probably participated in the 1904 Sunday school convention, because she and her parents, Dr. D. P. and Ella Webber Cook, were active in the Presbyterian church there, and she was 14 at the time.

In late September and early October, Elam and Rachel went by train to visit the World's Fair at St. Louis, Missouri. They were part of a tour group of 35 from Stockton, who found the excursion well worth the effort. On October 5: *And thus ended our most delightful trip to the great and unsurpassed "Louisiana Purchase Exposition" far surpassing anything yet the world has ever seen in the way of a World's Fair.* The fair celebrated the centennial of that great land acquisition.

Many descriptive details were recorded, but probably the most captivating exhibit to Elam was the *Electricity Building with all its varied wonders.* Displays from around the country and around the world were thrilling to see, especially in that pre-television era.

In late 1904, telephone service was about to reach the area where Elam lived. On November 1 of that year: *Purchased $25.00 worth of stock in the Bow Creek Telephone Association.* And by mid-November: *In the p.m., with neighbor Miller, worked at running out a line for our telephone line from the county line south one mile, preparatory to setting the posts soon.* On the next day: *In the p.m. we worked at setting telephone poles on the line run out yesterday.*

Telephone service finally began on Thanksgiving day, November 24: *Spent almost the entire day at completing our telephone line which we got into successful operation as far north as neighbor W. F. Miller's by night and talked forth and back over it!*

Full service became available on December 3: *Our telephone being connected today with the main line we are now able to communicate readily with points to the north, south, east and west of us!* Elam's ring was three longs. Ed's was one long and two shorts.

Ten days later, the phone was useful in an emergency: *In the afternoon we received a telephone message that Jesse was sick and was on his way home from Emporia, requesting us to meet him at Stockton tomorrow.*

December 14: *Went to Stockton in the morning and met Jesse at the 11 a.m. train and brought him home at 1:30 oclock. He has had forcible symptoms of coming down with typhoid fever, hence his home-coming before the holiday season. As to further developments in the case we are in doubt at present.*

Elam and Rachel must have felt their religious convictions shaken to the core. Their first son, dedicated to the ministry, had died just before entering seminary, and now the second one who planned to become a minister had a deadly disease.

On the 21st, Jesse's fever was *still quite high,* but eventually he did recover. He returned to school in Emporia after the holidays.

1905

Elam relished a surprise party given on June 9, 1905: *Birthday — age 53! It being the birthday also of our neighbor, Albert White, 57, he and wife and Dr. Bracken and wife of Phillipsburg came in the a.m. and took dinner with us but immediately thereafter a genuine surprise was duly "pulled off" on Mr. White and I by a large number of friends and neighbors who began to pour in until the house would not hold the crowd, so we all repaired to the nearby grove where games and various amusements were entered into by those present. Soon tables were spread and a most bountiful and elegant lunch made a speedy appearance which was soon closely investigated by the happy company assembled.*

Just a few days later, June 17, the Bartholomews began the preparations for the construction of their new home: *Elbert and Earl each drove to town and brought out two wagon loads of cement rock as a starter on the foundation of our proposed new house which we expect to have well under way next month.*

On his way to an International Sunday School Convention in Toronto, Elam stopped in Chicago to tour the city. He had visited in 1893 exclusively to see the World's Fair, but on June 20 and 21, 1905, he went to the usual tourist attractions: museums, Lincoln Park, and the lakefront. Especially interesting to him was touring the thriving mail-order houses of Montgomery Ward and Sears Roebuck.

June 22: *Visited the postoffice building in the early morning and thence to the Board of Trade Building where I witnessed for some time the cavort-*

ings of the howling mob of bidders in the grain market. The scene surely beggars description!

Taking my baggage I then went to the Polk St. depot where at 11 a.m. I resumed my journey toward Toronto.

Upon leaving Toronto Elam took time to visit Niagara Falls, Rachel's sister Celia and husband, J. D. Fink, and *the National Food Co's. factory where "shredded whole wheat biscuit" is made.*

On the return trip he went to see Rachel's brothers, Robert Montgomery and Thomas Montgomery, who had moved to Parnell, Missouri, and Savannah, Missouri, respectively.

Work on Elam's new house began in earnest on July 26: *With W. E. Allis as boss carpenter and three assistants, Jones, Kay and Hollingsworth, started the erection of our new house which is to be 28x30 with addition of 16x19. I did some work and a great deal of looking on!*

The entry for August 10, when Elam and Rachel and several others went to a Chautauqua gathering, first mentioned Lily, the girl who eventually became Lee's wife.

Delivery of mail to rural residences actually began on August 31: *By the establishment of rural route No. 3 from Stockton the Rockport post office, which we have had since April 3, 1895, ceased to exist today. The office was established in 1873 with Jas. Stroup as postmaster. Then followed S. A. Hebrew, A. B. Wilson, Elam Bartholomew and last Mrs. R. I. Bartholomew* [Rachel].

October 7 was a big day: *Continued moving into the new house until 11 a.m. at which time with Lizzie made a business trip to Stockton where among other things we purchased a fine piano of Harley Viers.* The piano was Lizzie's wedding present from Elam and Rachel.

Costs of the new house were calculated December 22: *Worked nearly all day at cleaning up the yard of old lumber and other rubbish about the house, such as has accumulated since the 26th of July when the first nail was driven. Now that the house is practically completed, in looking over the various bills I find that the structure has cost us about $2100!*

Elam's new house, built in 1905.

1906

First mention of the man whom Elizabeth eventually married was made on January 2, 1906: *Mr. Chester Ingle of Chickasha, Indian Territory came at 11 a.m. for a visit with us for several days.* (The area known as "Indian Territory" later became Oklahoma.) Chester was an attorney. They had met at school in Emporia.

Rachel had to make a quick trip back East on February 20: *In the p.m. took wife to Stockton from whence at 6 p.m. she took the east bound train for Jacksonville, Ill. to be at the bedside of her mother who has been dangerously ill for several weeks.* Then on March 4: *About 5 oclock p.m. rec'd. a telegram from wife announcing the death of her mother, Mrs. Elizabeth Montgomery, early this morning!*

Earl was in his final year of high school at Stockton when on November 26 Elam wrote: *At noon we received a telephone message from Stockton stating that Earl had taken very sick last night at Mrs. Mead's, his boarding place, that the Dr. had been called, and for some of us to go over at once, so wife and Beth went.* (Elizabeth, previously called "Lizzie," was now known as "Beth.")

Each day one or more members of the family went into town to spend time with Earl, until on December 4: *With Beth went to Stockton to see Earl whose illness continues to grow more serious every hour! At 1:30 p.m. a consultation of physicians, consisting of Drs. Book and Callender, was held and it was found beyond a peradventure that he is in the grip of a well developed case of appendicitis which, unless relieved by treatment in the next 24 hours, must be operated on by a skilled surgeon! The ice or freezing treatment was commenced in the afternoon and we kept it up throughout the night with gratifying results.*

Improvement was noted by the 6th: *Went to Stockton in the p.m. to see Earl who seems to be improving with the ice treatment which consists in the placing of an ice bag containing pounded ice across the abdomen, covering the appendix. Remained all night.*

The family was understandably worried — eldest son George had died just six years earlier from a ruptured appendix. But there was no way that Earl could be transported to a location where an operation could be performed, so on December 13: *At 6 p.m. wife, Elbert and Earl came over from Stockton in a closed surrey, taking 3 hours to make the 10 mile trip — Earl standing the trip quite well considering his enfeebled condition.* Then he was better for a few days, with another brief relapse on the 20th, after which recovery was complete.

Beth's fiancé came for a visit on December 22: *Mr. Chester R. Ingle, our prospective son-in-law, now of Liberal, Kansas came in today for another important visit!*

1907

The first child of Elam and Rachel to be married was Beth. On January 3, 1907: *All things having been prepared for the marriage of our daughter, the ceremony was duly performed by Rev. R. Arthur in presence of a housefull of guests after which the wedding dinner was served and the remainder of the day spent in social commingling of our various guests.* Elizabeth had been born on this same day in 1881.

Then, on February 26, sadness returned to Elam's life: *At 6 oclock p.m. we received a message announcing my Mother's death today at 1 oclock at the home of my sister at Louisville, Kan. where I visited the latter part of last Sept.*

The next day held deep frustration: *Unusual storm of rain, sleet, hail and thunder and lightning today! No further word from Louisville. No communications as telegraph lines are down from the ice! Do not know what to do! Cannot tell whether funeral is to be here or there. Ed and I would go down if we were not afraid we would miss them coming up!*

The following day was filled with remorse: *Still no word and we sit in suspense! No arrival on the noon train so we infer that the funeral has occurred at Louisville today. Brother Ed was in waiting at the station!*

On Jan. 3, 1881 my father passed away at the age of 66 years, 1 month and 10 days and now it is mother at the ripe old age of 82 years, 10 months and 4 days! "We spend our days as a tale that is told!"

The writer hereof comes plodding along in his 55th year realizing that with him also the tale will soon be told! (Elam lived another 27 years — to the age of 82).

Earl graduated from Stockton High School on May 24, the only boy in a class of five. *Earl's oration was excellent and well delivered.*

In August, while on a botanical trip to Colorado, Elam saw his first movie — in Denver: *After a restaurant supper went on out to Bethel's and thence for an evening out to the City Park to hear the music and to see the public exhibition of moving pictures.*

But two days later he had to cut short his visit: *After remaining down town for supper, shave and shine went out to Bethel's where at 8 oclock I received a message from home that daughter Beth is lying very low with some form of heart trouble. I packed my luggage at once and with Prof. Bethel to help me, went to the Union station where at 10 oclock I bade my good friend good bye and taking the east bound train over the Rock Island sped away across the plains in the darkness.* Soon after Elam returned home, Beth recovered, and she and her husband returned home to Liberal, Kansas.

Elbert, having completed his studies at the State Normal College in Emporia, was immediately engaged as a teacher at the same institution in September.

On September 9, Elam and Rachel took a trip back to Illinois, where they spent many days visiting old friends and places of the past. Elam took special delight in making treks over many of his boyhood haunts collecting botanical specimens. Some of his old friends had purchased automobiles, so numerous trips were made in them. This was Elam's first mention of the new type of conveyance.

On the return trip there was an extended layover at Galesburg, Illinois, so Elam and Rachel went *to the big tabernacle to hear a sermon by "Billy" Sunday, the great revivalist.* It is interesting to note that Elam makes no critique of this sermon, something he commonly did when hearing other speakers, which may imply he was not significantly impressed.

Because Elam and Rachel were both musically inclined, it was inevitable that they would purchase a phonograph as soon as possible following its invention. The first mention was made on the last day of December: *In the evening we all went over to neighbor Mrs. Sarah Privett's where we spent the time in social visiting and returned at 10:45 oclock. Took our Phonograph along for part of the entertainment.*

1908

The phonograph became a focal point for visitors on January 22, 1908: *Neighbors, Mrs. Sarah Privett, Mr. & Mrs. Willis Privett, Mrs. Cora Johnston and daughter Irene, Mrs. Susan Foote and Miss Winnie Hopkins having all come in to visit us the day was spent in social chat, listening to graphophone music, etc., etc. until evening when the guests departed to their homes.*

While attending a presbytery meeting in Hays on April 11, Elam visited scenic attractions: *The whole Presbytery took carriages which were in waiting for us and embarked at once for a trip to the Agricultural Experiment station, around by old Fort Hays and thence back to the State Normal school and out north to the once famous but now rapidly disappearing "Boot Hill" where are buried, in unmarked graves, a large number of toughs, thugs, gamblers and cow-boys who yielded up the ghost, with their boots on, at the too close proximity to the muzzle of a loaded gun or revolver.*

Then in company with Prof. Kent went out to the Normal where we met Supt. Picken with whom we went over the entire building which surely is a fine institution. (Elam took a position there in the botany department 21 years later.)

A major shopping trip on July 29 helped furnish the new home and solved the transportation situation: *With wife went to Stockton in the spring wagon on a shopping expedition and came home at 3:30 p.m. While in town we bought a $135 surrey, a $35 harness, a $12 oil stove, a $6 rocker, $37 worth of rugs and other smaller articles too numerous to mention.*

When Elam got home from a botanical trip to Arkansas, he learned that Earl had become seriously ill when he began his second term of teaching at the Bethel school. On October 14: *While in Stockton before starting home we learned that Earl was sick so soon as we got home Lee went up*

after him and returned at 4:30 p.m. He was in a precarious condition and soon as he got here he had a violent hemorrhage of the lungs and lost about 1½ pints of blood. Dr. Book was called over the phone but did not get here until 6 oclock. Remedies were administered at once, but the patient went into the night in a distressed condition. After several days he recovered.

Beth and Chester decided to move west. On November 13: *About 3:30 p.m. Lee drove in with our daughter Beth (Mrs. C. R. Ingle) whom he had gone to meet at Plainville. They have sold out their interests at Liberal, Kansas and will move, in about a month, to Seattle, Washington.*

1909

It was decided on March 13, 1909, that it was no longer necessary to have such a large investment in transportation: *While in town Earl sold my pony driving team for $125 which I bought 6 years ago for $110.* Was Elam preparing to buy an automobile? Not just yet, but he probably realized that the demand for horse-drawn transportation would be declining in the days ahead.

Son Jesse completed his college education on June 7: *After dinner with wife drove to Stockton where at 6:30 she took the east bound train for Emporia to be present at Jesse's graduation from the College of Emporia next Thursday.* Elam had obligations with various Sunday school conventions. In September Jesse went to Chicago for three years' study at McCormick Theological Seminary.

On October 24, the name "Hale" came into the picture: *Sunday school at Mt. Nebo at 10:30 a.m. and home with W. H. Hale for dinner after which with him in his buggy drove to Stockton where at 2:30 p.m. at the Christian church we attended the funeral of Dan Laird. Went thence to the cemetery and back with Mr. Hale to his place where I found my team and buggy which Earl had left there for me on his way to his boarding place at Bethel.* Alice Hale would eventually become the wife of Earl, and this explains why he had been to visit at the Hale residence.

The little town of Marvin, north of the Bartholomew homestead and south of Phillipsburg, was frequently the place of choice for marketing livestock and grain and sometimes where visitors arrived and departed by train. But there was a name change, after which it became Glade. The last time that Elam referred to Marvin was on November 27, and the first entry referring to Glade was February 19, 1910.

1910

Mrs. Foote died on January 23, 1910. Elam had stayed at the Footes' home during his first years in Kansas.

A fund raising event on March 24 was a bit unusual: *At our home was held a "Hard-times" Social, the proceeds of which went to the Bow Creek Cemetery improvement fund. About 75 people were present. Refreshments consisted of mush and milk, with cake!*

Even though times were hard, Elam had made a special event out of February 22, just one month earlier: *Wife's birth-day! Age 55! Bought for her a fine $25 china closet, a $12.50 set of dishes and a $4.75 set of knives and forks.*

Lee's birthday was of special note on March 8: *Today is the 21st birth-day of our baby-boy, Lee and thus passeth out to his majority the last one of our 6 children.*

After attending the World Sunday School Convention, Elam began a nostalgic trip on May 28: *At 7 a.m. left Washington over the B.&O. road for Philadelphia at which place I arrived at 10:30. I then proceeded to hunt up my oldest brother, Amos, whom I had not seen for 34 years (summer of 1876) and found him and wife at 711 Wood St. and in rather strait-ened circumstances in a rented house with no accumulation of property.*

With him I visited the old Independence Hall and thence down to see the shipping on the water front, and on the return I said good by to him and went over to visit the great Witherspoon building which ended the day. Secured lodging at 2060 Chestnut St.

Obviously the visit with Amos was a disappointment, for there was little they had in common except their genetic relationship. There is no diary entry mentioning Amos in the summer of 1876; maybe he came to the wedding of Elam and Rachel. We know that Amos served in the Union

Army in that most terrible of wars. One could speculate that he never quite healed from that traumatic event.

Much more gratifying were visits with other kinfolk in the area of his birthplace on following days, beginning May 31: *Went to the Pa. R.R. station at 11:30 where I took the train west to Lancaster, some 60 miles, where I arrived at 2 oclock p.m. and went at once to the home of my cousin David H. Bartholomew on the hill south of Conestoga creek where I spent the rest of the day doing some botanical work and remained for the night.*

June 1: *With cousin Dave took a trolley car out to Strasburg about 10 miles S.E. to see the old two story brick house in which I was born 58 years ago. After about an hour spent in the little town which has a population of 900 or 1000 people we started back toward Lancaster along the car line and adjacent fields botanizing as far as to the quaint little cross roads Lampeter Square of which I have often and often heard my parents speak many years gone by! We took the car again and got back to Lancaster at 5 oclock.*

After caring for my specimens collected today went with cousin up town where I met another cousin on my mother's side of the house, Ben Esbenshade, with whom I had a pleasant chat after which Dave and I attended the mid-week meeting at the Memorial Pres. Ch. and heard a good talk by Rev. H. W. Haring.

June 2: *With cousin Dave went up town in the morning and called on cousin Jennie Bartholomew, widow of the late Ben B. and thence to visit cousin Nat Ryan, wife and daughter and through the cemetery to the James Buchanan monument and returned home at noon. In the afternoon we took several car-riding trips over the city seeing the many things of interest. Toward evening met another full cousin in the person of John Esbenshade.*

Then Elam made his first visit to New York City, seeing many of the sights there, walking across Brooklyn Bridge, and touring the Wall Street area.

The next stop was at Newark, Ohio, on June 17: *Reached Newark at 7:30 a.m. and taking the interurban for Granville, 5 miles west, reached there at 8:20 and about 9 struck out afoot for a 5 mile walk up north to the*

old neighborhood where I used to prance around as a boy 45 years ago and from whence we moved to Illinois in March, 1865.

Got a ride on a load of lumber part of the way and reached the old stomping ground about 11 oclock. Stopped first place at the home of an old school mate Frank Jones with whom I took dinner. In the afternoon Mr. Jones and I spent the time walking about from place to place doing some botanizing and making a visit to the home of Sam and Helen Devenney, the former being a school mate and the latter one of my school teachers in 1862! The brother and sister have neither ever been married. Past the night with Mr. Jones.

The next day: *With Frank Jones took a buggy drive up N.W. 2 miles to the little cross-roads town of New-way and thence on west 6 miles to Johnstown where we arrived about 10 oclock where we remained until 2 p.m. visiting at the home of Mr. and Mrs. H. B. Rusler. Mrs. R. is a sister of Mr. Jones and also one of my old school mates — Sarah Jones. While there we took an auto ride with Mr. Rusler out west into the edge of Delaware Co. and back.*

At 2 oclock we started on the way back by another route calling at the home of Mrs. Elizabeth Ramey where I met two more of my old school mates in the persons of Gifford and Alice Ramey, two more of the unmarried tribe! Got home at 5 oclock. In the evening still another old school mate in the person of Andy Millburn called to see me.

On the following day, Elam reminisced further: *In the a.m. went again with Mr. Jones on a drive of 6 or 7 miles south to the home of his brother John A. ("Bub" of yore!) my especial crony of 45 years ago with whom I used to cut up all sorts of boyish pranks as well as fish, fight on the road home from school when the provocation was thought to be past endurance and to play hookey to go bathing in the "old swimmin' hole!"*

Elbert left for graduate school on September 23: *At 3 p.m. Lee took Elbert to Stockton to take the evening train for Madison, Wisconsin where he goes to take a year of post-graduate work in the State University, he having gotten a year's leave of absence from his work at the State Normal at Emporia.*

Jesse took the train back to his studies in Chicago. When it made a stop in Clay Center, Kansas, two passengers got on: Ernest Brown, a classmate of Jesse; and Ernest's friend, Florence Cook, who was going to Chicago for two years' organ study at the conservatory. Florence later became Jesse's wife.

1911

On February 6, 1911, Elam reported: *In a letter today from our son-in-law C. R. Ingle, at Bremerton, Wash. learned that we have become grand-parents to a fine boy* [Chester, Jr.] *born to their household Jan. 30th! And we rejoice!*

In April, as Jesse was about to complete his seminary work, he wrote the following letter, which his parents kept and treasured:

> 2330 N. Halsted St.
> Chicago, Ill.
> April 10 1912

Dear Mother and Father:

As the school year is drawing to an end and commencement is so near I can not help but think of three years ago this Spring when I finished college. I well remember how glad I was at that time. Now it seems, as I am about to start out into my life's work, that that joy is increased many times. Then, I knew that there was another delay ahead, now it seems as if the way is clear, and I can get out into the world and undertake various enterprises, such you know is the desire of all young men, and many of them can not hold back long enough to go through college. In the business world many would say that my long preparation has injured my future success as much or more than the real benefit. But in my chosen profession I doubt if you could find many who would not say that my lengthy school course has not been a waste; but rather tends to insure my success. A man needs the years and experience before preaching, as well as the education.

Indeed, I truly thank you both father and mother for what you have done to help me financially; but most of all for the words of encouragement and advice to stay by it as I have done. Perhaps you know it not; but I feel sure that we have lost at least one tenth of our class-mates (50 in class) — I mean lost as to their succeeding in the ministry — because of their parents lack of teaching them a vital religion. They are carried away by every theory and do not know where they stand. They had no sound religion when they came here and they do not seem to have any yet. They are not sure of anything and all is <u>doubt</u>. However, we as a class think that the most of these fellows (about 5 or 6) will be shaken up by the Holy spirit before they preach very long. Aye, I guess each class has two or three who never can combine piety (religion), education, and common sense. A tale out of school? Well, I wanted to tell you one thing more what I was truly thankful to you both for. Again, sometimes when some of my friends (?) here would go back on me, or give me a snub, I always assured myself that back home I had some friends who understood me and would stay by me through anything. And — the "Friend" — ever helped me.

Easter day here, beautiful and just after a shower that fell the night before. A little cool but the air was so pure and in the churches "fragrance everywhere pierced the air".

I am quite well and I hope this will find you all well and happy.

Affectionately your son,
Jesse E. Bartholomew

1912

Lee was married to Lillian White on June 2, 1912, at the same time the Mt. Nebo church was dedicated, with newly-ordained minister Jesse conducting the ceremony.

On July 9, Elam and Rachel began a three-month trip to the Pacific Northwest. On the way they stopped at a historic site. On July 11: *Passing over into and through the west end of Nebraska we reached Edgemont, So. Dakota at 7:50 a.m. and thence on over into Wyoming to the northwest and on over the line into Montana and by the monumented battlefield, near the Crow Agency, where General Custer and his command consisting of five companies of soldiers were all slain by the Indians under Sitting Bull, a Dakota chief on Sept. 25, 1876.* This event had special meaning for Elam and Rachel, for they had gone to western Kansas as newlyweds to take up their homestead just two weeks before that date.

1913

Earl was married on April 23, 1913: *At 4 oclock p.m. with wife, Lee and Lily, in the surrey, drove through a fierce north rain to W. H. Hale's, 5 miles S.E. where we arrived at 5 oclock at which hour we witnessed the marriage ceremony, performed by Jesse, which united as man and wife son Earl and Miss Alice Hale. Supper followed. We, with Jesse, came home at 7:30 oclock and a half hour later Earl and his bride came to pass the night at the paternal home.*

The next day: *At noon a goodly number of guests came in to attend the infare reception given to the new bride and groom. A sumptuous 2-course dinner was served at 2 oclock p.m. to which all seemed to do ample justice. Guests all departed before 6 p.m. at which time Earl and Alice drove to their newly furnished home, on the Stroup farm, two miles west.*

Elam, Rachel, and Elbert then traveled to Montana, arriving on August 15: *Reached Billings, our destination, at 7:45 p.m. where we were met at the station by our daughter Beth and son-in-law C. R. Ingle, who moved here from Bremerton, Wash. last winter.*

In October, Jesse moved from Glasco to take up pastoral duties at Solomon, Kansas.

1914

By February 19, 1914, sister Emma Hebrew had moved to Minneapolis, Kansas, where Elam and Rachel stopped on a return trip from Topeka: *In the a.m. with wife, brother-in-law W. J. Hebrew and his daughter Alice went in the surrey out S.W. a mile to the recently purchased Hebrew farm to which they are about to remove from town.*

On March 5, Elam expressed compassion for an older brother, who had met an untimely fate: *How well I remember this day, 50 years ago, when my brother David having enlisted as a soldier in the civil war, in the 76th Ohio Volunteer Infantry, and shouldered his knapsack at the old home near Granville, Ohio, at the age of 18 years and turned his face to the foe in the southland never to return! He was with Sherman in his march to the sea and laid down his life for his country at East Point, Ga. Sept. 24, 1864.*

More grandchildren were born to Elam and Rachel. Lee and Lily became parents on March 31: *At 3:30 p.m. Lee and Lily became parents*

to a 9-lb. girl baby [Rachel]. Earl and Alice became parents on May 14: *At 10:30 oclock last night an 8-lb girl* [Elizabeth] *was born to Earl and Alice.*

The next month, however, a dear friend and spiritual mentor died. On June 11: *In the forenoon came the sad news over the wire of the death, at the Presbyterian Hospital in Chicago, of our best of all and most valued old time friends, the Rev. Dr. Theodore Bracken of Phillipsburg. The dearest of earthly friends — true and tried throughout all the changing visissitudes of life for 36 years, his straightforward life has been a constant benediction to our family! No other earthly friend can ever take his place!*

The funeral was on the 15th: *With wife, Earl and Lee in the surrey set out for Phillipsburg over very heavy and muddy roads and arrived there at 2 oclock and went to the Presbyterian church where at 2:30 the services were conducted by Revs. J. C. Everett, John C. Miller, S. J. Ward, D. C. Smith, S. L. Allison and W. B. Brown. Dr. Miller making the principal address, and a grand one it was indeed!*

We went thence to the cemetery and laid at rest our much loved and valued friend whose dust shall go to be a brother to the insensable clod while his spirit has gone to God who gave it! As we think of the precious memories of the past 36 years of a close friendship when the clouds were dark and heavy as well as in the time of joy and gladness, the tears well unbidden to our eyes when we realize that this most enjoyable earthly comradship has past away forever.

Elam became interested in buying an automobile on July 14: *Geo. P. Taylor, Maxwell auto agent of Stockton, called on us and including the taking of daughter Beth, Lily and I for a ride up northwest four miles, remained until 6 oclock when he returned to town but sold no auto although we may be considered to be in the market.*

The next day: *From 8:30 to 9:30 a.m. Taylor, the auto man of Stockton, with his wife and two little boys made us a semi-social call — not to sell a machine of course but only to show its good points.*

The following day: *At 8 a.m. Fred Lambert of the Griffen garage at Stockton came out in an auto and with him, wife, Beth and Chettie and I went to Stockton where we spent the day in business and visiting, taking dinner at T. R. May's and returning home at 7 p.m. the same way we went*

Bow Creek

18	Adams, W. C.	L		35	Low, J. B.	3 L
59	Andrews, R.	2S L		36	Low, C. W.	S L 2S
				37	Low, A. D.	S 3 L
69	Bartholomew, Elam	3 L		64	Lyon, Elmer	2L S L
27	Bartholomew, Ed.	L 2S				
75	Blauer, A.	L S		70	McCue, Tom	3 L S
67	Boler, Geo.	S L		51	McNulty, Harry	L S L
				43	McKenzie, Wyatt	S 2L S
14	Chaffin, Geo.	L 2S L		45	Martin, Wm.	4 L
				47	Mayer, Herman	L S L S
66	Delay, Arnold	S 2L		26	Meracle, John	L 2S L
				56	Miller, W. F.	S 2L S
9	Elliott, Wm.	L S 2L		53	Mellon, J. M.	L 3S L
10	Elliott, L. F.	2L 2S		38	Muir, Geo.	L S L
11	Elliott, Albert	S 2L S		39	Muir, Alex	2S 2L
12	Elliott, Frank	S 2L		40	Muir, G. B.	3S L
13	Elliott, J. M.	S L S				
15	Elliott, Fred	2S L		62	Odle, Bert	2S
29	Groner, Mrs.	S 2L		77	Reimal, R.	L S L S
22	Gallagher, Wm.	3S				
7	Gibbs, N. W.	S L		52	Senior, C. P.	L 2S L
50	Graham, A.	4S		54	Senior, Art	3S L
				57	Shaw, John	S L S
5	Hardman	L 3S		58	Shaw, Mrs. Wm.	L S
61	Horn, Theo	2L 2S		73	Shaw, Dan	L S L
28	Hopkins, C. E.	S L S		16	Shaw, Lew	L S
55	Hulse, Bert	L 2S		68	Short, Roy	L
32	Hopkins, C. C.	2L 2S		42	Southard, W. S.	S L
78	Hulse, H.	L 3S		44	Southard, Fred	2L S
41	Hubble, Ustel	L 3S				
30	Hebrew? Evan	2L		63	Teagarden, S.	3S
48	Hebrew, J. A.	2L S		72	Townley, J.	3 L
8	Iman,	2S L S		3	Van Allen, Geo.	3 L S
				24	Van Horn, Q.	2 L S
60	Jerby Bros.	4 L		20	Vincent	L
65	Jones, A.	2S L S				
33	Johnston, G. L.	2S L S		46	White, Albert	3 L S
				76	Whitney, E. E.	2S L
4	Keeten, T. N.	3 L		21	Wiliams, H.	S L
19	Keeten, M.	2L S L				
23	Kincaid, P. E.	4 L				
49	Koons, Milt	2 L S				
34	Kemmler, Mrs. C.	L S		2	Zink, F.	L S L

The Stockton Telephone Exchange of April 1913. Elam's ring was 3 longs; Ed's 1 long, 2 shorts.

over. The car was a 5-passenger Ford touring car and I drove most of the way in and all the way out. My first drive!

Finally on the 17th a sale was made: *Quite early in the forenoon W. R. Griffen and his man, Glenn Heiner, drove in from Stockton with two Ford touring cars which were demonstrated about the yards and nearby roads until noon after which I proceeded to buy one of them at $585 cash in hand. Later Lee and I with Griffen and his man drove the two cars over to brother Ed's where we stopped some time and then we all, including Ed and his two boys Floyd and Marion drove back to our place and our new car was run into the auto shed and the other folks returned to their several homes.*

On July 29, a special outing was begun: *Spent the a.m. knocking about getting ready to attend, at Stockton, the Chautauqua, so about 12:30 oclock with wife, Beth and Chetty, Lily and baby, Alice and baby drove to town in our auto and securing two tents in the McNulty grove which we furnished with the necessary accoutrements from home which were taken over in the wagon by Earl, we settled down for an 8-days outing attending the first session at 2:30 p.m. and also the evening concert, camping for the night on the grounds.*

It ended on the 5th of August: *All of us being pretty well worn out on account of the very hot, dry weather we broke camp at the close of the afternoon lecture and Lee taking our goods home in the wagon I took the auto and with wife, Beth, Chetty, Lily and baby, Earl, Alice and baby — 9 of us — came home at 7 oclock, Earl being quite sick, and thus ended a most excellent Chautauqua program.*

Elbert completed his post-graduate work, so Elam recorded on August 7: *With Lee in the auto left home at 5:30 a.m. and driving to Phillipsburg met Elbert who is home on his summer vacation as a recently dubbed Ph.D. by the University of Wisconsin.* He returned in September to resume teaching in that institution.

A new lighting system was decided upon on October 22: *Spent the day making preparations and in assisting a workman of the Wichita Acetylene Light company who is installing a plant for us at house and barn.* This would be much cleaner and give better light than kerosene lamps. It was finished five days later: *At noon Mr. DeVries, the light man, finished his work of installation consisting of double chandeliers in the dining room, library, and parlor with single lights in the kitchen, the two hallways, the five bed rooms and the porch and two in the barn. It is a most excellent system and produces a most excellent result.*

Another wedding was celebrated on December 23: *About 9:30 a.m. Jesse, Earl, Alice, Lee and Lily started in the auto on a trip down near Alton to attend the wedding at high noon of Nephew Floyd Bartholomew to Miss Edith Osborne, daughter of Nate Osborne. Jesse performed the ceremony.*

1915

Rachel reached a birthday milestone on February 22, 1915: *Spent the time at botanical work in the laboratory with wife until nearly noon, just previous to which several of the neighbors had gathered in to surprise wife on her 60th birthday; and it was a complete surprise to her indeed!*

A bountiful dinner was served from 12:30 until 2 p.m. the greater part of which had previously been prepared secretly by daughters-in-law Lily and Alice to whom much credit is due with the help of Earl and Lee for the excellent way in which their previously arranged program was carried out.

Many little mementoes of considerate regard were presented to the lady of the house including $60 in gold coins from husband and the five children. It was a most pleasant party and the jolliest of good cheer continued from the start until the last guest left at 5:30 oclock.

Later, a trip to the West Coast in the summer provided Elam a pleasurable *first experience in the briny deep* at Long Beach. Then on to the World's Fair at San Francisco.

From there they proceeded to Portland, Oregon. On August 19: *We took an Alberta St. car out to 575 Webster St. to the home of brother Frank where we arrived at 9:30 oclock. Frank soon came home from his office with the Scribner Bros. at 2nd and Stark Sts. so the rest of the day was spent in social visiting and in looking about.*

Returning by way of Denver, Elam met another interesting person. On

September 20: *Made a pleasant call on Geo. W. Bartholomew (no relation) editor of the old 1885 edition of "The Bartholomew Family", then of
Austin, Texas, who is now auditor of the Colo. Portland Cement Co.*

On November 8, Elam responded favorably to a solicitation to benefit
both the Presbyterian college and some students who could get the education he had never had: *Mr. A. S. Wilson of Emporia, financial agent of the
College of Emporia, drove in in his auto and stopped with us for dinner
after which some time was spent in social and business chat relative to
endowment subscriptions to College, and after due consideration with
wife and I, took out a $1000 scholarship to be known as the "George E.
Bartholomew Scholarship" in memory of our oldest son.*

1916

On February 14, 1916: *A carefully planned surprise party for Lee and
Lily brought out 30 of the neighborhood young folks at 8 oclock p.m. so a
hilarious time with games and refreshments occupied their attention until
the midnight hour soon after which time the last guest departed.*

February 25: *The p.m. was full of callers and general* <u>hubbub</u> *incident
to the departure of Lee and Lily for their new home in Wyoming. At 4 p.m.
they bade us a sad farewell and at that hour Earl took them in the auto to
Phillipsburg where they take the train for the west tonight.*

Then came a feeling of loneliness: *Two score years ago one bright September day in 1876 I came to the new homestead with my bride, but with
neither chick nor child. In the years that followed 7 children came to bless
our house, two of whom have fallen asleep and the others to homes of their
own and now the* <u>old</u> <u>homestead</u> *is as it was on that bright September day
in 1876!*

A new house was planned — for the hired man and family. On March
20, 1916: *With Jasper worked all day at excavating for a cellar under the
new dwelling house we are about to erect several rods N.E. of the Laboratory* [built in 1912]. The cement foundation was completed April 4.

Finally, on June 1, the new house was ready for occupancy: *Worked in the a.m. at putting the real finishing touches on the new house in the way of screening the porch and putting up the door and window screens. This evening Jasper and Clara got moved into the new house and we will be to ourselves again which, under the somewhat peculiar and trying circumstances, is a decided satisfaction!*

A death in the family had occurred on May 11: *Learned this afternoon of the death at Phillipsburg of our old friend and neighbor, Albert White, Lee's father-in-law.*

The next day: *At 1 p.m. with wife, Earl and Alice in the auto drove to Phillipsburg where at 2:30 oclock we attended Mr. White's funeral at the Presbyterian church which was conducted by Rev. J. C. Everett of Osborne who took for his text Phil. 1:23 — "For me to live is Christ, and to die is gain." Daughter-in-law Lily, who had come in to attend her father's funeral, came home with us bringing little Rachel with her.* (Lee and Lily were now living in Wyoming.)

On August 7, Elbert, who had married in recent months, came to introduce his wife, Lucille, to his family and friends: *Earl took the car and drove to Phillipsburg where he met Elbert and wife who were accompanied by Jesse. They got here at noon and the p.m. was spent in social visiting and general good cheer.* On the 9th, Elam and Rachel gave a reception for the young couple.

An extended auto trip, the first one, began on August 15: *With wife, Elbert and Lucille left home on our western auto trip at 8 a.m. and drove north to Phillipsburg where we made a short stop and then drove on to Alma, Neb. at 11:20 where something got wrong with our car and it balked on us completely and in getting it repaired we were held up at the Moore garage until almost 6 p.m. at which time we resumed our journey northward to Bertrand, Neb. Had two tire punctures between Alma and Bertrand.*

The following day: *We left Bertrand at 7 a.m. and drove north about 25 miles to Lexington, north of the Platte River where we arrived at 8:20 and stopped for breakfast. Being now on the much-talked-of "Lincoln High-*

way" from Omaha to Cheyenne, we resumed our journey toward the west. Drove to Ogallala where we stopped for the night. Drove today 165 miles.

The next day they arrived at Lee's place: *Arrived at Burns, Wyoming at 3:30 p.m. and then on out to son Lee's 7½ miles S.W. at 4 oclock. On our arrival Lucille found a telegram awaiting her stating that her father was critically ill and not expected to recover so Lee, Elbert and she and I drove at once to Carpenter where they wired back to Columbia, Mo. for further information after which we returned to Lee's for the night.*

Then on the 18th: *Lucille received a wire this morning announcing the death of her father on Tuesday and his funeral on Wednesday. A sad stroke indeed to the poor girl and she so far away!* This was Friday, and it was all over, so there was nothing she could do.

Circling back through Denver, the travelers returned home on September 2 — a 1300-mile trip. (On good roads from Limon Junction to Burlington, Colorado, they made 30 mph!)

1917

After having several problems with the car, Elam decided it was time to get a new one. On January 6, 1917: *In the p.m. with Lee* [who had returned to live at the homestead in late 1916] *made a business trip to Stockton in our new Ford 1917 model touring car which the dealers, Griffen and Beckley, brought over for us yesterday morning.*

Lee and Lily had another baby, Margaret, on February 6: *About 4:30 p.m. was re-christened grandfather to a 9½ lbs. girl born to Lee and Lily at that hour!*

On April 14, Jesse decided to move on: *Jesse has resigned his pastorate at Solomon and will be at home for a few days before seeking work elsewhere.* By May 17, a new location was planned: *Went to Stockton where we said good bye to Jesse as he took the 6 oclock train for Clyde where he expects to locate if all goes to suit him.* (It did.)

On June 9 Elam did a little sleuthing while on a trip to Colorado: *Left Denver at 8:15 over the Moffat road for Rollinsville where I arrived at 11 and soon thereafter started out on a 3-mile hike up the gulch S. and S.W. to the site of the Penobscot Mining & Milling Co. where I stopped for a short inspection and the only evidence of life about being a rather savage*

looking dog sitting in the mouth of the tunnel I tarried not but kept on going up the gulch to the bunk house of the defunct Gold Dirt mine where I met a Mr. Wherrey and a Mrs. Spears, the latter being the wife of the Penobscot engineer, but as he and Mr. P. J. Hamble, the mine supt., were out on a tramp on the mountains I shortly started down the trail toward Rollinsville and when within about a half mile of town I was overtaken by Mr. Hamble and Mr. Spears in an auto who insisted that I should go back to the mine and give it an investigation, but I declined, so we drove to town where I visited an hour or two with them and taking the 7:30 train back to Denver got here at 9:30 and went to my hotel for the night.

My real object in visiting the mine was to try to find out whether or not some of our Kansas neighbors who have taken stock in the mine have been buncoed [swindled], *and I think they have.*

A quick trip to botanize in the Lake Michigan area ended on a disagreeable note on September 26: *I very gladly said farewell to the smoky, bum and booze afflicted burg of Michigan City and at 6:40 a.m. took the Interurban train for Chicago where I arrived at 9:15 and as my train for the west does not leave until late this afternoon I spent the day about the city somewhat, among other things visiting the Chicago Art Institute on Michigan Boulevard, and the nearby Marine training camp watching the maneuvers of the soldier boys at drill and play, including machine-gun drill, wig-waging, target practice and base and foot ball.*

En route home, a few days were spent with Rob Montgomery and family, Addie, Beryl and Garland, who now live eight miles southeast of Hopkins, Missouri. Elam enjoyed seeing the *new, modern $3500 house which the Montgomery's are erecting and have nearly completed.*

The next day was Sunday, and Elam became agitated: *Spent the a.m. in social visiting with the Montgomery's. About noon their two sons-in-law Nelson Killam and Alva Sparks with their wives, Lizzie and Fannie, respectively, and their three children, each, drove in in their Fords and much gabfesting resulted. At 2 p.m. Rob, Killam, Sparks and I got into the Sparks auto and took a spin over S.W. 14 miles, to Maryville, and returned at 4 oclock. This was* <u>not</u> *"a Sabbath well spent"!*

On October 22 Jesse drove in to visit his parents to show off his new Dodge.

The day after Christmas, Lee had to go to Stockton for his military draft examination. He was deferred.

1918

A brother's wife died in January of 1918: *Word received by mail today conveyed the sad news of the death of Mary, brother John's wife, at their home at Howard, Kansas, last Monday, the 21st.*

Another grandson, Earl Robert, Jr., was born on February 5: *About 4 p.m. today Earl and Alice had born to them an 8-pound boy: second child — first son!*

The first mention of the family into which Jesse later married occurred on August 14, while Elam and Rachel were on an auto trip with Jesse to eastern Kansas: *Left Clyde at 10:30 a.m. and drove to Clay Center where we got lunch and made a call at Dr. Cook's.*

A visit to relatives at Louisville, Kansas, turned out to be a sort of pilgrimage for Elam. On the 15th: *About 4 p.m. drove out to the Louisville cemetery where, for the first time, I visited my Mother's grave.*

Elbert and Lucille came through on a visit after completing a year's work at Stanford University in California. Then on September 12: *Elbert and Lucille left us at 8 oclock p.m. on their way to Madison, Wis., where Elbert goes to resume his labors as Assistant Prof. of Botany in the State University.*

1919

Neighborhood celebrations were in order when military service ended and sons returned safely. On June 10, 1919: *In the evening with wife and Lee's folks drove in the car over to brother Ed's where a surprise party was given in honor of nephew Marion who recently returned from the army in France. About 50 persons were present and all seemed to have a good time.*

While on a botanical trip, Elam again stopped at Niagara Falls, New York, to visit Rachel's sister Celia and her husband, John Fink. On September 7: *At 4 oclock John and I walked out east about a mile to see the aviation field where we saw several flights and landings. One passenger was taken up on each trip. Fare $10 for a 10-minutes flight!* This was probably the first time Elam had seen airplanes.

After traveling to and through most of the states of the northeast, Elam returned by way of Farmington, Illinois, where Rachel had already been for several weeks. Together they spent over three weeks in and about that area seeing relatives, old friends, and familiar places.

On December 4, Elam was really upset by news: *In the evening we received a phone message from Stockton saying there was some newspaper report of son Jesse's marriage at Topeka, yesterday.* Then the next day: *In the Topeka State Journal this evening we saw a brief notice of Jesse's marriage to Miss Florence Cook of Clay Center so it must be true.* Finally on the 6th: *Got letter this evening from Jesse confirming all reports as indicated.* The disturbing factor was that after Jesse's courtship of seven years Jesse's parents seemed to be "among the last to know" about the marriage, and that by way of newspaper accounts.

The newly married couple came on December 22 to spend Christmas: *At 1:30 p.m., Lee having gone to town for that purpose, brought out from the train Jesse and his brand new wife so the rest of the day was spent in social visiting with the newly weds.* Florence soon began to assist Elam in his botanical laboratory, which helped appease his discomfort with the situation.

Then a special treat began the day on December 25: *A Christmas Day of rejoicing and good cheer which started very early — 1:30 a.m. — by the birth to Lee and Lily of a bouncing big baby boy* [Elam]*! This started the ball rolling, and merriment and general hilarity was kept up throughout the day.*

1920

Influenza became a problem in early 1920, thus a ban on public gatherings. Then on February 17: *Earl's all being down with the flu wife went over this evening to care for them through the night.* On the 20th: *Wife returned this morning and found Lee's folks also going down with it, little Rachel being in a very critical condition. Dr. Book was called at once.* The next day: *Lee's folks, all 5 of them, are now down in severe condition with the flu. We got a nurse from Stockton, a Miss Gillenwaters, to come out to help care for them.*

The following day, February 22: *Wife's 65th Birth Day but not a very happy one by any means owing to her strenuous work in helping all last night and today in caring for the sick ones at Lee's. Little Rachel has hovered on the border land all day with little hope of recovery.*

February 23: *About 3 a.m. we telephoned for Jesse to come so he and his wife came up on the morning train. The sick folks seem to be doing as well as could be expected with the exception of Rachel and with her the fight still goes on with Dr. Book, the nurse and wife straining every effort to pull the little girl through.*

February 27: *Little Rachel is some better but still very low and by no means out of danger. With her strenuous work of the past 10 days in nursing at Earl's and Lee's, wife is very much worn out and went under the doctor's care this afternoon.*

Finally by March 4 both Rachels were much improved, as were also the others. The public meeting ban was lifted by the 14th.

While attending the state Sunday school convention in Topeka in early May, Elam was provided lodging and meals at the home of C. M. Morrow, a high school principal in North Topeka. He also went to visit the principal of the main high school: *At the noon recess called on Prof. R. R. Cook at the Topeka High School of which he is the very efficient principal and Brother-in-law to son Jesse. At 5:30 met Prof. Cook again and went with him for supper out to his home at 1207 W. 16th St. Spent the night at 715 West Tenth St. at the home of cousin Ed Montgomery.*

In September, while on a botanical trip to the Southeast, Elam fulfilled a long-term ambition on the 29th at Marietta, Georgia: *In the morning took a half mile walk out east to the National Military Cemetery where I met Supt. Pierce and soon had a half-century longing gratified by*

being permitted to see and stand by the grave of my long-dead brother David!

He was a member of Co. B 76th Ohio Volunteer Infantry, Col. Wood commander. He died at Eastpoint Ga. (now a suburb of Atlanta) of diphtheria, Sept. 24, 1964, aged 18 years, 1 month and 17 days! He was with General W. T. Sherman on his memorable "March to the Sea"!

It was 56 years last Friday since the dear brother past over "the long, long trail". The grave is in section E No. 6400 and is about 25 feet southwest of a moderately large laurel oak tree whose branches extend over the grave.

In this cemetery there lie buried 10,132 soldiers who laid down their lives for the preservation of the Union in the dark days of 1861-1865.

Botanized quite successfully awhile to the northeast a short distance and then returned to the cemetery and gathered some fallen leaves from brother's grave and also some from the tree mentioned above, and then going to a nearby rose bush I cut off a fine spray and placed it on the grave by the headstone.

Another grandchild, Marie, was born on December 22: *At 7:00 oclock this morning a bran new little girl came to take up her boarding place with Earl and wife; third child; two girls and one boy!*

At the end of 1920 Elam proposed terminating his diary:

And thus endeth the labors of one more year, in these latter days, of my life's history.

For a full half century — 18,262 days — my pen has been unflagging in the writing of this diary!

The first entry was made January 1, 1871 and has continued without interruption or the omission of a day from that date to this!

When the first day's record was made I little dreamed that it would be carried through to an unbroken record of 50 years. Few men may boast of so unique an undertaking.

If my life is spared to do it, I may record, in the following pages, such events as may seem worthy of particular note but as to the keeping of a Diary I herewith lay down my pen and write the word

FINIS

One reason to cease writing was that his hand was getting shaky. But despite that, he kept right on going without skipping a beat. Nevertheless, it is noted that subsequent entries are briefer and more cryptic.

1921

An investment was made on May 21, 1921: *While in town made a purchase of $2100 worth of 3rd Liberty Loan 4¼ percent bonds.* The deal was concluded on the 28th: *While at the Stockton Nat. Bank rec'd the $2100 3rd Liberty loan bonds purchased last Sat. They cost me $1906.10 at 90.77.*

Another purchase was made on June 14: *While in town bought $400 more of Liberty loan Bonds which we deposited in the Stockton National Bank with the $2100 purchased previously.*

Elam secured a new record player on November 3: *Purchased and had it brought out from Stockton a $295 Edison phonograph.* This was probably one that used flat disc records instead of the cylinder type previously used. Nevertheless, that was a lot of money to spend for a wind-up record player. Elam seemed devoted to quality sound reproduction.

1922

A new lighting plant was necessary on March 21, 1922: *We decided to cast aside the Wichita acetylene gas generator which we installed 7 years ago as it was doing very poor work. We were induced to purchase a new Eclipse generator and they proceeded at once to begin its installation.*

The next day: *Worked with the men and Lee on the installation of the new plant and taking out of the cave the old generator and turning it over to Mr. Garlow. The old plant cost us, including all the fixtures, $225. The new plant, by using the already installed fixtures and tubing cost us $90, Lee paying 25% of the bill.*

A new grave marker was purchased on April 14: *Had Lily take me in the car down to the Bow Creek cemetery where I met the Marble Cutter, C. W. Totten, and two of his men and we proceeded to put up a $435 monument on our lots. Total weight 3800 lbs.*

In early June, one of the prominent businessmen of Stockton died, so on the 4th Elam wrote: *In the p.m. at 2:30 with wife, Lee, Lily and their 3 children in the car we drove to Stockton to attend the M. J. Coolbaugh funeral. As the crowd was too big to be accommodated by any building in town the services were held in the front yard of the mansion home, the throng extending beyond the sidewalk and out onto the street. I think that perhaps in every respect it was the greatest affair of this kind that I have ever witnessed.*

Elam was elated with the importance of June 9, 1922: *1852-1922 Birth Day! The most important one I have ever had! Three score years and ten! A red letter day!* But then a funeral of a long-term friend that afternoon: *With wife and Earl in his car attended the Jack Shaw funeral in Stockton.* Then in the evening: *Later 20 friends and relatives called to pay their respects and congratulate me on my 70th birthday. Music, ice cream and cake kept all in good spirits until 12:30 oclock when our guests departed.*

Dental work was necessary on August 31: *With Lee in the car made a trip to Stockton to have dentist R. H. Ewing commence on the making of the plates for my false teeth which has been in preparation since last April when he started to clear my mouth of useless and broken rubbish.*

The project was finished on September 12: *With Earl in his car made a trip to Stockton where I received from dentist R. H. Ewing my upper and lower plates in the case of a set of false teeth. Came home at noon with a mouthful of unutterable things which gave me no hilarious pleasure, I tell you!*

A new car on November 18 had more modern features: *In the p.m. with Lily in our new self-starting Ford touring car, purchased of the Coolbaugh Motor Co. made a trip to Stockton, where at 3 oclock we met Professors L. E. Melchers and R. P. White of the Botanical Department of the State Agricultural college at Manhattan.*

Another investment was made on the same day: *Purchased $1000 worth of stock in the United Telephone Co.*

At the end of 1922, Elam made another vow to discontinue the diary: *Two years ago this evening when, after the keeping of this diary 50 even years comprising 18,262 days, little did I think that through force of habit I would ever take up my pen to continue my life's story, but I have done so and added 730 more days to the 50 years, now making a grand total of 18,992 in the 52 years record.*

The year closing with today has been one of no particularly important event with perhaps the exception of the two botanical collecting trips to the Black Hills of South Dakota and to Ohio, West Va. and Kentucky.

To complete an even 19,000 days period I may continue this record in the following pages for the coming eight days when I promise faithfully that as a diary writer I will lay down my pen forever!

1923

Elam reaffirmed his vow on January 8, 1923: *In accordance with my solemn promise made in this diary eight days ago I am now laying my pen down forever as a daily chronicler of the events in my earthly pilgrimage! This day rounds out the even 19,000 days in this record of my life's events.*

From that date begins monthly summary notes, but he reverts to daily entries frequently when situations merit that kind of record.

In June, another relative moved west: *Brother John of Howard, Kans. paid us a short visit and left on the 19th. He has sold out at Howard and will soon move to Fresno, Calif.*

Elam decided on July 3 to unload some of his archives: *County Commissioners Reed, Thomas and Robinson called on us today and I presented the county with 45 volumes of Rooks county newspapers beginning Jan. 1st 1876 and ending Dec. 31, 1920 — each volume complete.* Obviously storage space had become a problem, but he was now 71 years old, and he may have been thinking about a move that would take place before long.

Jesse and Florence's first child was stillborn on September 25; nevertheless, it was given a name: Robert Daniel.

1924

While Elam was on a trip to Wyoming in 1924 to botanize and visit Beth and family at Thermopolis, he went on a camping trip that included a stop of special interest. On July 4: *At Cody attended the demonstration and heard the speeches connected with the unveiling of the heroic equestrian statue of Col. W. F. Cody (Buffalo Bill) one half mile northwest of town. Probably 25,000 people were present and the greatest number of autos that I have ever seen at one time and one place.*

On September 28 Jesse paid a brief visit: *Jesse, having resigned his charge at Clyde, Kan. is now in transit to his new field at Oberlin in this Presbytery where he will have a much larger field for usefulness.*

During an October trip to southeastern states, Elam made a stop in Atlanta. On the 8th: *Took a trolley car in the morning and went out to the famous Stone Mt., 16 miles N.E. of the city where I botanized and climbed to the top of the mountain and over to the east side and then back to the west side and thence along the north side where the sculpture work under Gutson Borglum is going on to commemorate the lost cause and fall of the Southern Confederacy in 1865! It will cost millions of dollars, be a useless and foolish waste of money and subserve no good end whatever!*

In 1924 Elam and Rachel had only two grandsons. One of them contracted a deadly disease on November 12: *Last night Earl's boy "Bobby" developed a mild case of Infantile paralysis which grew more pronounced as today passed.* On the next day: *Little Bobby much worse!*

Then on the following day: *Up with little Bobby until one oclock. Doctors in consultation gave up all hope for the recovery of the child!* On the 15th: *We went over to Earl's where at 4 p.m. the gentle spirit of dear little Bobby passed over into the summer land of song! Age, 6 years, 9 months and 10 days. Why was it so? Only the dear Lord knows.*

November 16: *In the p.m. Lee and I made a necessary trip down to the Bow Creek cemetery and over to Earl's.*

November 17: *With wife, Jesse and his wife and Lee and Lily attended the funeral of our dear little Bobby, and the end for all things earthly was a sealed book!*

1925

A special day for Rachel was celebrated on February 22, 1925: *Wife's 70th Birth Day and from some one, some where she got a present of $70 in gold in the form of 14 five dollar gold pieces!*

On March 31 Jesse came for a brief visit to show off his new 1925 Dodge sedan.

Another grandchild, Roberta, was born on December 5: *A new nine pound daughter came to son Earl's home this afternoon.*

1926

Elam testified in court on behalf of a friend on January 26, 1926: *At 2 oclock was put on the witness stand in the district court to testify to the general character of Geo. Bigge who recently confessed to the crime of arson in the burning of one of the Stockton grain elevators last fall.*

Fifteen men testified to the previous good standing of the culprit but nevertheless and notwithstanding Judge Sparks sentenced him to an indefinite term in the Kansas penitentiary at Lansing. That "The way of the transgressor is hard" goes without saying!

Possibly this act was committed as a result of a financial crisis. Things were going from bad to worse for many individuals and businesses. Banks were closing and businesses going bankrupt at an accelerating rate. Economic chaos was infiltrating life at all stages. Newspapers told increasingly of people setting fire to commercial buildings and homes. Suicides were becoming frequent. People today remember the Wall Street collapse in October 1929, but forget that the problem had been brewing for years before that.

All the children and grandchildren, plus Rachel's brother and wife, George K. and Hattie Montgomery, of Middlegrove, Illinois, converged in early June to get ready for the big event of June 14: *Our Golden Wedding Day! Shortly after noon today we partook of a most bountifull Anniversary "feast of fat things" prepared for the occasion, with about 30 of our friends and relatives. The last arrivals being son Jesse and Florence of Oberlin with Florence's mother, Mrs. D. P. Cook of Clay Center, who drove in at noon.*

About 5 p.m., when most of the people had assembled, who came to attend the public reception, all preparations and decorations in the grove, near the laboratory, having been most tastefully arranged, including a leafy bower for the reception of the prospective bride and groom, the wedding march was played on the piano by Mrs. Florence Wallace of Stockton, and marching out along the pathway with wife we took our appointed place in the bower.

This portrait of Elam and Rachel on their golden wedding anniversary was actually a composite from two photographs. Elam, being of wry wit, had shaved off his moustache that morning. Because it had been many, many years since he had not had one, and he let it grow out again after the anniversary, they wanted the portrait to include the moustache.

*Son Jesse in a few well chosen words of eulogy and congratula-
tion piloted us through the ceremony which was followed by the best
of good wishes by the many friends who were present. Refreshments in
the form of ice cream and cake were served. The weather was cool,
pleasant and ideal. The late afternoon passed away in a blaze of glory*

The golden wedding anniversary of Elam and Rachel Bartholomew, June 14, 1926, with children and grandchildren.

This is the actual photograph of Elam and Rachel on their golden wedding anniversary, June 14, 1926, he without a moustache.

for us and our fiftieth wedding anniversary became a matter of history.

About 160 of our relatives, friends and neighbors were present to greet us. A number of presents were received including $110 in Gold!

A new grandson was born two months later, on August 16. Elam wrote on the 17th: *Received a message this afternoon from Jesse that there was born to himself and wife, at Oberlin, Kansas, yesterday at two oclock a.m. a 9-lb. boy who goes as Robt. Daniel.*

1927

With inflation raging, Elam succumbed to the temptation to shift invest-ments from safety to higher yield. On March 31, 1927: *In the morning Mr. Bradley Young of Salina, a Public Utilities Bond agent came along and talked with me until after dinner when in the rain and over very muddy roads we drove to Stockton where I transferred two 1000-dollar 4¼ Lib-erty bonds to his company, taking in exchange one 7-per cent and one 6-per cent $1000 Gold bonds in the Central States Telephone and Power Co.* It was not a wise choice ultimately, his heirs later learned when trying to collect on them.

Returning from a trip to Oberlin on May 3, a Tuesday: *A shock awaited us as a telegram had come from brother last Saturday morning announc-ing the death of sister-in-law Bessie, brother Elias' wife, at Louisville, Kansas that day. No particulars received to date.*

A prominent local bank folded on November 14: *In the p.m. with Lee in the car made a business trip to Stockton principally in connection with the closing of the doors of the National State Bank this morning marking the collapse of the Coolbaugh banking institution, a firm of long standing. It is by far the greatest financial crash that this county has ever experienced! Yes, we lost a little, about $150. Not a bad break for us!*

At age 75 Elam got a typewriter. On December 10: *I have taken up and am trying to learn type writing. Am using a Royal machine!*

Brother George, of Casper, Wyoming, dropped in from time to time when he pursued his business of oil well prospecting to the south and west of Rooks County.

1928

Radios were becoming more common, but not everyone had one and sometimes reception was disappointing. On May 24, 1928, Elam wrote: *In the a.m. with wife and Lily drove over to brother Ed's to hear over the radio Dr. Speer's opening sermon at the Presbyterian General Assem-bly at Tulsa, Oklahoma. From some unknown cause we could not get Tulsa, so heard nothing and came home, considerably disappointed, at noon.*

A new car was purchased on August 20. *Lee and Lily went to Stockton this afternoon and brought home our new Plymouth Chrysler sedan, 4-door car! It is a beauty.*

On October 9 to 11, Elam and Jesse attended the synod at Hays. Then on the 12th: *Rainfall last night just even 2 inches! Nevertheless at 5:30 a.m. Jesse pulled out, through deep mud, for Oberlin on a hurry-up stork call! About 4:30 p.m. we got a phone message that he had made the trip with much difficulty and reached home at 11:15 oclock and at 1:30 p.m. a new son was born to their household.*

The new baby was called David, partly to honor Elam's recently departed cousin and Elam's brother, who had died in the Civil War, but largely because in the Bible David was the son of Jesse. (This grandson of Elam and Rachel is the author of this book.)

Elam marks the end of an era with the death of a dear friend on November 27: *Learned today of the death, at Topeka last Saturday, of our old time friend and pioneer neighbor, D. A. Duff. And now all of the older generation who were as old as 25 or 30 years when I came here, in March 1874, up and down Bow creek, from its source to its mouth, have one and all passed over the long, long trail, and the places that once knew them as active men and women shall know them no more forever! Truly, as the song says, "We are going down the valley one by one"!*

The next day Elam, who had been suffering physically for some time, received a definitive diagnosis: *Called on Dr. F. E. Richmond, as I have done several times recently, and he pronounced me, after examination, to be in one stage of Diabetes! Foot dressing, diet and medication were established as a necessary procedure.*

1929

After 55 years on the farm, Elam and Rachel decided to move. On May 13, 1929: *With Lee and Lily in the car drove to Hays by 11 a.m. where we transacted some business in the way of house-hunting as, no preventing providence, it is the purpose of wife and I to leave the farm and move to that place in the near future. Looked at a number of places but made no agreement to purchase any of them.*

A deal was finalized on June 18: *With Lee and Lily in the car drove to Stockton in the early morning and at 9:15 oclock we took attorney*

F. E. Young aboard and drove over to Hays where we spent the greater part of the day in completing the deal in the purchase of the residence property at 415 West Sixth St., Lot 3, Block 2, Reeder's Addition to Hays, of M. J. Goff and Adah Cain for the consideration of $7000, one half paid down in cash and the remainder on one year's time at 7 per cent interest.

The big move to Hays began on July 30: *With J. W. McCauley of Stockton and Loyd and Dwight Garrison of Glade with 2 truck loads of material from the laboratory and another load on our car, with Lee as driver, set out for Hays at 10:30 a.m. and arrived there at 12:30 and proceeded to unload our stuff at room 307 in the new Science Hall on the Campus of the State Teachers College.*

After the farm was sold, Lee and family also moved to Hays. August 26: *Lee's moved over from Bow Creek today. Their new home is at 311 Ash St.*

Another trip to Colorado in August included witnessing something new: *Before taking a late train home from Denver we went to a "talkie" show on Curtis St.* Until this time movies had been silent.

Arriving home from Colorado, Elam took sick. On the 25th: *Feeling quite "punk" from our western trip.* Then on the next day: *Still feeling from punk to punker!* On the 27th: *Sicker and sicker! Dr. Meade visited me this evening but apparently to no purpose.*

Then on the 28th: *Woefully sick all last night with a major attack of the* giant hives*! Most probably superinduced by indigestion and the drinking of cherry juice punch at Boulder. Dr. C. D. Blake was called at 8:30 a.m. and hurried me away in his car to the Protestant Hospital on East 7th St. Had a rather bad day with very little relief.*

From then on there was steady improvement, so that on September 1: *The doctors pronouncing me OK discharged me from the hospital at 4 p.m. today and thus ended my first experience in that line.*

Christmas day 1929 was enjoyable: *At 10:30 a.m. with Mr. and Mrs. Carl Whitsett and their 3 boys of Phillipsburg, Lee, Rachel, Margaret and Elam Jr. went over to my office in the Science Bldg. for a short visit and thence out west a mile to the airport where we witnessed the coming in and going out of the Denver-Kansas City commercial airplanes.*

In 1929 Elam and Rachel moved to Hays and for the first time had a home with the modern conveniences of electricity and indoor plumbing.

1930

Lee decided to find other sources of income since he was no longer living on the farm. One of his first jobs was selling tires. Elam helped out on January 1, 1930: *From 2 until 4:30 p.m. I went out with Lee and Elam in the car to put up some National Tire signs, about 2 miles north, 2 miles east and 2 miles south.*

Elam and Rachel had space enough in their new home to rent rooms to college students. They lived very close to the campus. Elam listed the first students: *Alma Bowen and Tressie Yeager of Covert, Shirley Caissman of Russell, Alma DuPree of Waldo and Pauline Bremgardt of Collyer.*

The purchase of the home in Hays was finalized on February 22: *Went up town to the First National Bank where I paid off my entire unpaid obligation of $2650 to Mrs. Adah Cain (now of Salina) and the $7000 property purchased of her last June became ours in fee simple and, happily, thus ends that transaction.* This date was also Rachel's 75th birthday.

Now that he was part of the college scene, Elam tried to get interested in basketball. On March 15: *In the evening attended the basket ball tour-*

nament and I surely got enough of that game for one while at least. The games were OK but the deafening racket of the rooters was a positive disgrace in its many forms! (Note here the first use of the term "OK.")

But on the 20th he appreciated the enthusiastic response *he* got: *In the evening, at the Chemical lecture room at Science Hall, made an address on "Fungi and Some Other Things" to a good and enthusiastic audience which applauded me to the echo which was most gratifying!*

On May 22, at the first graduation Elam attended as a member of the faculty, he was given a place of honor: *At 10 oclock the faculty and student class marched in double column to the Sheridan Coliseum where the faculty took seats on the platform and the graduates on the floor to the front.*

In the march Dr. Lewis on the right and Dean Lee on the left headed the column followed by President F. D. Farrell and myself, respectively. Another honor!

In September, grandson Elam developed an ailment of serious concern. On the 22nd: *At 9:45 with Lee, Lily and Elam Jr. in their car started eastward — I to stop off and botanize at Russell while the others to continue on to Kansas City, Mo. where they are taking Elam to a clinic to inquire into his peculiar anemic condition which has knocked him out in a great measure for the past six weeks. Botanized successfully about Russell the remainder of the day. Came home by bus at 7:30.*

Two months later young Elam was no better: *Lee and Lily drove in our car yesterday to take Elam Jr. to the famous Hirschler Hospital at Halstead, Harvey Co. Kan. to have him examined again by experts as to his peculiar anemic physical condition which has been with him since last July. A bad report was brought back when the folks returned this evening, declaring that the ailment was not pernicious anaemia as previously reported from other sources, but False Leukemia or Hodgkin's Disease, that dread malady from which there is no known cure! This was the saddest of all sad reports. They claim that it is only a question of varying time until the patient must succumb to the inevitable!*

Five days later, on November 30: *The doctors here were not satisfied with the diagnosis of Elam's case at Halstead so advised that he be taken to the celebrated Clinic and hospital of the Mayo Brothers at Rochester,*

The four sons of Elam and Rachel Bartholomew. Top left to right: Elbert and Earl; bottom left to right: Jesse and Lee. Elizabeth was not available for this portrait.

Minnesota. In accordance with this idea, at 2 p.m. today Lee, Lily, Rachel, Margaret and Elam drove in the car to Phillipsburg where Lee and Elam were to take the train for Rochester. The other members of the family returned to Hays at 8:30.

Then on December 6: *Lee and Elam returned last night at midnight. Lily drove over in the afternoon to meet them. The doctors up there say that he has leukemia but not Hodgkin's Disease! However the diseases are similar and to me there seems small hope for the boy's recovery.*

A new car was bought on the day after Christmas: *We and Lee's bought, in partnership, a new 6-cylinder Chevrolet motor car, trading in our Chrysler which we have run for seven years. We paid a difference of $350.*

But Christmas time had its sadness too. On the 27th: *Took little Elam to the hospital at 10:30 to administer a treatment of blood transfusion, of about one pint, from his father's body!* On the 29th: *The boy Elam does not seem to respond encouragingly from the blood infusion treatment.*

The end of 1930 brings another comment on diary-keeping: *Ten years ago, this day, I concluded to close the writing of this diary but reconsidered the proposition and continued on until this date having recorded the events of the 21,914 days transpiring in the full 60 years ending with today! This is a record few men or women live to accomplish and is one of the outstanding features of my life!*

1931

Rachel gave everyone a scare on April 6, 1931: *Wife taken down at 9 a.m. with violent hemorrhages of the lungs numbering about 10 attacks up to the morning of the 8th.* The children all came to be with her, but by the 12th the problem ended.

The first grandchild to graduate from high school, Rachel, received high honors on May 22.

Intense sorrow came to the family on September 3: *Went over to son Lee's (whence wife had already gone) to be with our dear little grandson, Elam, who was stricken some 16 months ago with a fatal, uncurable malady known as lymphatic leukemia. In all that time all that medical science could do for the poor sufferer was faithfully done, but to no permanent avail!*

At 12:25 a.m. as we all, including Rev. and Mrs. David McCleave, sat in grief by the bedside, the spirit of the little boy in his 12th year was carried by the angels over into "The Summerland of Song", and thus ended the earthly pilgrimage of this dearly beloved and bright intelligent little boy.

At the funeral the following College Professors were present: Dr. W. A. Lewis, F. B. Lee, Roy Rankin, C. E. Rarick. F. W. Albertson, F. D. Streeter and Dean Agnew.

There remained only the two sons of Jesse to carry the Bartholomew name. Thankfully they lived to have families of their own, with a combined total of three sons and one daughter.

1933

Elam gave everyone a scare on January 13, 1933: *At 1:30 p.m. in corridor in front of my office door in the Science Bldg. I became unconscious, slumped to the floor and became violently ill. Various persons soon came to my assistance. Also Dr. Morris, the college physician. They got me into a car and brought me home and put me to bed, the doctor coming along. He examined me with his instruments but didn't find anything particularly the matter with me.*

Dr. Brewer was called in the late afternoon who also examined me quite thoroughly and who also reported nothing serious the matter with me. Some medication and rest was prescribed with instruction to remain abed for several days.

January 14 to 18: *In bed most of this time trying to recover my usual strength; quite seriously "punk" most of the time but getting OK by the 18th.*

Elam's health grew worse on July 17: *Was taken with a general physical break-down today and became a very sick man!* Then by August 24: *Began a slow tedious recovery.*

In July, after receiving a master's degree, Jesse moved his family from Oberlin to Topeka, where he became pastor of the Third Presbyterian Church, later serving also the church at Wakarusa and the Second Presbyterian Church of Topeka.

Elam had recovered sufficiently by September 29 that Lily took him and Rachel to Topeka for a four-day visit.

Three days after returning home, Elam attended the funeral of Fred Arnhold, *who died from wounds received at the hold-up of the Farmers State Bank 2 weeks ago.*

1934

Lee, who had become involved in the trucking business, had a problem on February 2, 1934: *Lee went to Neb. this morning after a truck load of corn and on the road home when at Phillipsburg he was stricken by appen-dicitis and drove on home by 5 oclock. He remained at home for the night under the doctors care.* On the next day: *He was taken to the hospital today for an operation, but as he felt so much improved no operation was made.*

Elam and Rachel were proud grandparents on May 23: *At 8 p.m. with wife attended the city High School graduation exercises at the H.S. build-ing to see our granddaughter, Margaret, graduate. Large attendance and fine meeting!*

On August 28, sadness came to brother Ed and his family: *At 11 a.m. today sister-in-law Myrtle, Brother Ed's wife, past over to the great beyond from the effects of an interior cancer.* Then on the 30th: *With wife, Lee, Lily, Rachel and Margaret drove to Stockton where we took dinner and drove thence on to brother Ed's where at 2:30 p.m. we attended the funeral services of sister-in-law Myrtle conducted by Rev. Spalding of Stockton. After being held up a half hour by a thunderstorm we drove on north over to the Bow Creek Cemetery where the interment was made.*

Elam made his last journey to Bow Creek Cemetery less than three months later.

Chapter 7

Debates

*D*ISCONTENT WITH THE LACK OF stimulating discourse among those who were consumed with the daily
concerns of Western frontier life, several people formed
an organization to discuss current events. These gatherings focused on a broad spectrum of political and economic issues, with obvious tangential religious perspectives.

1879
The discussions began Saturday, November 22, 1879, three years
after Elam had brought his bride to their new home, and one year following the Indian massacre two counties to the west.

The group, called the Adelphian Literary Association, met at the
newly-built sod school house. *The exercises of the society are to be:
Debate on select questions, Essays, Select Readings, Declamma-
tions, Dialogues and reading of the Society Paper.*

At the first meeting the topic of discussion was "Resolved that Negro emigration to the State of Kansas is detrimental to the best interests of the State." Elam took the negative side, which was declared the winner. Obviously this topic was of no minor importance, because the Civil War had ended only 14 years earlier. The prominent place of Kansas in that war could not be forgotten. The decision that Kansas could become a state only on the condition that it be a free state instead of a slave state had precipitated the hostilities in 1861 that continued until 1865.

The second gathering of the literary society, one week later, did not go smoothly. The topic: "Resolved, that the works of nature alone are sufficient to demonstrate the existence of a Supreme Being." Elam took the affirmative side of debate, but lost, agitating him considerably: *Our side was beaten in a very shabby manner through the babblings of W. S. Thomas who allowed our side no chance whatever to make our argument but managed to cut us off with about 20 to 25 minutes while his side occupied the floor nearly one hour.*

The next meeting, on December 12, ended in a frenzy of excitement and despair. *Bill Stockman, a noted "harem-scarem" of this vicinity put a quantity of dry bark into the stove, while a roaring fire was already in progress, which heated the stove pipe red hot and caused the roof to take fire on the inside and no water being at hand the fire spread rapidly and the sod school house which has cost us so much time, labor and vexation was soon reduced to a wreck.*

The roof was quickly replaced, and the next meeting was held December 26. The topic was more sublime, and so was the meeting: "Resolved: That the reading of fictitious literature is injurious." Elam took the negative side and won.

1880

Weekly meetings continued into 1880. On January 2 Elam was chief disputant for the affirmative of "Resolved that poverty tends more to develop the character than riches," and was the winner.

On January 9 Elam won on the negative side of "Resolved that the signs of the time point to the downfall of the US Government." It was 1880, just 15 years after the so-called "Civil War" had ended. It was surely uncivil in the extreme, with members of the same family sometimes on opposing sides in the brutal slaughter. For many years it was called "The

War of the Rebellion" instead of "Civil War." Political, economic, and emotional turmoil prevailed for a long time.

Following such chaos it takes time to restore a country to a sense of self-worth. It takes time to establish governmental functions with any degree of respect from multiple political factions. Pride from one side has always the shadow of shame from the other. A monstrous task, indeed, of assimilating all factions and instilling a sense of equilibrium in a government spinning out of control.

Assuredly the greedy opportunist and shady politician were taking advantage of the chaos in every way possible. Senators in the U.S. Congress were chosen by state legislatures until passage of the 17th Amendment to the Constitution in 1913, and it was easier to "buy" members with financial support from railroading, oil, textiles, mining, and iron and steel manufacturers. The fledgling civil service system was corrupt.

Venomous campaign oratory refused to let the Civil War die. Republicans charged that the men who shot Union soldiers and the man who assassinated Lincoln were all Democrats.

Even people on the Western frontier were aware of all this, although communications were still comparatively primitive. Settlers had gone west for various reasons, one of which was to escape all those evil forces that plagued the more "civilized" states of the Eastern Establishment, but they still had family ties back East, and the newspapers of the frontier carried the news, albeit usually with a profound bias one way or the other. Not all the frontier folk were taken in by radical rhetoric, and not all were willing to be bystanders, watching evil forces consume the democratic form of government they dearly believed in. One of these champions for governmental decency was Elam Bartholomew.

On January 16 the literary society debated "Resolved that man gains more information by travel than by reading." Elam had the affirmative side, but the negative won. Then the following week he did not attend *on account of the thing about having run into the ground, there being too much "society" and not enough "literary."*

1886
Finally the literary group became dormant, but it was reorganized in

1886 and took on new life; it again became involved in serious matters. On January 22 the debate topic was certainly not frivolous: "Resolved, that the coinage of the silver dollar should be suspended." Elam took the affirmative side and the judge ruled in his favor.

This was indeed a serious matter. Issuing coins made of silver pleased only silver mining interests, and it was fraught with political chicanery. It was more inflationary than the gold standard, but less than issuing more paper money, preferred by the newly organized "Greenback Party."

In January 1875 President Grant had persuaded Congress to pass legislation requiring that in four years the paper money floated beginning in 1861 to finance the Civil War be redeemed in gold, to restore stability and confidence in the U.S. economy. At the beginning of 1879 President Hayes ordered that this begin, but Congress passed — and sustained over his veto — the Bland-Allison Act, authorizing a return to unlimited silver coinage (which had been suspended in 1873).

The resulting financial panic was followed by a three-year depression. Greenbackers, mostly farmers, favored currency inflation that made it possible to pay off debt with cheaper money. "Free Silverites" prevailed, and just four years after this debate, the Sherman Silver Purchase Act of 1890 nearly doubled the amount of coined silver.

The government issued silver certificates in addition to gold certificates, helping to mollify the Greenbackers. Predictably this caused a panic in 1893; people rushed to redeem their paper in gold, causing the repeal of the Silver Purchase Act that year. William Jennings Bryan, who led the Free Silverites, lost the 1896 election to William McKinley, who favored the gold standard.

On January 29, 1886, the literary society debated a much more dogmatic issue, obviously wishing to gain respite from the previous week's contentious subject: "Resolved, that all laws, just or unjust, should be obeyed." It was decided in the negative. A large crowd attended. They had heard about the previous debate, but no doubt this time they were disappointed.

The next week, though, another hot topic came up: "Resolved that our [Kansas] prohibition law should be repealed and high license substituted in its stead." The *question was left to the house for decision and decided in favor of the negative*, the side taken by Elam, an ardent opponent of those who could not control their passion for intoxicating beverages.

Following a topic of such keen interest, the February 12 crowd was large, but they must have been disappointed by the relatively mundane topic: "Resolved that the author has done more for mankind than the warrior." Elam debated the affirmative, but his side lost.

The next week carried a rather titillating topic: "Resolved that man will do more for the love of money than he will for the love of woman." Elam took the negative, and the judges decided in his favor. Elam reflected: *A goodly number were out and a pleasant time was indulged in by all.*

For some reason, February 26 saw the repeat of the December 26, 1879, topic: "Resolved that the reading of fictitious literature is injurious." Elam again took the negative and won, but this time the decision was left to the audience. In his diary he attempted to explain why there was so much interest in the topic: *A number voted in favor of the negative simply to justify their practices of reading trashy stories — unworthy the name of literature.*

The next topic was "Resolved that a limited monarchy is preferable to a republican form of government." It is no surprise that Elam took the negative side, but it is surprising that *the question was left to the house and decided in favor of the affirmative.* These were frontier people, rugged individualists, usually thought of as being revulsed by any kind of subjugation. Obviously they were "fed up" with the greed, graft, and corruption engaged in so persistently by politicians regardless of party, and they were feeling the repression of big money barons in railroading, oil, textiles, steel, and so forth. They must have been disgusted and oppressed, to have cast a majority in favor of such an issue.

Only once during the 1886-1887 season did Elam attend literary society meetings, because of the death of an infant son and other conflicting events. The topic "Resolved that the government should own and operate the rail roads of the U.S." commanded his attention, but he only listened. The topic was decided in the affirmative. This may sound incongruous with previous denouncements of evils of government, but the people evidently resented the power play by large moguls in the industry and felt the futility of trying to change the system.

Chapter 8

Politics and Government Affairs

*A*T THE AGE OF 20, in summer 1872, Elam was approaching adulthood and voting age, and he began to show interest in political issues. On July 30: *As I am a Republican and as this is a presidential year I attended an enthusiastic Grant &* [Henry] *Wilson ratification meeting at Farmington in the evening.*

He never mentions Abraham Lincoln, but he was certainly aware that Lincoln also was a product of Illinois, just 53 miles south of Farmington. Elam had been almost 13 when in March 1865 the family left Ohio and settled in Illinois. At that age he must have been deeply impressed by events just one month later: the Civil War ended and Lincoln was shot.

Elam may also have known that Grant, a native of Ohio, had lived for a while at Galena, Illinois, just five counties north of Farmington, and at Springfield.

1874

Elam arrived at Stockton, Kansas (in Rooks County), on March 19, 1874, to establish residence on a homestead claim near there. This he did 6 days later. Just 13 days after that, April 7, he attended the township election to get acquainted with his new neighbors, knowing he was not yet eligible to vote. Nevertheless, he was thrust into the political scene quite to his surprise (and with some unease): *Attended, with Mr. Foote and Eli, the township municipal election for this, Bow Creek, township at the Rockport postoffice 4 miles west and although not yet a legal citizen of the state I was called on to act as one of the clerks of election because there were not enough persons present to form an election board. Was also elected township clerk for the coming year.*

August 8 finds Elam again getting involved in the local political scene: *Attended a mass Republican convention in Stockton held in the upper room of the stone store building, called for the purpose of electing delegates to the state and congressional conventions to be held respectively at Topeka and Leavenworth. Acted as secretary of the convention.*

Election day was November 3: *Attended the fall election at the Rockport postoffice 4 miles west and acted as clerk on the election board.*

1876

Exactly two months after bringing his bride to Kansas in 1876 Elam found himself again getting involved in things political, but not necessarily to his liking. On November 5: *Was informed today by Jim French of Stockton who called on us about noon that I had been nominated yesterday on the Independent ticket as a candidate for Clerk of the Dist. Court for Rooks county, against which I protested vigorously and wrote a withdrawal of my name from said ticket, for publication and distribution throughout the county tomorrow. Being a Republican I have no use for Independent tickets at present.* And on the 6th: *While at Mr. Foote's I met G. W. Patterson and Tunis Bulis of Stockton who had come over to see me and try to induce me to withdraw my card to the public, of yesterday, but I positively refused to consider the proposition.* But all to no avail. On the 7th: *Went to the election at Rockport P.O. and acting as one of the clerks of election did not get home until 8 oclock p.m. Was elected to the office of trustee for this (Bow Creek) township and in spite of my former protests carried the township against J. R. Marshall for Clerk of Dist. Court.*

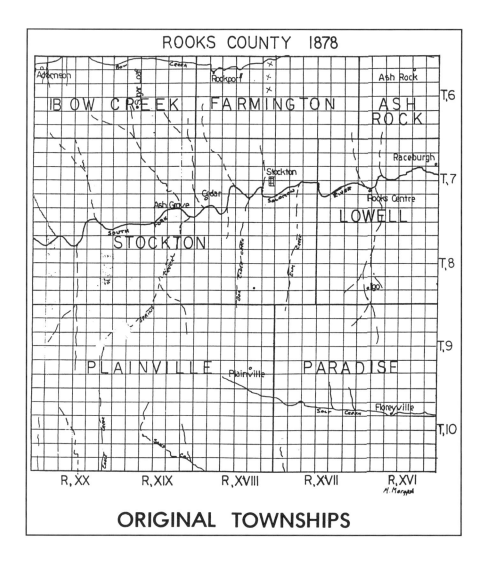

ROOKS COUNTY 1878

ORIGINAL TOWNSHIPS

1877

One of the tasks that Elam had to perform in political office was described on March 20, 1877: *As Tp. Trustee and overseer of the poor, went to the home of Jacob Shell and Mrs. Mary Messinger to make arrangements for their maintenance by the county as they had applied to me for such aid.*

Even though the first child of Elam and Rachel was born on May 1, it was time to begin the duty of township assessment, so on the next two

ROOKS COUNTY, KANSAS

	20	19	18	17	16	
T.6	Bow Creek *5*	Sugar Loaf	Farmington	Lanark	Ash Rock	6
T.7	Alcona	Belmont *6*	*3* Stockton	*2* Iowa	*1* Lowell	7
T.8	*7* Richland	Rush	*4* Hobart	Greenfield	Medicine	5
T.9	*8* Northampton	Logan *10*	*11* Plainville	Twin Mound	Coring	
T.10	*9*	Walton	Plainville	Paradise *12*		1

PRESENT TOWNSHIPS

days: *Worked both of these days at assessing the property of residents of this (Bow Creek) township. Came home each evening.* But on the 7th he had to stay overnight with a friend, because the work had taken him 15 miles away from home. After the job was completed there was some time for family May 10 to 12: *Spent each of these three days in and about the house acting as "chief cook and bottle washer" in house work!* And on the 27th there was time for an outing with the family: *Rachel, the new baby George and I went out for a walk over the farm and to view the high water in Bow creek from the hill a half mile east of the house.*

The next five days District Court was in session, so Elam had to stay in Stockton four nights. Then on June 4 he had another civic duty in Stockton: *Was appointed by the county commissioners as one of the Teachers Examining Board.*

1878

More settlers moved into the area, filling up vacant land. It was decided on November 5, 1878, that Bow Creek township was too large: *Our township, Bow Creek, which was 6x21 miles in extent, having recently been divided into a 6x12 mile territory and named Farmington for Farmington, Ill. our old home town, and the place of holding the elections having been transferred from Rockport to the residence of A. G. Muir 5½ miles southeast of here, I went over there early in the morning. I attended the election and sat as one of the judges on the election board.*

1879

On February 22, 1879: *Went to Stockton on business connected with the office of Township Trustee, and to carry to the Co. Supt. of Pub. Inst. our petition of Jan. 27 requesting the organization of a school dist. in this locality. Petition granted and notices of formation sent out to be posted in the new dist. 10 days after which notices calling a meeting for the election of officers will be likewise posted.*

Annual assessment duties began on March 4, covering the township 6x12 miles. It is intriguing to note that Elam ate dinner wherever he happened to be at noon, and some families even provided supper and overnight lodging. The work was completed on March 26.

In Kansas, as well as in Illinois, it was general practice for local residents to work on the roads in lieu of cash payment of a $3.00 tax. One such occasion was August 5: *Spent the day in working out one day of my poll tax on the roads two miles east of here under J. M. Mellon, Road Overseer.* There were similar work days, too numerous to mention.

On October 25: *As the day of election comes nearer the politicians of the day become very animated and as a consequence thereof Stockton was boiling over with politics and politicians and being somewhat of a poli-*

The Latest Wonder of the Telegraph.

The readers of the Traveler have been made acquainted with the wonderful inventions of Professor Bell, by which musical and vocal sounds can be sent over the electric wires; but few if any are aware of the wonderful results which are sure to follow these improvements in telegraphy. A few nights ago Professor Bell was in communication with a telegraphic operator in New York, and commenced experimenting with one of his inventions pertaining to the transmission of musical sounds. He made so of his phonetic organ and played the tune of "America," and asked the operator in New York what he heard.

"I hear the tune of America," replied New york; "give us another."

Professor Bell then played Auld Lang Syne.

What do you hear now?"

I hear the tune of Auld Lang Syne, with the full chords, distinctly," replied New York.

Thus, the astounding discovery has been made that a man playing upon musical instruments in New York, New Orleans, London or Paris, is heard distinctly in Boston! If this can be done, why can not distinguished performers execute the most artistic and beautiful music in Paris, and an audience assemble in Music Hall, Boston, to listen?

Professor Bell's other improvement namely, the transmission of the human voice, has become so far perfected that persons have conversed over one thousand miles of wire with perfect ease although as yet the vocal sounds are not loud enough to be heard by more than one or two persons. But if the human voice can now be sent over the wire, and so distinctly that when two or three known parties are telegraphing, the voices of can be recognized, we may soon have distinguished men delivering speechs in Washington, New York or London, and audiences assembled in Music Hall or Faneuel Hall to listen!—Boston Travel·er.

The September 14, 1876, edition of *The Stockton News* describes a thrilling discovery, which enlarged the utility of the telegraph. Soon thereafter, in 1895, the radio was invented by Marconi who said, "I have discovered how to telegraph without wires."

tician myself, though rather in a passive form, had frequent conversations with several of them.

In accordance with announcement in Stockton News and other previous arrangements Dr. E. J. Donnell and C. W. Smith of the Stockton News came over from town with us in the evening in a buggy and after partaking of supper at our house we repaired to the school house and listened to able discourse upon the political issues of the day from both of the above named gentlemen. L. C. Smith, Sorehead, also spoke but made a bad fizzle.

Those who split off from the Republican Party for one reason or another found no support from Elam. On October 29: *About 9 a.m. was called on by D. J. Moore, Trustee of Bow Creek Tp. and E. F. White of the same Tp., the latter named man being a candidate for the office of Register of Deeds on the ticket of Sorehead or Bolters faction of the regular Rep. Co. Con. on the 4th. Spent about 30 minutes in conversation with them, in which time I let them know in a very point blank manner that I am a full blood Rep. and believe everything that leads from the true Rep. Party leads direct into the detestable ranks of the Democracy. In consequence of which I told them that I could give the nominees of their faction no support whatever and would use my influence toward the election of the straight Rep. ticket. Being disgusted, they departed.*

1880

On township election day, February 3, 1880, Elam confronted an irregularity that appeared to be fraudulent manipulation of the results: *Today being election day for township officers and for voting on a $4000 proposition for bonds to build a court house, said election to be held at the residence of A. G. Muir, the usual place of holding elections, about 5 miles S.E. of here, and being Tp. Trustee and by virtue of said office, one of the judges of the election, and the polls having to be opened at the hour of 10 oclock a.m. in accordance with Sec. 7 Chapter 110 of the Revised Statutes of 1879, I repaired to the place of holding elections shortly before ten oclock and found on arriving that the polls had already been opened and the judges were receiving votes. Said board consisting of W. C. Sanford, Wm. F. Titus and A. J. Muir as judges and A. G. Muir and J. P. Shirley as clerks.*

As neither one of the "board" were the proper election officers, and as its organization had been completed so early in the morning that there were not sufficient men there from which to form a board without putting two of the Muir family on, and two of their particular "friends" (Sanford and Shirley) and A. G. Muir being his own candidate for Trustee on the Bailey-Smith ticket against S. R. Guthrie the straight Rep. man, and, from the complexion of the case believing that there was "Something rotten in Denmark", I walked into the room and demanded to know by what authority they had formed themselves into an election board and were receiving votes, telling them at the same time if they carried the returns of their "board" to Stockton, when the county Commissioners came to canvass the vote of Farmington Tp. the returns would be thrown out on the score of the board having been illegally formed by unqualified persons previous to the hour established by law.

Previous to my arrival I presume they were very much gratified to think that they would have everything their own way, and to make doubly sure the bogus "board" had deposited each man his own ballot in the box, as had also one Chas. H. Miller who was candidate last fall on the "Sorehead" ticket for Sheriff and who was working might and main for the election of Muir for Trustee.

No other votes had been cast. J. A. Southard, one of the justices and a member of the board, arrived before I did and the "board" being in session before he got there, he as a natural consequence got no seat thereon, and perhaps thinking that they calculated to carry their scheme out on the "Mississippi plan", he went home in high dudgeon even refusing to vote. Mr. Southard had gone home before my arrival.

Such however was not my intention (although perhaps it might be said I was in "high dudgeon") for I calculated to see the matter out if it took all day. So after making the demand and assertion above recorded A. G. Muir said he had consulted with the County Atty., A. L. Patchin, who told him that the polls must be opened at 8 a.m. instead of 10. I told him that Patchin had no authority to give any such advice, and having a copy of the revised Statutes of 1879 along with me I produced the section and chapter above referred to and by my request the law on the subject was read by W. Thomas to the crowd of people assembled within the house.

The effect was sensational! Muir tried to shield himself by saying that as a bond election was combined with the township election it would change the time to 8 oclock. Laf C. Smith, lawyer, former Co. Clerk and general political dead beat agreed with Muir as did also our angel of purity and political reform J. A. Bailey. By reference to Sec. 5 of Chap. 12 of the revised Statutes it was found that bond elections must be governed by the "rules and regulations provided by law for holding elections in any such county, city or township" and that "such election should be conducted by the officers or persons provided by law".

Here their game was blocked again, as the "board" was illegally formed throughout and they were all willing, yea anxious *that the board should be reorganized, a step which I did not feel like taking as Muir and his clique had considered themselves competent to carry things through* *without any aid from the proper election officers. So I held off for about half an hour before I consented to take a seat on the board and reorganize it. In the meantime Smith, Bailey and Muir had become <u>very</u> <u>anxious</u> to have a new board formed which was then done consisting of W. C. Sanford, W. F. Titus and myself as judges and H. E. Williams and A. G. Muir clerks, the ballot box being opened and the six votes cast being thrown out.*

The whole blame in the matter attaches to Muir who had undoubtedly put up the game for a big "beat", as on last Friday, knowing his duplicity but thinking he could be trusted that far I had allowed him to carry home the blank poll books from Stockton and on Saturday at the township meeting I had told him expressly that under the new law the polls would not be opened until 10 oclock and that previous to that time I would be on hand and seeing Mr. Southard yesterday in Kirwin he said that he also would be there about nine oclock and fulfilled his promise by being there at that time.

Muir was determined to be elected Trustee at all hazards, so yesterday he got a large number of tickets printed with his name on for that office, and having a number of fellows of "Sorehead" notoriety to work for him and scatter his tickets through the crowd he was elected over Guthrie. No other events worthy of mention transpired during the day and I left for home at 8:30 p.m. arriving at 10 oclock.

This whole affair greatly offended Elam's sense of ethical behavior and from that time forward hardened his relationship with those involved. Stimulated thereby to attain authoritative knowledge of laws pertaining to local affairs, Elam devoted February 9 and 14 as follows: *Spent almost the entire time of each day in reading, writing and study. Having the Gen. Statutes of Kan. for 1868 and all the Session laws from 1870 to 1879, both inclusive, by far the greater part of these six days was spent in making a <u>complete</u> <u>revision</u> of the entire code of Kansas laws, which was done by marking all the amended and repealed laws of the whole code and transferring to the Statutes of 1868 references to all the state laws as they now appear in the Compiled Laws of 1879.*

Did the above work as a pastime and also that I might have a compendium of the laws as they now are without going to the expense of purchasing a copy of the Revised Laws of 1879.

When the November 2 election day came, Elam's adrenaline ran at high speed: *About 8 a.m. went over south two miles to John Farnsworth's place to attend the election and being Tp. Trustee acted in the capacity of Judge of election, Chas. H. Buschman and C. H. Buschman being the other two judges and S. R. Guthrie and Sam A. Hebrew the clerks. 60 votes were cast by 6 p.m. at which time the polls were closed, and I being selected to make the returns to the county clerk at Stockton and the vote being counted by 8 oclock I and Dr. H. J. Fuller went home with C. H. Miller where we took supper and immediately thereafter Mr. Miller, Dr. Fuller and myself started for Stockton, getting there about 10:30 oclock.*

Republican head quarters was located at the court house (Ecker building) in front of which a number of glass torch lights were burning. In a moment I was on the inside and handing a copy of the Farmington vote to Laf. C. Smith, Chairman Cen. Comm., he jumped onto a chair and read the result of our vote to the crowd of excited men and anxious candidates who filled the house. We having given a clear majority of 30 to the whole Republican ticket, Mr. Smith proposed three cheers for Farmington which were given with a vim that seemed to make the very rafters tremble. Farmington was the first Tp. to make returns in the county. Shortly after, Miller, Fuller and I were taken to a neighboring restaurant by Mr. Smith and given a midnight lunch, after which we all returned to the court house to await further returns.

But on the next day bitterness rises to a fever pitch on the outcome of one race: *Mr. Smith having requested Dr. Fuller and I to keep a full report of the returns as they came in from the various Tps., we complied with his request, until about 10 a.m., (having been up all night) when we were relieved by T. C. McBreen of the Record (the local newspaper). By noon the returns were about all in and we were assured that the whole Rep. Co. ticket had been elected over the Greenbacks-Democratic Fusion ticket with the exception of Dr. E. J. Donnell whom we found to be defeated by one A. B. Montgomery by about 65 or 70 majority.*

In the defeat of Donnell Rooks Co. has met with a misfortune indeed as

Donnell is undoubtedly one of the ablest men in western Kansas, he being a graduate of Dartmouth College, N.H., and as a consequence he is a ripe scholar, a polished gentleman, a zealous Christian man and an active worker in the cause of temperance.

On the other hand Montgomery is a man of small experience, little learning, weak influence only with the lower classes, a back-slidden Baptist, a confirmed spiritualist and a man whose mouth is sealed on the temperance question. If these things be true in regard to each man's character and standing the reader will at once inquire why Donnell was defeated while Montgomery was elected!

The answer is at hand. Donnell is a resident of Stockton, his property is located there and as a consequence all his interests are there. Stockton is the county seat. Montgomery lives south of the river in Twin Mound Tp., in the Plainville country. His interests are there, Plainville wants the county seat and is opposed to Stockton, Stockton men, and Stockton institutions. The south side of the river holds the balance of power in voting, hence Montgomery's election and Donnell's defeat. As a consequence of yesterday's election stirring up sectional strifes and jealousies a county seat war is beyond question in the near future.

Besides the above causes the opposition headed by W. T. Donnell, (brother of E. J. and chairman of the Rooks Co. Dem. Cen. Com.) T. T. Tillotson and H. A. Hart (Fusion candidate for probate judge) resorted to the lowest, meanest and most contemptible calumny imaginable, to defeat E. J., going so far as to assert by bogus affidavits (that were exhibited at out-of-the-way precincts in the county) that Dr. E. J. Donnell had been carried into the hotel at Stockton on a recent occasion, dead drunk! While at the same time every body in the county that is acquainted with Donnell knows that there is not a more strict temperance disciple to be found in the land.

At one p.m. I started home arriving at 3 oclock feeling blue as indigo over the defeat of our worthy Donnell knowing that Rooks Co. will be the same as unrepresented in the Legislature this winter.

A few days later there was good news about other parts of the election. On the 6th: *Went to Stockton on miscellaneous business and while there learned of the complete triumph of Republican principles in the election of Garfield and Arthur, the whole state ticket, election of G. A. Smith for Dist. Judge and my old friend A. L. Patchin for state Senator for the 35th dist.* And also on the 13th: *Went to Stockton on miscellaneous business and while there learned that the temperance amendment to our state constitution had been carried by a good majority at the recent election, which news was extremely gratifying to me.*

1881

On Sunday, July 3, 1881, following church services, some stunning news was received: *At the close of the services we learned from Mr. Bracken the startling intelligence of the attempted assassination of President Garfield which sent a thrill of sorrow and profound regret to the hearts of those who were present, as the wounds received, it was believed, would prove fatal in a short time.*

President Garfield died on September 19, but the news did not reach Elam until two days later: *In the p.m. went over to mother's on an errand and while there learned the sad news of President Garfield's death.*

1882

Elam could get passionate on the subject of prohibition. On July 25, 1882: *Went to Kirwin in company with S. A. Hebrew and his father to hear a temperance lecture by Gov. St. John. Left home at 6:30 a.m. and got there at about 10:30. The address was delivered at 2 p.m. to a very large and appreciative audience, and was a masterly effort on behalf of Prohibition being loudly applauded throughout, and in my opinion Gov. St. John is the coming man who will be looked on in the near future as the commander in chief of the great army battling so nobly for an absolute prohibition of the rum traffic in the U.S.*

May God hasten the day when all the States forming our fraternal union will be as free from the bliting effects of the withering curse of alcoholism as our own fair state of Kansas. God bless Gov. St. John in his noble efforts to rescue fallen man from his thralldom, and may his labors in that direction be crowned with the fullest success, and his crown of rejoicing be studded with numberless stars when the great king cometh to make up his jewels. In the presidential election of 1884 Governor St. John of Kansas was the candidate of the newly formed Prohibition Party. Democrat Grover Cleveland was the winner that year.

Another speech, on October 9, was even better: *Went to Stockton in company with Rachel, Geo., Elbert and Mrs. S. A. Hebrew to hear a speech by Gov. St. John which we heard and were entertained and gratified in the highest degree. The court house was packed with a large and enthusiastic audience. The speech surpassed in intensity of interest the one delivered at Kirwin July 25th and was the best and most forcible piece of oratory to which I have ever listened. Dozens of those who have hereto-fore been his enemies were ready and willing to admit their delight and gratification and desire to place St. John hereafter among the list of the "big guns". His friends were enraptured, the luke warm were delighted and his political opponents were silenced.*

Sad news of the election came on November 10: *While in town learned that the report of Glick, Democrat, being elected over St. John was only too true, and thus has been sacrificed a great and good man on the altar of the sensual devotees of Bacchus.*

1884

Some Republicans bolted the party during the campaign of 1884 and supported Cleveland. They were called "Mugwumps." A supporter of Blaine, the Reverend Burchard, labelled the Democrats as a party of "Rum, Romanism & Rebellion," creating a backlash that was damaging, rather than helpful, to Republicans.

Then there was the new Prohibition Party, whose candidate was former Kansas Governor John P. St. John. (Elam knew that he stood no chance to win, so he did not waste his vote on his friend.) St. John conducted a fiery campaign against Blaine as well as "demon rum," which took more votes from Blaine than Cleveland.

These divisive tactics threw New York state's 36 electoral votes to Cleveland by a plurality of just 1,149 popular votes, and that put him over the top — this despite Cleveland's forthright admission during the campaign that he, though a bachelor, had fathered a child out of wedlock.

It is worthy of note that Elam remained faithful to the Republican Party even though he had strong convictions on the subject of prohibition. He was not a one-issue campaigner or voter. He refused to go along with splinter factions on other issues as well: groups such as the Greenbackers, Stalwarts, or Mugwumps.

1885

Elam's disgust for local politics intensified on January 31, 1885: *In the p.m. at two oclock attended the caucus of the township which proved to be about as inharmonious, wrangling, jangling, farcical affair as I have seen for a long time. The nominations were nearly all of the shallowest mater-*

ial in the township headed by the inefficient and illiterate Jim Richardson for Trustee.

Situations like this were taken hard, because he loved the democratic system of government but often found his moral and ethical convictions were in the minority. Then in his concern, he took action on February 25: *There being a very great dissatisfaction in regard to the nominees of last Saturday's caucus, I with several others, passed the day in canvassing the township in the interests of an opposition ticket.*

On the next day his viewpoint was vindicated: *Spent the whole day at the election or here and there over the township working hard for the election of the ticket as spoken of yesterday. In the evening about 7:30 oclock learned that our ticket had all been elected with the exception of Wilkin who was defeated by one majority for Coy. And thus, at last, has come to grief the Galvin-Richardson-Buschmen gang. Good!*

There was a campaign on April 3 to finally bring railroad service to Stockton: *In the evening Hon. W. H. Barnes and H. A. Hart of Stockton called on us, took supper and thence repaired to the school house where they addressed a moderate sized audience on the subject of voting $60,000 to aid in the construction of a railroad from Bull's City* [later renamed Alton] *to Stockton* [a distance of 17 miles].

Interest grew. On the 11th: *A very large number of people were in town and the all-absorbing topic of conversation was the $60,000 Railroad bond proposition to be voted on the 21st.* More attention was paid to the subject on the 17th: *M. C. Reville and J. W. Callender of Stockton took supper with us and immediately thereafter we repaired to the school house where a joint discussion was held on the railroad question with A. Nicodemus of Plainville. The former gentlemen favoring the $60,000 bond proposition while the latter opposed it. Not an anti-bond man was to be found at the close of the speech.*

The issue was successfully passed on the 21st: *From 7:30 p.m. until this writing (11:30 oclock) much cannonading has been heard in the direction of Stockton which we interpret as a jubilee given in commemoration of the success of the bond proposition.*

A school bond issue passed unanimously on June 10: *Our school district bond election coming off today, went down to J. A. Hebrew's, the place of election, and served as one of the judges of said election. Polls closed at 6 p.m. and a canvass of the vote showed 30 votes for the bonds ($350) and none against.*

Work began on September 3: *Worked over at our school house site, with several other of the neighbors, at dressing stone for the foundation.* And on September 19: *Met J. A. Hebrew at Kirwin and we proceeded to the Chicago Lumber Yards and proceeded to select a bill of lumber for our school house, said bill amounting to $207. Previous arrangements having been made ten teams were on the ground by noon which were loaded as fast as possible.* A contractor was secured on October 3: *In the p.m. went to Stockton in company with J. A. Hebrew to arrange definitely the matter of engaging a contractor to put up our school house. Secured J. M. Fike who proposes to commence work on the same next Tuesday morning.*

Finally, on Sunday, November 15, use of the new building began: *Attended Sab. school at 11 a.m. at our new school house which was the first public meeting held therein. The house is now complete and it is a neat, commodious and comfortable building and is spoken of highly by all with the exception of the proverbial chronic faultfinder who always makes himself a nuisance in any community.*

On November 5 Elam saw the results of the bond issue that had passed in April: *Took a grist of wheat to French's mill and leaving it drove up to Stockton and when within a half mile of town saw the construction train on the track and the tracklayers busy at work on the extension of Mo. Pacific R.R. into Rooks county which certainly is a grand achievement for the people of this part of Kansas, as this county has certainly squandered tens of thousands of dollars in building up towns in Phillips, Osborne and Ellis counties by giving them the benefit of our extensive shipping trade.*

Two days later: *Went to Stockton and from the hill on this side saw the construction train on the new R.R. in town! Whoop, La, Hurrah!!*

Elam assumed a new political role on December 8: *Went to Stockton on*

a miscellaneous business trip — among other things to pay our taxes. Last week I received a commission and appointment from the Governor as Justice of the Peace for Farmington Township, to fill the vacancy caused by the resignation of J. S. Travis, so while in town I took the oath of office, filed my bond and became a full fledged "squire". Mr. Travis has moved to town and by invitation I took dinner with him and family and while there he delivered to me the Docket and other effects of the Justice's office.

1886

A tough battle was waged for nomination of a candidate for Congress from the 6th District at the convention held in Stockton beginning July 14, 1886. Three ballots that day were indecisive. The second day, 70 ballots were taken, still without a sufficient majority for any one of the candidates. Finally on the third day: *Went to Stockton to witness further the proceedings of the Congressional convention, and when about a mile from town heard the din of exploding gunpowder and knew that the labors of the convention must have just come to a close.*

On reaching town learned that E. J. Turner of Sheridan county had received 61 votes on the 109th ballot and was declared the nominee amidst the wildest of cheering. Spent the day about town having a good time with various friends and acquaintances. Also met Mr. Turner at his room and congratulated him on his success.

1887

An organization was needed to assure the care and maintenance of the growing Bow Creek Cemetery, so on February 24, 1887, the Bow Creek Cemetery Association was established.

1888

Having been selected a delegate to the 6th Congressional Convention in Oberlin, Elam left on May 15, 1888: *Having made all necessary preparations had George take me over to Marvin in the morning to take the 10:45 a.m. train to attend the Oberlin convention. Arriving at Marvin learned that the train would be 5 hours late owing to a wreck near Concordia, so I sent George home while I proceeded in the most systematic manner to kill time. Called on Rev. A. F. Cumbour with whom I took dinner and passed several hours in pleasant social chat.*

At 3 p.m. a freight train came up the road which I boarded for Lenora.

On it I found a number of delegates from different counties down the road including three of our Rooks county delegation, viz. J. G. Smith, W. R. McNutt and J. C. Denney. Also met the two most prominent candidates for delegates to Chicago in the persons of W. W. Watson of Osborne and M. H. Johnson of Kirwin.

Arriving at Lenora, the railroad terminus, at 5 p.m. we all (about 40 of us) took 6 hacks in waiting for us and proceeded to make the 14 mile drive across to Oronoque at which place we arrived pretty thoroughly chilled at 7:30 oclock. After an excellent and refreshing supper at the hotel we boarded another abominable freight train in which we rode with much discomfort, reaching Oberlin about 10:30 oclock.

We were met at the train by a reception committee who conducted us with band music and a grand torch light procession to a large banquet hall where a most magnificent spread was prepared by the ladies of Oberlin. To this we certainly all tried to do ample justice. In saying that the banquet was <u>*magnificent*</u> *the subject was by no means overdone and it will no doubt long remain a pleasing thought in the memory of every delegate and visitor present. A social hop followed the banquet which I did not attend.*

Elam received a distinct honor on September 17: *Went to Stockton as a spectator to the proceedings of the Republican county convention. Went over in company with J. H. Disler and I. C. McMillan. Soon after arriving in town I learned that there was being quite a pressure brought to bear in favor of springing my name on the convention as a candidate for Probate Judge.*

After due consideration and urging by the delegation from our township I consented to allow the use of my name. When nominations were being made, D. H. Budd, the present probate Judge withdrew his name from the contest. U. S. McCollum and J. A. French were candidates of long standing. John Mullen of Plainville and myself were nominated as "dark horses". There were 91 votes in the convention, 46 being necessary for a choice. After several ballots were taken my vote ran up to 42 but got no higher than that. Two or three more ballots were taken when Mr. Mullen, having received a majority of all the votes cast was duly declared the nominee.

1889

Being Justice of the Peace can produce some tense moments. On May 22, 1889, Elam recorded: *Early in the morning was called on by two men from Custer Co. Neb. accompanied by constable Landreth of Marvin who wanted a warrant issued for the arrest of one Jas. McEndaffer, of whom they were in pursuit, for the unlawful selling and absconding with property under chattel mortgage.*

After due inquiry, warrant was issued and placed in the hands of constable A. B. Wilson who in company with the other three men resumed the chase, coming up with McEndaffer about three miles S.E. of here, proceeded to arrest him and brought him here at 9 oclock a.m. for a hearing of the case. The parties were given time to see if a settlement could not be arrived at without further legal proceedings.

After a parley lasting until after noon a settlement was agreed on (the amount being about $1,000) some deeds were drawn up conveying certain real estate and at 2:30 p.m. the case was dismissed and the costs taxed to the complaining witness (Elijah Stoddard), the prisoner discharged and court adjourned, and then went with the parties over to where the arrest was made to acknowledge the signing of the deeds by Mr. & Mrs. McEndaffer. Home at 6 p.m.

Elam again became a candidate for public office on August 13: *Went to Stockton to mill and to attend to quite an amount of miscellaneous business and returned home at 8:30 oclock p.m. While in town inserted a notice in the <u>Rooks</u> <u>County</u> <u>Record</u> announcing myself as a candidate for the office of County Clerk subject to the action of the Republican county convention to be held on the 23rd of Sept.*

But he lost: *With the following delegates, G. T. Granger, Wm. Broughton, Wm. Hall and E. N. McMillan, and the following alternates, Wm. Hebrew, Wm. Titus, J. B. Hubble and John Potter from this township, went to Stockton to attend the Republican convention. Convention met in the opera hall at 1:30 p.m. and proceeded to nominate the following county ticket to be voted for at the Nov. election: Treasurer, G. N. Mickel; Sheriff, R. Delay; Surveyor, J. T. Locke; Register of Deeds, W. R. McNutt; Co. Clerk, F. P. Hill; Coroner, Dr. W. A. Leigh.*

By this it will be seen that your humble servant was not the holder of the lucky ticket which drew the prize for county clerk!

It is usually the case for defeated candidates to be able to give loud and long reasons why they failed to get there, and so, in a measure, it is with me. Certain combinations between Hill and McNutt with the "old soldier" racket playing in Hill's favor were too strong to be overcome. McNutt did considerable double dealing by making pledges entirely at variance with each other. After all, probably the best and most sensible reason why I failed to receive this nomination was that <u>I</u> <u>didn't</u> <u>have</u> <u>the</u> <u>requisite</u> <u>number</u> <u>of</u> <u>votes</u> <u>to</u> <u>make</u> <u>the</u> <u>riffle!!!!</u>

A second term as Justice of the Peace was decided on election day, November 5.

1890

One more obligation came Elam's way when on February 10, 1890: *In the evening went over to the school house where a public meeting was held and C. R. Webbert, Farmer's Alliance organizer, proceeded to form an alliance. I was elected Secretary.*

The Republican nominating convention for the 6th Congressional District, beginning on May 7, was split precariously by the Farmers' Alliance faction: *In company with E. F. Randall, J. T. Locke and others enroute for Colby, left Stockton about 6 oclock a.m. by carriages for Plainville where we arrived about 2½ hours later and met with a number of Plainville folks who were also ready to embark for Colby. We left Plainville about nine oclock and having accomplished a very pleasant 100 mile ride, arrived in Colby at noon and took dinner at the Opelt House where we secured lodging for the time of our sojourn during the convention.*

We found an immense throng of delegates and interested spectators already on the ground. At 4 p.m. an informal meeting of the delegate members of the convention belonging to the Farmer's Alliance was held in the opera block. The meeting was called to order and S. H. Thomas of Ellsworth county was elected chairman and E. Bartholomew of Rooks, secretary. *The object of the meeting was to prepare resolutions at tomorrow's convention, so a committee of three was appointed to draft resolutions to be submitted to the Alliance members at 9 a.m. tomorrow. Passed the evening about the hotel and at our room getting acquainted with delegates and politicians.*

May 8: *Met with over 40 other delegates in the Alliance caucus at 9 a.m. and participated in its proceeding. We soon agreed on a good set of demands to present to the committee on resolutions in the congressional convention when the caucus adjourned to meet on the call of the chairman.*

May 10: *The chairman of the committee, C. J. Evans of Ellsworth county, submitted a partial report, seating 36 Turner delegates and 36 anti-Turner men. This created a great deal of dissatisfaction as nothing less than a full report could be accepted according to parliamentary rules in a case of this kind. After a great deal of speech-making and jangling, that part of the report was adopted by one of the Turner men from Decatur county voting with the opposition.*

Then the committee proceeded to make a specific report on each one of the contested counties, beginning with Jewell. This case was brought up and by another weakening by one of the Turner men the nine Hanback delegates were seated and the convention was then in the hands of the anti-Turner factions and beyond control. The counties of Mitchell and Rooks were next taken up and the Turner and Hanback delegates were given a half vote each.

The mill still went grinding on, unseating the properly and indisputibly elected Turner delegates from Gove, Sherman and Wallace counties, but the steal becoming so flagrant and villainous and the cry of fraud rising louder at each fresh indignity, the convention in its great magnanimity concluded to seat the Turner men from Logan county, which they did.

This took until quite late in the afternoon. The candidates were then placed before the convention in nominating speeches after which balloting commenced, resulting as follows on the first ballot: Turner 45, Hanback 36, McLennan 8, McNall 7, Hamilton 8. Several ballots were taken and after supper voting resumed until about 11:30 p.m. with very little variation; 72 ballots were taken. And adjournment was taken until 8 a.m. Monday morning, May 12.

May 12: *At 4:30 the convention was again called to order and on the first ballot the combined anti-Turner forces controlling 61 votes were cast*

for Webb McNall of Smith county which made him the nominee of the con-
vention, Turner having received only his original strength — 45 votes.

And thus came to a close one of the most remarkable congressional
conventions ever held in the state of Kansas. For downright political chi-
canery, double distilled political intrigue, fraudulent complexion and gen-
eral rottenness, combined with its manifest unfairness and arbitrary pro-
ceedings, it certainly is entitled to a place in our political history as one
of the flattest farces and largest aggregations of fraudulent "Tom-foolery"
that has ever stood up to be counted.

Taking into consideration the methods that were used to secure
McNall's nomination it cannot but bring the greatest dissension in the
Republican party for it is not ready to perpetration and then the perpetu-
ation of the fraudulent action of the convention. The Republican majority
is very large in this district but it seems to me to be very doubtful if the
party is able to carry so heavy a load as that which it will be compelled to
bear up under during the coming campaign, and I for one will not vote for
the nominee of the Colby convention.

On June 17, at the annual election of officers for the Farmers' Alliance,
Elam refused to continue as secretary, but was named "Lecturer." He was
beginning to get uncomfortable with the direction that organization was
going, and he sought a graceful way out.

Still he relished the social relationships offered by the Alliance, as can
be seen on July 18: *Went to Stockton in company with wife, Lizzie and Earl*
and Mr. and Mrs. A. B. Wilson to attend the big Alliance picnic in the
McNulty grove. A very large concourse of people were present and a good
time apparently was enjoyed by all. Van B. Prather, the assistant state Lec-
turer of the Farmer's Alliance, and Martin Mohler, Secy. State Board of
Ag. were present and delivered addresses. I think that for the size of the
crowd I met more persons with whom I was acquainted than in any other
gathering I have ever attended.

Despite this positive note, Elam began to smell a seductive plot, as he
revealed on August 12: *Attended our Alliance in the evening at the school*
house and came home at 11 oclock. Myself and wife have about concluded
that the Farmer's Alliance is a humbug, as nothing whatever seems to be
done but rushing headlong into Alliance politics for the purpose of form-

ing a new party on the plan of the <u>union</u> <u>labor</u> <u>party</u>. The whole busi-ness at this stage of the game seems to me to be a farce, a delusion and a snare.

Another gathering on the 23rd confirmed this attitude: *Went to Stockton to hear Wm. Baker, the Alliance candidate for Congress, make a speech. The meeting was held in the opera house at 2 p.m. and was well attended. O. L. Smith, the dist. lecturer also spoke. Both addresses were simply rehashes of the old Greenback and Union Labor Party doctrines we have been hearing for the past 10 or 12 years.*

A political speech of September 26 was a welcome respite from the dis-tasteful events of recent months: *Went to Stockton to hear a political speech by Ex-Gov. Geo. T. Anthony. The speech was delivered in the opera house at 2 p.m. to a fairly well filled house and was one of the most dig-nified and masterly efforts I have ever heard from a public speaker! Mr. Anthony is certainly an orator of no inferior ability and his smoothly rounded periods and his elegance of diction were an intellectual as well as a political treat.*

Election day, November 4, was a major disappointment: *Learned today* [the 6th] *of the election of the whole Alliance ticket in Rooks county, and many Alliance victories all over Kan. It seems to be a bad "wash-out" for the Republican party, but it certainly is to be hoped that the temporary success of this mushroom party will only cause the people to see more clearly that it is the supremest folly to elect inefficient men to responsible official positions.*

1891

More problems with the Alliance surfaced on November 11, 1891, in connection with the fifth annual Sunday school convention in Farmington township: *The weather was quite cold and blustery and the attendance was not as large as usual. Another cause to make a light attendance was the successful work done in the community by several of the old Nick's agents who not only boycotted the convention themselves but did all that lay in their power to induce others to stay away.*

The parties engaged in this disreputable and unchristian work are members of that delectable and highly moral organization known as the

"Farmer's Alliance". It seems to be the practice and principle of this decaying humbug to oppose almost every effort put forth for the moral and religious development of any given community as is evidenced by the infinitely small number of professing Christians who are connected with it, and its general opposition and hindrance to Sab. school work in all parts of this state!

1892

At the Republican county convention on May 2, 1892, Elam was chosen chairman of the delegates to the gubernatorial convention at Topeka on June 30. This convention would be unique: There would be a speech pleading for women's right to vote, and there would be a candidate for state office of African-American descent.

June 30: *After breakfast spent the time until 10 oclock a.m. in looking about here and there and in conversing with various friends and new-made acquaintances. Among others, had the pleasure of an introduction to my man for governor Hon. A. W. Smith.*

At 10 oclock the convention met at the State house in representative hall and was called to order by W. J. Buchan, chairman of the state central committee. After prayer by Rev. F. S. McCabe the convention proceeded to elect Judge Frank L. Martin of Reno county for Temp. chairman and Chas. M. Sheldon of Osage Co. for Temp. Secy. Then came the usual appointments of the various committees and while waiting for their reports we listened to good and stirring addresses by F. C. Dawes, Susan B. Anthony, J. R. Burton, C. I. Long and J. R. Hallowell.

After the report on permanent organization, making W. P. Hackney permanent chairman, was adopted the convention took a recess until 8 p.m. at which time while waiting for the report of the committee on resolutions we listened to a good address by Chas. Curtis,* candidate for congress in the 4th district. Then came quite a war on the adoption of the platform but it was finally adopted without material change amid great enthusiasm.

July 1: Attended the convention at 9 a.m. and the balloting for governor proceeded. On the second ballot this morning the vote stood as follows: Smith 375, Morrill 279, Murdock 51, Baker 10, and Wright 5. This nomi-

---

* *Charles Curtis, born in Topeka, Kansas, in 1860, served in the U.S. House of Representatives from 1893 to 1907, and in the U.S. Senate from 1907 to 1913 and 1915 to 1929. He was Vice President under Herbert Hoover from 1929 to 1933. His mother was part Kaw Indian.*

nated Smith and of course as is always the case the convention went wild for some minutes in cheering, etc.

From this time until about 2 oclock at night the balloting was almost constant on the other state officers resulting in the following selections: Lieut. Gov. R. F. Moore; Secy. State W. C. Edwards; Auditor B. K. Bruce (colored); Treasurer J. B. Lynch; Atty. Gen. T. F. Garver.

Final results became known on November 14: *Learned today of the positive defeat of the whole Republican state ticket and the consequent election of the whole Demo-Alliance gang! Ah Me!*

1893

By early 1893 the Populist movement in Kansas had become overbearing, bordering on anarchy. What could be called an insurrection took place at the state capitol in Topeka. Situated in that building was B. B. Smyth, librarian for the Kansas Academy of Science and, therefore, a close friend and professional associate of Elam, who by now was maturing in botanical studies. On February 25, Mr. Smyth sent Elam an extensive account of what was going on in the political arena where his office was located.

> The populists having all the state officers, including the treasurer, and the senate without question, do not care for the supreme court, as they can afford to ignore that for the time being, since they are morally certain it would not decide in their favor. Their motto "Rule or Ruin" should be written in letters of fire on their banner instead of the Abraham Lincoln sentiment "a government of the people, by the people, for the people".
>
> The most of them belong to a secret order which holds them by virtue of their oaths. They dare not resist the commands of their leaders. They consider that the governor has imperial powers, and do not consider that he is amenable to law or governed himself by it.
>
> Hence, when the governor ordered Col. J. W. F. Hughes to remove the Republican house from representative hall, they thought he must do it. But Col. Hughes was better posted on law and right than the governor was, and assured the republican house of his protection. The governor, of course, lost no time in dismissing Col. Hughes for insubordination and appointing one of his friends in his stead.

But the new commander found difficulties he little dreamed of on arriving on the scene of action, and found that it was absolutely impossible to do as he wished. What he wanted was to turn the Gattling gun on a lot of unarmed and defenseless men and women, and could find no way to have his desires consummated.

My room is at the foot of the stairs to representative hall — the west stairs. I have not yet been removed from the state house. They have overlooked me so far. Tuesday afternoon the pops brought in some new recruits with loaded guns and marched twenty-five of them up the west stairs to take possession of representative hall. In the meantime recruiting had been going on upstairs. Friends had flocked in, and at the time the pops and the militia came in to go up (about 2:30 in the afternoon) there were fully fifty or more assistant-sergeants-at-arms in the stairs, armed with sticks and two or three revolvers.

About 10 minutes before, I had gone up to the ladies' gallery with two young ladies (my daughter and another who came in with her) and the stairs were so well filled with people that it was not without some difficulty we worked our way through. I watched from the foot of the stairs the militia and pops going up. They didn't go far. They went up the first flight and part of the second. In the scrimmage that ensued one militia man and five pops were disarmed, and the arms carried up stairs to the hall. The militia and pops quietly retired.

The sergeants-at-arms then barricaded the door into the corridor above. One sergeant-at-arms (a student from Washburn college) got his hand squeezed against the wall and cut. That was the only blood drawn. In three minutes the sergeants-at-arms were down at the foot of the stairs searching for some more "pops with guns".

At 5 oclock reinforcements came back for the governor — recruits — such a forlorn and distressed-looking crowd, carrying guns and belts of ammunition from the arsenal, and headed by Hank Lindsay with a drawn sword. As they entered the lower door Lindsay said to his men, "We'll have them out of there, boys, or die in our tracks! Come on now, and have your guns ready!" Such a motley crowd. No militia among them this time, but ragged and desperate looking.

They went up one flight, Lindsay hesitating on every second step to look up. On the first landing he stopped to wait for his men. No man of his was within three steps of him. Half a dozen sergeants-at-arms on the steps just above him had menacing clubs. From the landing above a revolver in the hands of Dr. DeObert pointed directly at Lindsay and a clear voice called out "Stop! Advance one step further, and I'll blow day-light through you!" The men (pops) in the vestibule stepped into the corridor, the men on the lower steps did the same, and in less time than I write it they were all in the corridor, Hank Lindsay and all.

In a few minutes I went up to the ladies' gallery to see if any one was frightened on account of the battle but found every-thing serene. The ladies in the gallery — about 40 of them — seemed to be enjoying themselves greatly and had two of the captured guns in their possession.

A few minutes after 6, and before the ladies had all retired, the pops came again, this time headed by "Lieut." Bennington, who placed guards on all the doors around the capitol and two guards in front of my door with instructions to let no man pass in or out. I stood just inside the door in the vestibule, bare-headed and empty-handed, as I had been all the afternoon. The two sergeants-at-arms that were guarding the door quietly with-drew and retreated up stairs. Presently three ladies came down and wanted to go out. The guards stopped them saying they had orders to let nobody pass. After some parleying, and seeing the ladies were badly frightened, one of the guards said he didn't believe the order was intended to stop ladies from going out, so they allowed them to go.

Just then a half dozen or more sergeants-at-arms came down. I closed the door quickly and locked it, and they took my heavy boxes of books that were in the vestibule and piled them up against the door, and with plank reaching to my paleontological cases against the opposite wall effectually barricaded that door. I then locked the inside door and went out and home through the museum door.

Next day, by order of the governor, no provisions were allowed to be taken up to the besieged party; so it became necessary to invoke the aid of government and send coffee and sandwiches in through the mail by a mail carrier and about twenty assistants. This frequently during the day. About 250 persons were confined there the first night, among them a number of ladies. The number was constantly increased by reinforcements who came in with the provisions and otherwise until on Thursday there were hardly less than 600 persons besieged.

Our mutual friend Prof. W. A. Harshbarger was among those who did valiant service there from first to last. I visited those in the hall every day and gave them such encouragement as I could, passing boys with baskets through my doors and window, but in every case they had to run the gauntlet of the guards which, after the first evening were militia and not populists.

I never saw a happier crowd than the people in representative hall were Thursday morning. A large 50 foot flag had been raised over the west wing and little flags were flying out of every window. The big flag was taken from the speakers stand and the little flags from the wall decorations. At 3 p.m. the people in the hall were released.

The failure of the governor to get the militia to oust the representatives from their hall, and the presence of 1200 deputy sheriffs outside menacing the capitol did more to bring the governor to his senses than anything else. He begged the sheriff to dismiss his deputies, saying he would send the militia home and leave the reps unmolested. He did not, however, send all home, but kept his most reliable company until the following Monday. Sheriff Wilkerson was, however, fully prepared for any move the pops might make, and therefore, knowing that, they made none. A heavy fall of snow Wednesday night no doubt assisted in cooling off the belligerents.

There. I have written of incidents and scenes not generally published. Do not publish this. As you value my usefulness here hereafter do not publish any part of this letter that will give any clue to my identity.

Elam found a September 23 political speech to be obnoxious: *That far-famed populist orator Mrs. Mary E. Lease being billed to speak at the grove* [near Stockton], *wife and I went down to hear her wail a calamity howl or two and got too much in 15 minutes so we went up into town again. A very large crowd of people were in town.*

1894

There was increasing agitation by people desiring voting privileges for women. On June 1, 1894: *At 6 p.m. in company with wife and Mr. and Mrs. A. B. Wilson went to Stockton to hear a woman suffrage lecture by Mrs. Carrie C. Catt** of New York. It was a fine speech to a large audience in the opera house. Got home at midnight.*

And on the next day: *In the p.m. with wife went to Stockton to hear suffrage speeches by Mrs. Catt in the grove at 3 p.m. and by Mrs. Theresa Jenkins of Wyoming in the opera house in the evening.*

It is obvious that Elam was open-minded on the gender issue and favored the suffrage proposition. On September 24 he wrote: *Mr. and Mrs. King came on a visit so the time until noon was spent in social chat, after which we all went to Stockton where at 2 p.m. we listened to a most eloquent address by that famous woman lecturer and politician Mrs. J. Ellen Foster. A very large audience was present.*

1895

The Rockport postoffice moved again. On April 3, 1895: *A. B. Wilson, the Rockport postmaster, being about to leave the county and I being one of his bondmen, with a prospect of shortly being appointed to the office, I removed the office to our house this morning and spent the a.m. in fixing it up in proper shape for my own convenience and for the benefit of the public.*

** *Carrie Chapman Catt, born in Ripon, Wisconsin, in 1859, began organizing suffrage groups in 1887. She was president of the National American Woman Suffrage Association in 1900 to 1904 and 1915 to 1920, when Congress finally extended voting rights to women. Then she founded the National League of Women Voters to help women vote responsibly.*

1898

On August 23, 1898, the county convention nominated Elam to an office of high respect: *Went to Stockton to attend the convention and after being in town a short time I was prevailed upon to allow my name to come before the convention as a candidate for Representative to the Legislature which I did and when the convention met in the afternoon I was nominated on the first ballot.*

This new position necessitated contingent action on the 29th: *While in Stockton resigned my position as postmaster at Rockport on account of being candidate for the legislature. Wife will be recommended for appointment in my place.*

Son George made a special trip home on November 7 to vote for his father. But Elam failed to gather a majority of the votes. On November 9, the day following the election, he recorded: *In the p.m. with Earl went to Stockton where I learned of my defeat as candidate for Representative of Rooks county and the election of my opponent, E. E. Smith. And thus endeth my ambitions to sit as a member of the Kan. legislature!*

To help absorb the shock of defeat he took a trip east the next day to visit relatives and have some sharing time with son George: *Left Stockton on the 6:30 a.m. train for a short visit at cousin Aldus Sharp and family [at Blue Rapids].* Two days later: *With one Ora Ritchie as driver went out with one of Sharp's livery teams 7 miles northeast of town to a Mr. Holt's to see him on business connected with the sale of some cattle which I desire to sell. Meeting no success we returned to town at a little after noon and at 1:40 p.m. I took the east bound train for Kansas City.*

By previous arrangement, George was on the train on his way back to college at Emporia so we journeyed together to Kansas City where we arrived at about 7:30 oclock and getting off at the Wyandotte depot we went direct to brother-in-law John Fink's, 632 Shawnee Ave where we staid all night.

On November 15 George went on to Emporia and Elam went home: *My 6 days outing was a pleasant one indeed after the excitement and vexations of a heated and losing political campaign.*

1900

An attempt was made on April 10, 1900, to provide for a public high school: *From 3 to 4 p.m. was spent in attending the election and voting "yes" on the proposition to establish a high school in Rooks county.* But then, as now, those things are sometimes hard to pass. On the next day: *Went to Stockton on business in the p.m. and while there learned of the defeat yesterday of the county high school proposition.* Soon thereafter, however, one did pass, and son Earl was one of the first students.

Every ten years it was time to take the census, so on June 1, 1900, Elam began again, covering Farmington, Lanark, and Iowa townships. This time he had more stylish government transportation, *travelling in a two-horse top buggy.*

An impressive campaign speech was heard on September 28: *With wife and Mrs. Bracken drove up into town and thence to the R.R. station at 10 oclock where, a half hour later, Governor Theo. Roosevelt of New York, Vice presidential candidate on the Republican ticket with McKinley, passed through on his way east from a campaigning tour in Colorado and stopped long enough to make a stirring little speech. Being quite close to the car we had a good position and could hear every word distinctly.*

Things went well for the Republicans on November 7: *While in town learned of the re-election of President McKinley and the whole Republican state ticket.*

1901

But national tragedy struck on September 6, 1901: *Just as we were about to leave town* [Stockton] *learned of the assassination of President McKinley at Buffalo, N.Y. this afternoon!* Actually he did not die until the 14th, the first anniversary of the funeral of son George.

1903

While on a trip farther west in Kansas on his duties as Sunday school missionary, Elam felt compelled to make a political observation. On June 18, 1903, at Sharon Springs: *The meeting was held in the neat brick church in which President Roosevelt attended services the 3rd of last month while on his trip to the Pacific coast. Sat part of the day in the same pew in which "Teddy" sat, but I have a very severe headache this evening! Was the strain too much for me, I wonder?*

1904

The elections of 1904 went exactly as Elam had hoped. On Wednesday, November 9: *Learned this morning by the mail carrier of the overwhelming election of Roosevelt and the Republican state and county tickets. Am I feeling jubilant? Well, I guess yes!*

1908

On March 26, 1908, Elam was a delegate to the Congressional District Convention to select two delegates to the Republican National Convention at Chicago in June. One of those chosen was Otis Benton of Oberlin. Benton Hall, on the campus of Washburn University in Topeka, was named in honor of this family.

Elections of 1908 went well again for the Republicans. On November 4: *Learned today of the election of Taft and the whole Republican ticket generally as voted for yesterday.*

1910

Again in 1910 Elam was Census Enumerator for the same three townships, beginning on April 15 and finishing on May 11: *Thus ended my term as enumerator in this county — 1890 — 1900 — 1910. Compensation this year $5.00 per day of 8 hours.*

Most of the remainder of the month was spent in Washington, D.C., attending the World Sunday School Convention. Naturally he found time to see various sights about the area. Kansas Congressman W. A. Reeder escorted him on more than one occasion. One outstanding event was a personal visit with President Taft at his office on May 23.

1912

The election of 1912 obviously did not go well for Republicans, because Elam makes no comment. The organization was split by formation of a Progressive Party, which nominated Teddy Roosevelt again for President, while Republicans stuck with Taft for a second term. The result was a huge victory for Woodrow Wilson and the Democrats.

1914

Elam dallied for a time with the Progressives, also dubbed the "Bull Moose" Party. (They tried to nominate Roosevelt again in 1916, but he refused, and the party went into hibernation.) As a delegate to the

Progressive Party's state convention in Topeka, Elam was impressed by speeches on February 12, 1914: *At 2 p.m. went with wife and cousin Tillie Montgomery to the Grand Opera House to attend the big mass meeting where addresses were made by Congressman Victor Murdock, William Allen White, Henry Allen and that matchless orator, Raymond Robbins of Chicago. I, in my time, have attended many political meetings but I think this one eclipsed, in enthusiasm, anything I have heretofore witnessed.*

Despite Elam's enthusiastic response to the convention, he never mentions the Progressive Party again. He was losing his political vigor of younger years as he became increasingly involved in botanical matters, so he essentially dropped out of political action.

1916

One of the most influential of all Kansas politicians of that era gave a speech on October 11, 1916: *With Earl, Alice and wife drove to Stockton where at 10:30 a.m. we went to the opera house and heard a political address by Gov. Capper on the issues of the day.* Capper, a Republican, went on to become a U.S. Senator for 30 years, from 1919 to 1949. He was a newspaper publisher, he had two radio stations, and he published a group of farm periodicals.

Another prominent politician of Kansas origins had been on the campaign trail earlier that year while Elam was in Denver. On August 26 Elam wrote: *In the evening at 7 oclock I went to the auditorium and by 8 a 15,000 audience had gathered to greet and hear a speech by Hon. Chas. E. Hughes, Republican candidate for president. It was the greatest and most inspiring political gathering I have ever seen or ever expect to see!*

1917

Deterioration of the political scene in Europe reached a climax on February 3, 1917: *While in town heard by telegram that the United States had severed diplomatic relations with Germany at 8:30 a.m. today, and that a grave national crisis is at hand.* In April the U.S. entered the war.

A recently installed minister stirred things up on December 30: *Attended S.S. at 10:30 a.m. at Mt. Nebo and at 11:30 listened to a ridiculously semi-pro-German sermon by Rev. Haberly from 1st Tim. 6:12 which was anything but edifying!*

1918

During 1918 Elam and his family became heavily involved with the war effort, especially War Bond and Red Cross campaigns. On May 20: *As township chairman of the Second Red Cross War Drive I met, at 7 a.m., W. S. Southard, Earl Bartholomew, L. L. Marshall, Tom Shaw, Harvey Cooper, Floyd Bartholomew and A. S. Foster at the home of the latter and we soon arranged the company into three soliciting committees to canvass the township for the purpose of raising the sum of $270 which is our quota.*

Foster, Marshall, Cooper and I took the south half of the township and the other fellows the north half. In the south we used one car and in the north two were used. We closed the campaign at 4 p.m. with $280! The one committee on the south side raised $151 while the two on the north side raised $129!

While on an auto trip, Elam saw the major military establishment in Kansas in war readiness. On August 16: *Went to Camp Funston for a view of the great Cantonment, to the high hill at the north where almost every building in the great group is visible at a glance! About 60,000 soldiers are now encamped at this place, many of which are negroes from the southern states. A grand and never-to-be-forgotten sight! We then past by the lower detention camps and on through the grounds of Fort Riley and past the upper (negro) detention camp to Junction City.*

At the county fair on September 6: *The military display made by seven companies of Uniformed State Guards from the surrounding towns was fine indeed. In the evening, up town, the band concert and the lowering of the flag service were also very fine.*

There was great jubilation on November 11: *Learned this afternoon of the signing, in Europe, of the great world war armistice! And thus has fallen autocracy by the unconditional surrender of Germany, Austria, Turkey and Bulgaria to the victorious armies of the Allies! Praises be!*

1919

While at Smith Center on April 16, 1919, to attend the presbytery, the group took a recess to participate in a fund-raising event to help retire the war debt: *At 3 p.m. we took a recess to see the great war tank demonstration in boosting the 4,500,000,000 Victory loan!*

1920

When attending the state Sunday school convention in Topeka on

May 4, 1920, Elam was paid a real compliment: *Judge John Dawson of the state Supreme Court complimented me very highly on the write-up given me in the American Magazine last November and remarked in passing that "when a man breaks into the magazines the next step is to run for United States Senator!"* Of course, he never did.

Election day on November 2 found Elam again strongly in favor of the Republican ticket: *In the p.m. with wife, Lee and Lily in the car drove over S.E. two miles to the polling place at Wyatt McKenzie's where I exercized the rights of an American citizen by casting a most emphatic vote for the Republican ticket from Harding and Coolidge down to the township officers with the exception of one man on the county ticket!*

Then the next day: *Learned of the definite and overwhelming election of Harding and Coolidge and all the state and county ticket with the exception of J. W. Burton for Probate Judge. It is a most glorious Democratic washout!*

1921
The new President took over on March 4, 1921: *The last day of Wilsonism and autocratic government for the U.S. for awhile at least!*

One of the young men of the neighborhood was a casualty in the World War. On June 26, 1921: *Drove to Stockton where at 3 oclock at the cemetery we attended the military funeral of Chester Bird who lost his life in the battle of the Argonne Forest in Sept. 1918 and was returned from France. Impressive service and large crowd present.*

1922
With economic inflation following the war, taxes went up, and so did the tempers of taxpayers. On February 2, 1922: *In the p.m. with Lee and Lily drove to Stockton in the auto and at 2 oclock attended, at the court house, a mass meeting called for the purpose of organizing a "Tax Payer's League" as a protest against the rapid increase in general and especially school taxes as manifest in the exorbitant wages asked and paid to the country district school teachers, ranging from $85 to $125 per month!*

A. G. Schneider was made chairman and Carl Brown Secy. I was made chairman of the committee on resolutions with four other members.

I think I may safely say that it was the largest civic county meeting ever held at Stockton. The temporary organization was made permanent. Enthusiasm boiled and boiled and boiled and ran over!

1923

Another President died while in office, but not by assassination this time. On August 3, 1923: *About 2:30 p.m. today we got the sad news of the sudden and unexpected death of President Harding at San Francisco last night at 7:30 oclock.*

1928

A crucial election on November 6, 1928, brought out voters' biases and caused considerable polarization during a time of social upheaval: *We all voted for Hoover & Curtis, with all our might praying that the wet Catholic, Al Smith, and all that he stands for will be everlastingly snowed under!* At issue primarily was Smith's affiliation with the Tammany Hall machine of New York, and his opposition to prohibition. His religious orientation was interjected by opponents as a convenient wedge.

The next day: *Learned rather early last night that in all probability Hoover was overwhelmingly elected and that was that! While in Stockton learned for a fact that the National Republican ticket was elected by the most emphatic majority ever given to any presidential candidate.*

Seemingly almost everything north of Mason & Dickson's line and much south of it slid over into the Republican camp! Kansas reported over 300,000 majority for Hoover! This was the most gratifying all round election I have ever known! Amen & Amen!

1930

Elections of 1930 were disquieting. On November 5: *Up town on business awhile and getting the astonishing election news resulting from the action of the people yesterday, not only in Kansas but throughout the United States wherein there was a veritable landslide to the Democratic nominees!!!*

1932

Elam was obviously apprehensive about results of the 1932 election. On November 9: *Learned today of the defeat of President Hoover for re-elec-*

tion and the success of Franklin D. Roosevelt for the place. Seemingly pretty bad medicine!

1933

One of his worst fears was realized on February 20, 1933: *Congress disgraced itself today by voting to submit a repeal amendment to do away with the 18th or Prohibition amendment to the U.S. Constitution! And may the Devil take the foremost as well as the hindmost too!*

Chapter 9

Botanical Interests

ARLY ON, Elam grasped the significance of fungi as the cause of many plant diseases, and he set about collecting and correctly identifying those that are parasitic on grasses and other plants. It was not long before he clearly knew more about fungi, particularly the plant-parasitic fungi, than anyone else did for this part of the world.

Any mycological herbarium or laboratory with pretensions to the ability to identify fungi and sort out the correct names for them must either possess or have access to Elam's work. His work retains its utility in large part because of its thoroughness and accuracy. From our time, we biologists look back at him in admiration.

Theodore M. Barkley, professor and curator
Herbarium, Kansas State University, Manhattan

1882

The year was 1882. Elam was 30 years old, and it was eight years since he had first come to Kansas, six since he had married and permanently settled on his homestead. A lot of things were different from what he had known as a child in Ohio or as an adolescent and young man in Illinois. The greatest difference was in the grasses, wild flowers, other plants, shrubs, and trees, though some were similar. With these he was especially fascinated; they presented his keen, inquisitive mind with just the right amount of challenge.

On August 11, Elam first revealed an interest that was destined to become his career and major passion for the next 50-plus years: *Went up the creek about two miles in the a.m. collecting botanical specimens and getting home at noon worked in the p.m. for Theo. Allen raking hay.* He took the plants home so that he could identify them either from books on hand or by asking neighbors and visitors if they could identify them. He would not be content until names were known for everything growing in the area. It was intolerable to be asked "What is that?" and not be able to answer.

1883

The next date on which the subject was mentioned was six months later, on February 24, 1883: *The weather being blustery the day was passed in reading and botanical study.*

Another brief comment appears on July 4: *Very independent indeed! Did no work whatever! Spent the day in botanizing, reading and recreation.*

1884

On February 21, 1884, Elam wrote of his interest in botany to his close friend, who was a spiritual companion: *Went to Stockton to mill and to attend to other business. Took dinner by invitation at Rev. F. E. Sherman's where I spent several hours very pleasantly conversing on botanical and other subjects.*

A botanical expedition is combined with a family outing on June 14: *Went to Stockton on miscellaneous business. Georgie and Brother Frank were along and we spent several hours above the mill fishing and botanizing. Found few new specimens and fewer fish.*

Major inspiration was received when a professional in botanical sciences came for a visit on August 7: *In the evening Prof. E. N. Plank of Independence, Kan. came to our place on a botanizing tour and put up with us for the night. Mr. Plank is a botanist and lecturer of considerable note in this state and is engaged in the compilation of a Flora of Kansas. As I have been paying some attention to botany for several years Mr. P. will remain with us some days investigating my botanical labors and botanizing in this part of the country.*

The next five days were very affirming, fixing indelibly the course of the remainder of Elam's life. Then on the 12th: *Took Prof. Plank over to Marvin in the morning and returned home at 2:30 oclock p.m. working the remainder of the day at stacking wheat as yesterday. Mr. Plank expects to take the morning train for Beloit at which place he expects to lecture and botanize for several days. We found the professor to be a genial, intelligent, well bred gentleman, also a student and worker.*

1885

A major event occurred on July 16, 1885: *About 4:30 p.m. Profs Geo. H. Failyer and Wm. A. Kellerman of the Ag. College at Manhattan (established in 1863), accompanied by two of the students of that institution pulled in to our place expecting to spend several days in scientific research in this vicinity.* On the next day Elam was given more specific focus for his scientific interests in botany, but geology was enticing also: *In company with Prof. Failyer went over NW about eight miles on a geological exploring expedition to a place where a large number of exceedingly large fossil bones have been found and carried away. After quite a long and arduous search we returned at 4 p.m. having obtained very little to reward us for our trip. Later in the evening Prof. Kellerman and I spent some time in looking over my botanical collections and discussing the flora of this region. Last evening both the professors spent several hours discussing scientific subjects with us. They have their tent pitched on the north side of the creek opposite the house.*

A lifelong professional friendship had been fixed into place. The pair left on the 18th: *About noon the scientific company struck camp and proceeded eastward, they having been out to the west line of the state. We found them to be exceedingly agreeable and entertaining sojourners.* Before departing they "inadvertently" left behind a microscope for Elam's use — something he could not afford. Its "mysterious disappearance" enabled it to be written off college inventory.

Kellerman and others returned often, and the Bartholomew farm became a place for agricultural crop experimentation. The hospitality was shared willingly, and Elam's fertile mind flourished under such scientific stimulus.

1886

Elam's interest in geology had been stimulated, as well, by the visit of the Kansas State professor. On January 7 and 8, 1886: *These two days being exceedingly cold the time was spent pretty closely within doors, devoting a large part of the time to reading "Geology" from LeConte.* The weather again kept him indoors from the 11th through the 13th, so he delved deeper into LeConte's book.

Elam decided to slightly enlarge his botanical horizon on May 28: *Took a load of corn to Stockton. After taking dinner at the Commercial house, brother Frank who was with me, Benj. Cobb, a student of the State University with whom we met in town, and I went over on the bluffs south of Stockton on a botanical expedition and returned to town at 4 oclock well paid for our trip.*

A surprise visitor arrived on July 17: *Shortly after 7 oclock who should come along but our old friend Prof. E. N. Plank. He's still at work collecting the flora of Kansas preparatory to publishing a work covering the state suitable for the schools as well as a book of reference for all lovers and students of Kansas botany. He will remain with us until Monday and then go to Stockton where he will make arrangements to lecture five nights next week on the subject of Botany.* The next day was Sunday: *Passed the time until 3 p.m. in reading and in social chat with Prof. Plank looking over my botanical specimens and then attended Sab. School and listened to a good talk by Mr. Plank.*

Elam had to work around the farm the next week, missing the nightly lectures, but on Saturday the 24th he had a unique experience that delighted him considerably: *Went to Stockton where I arrived at noon and took dinner by invitation at the residence of Rev. F. E. Sherman. After dinner Mr. Sherman and I went out botanizing NW of town about a mile where I found several plants new to the flora of Rooks County. In the evening attended the last of Prof. Plank's lectures at the Congregational church and was highly pleased and entertained with it. After the lecture the Prof. accompanied me home where we arrived shortly after midnight.*

Sunday the 25th was even more stimulating: *Passed the time until*

3 p.m. in social chat and in looking over his collection of southern Kansas plants and then attended Sab. school while the Prof. staid at home. Did not stay to hear sermon by Mr. Bracken. Started with Mr. Plank to Stockton where we arrived about 6:30 oclock. After supper at Rev. Sherman's went to the Congregational church where Mr. Plank delivered his celebrated lecture on "The Immortality of the Soul" which was one of the best lectures I have ever heard on any subject. His mastery of language and eloquence of diction coupled with his richness of imagery and delightful rhetoric made it a feast of fat things long to be remembered. In company with the Prof. put up for the night at the Commercial House.

Monday was another great experience: *Immediately after breakfast at the hotel attached my team to Mr. Sherman's buggy and in company with Prof. Plank started on a botanizing tour toward the SW part of the county. Went up the river from Stockton 10 miles botanizing somewhat on the way passing through Webster about 10 oclock and continuing on arrived at the residence of E. M. Backus 6 miles S of Webster at 11:30 oclock where we stopped for dinner. After dinner spent 2 hours botanizing on Lost Creek and then hitching up again went on SW about 5 miles to C. A. Fesler's where we put up for the night.*

Things took a turn for the worse the next day: *In the morning resumed our travels in a SW course passing the Amboy postoffice and down into Hamilton township, Ellis county, thence across the Saline River about three miles where we stopped at the residence of one Caleb Thayer where we took dinner. At this place I parted with Prof. Plank who continued on his journey afoot toward Ellis at which place he expects to lecture this week, while I turned to the NE and travelled in that direction until toward evening and put up at the Watson Bros. sheep ranch on Sand creek in the SE corner of Walton Tp. Rooks county 10 miles SW of Plainville. One of my horses, a sorrel mare recently purchased, seemed to be rather under the weather with an acute attack of dysentery and would eat no feed, though apparently suffering no pain. Late in the evening went to the stable and found her apparently better so retired for the night.*

Then matters became more distressing the following day: *On going to the stable this morning my feelings can better be imagined than described when I found my horse stretched out dead! Here was rather an unfortunate and embarrassing state of affairs and I 35 miles from home. After breakfast we hauled the dead horse out and one of the Watson brothers, Ed, put one of their horses in with mine and taking his saddle along accompanied me to Plainville where we arrived shortly before 11 oclock and stopped until after dinner. Here I got a horse at the livery stable to take me to Stockton while Mr. Watson took his horse and saddle and returned home. I arrived in Stockton at 4 oclock and after stopping there about an hour re-engaged my livery horse which was owned in Stockton, and came home where I arrived at 7:30 oclock.* (This horse had to be returned to Stockton the next morning.)

In a few days, however, there was an encouraging development that raised Elam's spirits. August 4: *Went to Stockton to mill, botanizing near there finding several plants new to any Rooks county flora.* And a month later, on September 6, Elam is pleased to have a visit from a local citizen who shares his interests: *At 3:30 oclock Benj. Cobb of Stockton, a student at Kansas University, came here on a botanical visit so further manual labor for the day was suspended and scientific research and mental labor were substituted. The gentleman came over to have me help him in his botanical investigations and stayed all night.*

1887

Profs Plank and Kellerman had stressed to Elam the importance of specializing in a specific aspect of botany if he wanted to make a significant impact. His focus becomes evident on February 19, 1887: *George and I went up the creek about two miles and spent the forenoon in botanizing among the mosses, lichens, and stump fungi.* This branch of botany, called mycology — the fungus diseases of plants — was just moving into the center stage of importance in the field of sickness and disease control for animals and humans as well as plants.

1888

The year 1888 began with Elam *classifying and arranging a number of botanical specimens (fungi)* on January 10 to 14. Then a most welcome visitor came on August 3: *In the evening about 7:30 oclock who should come down upon us but my old botanical friend, Prof. F. N. Plank of Wyandotte, who is on his last tour through the state previous to the publication of his Flora of Kansas.* Next day: *Passed the day in social and scientific chat and in botanizing in the neighborhood with Prof Plank.* Then the following day: *Attended Sab school at 10 a.m. and at 11 listened to a very interesting talk by Prof Plank on the subject of the importance of Biblical knowledge. Came home at 12:30 oclock and at 3 p.m. the Prof and I took a little 6 mile trip out to the Sugar Loaf mound returning home at 7 oclock.*

It is plain to see that Professor Plank was more than just a scientific mentor to Elam in his formative years in the studies of botany. The professor was his ideal — a person who was proficient in his field and at the same time a spiritual person who was not shy in proclaiming his religious convictions.

1889

Elam became more serious about his botanical work January 16 to 19, 1889: *Spent the four days in reading and writing and botanical study, also preparing about 100 specimens of parasitic fungi to be sent to Prof W. A. Kellerman of Manhattan for identification.* By February 22 he was positively elated with the results: *Returns received from the package of fungi sent away the latter part of last month prove to be very gratifying as a number of them were found to be entirely new to science. One of the species — Diplodina Bartholomi — being named in my honor as its discoverer.* From then on there was no way to slow him down in this scientific pursuit.

1890

By early 1890 Elam's work in botany was well enough developed that he felt justified in calling his specimen collection an herbarium. On January 20 to 25: *Spent these six days almost entirely in reading, writing and botanical study and work with herbarium specimens, sending plants away for identification or exchange to Profs W. A. Kellerman, Manhattan, M. A. Carleton, Wichita and E. N. Plank of Kansas City, Kan.*

On February 7, during the annual meeting of the Farmers' Institute, held at Stockton, Elam presented a talk entitled "What is the cause of the Corn-Stalk disease in Cattle?" He described it as *quite a lengthy paper advocating the "germ theory."* The topic was on the cutting edge of new developments in plant and animal science. The "germ theory of diseases" had just recently been publicized. A German physician, Robert Koch, grew a pure strain of anthrax bacillus in 1876 and then determined how to inoculate cattle as a preventive measure against the disease. This was the first such identification and cure. Then Louis Pasteur took these findings and in 1881 proved further that cattle and sheep could be protected from anthrax and chickens from cholera by vaccination. One year later came the control of rabies.

This progress assured Elam that he was on the right track in specializing in mycology. How exciting to be involved in the sector of science shared by Louis Pasteur and others! The world was slowly beginning to accept the idea that bacteria (germs) were the cause of many diseases and disorders and that behind many of those problems lay a fungus. The challenge was to discover which ones caused which problems. That was beyond the scope of Elam's capabilities.

What Elam could do, and in fact had begun to do just a few years after the Koch and Pasteur discoveries, was to systematically collect, identify, and classify fungus organisms and supply these to the scientists doing research on bacterial relationships to disease and disorders.

Elam's list of professional contacts increased on February 26: *The weather being still colder than yesterday the day was spent in reading, writing and preparing a lot of botanical specimens to send to Dr. J. H. Oyster of Paola, Kan.*

Elam's horizons expanded considerably with a visit to Kansas State College, where Dr. Kellerman taught. Elam had been to Louisville, Kansas — a little east of Manhattan — to visit his brother Eli. On October 21: *I took the 3 p.m. train from Wamego to Manhattan at which place I arrived a half hour later where I stopped off to pay a two day's visit to the Agricultural College. On going up into town I met Prof C. C. Georgeson. I told the professor I desired to be directed to the residence of my valued botanical correspondent, Prof W. A. Kellerman. The Professor kindly invited me to get into his carriage and he would take me up to the college where I would find Mr. Kellerman.*

On arriving at the college we did not find the object of our search so I was taken over to Prof. K's residence where I met Mrs. K. and the three children but had to wait about a half hour before the Professor came in. He greeted me very cordially and made me feel very welcome and perfectly at home. While at Louisville I had received a letter from him inviting me to share the hospitality of his roof while visiting the college.

After supper the Prof. and I took a stroll down to the residence of Prof. S. C. Mason, Foreman in Horticulture, where we spent a pleasant half hour. I had met Mr. Mason at our Institute in Stockton the 6th of last Feb. I then returned with Prof. K. to his house where I put up for the night.

The next day: *With Prof. Kellerman, went over to the college grounds where we visited his office in the Horticultural Building. Here I met Mr. W. T. Swingle, the assistant botanist, with whom I have had much correspondence relating to parasitic fungi. Mr. Swingle is certainly a man who will make his mark in the world as a scientist of a high order as indicated by papers already published.*

At 8:30 oclock we went to the chapel and I had the pleasure of occupying a seat on the platform where I had a good view of the 475 students present. The exercizes consisted of music, scripture reading, prayer and a short address by President Fairchild. Just before going into chapel I met Prof. Failyer. At the same time also met and had introductions to Profs. Lantz, Graham, White and Hood. Immediately after chapel I was conducted by Prof. Kellerman to hear a class recitation on horticulture by Prof. E. A. Poponoe whose acquaintance I then formed. He was a man I have long wished to meet. I then accompanied Prof. Kellerman to attend a class recitation by him on physiology. I then went to the botanical laboratory where I spent a short time in conversation with Mr. Swingle after which I went with Prof. K. to visit the workshop where we were shown about by Prof. Hood.

From there we went to visit the printing office where I formed the acquaintance of the foreman Mr. Thompson. We then visited the kitchen under the superintendance of the bright and vivacious Mrs. Kedzie. (By the way Mrs. K. gave both the Prof. and I each a dough nut!)

We then went to dinner at Prof. K's and immediately thereafter he hitched up to his buggy and we took a ride up N.W. about a mile to the old college farm, and on our return went to the propagating house connected with the U.S. Experiment Station, after which my friend, Mr. Mason, took me for an hour's stroll over the college campus and adjoining grounds to show me the trees, shrubbery, etc. etc. It was then sundown so I went back to Prof. Kellerman's for supper and to spend the night.

The visit to Manhattan ended the following day: *Went in the morning to the college grounds and going direct to the green house was shown through that splendid institution by Mr. Baxter the supt. I stayed here so long that I missed the chapel exercises. From the green house I went to hear a recitation by Prof. Georgeson's fourth year class in agriculture relative to stock breeding. After this time I spent a very pleasant hour with Prof. G. looking through the barn and stables. From there I went with my friend and botanical correspondent, Mr. W. T. Swingle, to the chemical laboratory where I saw a most magnificent mineralogical collection and other things of interest at the hands of Assistant Breese.*

I was then met again by Prof. Kellerman who took me to see the library, drawing room, music room and from there to the entomological department where I had an opportunity of seeing the insects and various sections of different woods. I then bade adieu to the college grounds and went with Prof. K. to dinner, after which he took me down town where I parted with him and getting aboard the 3 p.m. Rock Island train to the west for Phillipsburg, proceeding very pleasantly along a good road bed and arriving at Phillipsburg at 10 oclock p.m. where I met wife and Elbert who had come to meet me. We proceeded at once to Rev. Bracken's where we passed the night.

My visit to the college, my kind reception by Prof. and Mrs. Kellerman and the kindness shown me by each one with whom I came in contact will remain sources of lasting pleasure and gratification.

1891

After such an experience of immersion in academia, Elam is stimulated to assert himself in a more professional dedication to his botanical work. On January 14 to 16, 1891: *Worked hard each of these days and late at night in mounting botanical specimens to be comprised in the Stockton Academy Herbarium and in my own private Herbarium. The Academy Herbarium is to consist, as far as my mounting is concerned, simply of the plants of Rooks Co. Kan. while my herbarium will not only include these but also plants from many other parts of the U. S. and Europe.* (The academy was the equivalent of high school — in effect, a college prep institution.) From the 19th to the 24th: *Worked assiduously each of these six days and late at night mounting botanical specimens.* More again on the 26th and 27th: *Worked these two days at botanical work as last week, and about completed the work as far as I am able to go until I get returns from plants previously sent away for identification. I have mounted about 650 specimens.*

Elam's botanical skills faced a real challenge when he began a program in applied technology on October 9: *Worked on commencing the seeding of wheat on a 132 plot of land under the direction of the U.S. Department of Agriculture, treating the various plots in different ways for the prevention of rusts. I have been appointed a special agent for the prosecution of this work. It is a very difficult piece of business and will require some skill and much patience as well as some very fine work.* This appointment allowed him to experience the practical application of his interest in botanical science, and he became even more dedicated to his vocational calling.

Tests began on October 29: *Worked at spraying 20 of my experimental wheat plots with various fungicides.* And on December 17: *Prepared chemical solutions and did my regular 10-day spraying on my experimental plots.* Finally on the 19th: *Received today my commission as special agent of the U. S. Dept. of Agriculture at the salary of $20 per month.* And the work continued on the 21st: *Spent almost the entire day in microscopic work on parasitic fungi infesting wheat. My work was only satisfactory in part.*

On December 29, there was another enlightening experience: *H. B. Wilson and I went to Stockton to hear Prof. F. H. Snow of the State University lecture on "The Story of the Bacteria". We got to town about dark and after putting our team away we went to the opera house where through the kindness of my friend Rev. F. E. Sherman I had an introduction to the reknowned professor and also a pleasant chat on scientific subjects. The lecture, which treated much on the germ theory of diseases, and especially on the new mode of chinch bug destruction, was a most excellent one and attentively listened to by a large and appreciative audience. Came home shortly after 11 oclock p.m. well pleased with the trip.* Again Elam was affirmed in his dedication to collection and identification of fungi specimens, and he was greatly enlarging the scope of study and discovery in laboratories of research everywhere.

1892

The first day of 1892 began with a satisfying task: *Worked at preparing packages of fungi to send to the Division of Vegetable Pathology of the U.S. Dept. of Agriculture at Washington.*

More experimental work was begun on April 8, this time with spring-planted varieties: *With Elbert's help worked hard at putting in a 100-plot tract of wheat and oats similar to the one last October, for experimenting in the prevention of rusts.*

Assistance was requested for fungi specimens on the 20th: *Packed saprophytic fungi* [living on dead or decaying organic matter] *to send to Prof. A. P. Morgan of Preston, Ohio for identification.*

On October 13 Elam filed his 33-page report of rust prevention on wheat and oats — printed on large "foolscap" paper. A week later he was awaiting word from Washington about the next season's work, so he sent a telegram from Stockton. Instructions were received and the project continued — spraying every ten days after the crop sprouted.

1893

Elam gave a botanical talk on February 4, 1893: *At 9:30 a.m. went to the Stockton Academy and a half hour later delivered an address before the students and faculty of that institution on "Why Study Botany?" The address seemed to be well received and the reception and words of commendation given at its close were quite gratifying to myself.*

On March 10 Elam became a sales agent for fruit tree sprayers: *Being agent for the sale of the Wm. Stahl spraying machines I made a trip up north west and north about five miles, taking dinner at John Van Horn's. Met with fair success in the sale of machines and came home at five oclock p.m.* Similar trips were made. The units arrived on April 20, and he delivered them.

Later, while in Washington, D.C., as a delegate to the Presbyterian General Assembly, Elam found time to solidify and expand his botanical interests. On May 19: *Soon as I could get a bite of dinner (they call it lunch here) I made a trip down to the U.S. Department of Agriculture where I called on Prof. B. T. Galloway, Chief of the Division of Vegetable Pathology, under whose direction I have been carrying on the experiments looking toward the prevention of rusts in wheat and oats during the past 18 months. I found him to be very sociable and apparently well pleased to see me. I also met Prof. Erwin F. Smith and Mr. P. H. Dorsett of the same division with whom I had pleasant chats. Prof. Galloway took me to the division of Botany where I met Mr. F. V. Coville, the genial head of that division and with whom I formed a very pleasant acquaintance.*

Weather in 1893 did not favor the government field tests. On August 2: *Worked in the a.m. at making my report to the Sec'y of Agriculture on the Rust prevention experiments carried on here this year, which were a complete failure on account of drought.*

By December 15 Elam had accumulated 1,000 duplicate fungi specimens, so he exchanged them with other collectors for some he did not have. For example, on January 10, 1894, some specimens from

W. C. Blasdale of Berkeley, California, arrived. On the 30th others came
from C. L. Shear of Alcove, New York.

1894

Elam was becoming even more dedicated to his botanical vocation. On
February 13, 1894: *Having decided to compile for publication a complete
list of all species of Kansas Fungi so far as our present knowledge goes, I
devoted nearly all of the time today at work on this line. The work being
of a scientific nature, one must "hasten slowly" to avoid mistakes, so I will
be a number of days in completing the work — probably not having the
manuscript ready for the printer before May.*

A week later Elam sent some specimens to J. B. Ellis of Newfield, New
Jersey, for identification.

Elam's botanical interest made him aware of the medicinal merit of
some plants — and of the commercial value when suitable quantities
could be gathered. On November 21: *In the p.m. with Elbert went over
north about 7 miles to dig Echinacea roots for shipment to Lloyd Bros.
Wholesale Druggists, Cincinati, Ohio. We got 33 pounds of the green root
and came home at 4:30 p.m.*

Elam made collection trips on numerous days during the next four
weeks, going in various directions from the homestead. Then on December 22: *Went to Stockton to take over my first shipment of 100 lbs. of dried
Echinacea root for shipment to Cincinati, Ohio, for which I am to get
$25.00.* It is noteworthy that many people still prefer the medicinal preparations from this plant for treating colds and sinus conditions.

1895

Elam's fungi collection kept growing. On October 1, 1895: *Spent the
day mostly in making preparations for exhibits to be made at the county
fair which begins tomorrow at Stockton. One of my exhibits in the Scientific Department will be my cabinet which contains about 3200 specimens
of fungi from various parts of the world.* It seems safe to say that there
never was another county fair anywhere with such an exhibit, and it was
presented by a local resident.

Visual aids for speakers reached a new dimension when on October 19:
*Went to Stockton where in the evening at the Congregational church I gave
a stereopticon lecture on botany for the benefit of the church. Attendance
good!*

Handwritten labels were used on packets in Elam's file which he collected himself on dates specified.

FUNGI COLUMBIANI.———E. Bartholomew.

2785. Ramularia Desmodii, Cke.
1878 : Hedwigia **17** : 39.

On *Meibomia canescens.*

Emporia, Kansas, Sept. 17, 1908.   J. E. Bartholomew
E. C. Colpitts

Kellerman & Swingle—Kansas Fungi.

30. Aecidium tuberculatum E. & K.
Journal of Mycology, IV, 26.

On leaves of *Callirrhoe involucrata* Gr.

Rockport, Rooks Co., Kansas, May 20, 1889.
George E. Bartholomew.

These printed labels were glued onto handmade packets into which were placed individual specimens. The top line indicates which collection it was a part of. The bottom line identifies the collector, with location and date.

1896

A new piece of office equipment was of great help. On January 13, 1896: *Worked at making copy of exchange list of Kansas fungi and multiplying impressions of the same on the mimeograph.*

One of the botanists with whom Elam corresponded lived not far from where Elam had grown up. On February 1: *Spent the time until 2 p.m. in reading and botanical work — getting out for mailing 125 flowering plants for Dr. W. E. Damon of Williamsville, Ill.*

Elam's reputation as a good source for fungi specimens continued to spread. On March 12: *Completed the job of getting out 375 packets of fungi for Dr. Wm. Trelease of the Missouri Botanical Garden at St. Louis, and also 100 for Dr. L. M. Underwood of Auburn, Alabama.*

1897

Preparations were made on January 6, 1897, for even more exchanges: *Calculating to make some quite extensive exchanges in fungi with mycologists in various parts of the United States and Canada, the day was spent in making mimeograph copies of a list of such fungi as I have in duplicate for exchange — 445 types with their various hosts.*

It is especially satisfying for a botanical scientist to discover something new and be able to give it a name. Elam had such a thrill on January 18: *Spent the p.m. at work with the microscope among my fungi. Wrote three original descriptions of new species, viz. <u>Macrosporium negundinicolum</u>, <u>Cytospora Amorphae</u> and <u>Cytospora leucosticta</u>.*

More specimens were sent to New York on March 22: *Spent the day in writing and botanical work — got out 174 specimens of fungi for Prof. Geo. F. Atkinson of Ithaca, N.Y.* Two days later some were sent to Ohio: *Worked in the a.m. at getting out a lot of fungi for C. G. Lloyd of Cincinati, Ohio.*

1898

Nothing significant developed in botanical endeavors for the balance of 1897 and much of the next year. Elam devoted considerable time to the effort of establishing Sunday schools in the county. Then on November 24, 1898, came news of one of the most gratifying events possible: *A letter came today from Prof. Geo. L. Clothier of Manhattan announcing the rather pleasing intelligence that on the 16th the Regents of the State Agricultural College had conferred on me the degree of Master of Science for proficiency in botanical and horticultural researches.*

In consideration of this honor Elam began writing a scientific treatise on December 9 and 10: *Worked each of these two days in the preparation of a monograph on the "Kansas Uredineae" — the rust spores of fungus that spread to other plants.*

1899

More fungi specimens were requested, and Elam was glad to oblige. On March 29 to 31, 1899: *Having received an order for 500 fungi from Prof. F. S. Earle of Auburn, Alabama, spent each of these three days working hard at labelling and getting them out from my duplicates. Finished the job Friday — $25.00.* And the next day another shipment went to Professor J. B. Ellis of Newfield, New Jersey.

A contractual trip for collection of fungi took Elam for his first view of the Rocky Mountains on August 17: *Spent the time until 2 p.m. in packing my baggage for my Colorado trip in the collection of fungi for Arthur and Holway, publishers of "Uredineae Exsiccatae et Icones", and at that hour, in company with Earl we drove to Phillipsburg where after buying a ticket and getting my baggage checked to Denver, we went to Rev. Dr. Bracken's where we took supper, after which Earl started home, and I went up into town again and made a call at Rev. Shockley's. Then went to the station and getting aboard the 10:20 train turned my face toward the land of the setting sun.*

August 18: Just at sunrise we arrived at the little junction of Limon, Colorado, and as the train pulled out, off to the south and west the majestic pile of granite, Pike's Peak, came into view! As we passed on, it supposedly grew in stature and soon other peaks became visible until the whole western horizon banked by the interminable Rockies! A grand sight indeed and one, once beheld, never to be forgotten!

Arrived in Denver at 7:45 a.m. and spent the whole day looking about over the city visiting the various places of interest, but met no one with whom I was ever acquainted. Put up for the night at the Park Hotel near Union Depot.

August 19: Left Denver for Colorado Springs at 7:30 a.m. over the D. & R.G. Railroad and arrived at that place at 10:30 and at once took an electric car for Manitou where I arrived at 11 oclock. Then walked up the cañon a mile to the Iron Mountain Springs and later about a mile farther on up the cog road and returned to the cog station where at 1:30 p.m. I got on a car with about 50 other persons and began the ascent of this, the most noted of all American mountains — Pike's Peak!

At 3 p.m. we reached the summit. The sky was perfectly clear. A chilling breeze was blowing from the northwest though at the mountain's base it was calm and sweltering hot! The magnificence and supreme grandeur of the view from this summit with an elevation of over 14,000 feet, and an area of 40,000 square miles spread out before you, is beyond the power of my pen to depict or my feeble language to describe!

Our stay on the summit was 45 minutes which was surely long enough to suit me on account of the extreme rarity of the atmosphere. Arrived at the cog station again at 5 oclock. Took a car back to the Springs and after supper spent the time looking about the city until 9:40 at which time I took the train for Pueblo and thence on to Salida.

August 21: *Leaving my friends at 7 oclock a.m. I boarded the west bound train over the D. & R.G. for Gunnison, my objective point, and passing over the famous Marshall Pass at an elevation of nearly 11,000 feet arrived at Gunnison, the home of my brother George, at 10:45, but he having just left on a trip to Denver and Col. Springs I did not meet him as I had fondly expected. However, having telegraphed ahead I found George's room mate, Frank Hampton, awaiting me at the station with whom I went up to George's house, a sort of 2-room bachelor's hall, where we prepared us a dinner at noon. At the house was also stopping for a few days a young man by the name of Frank Mayhew who is teaching a new chemical process of enlarging and coloring pictures.*

Because this was Elam's first major botanical expedition and also his first experience in the mountains, he wrote detailed descriptions of each day's excursions. The trip lasted over four weeks.

Returning home on September 19: *And thus endeth one of the pleasantest months in my life's experience! The delightful collecting, the peculiar experiences, and the multitude of wonders beheld will ever constitute a series of gratifying rememberances!*

1900

Numerous days in the autumn were spent preparing fungi specimens in accord with the Colorado contract. Finally on January 8 to 11, 1900: *Spent each of these four days mostly at work with my fungi collected in Colorado last summer.* And on the next day: *Spent the day preparing the bulk of the fungi collected in Colorado last summer to send to E. W. D. Holway of Decorah, Iowa, under whose auspices I did the collecting.* But some time was taken in the midst of this to service another client on December 1: *Spent the day in reading, writing and botanical work — completing the getting out of 260 specimens of fungi for Prof. P. Sydow of Germany.*

1901

Elam found a market for another wild plant growing in the area, so on March 22, 1901: *With Earl went over east about 6½ miles where we spent the day digging wild Clematis plants for a firm at Boulder, Colo. Secured 650 plants.* Four days later another 400 were collected, and all were shipped the following day. Possibly these were for ornamental rather than medicinal purposes.

Another foreign request for fungi came on April 24: *Worked at getting out and labelling fungi for a European correspondent, Dr. Michel Gundogers of Arnas, France. I am to send him 525 specimens when I get them out.*

In the summer of 1901 Elam decided to begin his first really formal botanical procedure, organizing fungi specimens into indexed categories and preparing the publication *Fungi Columbiani*. This was a program begun in 1893 by two New Jersey botanists, Ellis and Everhart, that grew out of their earlier efforts called *North American Fungi*. By 1901 they both felt the need to retire from this activity. Everhart died in 1904 at 86 years of age, and Ellis died in 1905 at age 78. Ellis's friend, C. L. Shear, initially took over, but that same year he persuaded Elam Bartholomew to assume the duties.

One hundred fungi specimens, each identified in detail, formed a "century." Subscribers were notified when a new century was available for them to order. Each issue was limited to 70 copies. That meant 70 duplicate sets of 100 labeled packets containing fungi samples.

Elam did not collect all the specimens, nor did members of his family, who helped on some field trips. He received samples from other mycologists in exchange for some species from his own collection. Considerable correspondence developed in the exchanges and purchases. Some writers requested identification, and others challenged the identity of some of the fungi.

By the end of October 1901 Elam had concluded the purchase of rights to continue publication of the fungus collections under the title *Fungi Columbiani*. On October 29 and 30: *Having recently made arrangements to assume the continued publication of Ellis & Everhart's "Fungi Columbiani", as indicated in the attached "Prospectus", each of these two days was spent wholly in getting material ready for distribution in the publication.*

At the end of December work was completed on Century 16 — Elam's first century — of *Fungi Columbiani*. Seventy sets of 100 species each were prepared, with help of family members, to send to subscribers. There had been many trips to Stockton to supervise the label printing for the sample packets, because Elam detested errors in spelling, punctuation, and so on.

Neither would Elam tolerate inaccuracies in the work of others. Dr. George B. Cummins, now retired from Purdue University, wrote in July 1993 that he remembered one such instance:

> Dr. Joseph Charles Arthur, with whom I studied and replaced at Purdue University, was well acquainted with your grandfather but I was a mere graduate student illustrating Arthur's "Rusts of United States and Canada" published in 1934. In the first paper that I wrote concerning rust fungi I made a mistake in the spelling of a specific epithet. This prompted E. Bartholomew to write me about this mistake and urge me to be very careful about such matters in technical writing. This impressed me; favorable, I might add.

Elam was now fully committed to a career as a mycologist, and others in the field not only accepted him as one of their own but began to look to him as a source of knowledge and inspiration — and a source of herbarium material. Consequently Elam dedicated every possible moment to this work. It was a favorable time in his life. He was 50 years old. There were sons old enough to do the farm work. The oldest, Elbert, had gone away to college, and Jesse was due to leave in 1903. But Earl and Lee were coming along, and they were more inclined to make farming their vocation.

Elam sent out 36 mailings to the subscribers of *Fungi Columbiani*:

Century	16	Dec. 1901	34	Jan. 1911
	17	Sep. 1902	35	Dec. 1911
	18	Feb. 1903	36	Dec. 1911
	19	Dec. 1903	37	Feb. 1912
	20	Nov. 1904	38	Mar. 1912
	21	Jan. 1905	39	Jan. 1913
	22	Feb. 1906	40	Feb. 1913
	23	Dec. 1906	41	Jun. 1913
	24	Mar. 1907	42	Nov. 1913
	25	Dec. 1907	43	Feb. 1914
	26	Jan. 1908	44	Sep. 1914
	27	Jan. 1909	45	Oct. 1914
	28	Feb. 1909	46	May 1915
	29	Mar. 1909	47	Jun. 1915
	30	Nov. 1909	48	Jan. 1916
	31	Mar. 1910	49	Jan. 1917
	32	Apr. 1910	50	Feb. 1917
	33	Dec. 1910	51	Mar. 1917

1902

Another request for specimens came from Europe as Elam's reputation began to spread. On December 3, 1902: *Most of the time was spent in getting out and labeling 200 specimens of fungi for Prof. Tycho Vestergran of Stockholm, Sweden.*

1903

A local expedition on June 3, 1903, had exciting results: *In the p.m. with Jesse went up west 2½ miles collecting fungi and returned at 5 oclock, having made some excellent finds in the way of securing two species in quantity new to this region.*

1904

While visiting the World's Fair at St. Louis in 1904, Elam took time to satisfy his appetite for things botanical. On October 3: *We visited the Missouri Botanical Garden and beheld the wonders of that most beautiful resort. While there I met my old-time botanical correspondent Dr. Wm. Trelease, the director, with whom I had a pleasant chat.*

This gives an idea of the nature of Elam's first professional effort in the field of mycology.

Ellis & Everhart's

Fungi Columbiani Continued.

Prospectus.

—❦—

IN assuming the editorship and publication of this important work which has been so well established and ably conducted in the past by Messrs. Ellis and Everhart, the undersigned, by way of introduction, desires to address a few words to his patrons relative to future plans under the present management. No pains or reasonable expense will be spared to make the continued publication of FUNGI COLUMBIANI of such intrinsic merit and scientific value that it may stand second to no publication of its character in the world.

An earnest effort will always be made to issue nothing but neatly prepared material in ample quantity, as nearly representative and typical in character as possible.

A given species occuring on two or more hosts, will, in each subsequent issue, constitute a new number—there will be no "a", "b", and "c" packets.

For the purpose of showing ecological variation and geographical distribution, it will be considered allowable to reissue, in some instances, a given species on the same host when it comes from widely separated regions.

As the serial numbers running through the entire issue are merely arbitrary and possess no specific value, the relative number plan followed in Saccardo's Sylloge will be abandoned and the regular serial numbers will accompany the alphabetical list of each Century index.

If sufficient material can be obtained from time to time, it will be my expectation to issue two Centuries per annum, as uniformly as possible.

Each issue will be limited to 70 copies.

No bound fascicles will be issued.

The subscription price will be $6.00 per copy where no previous contract prices have been made.

That there may be a healthy and permanent growth, indicating a steady development of interest in the work, the editor urgently requests the hearty co-operation of mycologists in all parts of America to become contributing correspondents to FUNGI COLUMBIANI.

Very Sincerely Yours,

ELAM BARTHOLOMEW.

STOCKTON, KANSAS, October 25, 1901.

Elam in the Editor's Chair.

It is with pleasure we announce the practical good fortune that has just come to our botanical friend, Mr. Elam Bartholomew, M. Sc.

For over two years on account of failing health, the editor of "Fungi Columbiani," Prof. J. B. Ellis of Newfield, New Jersey, has been urging Mr. Bartholomew to assume the editorship and he has recently consented to take up the work and continue its publication here. While there is considerable printing connected with the business the work really has nothing to do with the publication of a magazine or journal as one might suppose, but consists only in the scientific distribution of carefully prepared and neatly labelled specimens of American fungi. The specimens are put up in bundles or fascicles of 100 species each and are sent to subscribers in all parts of the United States with a goodly sprinkling in Europe. While there are a few individual subscribers, the bulk of each edition goes direct to our American colleges and experiment stations.

Each edition of the work is called a "Century." Fifteen "Centuries" were issued before the work was taken up here, and Mr. Bartholomew has just issued Century XVI. It is his purpose to publish two editions per annum. He has now the largest and best private collection of fungi west of the Mississippi river and is a recognized authority both in this country and Europe on fungus plants and diseases and his editorship and publication of the above named work, which is the only one of its kind in America, will bring him in a handsome revenue and not materially interfere with his other lines of work. We are glad to know that we have one among us so well qualified to pursue this important branch of scientific research and predict for Mr. Bartholomew a large measure of success in his chosen field of labor.

From the January 18, 1902, edition of *The Home Visitor*, published in Farmington, Illinois.

1905

Elam attended a regional Sunday school convention in St. Louis late in 1905, but he took time on December 9 to attend to botanical interests: *Visited the Mo. Botanical Garden where I had the pleasure of meeting again, as I did last fall, the Director, Dr. Wm. Trelease, and a greatly added pleasure in meeting my much-admired but never-seen botanical correspondent Dr. J. C. Arthur of Purdue University, Indiana!*

1906

Sad news arrived on January 5, 1906: *Today learned by letter of the death of my old co-laborer and most valued botanical friend Prof. J. B. Ellis of Newfield, New Jersey with whom I have been intimately connected in the work for the past 15 years. And thus has passed away the greatest worker in mycological botany that America has ever produced. He was in the 77th year of his age and died at 11 oclock p.m. Dec. 30th 1905.*

1908

Elam was certainly proud of the development of Elbert in a scientific field similar to his own. On a visit to Emporia on May 9, 1908: *Went with Elbert to the science department of the Normal to see some of his demonstrations in plant physiology as teacher, which surely were remarkably creditable and of a pleasing scientific order.*

Elam needed more storage capacity for fungi specimens, so on May 18: *Made a trip to Stockton in the wagon to get a cabinet recently made to order, by Josh Reddish, calculated to hold about 6000 specimens of labelled fungi. Came home at one oclock p.m. and worked the remainder of the day mostly at giving said cabinet a coat of cherry stain. Cost of cabinet about $30.* Then on the 23rd: *In the p.m. worked at re-arranging the 13,000 specimens now in cabinets. Too tired by evening to stand up!*

A good friend made a stop at Elam's on August 27, following another collecting trip to Colorado: *Jesse drove in from Phillipsburg with Prof. W. T. Swingle of Washington D.C. with whom the p.m. was spent in social and business chat.*

On September 21, 1908, Elam began a collecting trip to a part of the U.S. where he had not previously been: *At 3 oclock had Lee take me to Stockton and while he drove back home I took the 7 p.m. train for various points in Arkansas where I expect to botanize for several days.*

Results on the 24th, near Rogers, were exceptionally good: *Botanized all day to the east of town down as far as the Electric Springs being most successful in my labors as I secured over 1100 specimens of fungi for distribution in Fungi Columbiani. This is the largest number of specimens ever collected by me in one day!*

Moving on to Batesville on October 3, Elam was favorably impressed: *This is a nice town of nearly 4000 inhabitants who appear to be wide-awake and up to date.*

The trip to Arkansas, ending on October 10, produced exciting results. *Botanized awhile near the S.E. part of town which rounded out my work in this state, where I have collected since Sept. 23rd about 10,000 specimens of fungus plants which constitutes a record probably unsurpassed by any American collector at any time or any place!*

1909

Before proceeding further, Elam decided it was time to issue a summary

=====INDEX=====

TO

Fungi Columbiani

Centuries I to XXX

COMPILED BY

ELAM BARTHOLOMEW,

STOCKTON, KANSAS.

NOVEMBER, 1910.

.RECORD PRINT, STOCKTON, KANSAS.

publication. On December 8, 1909: *Have begun the compilation of an alphabetical index of the first 30 Centuries of Fungi Columbiani to be published sometime this season.* Following several more days' work, on the 23rd: *Spent the past 4 days at the Index, nearly completing the first draft which will need to be re-written before going to press.*

1910

Elam attended the World Sunday School Convention in Washington, D.C., during May 1910. As usual he took time to visit with various persons at the U.S. Department of Agriculture. He had a unique experience on the 27th: *Took a car at 7:45 a.m. and went over S.W. into Virginia about 16 miles to the home of Prof. C. L. Shear where the time was spent in social chat and botanizing, returning to the city at 3:45 and 15 minutes later went out N.E. near Lanham, Md. with Profs G. N. Collins, C. S. Scofield and W. T. Swingle, where they all live, and botanized awhile nearby.* It was a special treat to be accepted into the companionship of persons of such high academic and professional standing even though he himself had never attended college.

After a visit to Philadelphia he made a pilgrimage on the 30th: *At 9 a.m. went down to the ferry and over to Camden, N.J. where I took passage on the electric road put to Newfield about 30 miles which was the home of my old botanical partner Prof. J. B. Ellis. I visited his tomb in the little cemetery and also his late dwelling which is now unoccupied. While I never met Mr. Ellis, yet a feeling of profound sadness came over me when I thought of our long and intimate correspondence and close relationship in the collection and determination of the fungi. He died Dec. 30, 1905.*

After this I took the electric on to Vineland, five miles, where at 520 Plum St. I met Miss Cora Ellis, daughter of J. B. Ellis with whom I had a pleasant visit and took dinner.

After a few days in the Lancaster, Pennsylvania, vicinity — his birthplace — where he did some botanizing, Elam moved on to New York City where he again spent most of his time on botanical matters. On June 3: *After lunch I took an elevated car up N.E. several miles to Bronx Park where I visited the New York Botanical Garden and meeting Dr. W. A. Murrill there was shown about the buildings and grounds by him and had the pleasure of meeting Dr. P. A. Rydberg, Dr. J. K. Small, Dr. M. A. Howe, Dr. C. E. Fairman of Lyndonville, N.Y., Prof. Fred J. Seaver and Mrs. N. L. Britton, wife of the Director of the Garden.*

Dr. Murrill pressed me to accept his hospitality which I finally did and went home with him near the Park, for supper and to spend the night. In the evening at the town hall, nearby, we attended a full fledged ward meeting called for the purpose of laying out new streets through the Park, so I very unexpectedly had the experience of attending a "New York ward meeting".

On the following day: *With Dr. Murrill went up to the Museum Building in the Garden where I met Dr. N. L. Britton, the director with whom I had a short chat, shortly after which I bade my Guide, Philosopher and*

Friend and the Garden good bye and walked down through the Zoological Park and out to the Westfield subway station.

Returning to Washington, D.C., on June 13: *Spent the whole day at the Department of Agriculture with Profs. Briggs, Mason, Swingle, Johnson, Kellerman, Long, Carleton and Jardine.* The next day: *Took a car and went out to Anacostia where I spent the a.m. botanizing and returning to the city put my plants in press and then went over to the Dept. of Agr. and at 3 p.m. with Prof. Swingle went out on the trolley to Lanham, Md. where we did some botanizing and later took supper at the residence of Prof. O. F. Cook.*

Another satisfying experience took place on the following day: *Went to the Dept. of Agr. at 9 a.m. where I met Prof. Swingle by appointment and at 10 oclock, after he had purchased an elaborate lunch, to take along, we took a car out to Cabin John Bridge 10 miles up the Potomac river above Georgetown where we spent the day botanizing in that vicinity. We collected about 1000 specimens of fungi for F. Col.*

Elam made stops in Ohio and Kentucky on the 20th: *Arrived at Cincinati at 1 oclock p.m. Left the train and went up to the great Lloyd Bros. Chemical laboratory at Court & Plum Sts. where I met my old botanical correspondent and the author of Lloyd's Mycological Notes, Mr. C. G. Lloyd with whom I had a pleasant visit and at 4:30 oclock I took a car and went out to the suburb N.E. and botanized awhile, getting some good things and returned to the city at 7 oclock and put up for the night with Mr. Lloyd at his rooms; 224 Court St. He is an old batch!*

The many conversations Elam had been having with leaders in the botanical sciences had emphasized that if he really wanted to make his mark in this field he had to specialize even more than in the past. What he had been doing in the general field of mycology was commendable, but it was too broad to make a significant impact. They urged him to specialize in one branch of the field, in the area of rusts. He already had experience in rust prevention in grain crops from experiments sponsored by the U.S. Department of Agriculture, and he realized the economic importance of this field of study.

1911

Thus on January 17, 1911, with gusto Elam launched into the specialization of rusts: *Spent 2 days hard at work determining and writing citations for about 100 species of fungi recently rec'd from E. W. Holway of*

Minnesota to be issued in my new publication North American Uredinales
[NAU].

Family members had been well-trained in the laboratory preparation of
fungi specimens. On March 2 Elam wrote: *Earl and Lee, with very little
assistance, distributed the packets and put up into century fascicles the
whole edition of 50 copies of our new publication N.A.U. Century I.*

From the vast material already on file in his laboratory Elam moved
rapidly with his new venture of *NAU*. Century II was completed at the end
of 1911; Century III on February 7, 1912; Century IV on March 8; and
Century V by April 29.

Elam sent out 35 centuries to the subscribers of *North American Uredinales*:

Century	1	Mar. 1911	19	Jan. 1918
	2	Dec. 1911	20	Dec. 1918
	3	Feb. 1912	21	Dec. 1918
	4	Mar. 1912	22	Jan. 1920
	5	Apr. 1912	23	Jan. 1920
	6	Jan. 1913	24	Feb. 1921
	7	Feb. 1913	25	Apr. 1921
	8	May 1913	26	Jan. 1922
	9	Jan. 1914	27	Feb. 1922
	10	Mar. 1914	28	Sep. 1922
	11	Jun. 1914	29	Jan. 1923
	12	May 1915	30	Nov. 1923
	13	Jun. 1915	31	Dec. 1923
	14	Nov. 1915	32	Dec. 1924
	15	Jan. 1916	33	Jan. 1925
	16	Mar. 1916	34	Nov. 1925
	17	Feb. 1917	35	Jan. 1926
	18	Nov. 1917		

An honored guest arrived on September 23: *At noon Elbert drove in
from Phillipsburg with Dr. J. C. Arthur of Lafayette, Ind. whom he had
gone over to meet by previous appointment so the p.m. was spent in very
pleasant social and botanical chat with the learned Doctor.*

1912

After construction was completed on the new house, new barn, and new church, work began April 18, 1912, on a building to be used exclusively for botanical laboratory work: *Worked with the boys in the p.m. at excavating for the foundation of a botanical office and laboratory to be of cement and practically fireproof.*

The next step came on the 22nd: *Left home in the wagon for Stockton at 7 a.m. and getting there at nine got a load of cement — 2300 lbs — a barrel of coal oil* [kerosene] *and Griffen's cement-block machine and started home at noon.* Two days later: *With the help of brother Ed who came over in the morning to "show us the way" worked with him and Lee in the a.m. at making cement blocks. Ed went home at noon and Earl and I worked the cement machine alone in the p.m.* The next day they started building foundation forms.

Elam and his family spent many days or partial days making blocks until that was completed on May 14: *With Jesse and Lee worked at making cement blocks until 4 p.m. finishing the job of making 525 blocks 8x10x20 inches in size.* The cement foundation was completed two days later, but some of it was unsatisfactory and had to be replaced on the 21st.

Erection of the walls began on the 23rd and ended on June 5. The cement floor was completed on the 11th. The laboratory needed to be as fireproof as possible, so on June 20: *Made an early-morning trip to Stockton in the wagon after a load of lumber and the steel ceiling and steel shingles.* On the same trip Elam brought home a relative who would provide some help: *Met at the 9:30 train Raymond Montgomery, son of cousin Ed Montgomery of Topeka, who has come to work on the farm for us for the summer.*

Plastering, installation of doors and windows, and painting were done in short order so that on July 8: *Spent the entire day in moving my botanical belongings of sorts into the new laboratory building. Had the assistance of Lee and Raymond Montgomery most of the day.*

1913

Specimens from a correspondent consumed most of May 13, 1913: *Spent the time until 3 p.m. in going over a lot of fungi from Dr. F. L. Stevens of Mayaguez, Porto Rico. Completed my Mycological Index which revealed the astonishing fact that I have no fewer than 867 genera in my herbarium!*

This structure was built in 1912 in the grove near the house to serve as Elam's botanical laboratory. The cement blocks were made from a borrowed mold.

On October 30 Elam summarized results of his recent trips: *And thus endeth east, west and south botanical trips for the year 1913 which have resulted in the securing of about 30,000 specimens of fungi for distribution in Fungi Columbiani and North American Uredinales, possessing a gross value of nearly $2000!*

A new piece of equipment was purchased on November 29: *Brought from the Stockton express office a fine $65 Spencer Lens Co. microscope manufactured at Buffalo, N.Y.*

1914

A trip to southern states began November 3, 1914. After stops in Tennessee Elam headed for Asheville, North Carolina, where on the 13th: *Took a car at 9 a.m. and went out to the little village of Biltmore, about 3 miles, and getting a permit to go into the grounds of the famous Biltmore Estate, property of the late Geo. W. Vanderbilt, and spent several hours strolling along the magnificent driveways and botanizing through the beautiful woods on up to the palatial grey-stone mansion of 127 rooms.*

The original estate, I am told, consisted of about 143,000 acres but by the sale of 86,000 acres to the government for a forest park and sales to other parties the estate is now said to contain only 12,000 acres. Taking it all in all it surely is one of the most enrapturing beauty spots in America.

Elam returned home on December 9 with this summary: *And thus endeth a rather notable trip of just even 4100 miles with R.R. fares of even $99.00 and hotel and transfers of $50.30. With this trip I have now visited every state in the Union except Nevada!* (That state was visited in 1917.)

1915

Some specimens were sent out February 12, 1915: *Worked two days in the laboratory, with wife, at getting out and labeling for shipment a large miscellaneous assortment of fungi for Purdue University, Lafayette, Ind.*

Other specimens were sent out April 10: *With wife worked about all day at getting out a large lot of miscellaneous fungi for the North Carolina Agr. Expt. Station at West Raleigh.*

Elam and Rachel left on June 24 for an extended trip to the West Coast. Stopping at Ogden, Utah, they spent time botanizing with Professor A. O. Garrett. They were joined by Dr. F. W. Pennell, of the New York Botanical Garden, who was also there for the same purpose.

While in California, Elam and Rachel went to the San Francisco World's Fair, where Elam participated in a professional gathering. On August 3: *At 10 a.m., on the University campus in the Hearst Memorial Hall, attended the opening session of the Botanical Section of the American Association for the Advancement of Science where we heard some fine addresses by Drs. J. M. Coulter, L. L. Burlingame and L. R. Abrams. Then came a special luncheon at the University Club. At our table sat the following more or less distinguished persons, viz. Wife, Prof. C. O. Smith, Prof. H. S. Fawcett, Prof. F. S. Earle of Cuba, Prof. A. O. Garrett, Prof. E. Bethel, Prof. W. T. Horne and I.*

At 2 p.m. we went to the Agricultural Building where we attended a meeting of the American Phytopathological Association at which addresses and demonstrations were given by Dr. C. L. Shear, Profs. R. E. Smith, Haven Metcalf, E. P. Meinecke, H. S. Jackson and others.

On the 7th, a special event took place: *This was an outing day for the scientists in general when all sections of the A.A.A.S. were to be conducted to the top of Mt. Tamalpais under the leadership of Dr. C. Hart Merriam of Washington, D.C. so we took car and ferry over to San F. where at 9:15 we took the ferry trip across the inner part of the Golden Gate to Sausilito and thence by train to Mill Valley where we took the Tamalpais train for the summit which we reached at noon.*

Shortly thereafter about 25 of us, headed by Dr. Merriam, walked down across the brow of the beautiful mountain about two miles to the first station below the summit, where, after a short stop, wife and I walked on, eating our lunch as we walked, while the others staid to lunch at the little station and were to follow us in the course of a half hour, which they did as we could see from a mile or more below.

But somehow they seemed to get cold feet and deflected from the trail, going back to a point on the railroad where they intercepted the down-going train. This left wife and I to shift for ourselves so we started down the steep canyon at the entrance to Muir Woods.

Down the winding, almost impassable water course we wended our way with as much haste as possible, climbing over logs, crawling along banks and holding onto bushes to keep from rolling into the gulch below, we reached the Muir Woods station at 4 oclock where we boarded the train back to Mill Valley and thence on back to the city and back to Berkeley to the hotel at 7:40 p.m. almost too fatigued to stand up!

The trip down the canyon was not devoid of accidents and incidents as it was the most difficult and dangerous tramps that we have ever taken or ever want to take!

From there Elam went to Portland, Oregon, where he engaged in successful botanizing from August 19 to 31.

1917

The benediction of *Fungi Columbiani* was finally pronounced in March 1917: *In the past 15 years we have put up 2527 copies of this publication comprising 252,700 labeled packets and the good wife has been a constant and faithful assistant in this great work, doing much of it with her own hands, unaided!*

On September 13 Elam left for a trip to the Lake Michigan area. He spent most of the time around Madison, Wisconsin — with Elbert — and in Michigan, where he collected many good specimens. But the last stop, Michigan City, Indiana, was fruitless. On September 25: *Took a hike out N.E. of town and on out to the shore of Lake Michigan over the sand dunes but found no specimens whatever owing to the dense clouds of coal smoke which nearly ruins the vegetation in this vicinity.* The concentration of steel mills and other factories in that area has been known to be hazardous to the health of all forms of life for a long time.

1918

A major request from Washington, D.C., was handled on November 13 and 14, 1918: *With wife, in the laboratory, worked each of these two days at getting out and packing about 20,000 specimens of miscellaneous duplicate fungi for the U.S. Dept. of Ag.*

1919

At the meeting of the Kansas Academy of Science in Manhattan, Elam made a presentation on one aspect of his vast experience in the field of fungus growths. On April 19, 1919: *At 11 oclock I read my paper on "Edible Mushrooms of Kansas" which was well received and highly commended.*

Later, while attending the Presbyterian General Assembly at St. Louis in 1919, Elam, as usual, found time for botanical pursuits. On May 21: *After lunch took a car out to the Botanical Garden where I met Drs. B. M. Duggar and E. A. Burt with whom I had pleasant visits. They are both old botanical correspondents but I had never met either one of them before.*

On August 18, Elam and Rachel departed on an extensive trip to the northeastern section of the country. After a number of days in the Madison, Wisconsin, area, Rachel went to the old home site in Illinois while Elam proceeded to Toronto, Canada, and New England, thence to New York and Washington, D.C., gathering numerous botanical specimens and seeing many colleagues along the way. One of the stops on the return trip was Grafton, West Virginia, a disagreeable place. On October 2: *Grafton is the last word in a smoke-begrimed town being the dirtiest and most uninviting place I have ever visited! In all ways it is a bigger freak than Barstow, Calif. and that is saying a whole lot! It is a town that should be spelled with a lower case initial — "grafton".* Then the next day: *With much satisfaction I held my nose (at least figuratively speaking) and bade a gratified farewell to the foul smelling town of grafton at 9:30 a.m. for Parkersburg, West Virginia.* After a pleasant day there: *This is a very decent town indeed, and coming here from grafton seems like a transit from the infernal regions to Paradise!*

In Cincinnati on the 7th, Elam made this summary of the trip thus far: *I find that I have collected over 12,000 specimens for issuance in N.A.U.! I think this is a fine record and seldom equalled by any collector of fungus plants.*

More collecting took place in Illinois. When the trip ended on October 30, Elam recorded: *Thus ended our big 10-weeks visiting and collecting trip in which I find that I have travelled in 21 states and Ontario, Canada making a total for the trip of about 6120 miles and the collection of about 15,000 specimens!*

A close friend prepared a publication that Elam was invited to critique. On November 11: *Most of the time was devoted to reviewing Prof. E. Bethel's manuscript paper on the "Rusts of Boulder, Colorado".*

Just three weeks after being married, Jesse took his bride for a visit at Christmas time, and she quickly became involved in the botanical experience. On December 26: *Finished writing the Century 23 labels in the a.m. and in the p.m. worked with wife and daughter-in-law Florence at placing fungi in the envelopes for Cent. 23 N.A.U.*

1920

Some specimens were received from Asia on February 17, 1920: *Prepared 200 specimens of fungi for the herbarium, which came rather in the rough, from the Philippines and "The Straits Settlements" at Singapore!*

Elam made further comment on this material one month later: *Spent two days at work in the laboratory at placing in the herbarium specimens of fungi recently received from the Philippines and Singapore Island at the Malay Peninsula. The specimens were collected by Prof. C. F. Baker and issued in "Fungi Malayana".*

At the end of February, Elbert took on a new position that became his vocation for the rest of his life. The following newspaper account was published:

Dr. and Mrs. E. T. Bartholomew of Madison, Wis., came in Saturday night, via Phillipsburg, for a short visit with the home folks on Bow Creek. Dr. Bartholomew has been one of the botanical instructors in the University for the past nine years. He has resigned his position of Assistant Professor of Botany to take a position in research work at the Citrus Experiment Station at Riverside, California. Mrs. Bartholomew has been employed by the Bureau of Plant Industry as investigator in pathology at the University which position she has also resigned.

Elam decided that it was time to take inventory on April 13: *Spent almost the entire day in completing the count of my labeled fungi in the cabinets. The count reaches the very gratifying number of 25,900. Aside from these I have on my shelves 61,600 additional labeled specimens and about 15,500 unlabeled specimens in bulk, which brings the grand total on hand, in the laboratory, at this date to 103,000!*

1923

On January 8, 1923, it was Elam's intention to terminate publication and distribution of specimens of *NAU*: *I went to work at throwing into the pigeon holes the 5000 packets of fungi which we recently put up for distribution in Century 29 of N.A.U., finishing the job at 1:30 p.m. Then, after a bite of dinner, wife and I worked at making up into fascicles of 100 specimens each, 2500 specimens working thereat the remainder of the day expecting to get not only Century 29 but also Century 28, which was put up last spring, late, into the mails in a few days and thus will end the many references to this sort of work which was commenced in 1901 since which time in Fungi Columbiani and North American Uredinales we have issued 36 Centuries in the former and 29 in the latter, making a total of 65 Centuries in both publications containing no fewer than 397,000 labeled specimens of fungi! Who will ever equal it?*

Elam found it was not easy to retire. He made subsequent trips with good results to Oklahoma and Texas, to Montana, and to the Missouri Ozarks, all in 1923. As a result, Centuries 30 and 31 were issued. Then in 1924 there were trips to the Western states and Southeastern states that resulted in two more centuries. The final two were sent in late 1925 and early 1926.

1925

Elam was privileged to speak at the annual meeting of the Kansas State Board of Agriculture in Topeka on January 15, 1925, on the subject "Some Enemies of Plant Life — An Unseen World," the topic he had spoken on in 1894 at the Rooks County Farmers Institute. A comparison of the two talks clearly reveals the advancement in maturity and experience during the intervening 31 years.

During February Elam spent much of the time, with Rachel's help, *preparing the herbarium envelopes and placing therein the packets of fungi that have accumulated in the past 12 months. The envelopes thus prepared are now ready to be placed in their proper order in our several cabinets. The number of specimens thus prepared, from North America, South America, Europe, Asia and Africa, total 1820, ready for the cabinets. Some work, I tell you!*

A major order was filled on March 9: *Spent the a.m. with wife in the laboratory at getting down and packing 33 Centuries (3300 specimens) of North American Uredinales for the State College of Washington at Pullman.*

A significant pair of visitors came to call on July 11: *Profs. [L. D.] Wooster and [F. W.] Albertson of the Hays Teachers College paid us a 2½ hours visit, spending the time mostly in the laboratory.* They may have proposed that Elam join the faculty at Hays, which he did a few years later.

Elam made a short trip to Denver on August 14 to 25 to botanize and to see his old friend, Professor Bethel.

But in a little over two weeks, September 11, came sad news: *When I reached home one of the saddest shocks of my life greeted me in a telegram from Mrs. Dorothy Bethel of Denver announcing the sudden death of her celebrated husband from apoplexy.*

Prof. Bethel was my dearest and best loved botanical friend with whom I have been intimately associated in work among the fungi for the past 26 years, our acquaintance dating from September 1899.

And then to think that only a few short days ago, Aug. 24th, I was enjoying the delightful companionship of the Professor and his good wife while now it is ashes and darkness! Oh the frailty and uncertainty of human life! Later that night he took the train to Denver to attend the funeral.

Elam recorded: *Rev. Mr. Hopkin of the Congl. ch. preached the sermon, after which we drove out to the fine Crown Hill cemetery where we laid at rest all that was mortal that remains of one of the dearest of all my dear friends, Ellsworth Bethel!*

September 13: *At 1 p.m. went down to Alice Bethel's and with she and Mrs. Bethel went down to 283 S. Lafayette St. to the old home and storehouse of Prof. Bethel where we looked over a multitude of piled up material of various kinds in the way of books and specimens of a botanical nature, but found little of real value owing to the careless way in which the material had been cared for.*

September 14: *Went up to the State Museum at 10 a.m. where somewhat later I met Mrs. Bethel and we spent the remainder of the day in going over some of the botanical material left by Mr. Bethel to me. The arrangement was then made that I should return in about a month and remove to Stockton, Kan. said botanical material.*

Another botanical trip — to southern Illinois, Kentucky, Tennessee, and Arkansas — began two days later. Even though the results were good, Elam felt this phase of his life drawing to a close. When he returned on October 3, he wrote: *It is my firm purpose now to make no more long collecting trips because it no longer pays expenses!*

1926

Elam prepared another publication on March 15, 1926: *Botanical work in the laboratory; especially at work on a list of the "Fungus Flora of*

Kansas" to be submitted to the meeting next month of the Kansas Academy of Science.

Foreign specimens were assimilated into the files on May 11: *Worked in the laboratory preparing fungi for our herbarium — 580 specimens received a few days ago from H. Sydow of Berlin.*

In July, Elam put his letter file in order, finishing it on the 31st: *Continued work arranging and putting in separate files the botanical letters which I have received from my various correspondents in the past 35 years, arriving at the astonishing fact that I have had the phenomenal number of 240 botanical correspondents! The letters number from 225 down to single letters in many cases! Can any American surpass this record? Perhaps not!*

Much of the correspondence received by Elam, totalling nearly 4,000 letters, is available for viewing in the archives of the Kansas State Historical Society in Topeka. George Washington Carver, of Tuskegee Institute in Alabama, was one with whom Elam exchanged botanical information.

On October 4, Elam took a bus to Manhattan for a significant experience: *I took the 10:20 east bound Kansas City-Denver auto stage for Manhattan where I arrived, over some good and some also mighty rough and muddy roads, at 8 oclock p.m. and put up at the Shamrock Inn, on Houston St. by the Postoffice.*

October 5: *In the early morning went to 617 Leavenworth St. where I called on our old Rooks county neighbor, Walter Low, who took me in his car up on the hill to the Horticultural Bldg. of the Agr. College where I met our old friends, Profs. L. E. Melchers and R. P. White of the Botanical Dept. I was soon at work in the Fungus herbarium getting out certain data for my forthcoming Bulletin on "The Fungus Flora of Kansas."*

At one oclock p.m. made a half hour's address to Melcher's biology class of 25 students and thence back to work in the herbarium, incidentally meeting Profs. E. C. Miller, C. O. Johnston and Price. About 5:30 Prof. Melchers drove me in his car to the Shamrock Inn where I got my luggage and went with him out to 1801 Leavenworth St., his home, where I passed the night.

October 6: *Back, in the morning, to work in the herbarium with Profs. Melchers and White and at 10:30, made a half hour's talk to 30 students in Prof. White's class in botany. At 11:30 went with Prof. Melchers to make a formal call on President F. D. Farrell at his office.*

After lunch back to work at the college herbarium. At 4:30 oclock met the Botanical Seminar, in the Horticultural Bldg. and made an address to this fine body of 18 Professors and graduate students. A fine time! Refreshments served! And all went merry as a marriage bell!

The new publication, begun in March, was finished December 17: *We completed the work having recorded almost exactly 1800 names, which, so far as we know, constitutes a list of fungus plants greater than that of any other state in the Union.*

1927

Finally, on April 20, 1927, Elam received news of the highest possible honor of his professional career: *Through letter from President Farrell of the State Agricultural College learned that it is the intention of the Board of Regents and the Council of Deans to confer on me the honorary Degree of Doctor of Science at the Annual Commencement, June 2nd of this year!*

The degree is termed "honorary" only in the sense that Elam had not been enrolled in academic studies on campus as a doctoral candidate. It was an "earned" degree in the truest definition through experiential accomplishment.

The big event began on June 1: *Reached Manhattan at one oclock p.m. Was met at the station by Dr. E. C. Miller of the Agricultural College who took me with him to his home at 211 N. 18th St.*

At 8 oclock with Dr. Miller attended the alumni senior banquet at the Gymnasium Building and was given one of the places of honor at the head table. It was a fine affair. 700 plates were laid.

June 2: At 10 oclock a.m., with Dr. Miller went to President Farrell's office where I was capped and gowned for the great Commencement exercizes at the Auditorium where I was given the seat of honor at the head of the first row of seats on the stage while the 330 members of the several graduating classes were seated in the body of the room below and in front of the rostrum, in their caps and gowns. All the dignitaries on the rostrum, including the three candidates of the degree of Doctor of Science, were all in full regalia.

At the close of the impressive presentation of degrees to the regular college graduates, Dean J. T. Willard in a few laudatory words introduced me to the assembled audience of some 2300 people after which another Dean placed the Doctor's graduating hood of yellow velvet and black and purple silk on me and turned me over to President F. D. Farrell who pronounced the words which conferred on me the degree of Doctor of Science with all the rights and privileges pertaining to that degree in token of which a duly approved diploma was presented to me.

This, aside from the event noted in this diary under date of June 14, 1876 [Elam's wedding date], *was perhaps the most notable and interesting event that has ever occurred in my life!*

By previously written invitation, I took lunch, with several others, with President and Mrs. Farrell at their home. W. Y. Morgan, President of the Board of Regents including the newly-made Doctors Boss and Knaus were also invited guests.

. . . At 2:40 with Farrell and Morgan took a motor train, over the U.P. railroad, for Topeka where I arrived at 4:15 and parting from my travelling companions put up for my stay here at the Throop Hotel on Kansas Avenue.

June 3: *In the a.m. called on B. P. Walker at the state printery and went thence to the Memorial Hall with him with framed picture of self to be hung in that building. Met Wm. E. Connally the Secy. of the State Historical Society with whom I had a pleasant visit.*

Unfortunately Rachel could not be with Elam during these events of great honor because she was in Oberlin caring for the baby of Jesse and Florence while they were in San Francisco attending the General Assembly of the Presbyterian church.

Using a newly acquired typewriter, Elam began a new book on December 16: *Worked quite steadily for three days with the typewriter at preparing copy on a new publication to be designated "A Handbook of the North American Uredinales including Citations and Synonyms".*

1928

Many days were spent working on the Handbook, which was mostly finished by February 22, 1928: *In looking over our manuscript today, of our Handbook on the N.A. Uredinales, I find that on the whole North American continent from the Isthmus of Panama to the Arctic Ocean, including the West Indies, we have a total, to date, of 1231 valid species with an unfortunate appendage of 3505 synonyms! The greatest number of synonyms attached to any one species is 51 belonging to Puccinia Clematidis!*

By this time Elam had a pretty good idea that he would one day be moving to another occupation, so he began a campaign to market as much of his botanical collection as possible. He was now 76 years old and definitely slowing down. Potential buyers knew this and became more aggressive in placing orders.

One order was filled on April 18: *We packed in box for shipment to Wellesley College, Wellesley, Mass., 25 copies of Fungi Columbiani at $6.00 per copy.*

Another shipment was made on the 24th: *Botanical work in the laboratory especially preparing quantity material for shipment to Dr. F. Petrak at Weisskirchen, Czechoslovakia.*

Elam was honored by visitors on July 1: *About an hour was spent in social chat with Dr. E. C. Miller, Prof. John H. Parker and Mr. Loren L. Davis all of the Botany Dept. of the State Agricultural College, Manhattan. These men made a detour of about 80 miles to visit our laboratory and us! Then they made a hurry-up drive for Manhattan. They drove directly here from Hays. Mercury 100 degrees.*

And an impressive order was filled on July 7: *Made a trip to Stockton with Lily and Rachel in the car to take over to express a full set of N.A. Uredinales — 3500 specimens for Rutgers College of New Brunswick, New Jersey.*

A major order was shipped on September 19: *With Lily in the car made a business trip to Stockton to take over 6400 specimens of fungi in F. Columbiani and North Am. Uredinales for the Egyptian Department of Agriculture at Cairo. Box sent by express. Value $419.00.* Payment was received on February 14, 1929.

Elam decided on November 27 to reduce his library, getting rid of books no longer needed, because he made plans to move soon: *With wife worked in the laboratory at packing a lot of botanical books — 40 vols. — for shipment to Fred. J. Dimler, Brooklyn, N.Y.*

On December 1, work progressed to the proofreading stage on the new publication: *The printers at Stockton having assembled a sort of "dummy" copy of our Handbook of the North American Uredinales, with wife in the laboratory spent all day at reviewing its 191 pages and noting down several errors to be corrected in the appendix. We did not find many, yet there were sufficient for a printed record. Index to the Handbook has 4745 specific names.*

Finally the new book was completed — on January 11, 1929: *With Lee in the car made a business trip to Stockton and brought home with us the full edition of the 200 copies of our just completed "Handbook of the North American Uredinales". It is a book of about 200 pages and is to sell*

*at $2.50 per copy. Total cost of the work, including some necessary sta-
tionery was $297.75.*

An order was prepared on December 17, 1928: *With wife worked in the
laboratory all day at assembling an additional copy of Fungi Columbiani
Century 21 from duplicate material on hand supplemented by a division of
about half of the copy from specimens in the herbarium bearing the same
numbers and dates of the original copies issued in March 1905. The copy
was put up for Dr. E. P. Meinecke of San Francisco, Cal.*

1929

Some miscellaneous orders were filled on March 15, 1929: *Sent out 400
specimens from our old duplicate material to Dr. J. F. Brenckle of
Northville, So. Dak., and got out more than 150 additional specimens for
J. M. Grant of Marysville, Wash.*

A major order was prepared on March 21: *Spent the a.m. at fixing up
for mailing 17 copies of Fungi Columbiani (Centuries 35 to 51) to be
shipped by parcel post to the Cawthron Institute of Nelson, New Zealand.*

A book revision was continued on April 12, 1929: *In the a.m. commenced work on the index to our revised and enlarged Handbook of the
North American Uredinales.*

Finally, on May 13, Elam prepared to move to Hays to become curator
of the mycological herbarium at Fort Hays State College.

The move began on July 20: *With Lee and Lily in the car and a good
bulk of laboratory matter also, set out for Hays and drove to the new Science Hall where we unloaded our stuff in room 307 which is to be my
office in the future.*

While on another trip to Colorado, on August 19: *Dr. and Mrs. F. J.
Seaver of the N.Y. Botanical Garden called on us for a pleasant visit.* Then
the next day: *Visited with Dr. Cockerell, Dr. Ramaley, Profs. Henderson
and Paul F. Shope at Hale Hall on the Colorado University campus.*

Back home in Hays, Elam received a visit from an old friend. On
September 9: *About 4 p.m. our good friend, Prof. L. E. Melchers, of Manhattan, lately returned from a year and a half sojourn in Egypt as an
expert mycologist for the Egyptian Dept. of Agriculture, called on us, took
supper and went to his hotel at 10 oclock. He told us many interesting
stories of the people and customs of the ancient land of the Pharaohs.*
Elam was especially glad to hear of the uses to which his specimen collection was being applied.

A welcoming event was enjoyed on September 17: *Spent the day mostly at my office. At noon lunched at the cafeteria with the College Faculty and College Regents, most all of whom visited my office after the luncheon — about 50.*

Elam made his first speech at the Hays college on October 29: *At home until 10 a.m. preparing an address on Mycology and then went over to the Picken Hall where at Assembly delivered the address before the College faculty and several hundred students. Occupied about 45 minutes. The effort seemed to be well taken.*

This was without a doubt one of the most euphoric times in his life. It is no wonder that in the diary no mention is made of the great crash on Wall Street that same day. While it may have come as a surprise to those traders in New York, it was seen by those out in the country as simply an extension of what they had experienced for several years when local banks and businesses had gone bankrupt.

A classroom event followed on November 19: *In the morning with Jesse went over to my office in the Science building and at 10 oclock took Prof. Albertson's class in Agriculture and gave the 17 young men thereof a lesson on the rusts and smuts affecting our economic field crops.*

1930

Elbert came for a visit in early 1930. He and Elam put up an order on January 3: *With Elbert spent the a.m. at my office in the Science Bldg. in botanical work, especially in preparing 1700 specimens of N.A.U. for shipment to the Cawthron Institute at Nelson, New Zealand.* The order filled a year before was for the same amount, but was of *Fungi Columbiani.* Apparently they liked what they had gotten, and they wanted more.

Elam made a donation to the college from his archives on January 25: *With Profs. Albertson and Walker worked at sorting over and classifying some 760 Bulletins and reports brought over from Stockton which have been accumulating with me for the past 20 years or more.*

On February 4, Elam wrote: *With Lily in the car left Hays at 8:40 and drove to Stockton on miscellaneous business. Took dinner at Mrs. T. R. May's. While in town made arrangements with the Record printing office* *to print the second edition of my North American Uredinales which is revised, enlarged and has appended a complete index. Printing to be completed in the spring or early summer. The work, unbound, is to cost $375. Cloth binding will be done at Topeka or Kansas City, Mo.*

A major project was begun on February 14: *All day at the office working at the matter of commencing the putting up and labelling 5000 specimens of miscellaneous fungi as the foundation of a good cryptogamic herbarium* [plants that do not produce flowers or seeds] *for the State Teachers College at this place. Wife assisted me awhile in the a.m. and awhile in the afternoon.*

Another big project commenced on the 20th: *With wife succeeded in getting out and ready for the label pasting all the duplicates of Fungi Columbiani in the 36 Centuries — 16-51 — of that publication yet on hand. The same was done for North American Uredinales on the 26th.*

A helper was hired on April 9: *Miss Claire Schueler, a college student of this town, has been typing for me in helping to get out our 5000 specimens for the College Herbarium. She worked parts of 11 days, beginning March 27th and closing today, having put in 52½ hours at 30¢ per hour.*

Elam frequently did some botanical collecting near his home in Hays when he needed to get out and about a few hours. Having been on a farm all his life, he could not remain confined to house and office as long as he was healthy. Fortunately Big Creek flowed through the campus, just a block from his home. Often he would take along students or faculty.

Sometimes Elam would go to locations farther out — when there was someone to do the driving. One of those times was September 27: *At 1:30 p.m. with Doctor Barton, Prof. T. W. Wells, Prof. F. W. Albertson in the latter's car drove to Ellis in the near vicinity of which we botanized with moderate success and came home at 5 oclock.*

1931

Numerous day-long collecting trips were made in 1931, radiating out from Hays in all directions. Often Professor Albertson and sometimes Professor Wooster and Dr. F. C. Gates would go along.

Another honor was received on July 27: *Was initiated into the Delta Epsilon scientific society.*

1932

By late 1932 Elam was definitely showing signs of slowing down. November 15 to 23: *Worked almost constantly these 9 days at lettering and placing in the herbarium the 750 specimens which have accumulated in the past year. A big and painstaking job.* In younger years he had processed thousands of specimens in that length of time.

1933

The new book was finished, and a bindery was selected on April 15, 1933: *With Lee in car left home for Salina at 1 p.m. and arriving there in due time did some business at the Hassler Book Bindery and left for home at 5 oclock.* The first shipment of the completed product arrived on May 27.

1934

Elam decided to share his botanical collection with an institution dear to his heart. On April 13, 1934: *Shipped to College of Emporia as a donation, 3500 specimens of labelled fungi today.*

This is the last entry in Elam's diary concerning things botanical. His health was failing badly. Death came later that year, on November 18.

Chapter 10

Religion

*F*OLLOWING THE AUGUST 25, 1926, funeral of a dear Sunday school associate, John W. Noyce, Elam relates this touching episode: *One time, at a Sunday School convention where I was present, Mr. Noyce told this incident: "One night, some years ago, I had a dream or vision, I don't know which. I thought that a man, who seemed to be an ambassador, came to me and wanted to know if I wasn't related to some King. I said No, I don't know what you are talking about but I'm not related to any King. Well, the ambassador said, I think you are and he wants you to do some work for him. Again I said, No, you are mistaken. I'm <u>not</u> related to any King and I don't know anything about his business. He persisted in saying that I was related to a certain King. I then looked on him again and said, Why, yes, I suppose I <u>am</u> related to the King of Glory. That's just it, he said, and he wants you to do some work for him. I said, all right, I'll do it.*

"Then I awoke and behold, <u>it</u> <u>was</u> <u>a</u> <u>dream</u>! The very next day a man came to me and said that he had some work for me to do and it was about the King's business. I then looked upon the man more closely and in much surprise I said, Well I declare, I believe you are the same ambassador I saw in my vision last night! Yes, I'll do anything you want me to do for the King. That man was Elam Bartholomew!" A most peculiar vision!

Very little is revealed about the moral, ethical, or religious background Elam's parents provided. But it becomes obvious that early in life he was deep-rooted in highest standards, and he grew in fertile soil, watering and tending his roots well. They flourished abundantly from adolescence to his last days. These exemplary convictions were the prominent feature of the entire multifaceted, complex fabric of his life.

The quality of his character is profoundly illustrated time and again, whether in religion, politics, social matters, scientific pursuits, economic factors, or in the rest of life's involvements. His was a keenly focused personality from which deviation was rarely permitted.

This did not endear him to some of his contemporaries, for it seemed to some that he was bullheaded, stubborn, and narrow minded, with little room for compromise. But such an appraisal must be viewed in context. Some of those who responded to the lure of life on the Western frontier were society's castoffs or misfits, or were rebels against established cultural norms back East. It was an annoyance to them that a champion of those norms had contaminated their fantasy of "free-wheeling" life away from it all.

With a keen sense of justice for all, Elam adhered strictly to the moral code so aptly stated, "Your freedom ends where my nose begins." This conviction was vigorously applied in neighborhood disputes, in school board and church board confrontations, and in local and regional politics. He railed against social evils created by alcoholic excess, while recognizing medicinal benefits from fermented products. He purchased cigars from time to time, maybe to provide relief from pesky insects that plague one who farms with horses, or maybe as gifts to those who helped around the farm. He resented the smoking of cigarettes and refused to converse with anyone who was smoking one.

Elam was ahead of his time in many things, but especially in his respect for women. He showed no evidence of taking a leading role as activist in such considerations, but he was willing to accept as equal with men those who preached the gospel, taught in Sunday school, and advocated female voting privileges. (Not until 1920 did women gain the right to vote, with ratification of the 19th Amendment. Congress had first taken up the issue 40 years earlier, in 1880.)

Elam harbored no bias against people of other races, showing full respect for those who had been freed from slavery during his younger years. When he referred to the nearby town of Nicodemus, Kansas, as a "darkie town," it was done entirely devoid of aspersion or malice. He supported a political ticket in 1892 that included a black candidate for state auditor. (It lost.)

1871

From the very beginning of the diary, in January 1871, when Elam was 18, he slowly revealed religious inclination. On Sunday, the 8th, he attended evening services at the Methodist church in Farmington, Illinois. He returned the next two nights. It is likely that religious interests prompted him to begin writing things down in a journal.

It is fair to conclude that the neighbor boys, Howard and Charlie Day, had something to do with Elam's religious development. Elam's diary contains frequent reference to their companionship at church and at their home.

Later in Elam's diary it becomes evident that Elam's mother was a positive influence in his early religious development, nurturing this young spirit, which grew stronger as the years rolled by. And strong it would have to be, for life on the frontier would test it to the core. On the other hand, his father was passive — a bystander. He did not interfere, and it was disappointing to Elam that there was no active participation in religious things.

The family had come from Strasburg, Lancaster County, Pennsylvania, leaving there when Elam was but two years old. The county is well known for its religious inclination, a concentrated area of "Pennsylvania Dutch," with many of the strict Amish beliefs. Since the family was not part of that persuasion, it is possible that they were repelled by those who were and that Elam's father never overcame that.

Elam, however, had no such personal experience to bias him against religious expression, and he was drawn to the teachings and life style of the principal Protestant denominations in the Midwest (Illinois) and the West (Kansas). Weekly church attendance on the frontier was not always possible, for there were not enough parishioners to maintain a full-time minister in most places. Sometimes several parishes shared a minister, and services were held only when he was able to come, or when a series of meetings was held on consecutive nights for a concentrated preaching mission.

Sunday schools helped fill the void when no preaching services were possible. They served a good purpose in their own right, providing instruction in Bible teachings to children and adults alike. Elam was a great champion of the merits of this training, and he carried his ideas to the frontier.

From the very beginning of the diary, Elam reveals a strict reverence for the sanctity of Sunday, most often referred to as "Sabbath." His entries typically say, *Spent the day in reading and rest.*

Elam attended church during the first eight months of 1871 at the Methodist church in Farmington, where several of his friends went. Then on September 17 he went to the Farmington Presbyterian church with his friend, Charlie Dunn. That was a major turning point in his life, for it was there that he found the girl who later became his wife, and there he began to come alive spiritually.

1872

On various occasions during the next nine months, Elam continued to attend the Methodist church. Then on June 30, 1872, he and Charlie Dunn went to Sunday school at nearby Liberty school, where Thomas Montgomery was superintendent. Just four years later, Mr. Montgomery would become Elam's father-in-law. This entry in the diary was marked by a border on all sides, signifying the importance felt in this event.

There followed fairly regular attendance at the 3:00 p.m. Sunday school at Liberty school house, and frequent attendance at Presbyterian services in Farmington, where Rev. Thomas Stevenson was minister.

On August 8 and 9 Elam helped Thomas Montgomery thresh grain. Previously Elam had worked for other farmers in the vicinity, but now he began helping Mr. Montgomery regularly, and the spiritual bonding deepened as the two labored together.

Shortly thereafter the social aspect of this relationship surfaced. On October 2: *With a party of five other young folks of the tribes of Bartholomew and Montgomery, went over northwest about 2 miles where we spent the day gathering hickory nuts. Had a most excellent time, got 3 bushels of nuts and came home about 6 o'clock p.m.* Six days later they collected four bushels.

1873

During March 1873 Elam attended revival services nearly every night at Pleasant Hill school house. On the 13th came a major milestone in his life. *In the evening attended meeting again at the school house and on the invitation of the minister I then and there publicly manifested my desire to have a change of heart and become a Christian! On my way home I stopped at Montgomery's and finding Rachel quite sick I remained all night.*

He felt great joy in his new commitment to the Christian life, for on the 14th he related: *In the evening attended church at Pleasant Hill and found sweet peace in accepting the Lord Jesus Christ as my Savior and King, resolving with God's help to henceforth live the life of a Christian man.* This was a covenant from which he would never turn back, living it out diligently to the end of his life, 61 years later.

Every evening through the 27th found Elam attending services at the school house, except for one when there was a severe snow storm. Rachel recovered from her illness and went with him on at least two occasions.

Then came the next big event in his religious experiences. On Saturday, March 29: *In the p.m. went to Farmington and at 3 oclock attended preparatory communion services at the Presbyterian church and heard a good sermon by the new pastor, Rev. W. J. Bollman after which I presented myself before the Session for examination with a view to uniting with the church and past a satisfactory examination. Past the night in town at the home of Mr. & Mrs. John Budd.*

Sunday the 30th: *Attended services at the Pres. ch. at 10:30 a.m. at which time I was baptized and received into full communion of the church. After listening to a good sermon by Mr. Bollman came home at one oclock p.m. having first participated in the communion service. In the evening attended church at our school house and on the way home called at Thos. Montgomery's awhile.*

Right away Elam began to broaden his religious orientation as much as was possible in a rural setting. On Sunday, April 13, he attended *an evening meeting in the interest of the American Bible Society held in the Methodist church.* And on the 27th: *In the evening Thos. Montgomery came over and we walked into town (2½ miles) to attend a temperance meeting at the Congregational church. As it rained on us the whole way home we had a muddy tramp of it!* The next Sunday he *attended a temperance rally in town at the Methodist church.*

Elam's 21st birthday, on June 9, was another occasion for celebration, both spiritually and romantically. In the evening he went to visit Rachel, and she gave him a "fine" New Testament. They became engaged three months later.

1874

Communion services were held in the Presbyterian church four times a year. It was a 19th-century practice to conduct a service of preparation on Saturday prior to the Sunday celebration of that sacrament. On Saturday, February 28, 1874: *Went to Farmington in the a.m. and remaining there attended preparatory communion services at the Presb. church at 2 p.m. after which I returned home and spent the evening in making a presumptively very necessary call at the home of Thos. Montgomery.* Then on Sunday, March 1: *Attended church and communion at the Pres. ch. in Farmington and came home at 2 oclock spending the rest of the day mostly in reading.*

After Elam went to Kansas in March to take up a homestead, it was some weeks before he got established sufficiently to find a place to worship on Sundays. Finally on May 24: *Attended church and Sunday school at the Saylor school house 5 miles N.E. and was gone all day.* He attended services there nearly every Sunday for the next six months. When there was no minister, he went to Sunday school. The minister, D. G. Kling, was affiliated with the United Brethren denomination. Frequently Elam ate Sunday dinner at the Klings' home and visited with Reverend Kling, a mentor for this fledgling Christian. In return, Elam worked many days at the Kling place stacking hay, digging a well, building a dugout stable, and helping in other ways. He enjoyed the companionship of Klings' son, John.

Then on November 17, a Tuesday: *In the evening attended United Brethren meeting at neighbor D. A. Duff's and heard a sermon by Rev. Schiesser.* The next evening: *Attended church again at Duff's and united with the United Brethren church."* Not long after that, on December 19: *Went down to Rev. D. G. Kling's in the morning and in company with him drove over onto Deer Creek 7 miles N.W. of Kirwin where we arrived at 2 oclock p.m. and went to the home of Mr. M. H. Gardner to attend the U. B. quarterly conference for this district. The conference met at 3 oclock and was presided over by elder Loggan. Spent the night at the home of Wm. Archer near by.* The next day was Sunday: *Attended communion services at Gardner's at 10 a.m. Sermon by elder Loggan after which the ice was cut and a Mrs. Henderson baptized by immersion in Deer Creek.*

1875

By April 4, 1875, it had occurred to Elam and at least a few others that there would be merit in organizing another Sunday school for the convenience of neighbors: *Attended the organization of a Sabbath school at D. A. Duff's in the a.m. with Samuel Hebrew, Sr., as Supt. and myself as assistant Supt. and chorister.* But this did not signal a break in the friendship with Rev. Kling or his son John, for Elam spent many spiritually and socially edifying hours at their place, and he remained active in their church. On June 5: *Went down to Mr. Kling's in the morning and with him went over S.E. some 14 miles to the mouth of Medicine creek to attend the U.B. quarterly conference.*

1876

In the summer of 1876 Elam returned to Illinois, where he and Rachel were married by the Presbyterian minister, Reverend A. R. Mathes, on June 14. Then on the 25th: *As a married couple we made our initial appearance in church at Farmington today at 10:30 oclock and heard a good sermon by Rev. Mathes.*

In early September Elam and Rachel prepared to leave for Kansas. Reverend Mathes went to see them on the 4th. Then they stopped by to see him in Farmington, on their way to the train station.

After arriving in Kansas, Elam and Rachel stayed at Footes' home while their own house was being completed. They attended Sunday services regularly at the Saylor school house. The day after moving day, September 15, Elam wrote: *We spent this, the first Sabbath in our new home, alone, in reading and rest. On this day we established the family altar in the home on which to offer, morning and evening, the sacrifice of prayer as long as the household shall stand!*

1877

June 17, 1877, was another milestone in the religious life of this young couple: *W. E. Foster of Osborne City, a S.S. Missionary for the American Sunday School Union of Philadelphia, Pa., came in last evening after having canvassed the neighborhood somewhat and stopped with us for the night. At 10 oclock a.m. he organized a Sab* [Sabbath] *school at our house to be held at the same hour each Sab. I was chosen Supt.*

1878

On April 6, 1878, Elam and Rachel vowed to lead a sober life: *In the evening wife and I attended a* <u>Blue</u> <u>Ribbon</u> *temperance meeting at the Rockport post office where we both signed the pledge to abstain from alcoholic liquors as a beverage.*

The Sunday school at Bartholomews' home went out of existence after a few months — a major disappointment — but another was organized nearby on April 28. This one met at Wilcoxen's, and again Elam was superintendent.

On Elam's 26th birthday, June 9, there was a happy event: *Rev. J. E. Young again conducted services at our house at 11 a.m. and after the sermon we had our little 13-months old boy, George, baptized, taking upon us the usual vows of the church to rear him in the ways of righteousness.*

October 18 was an outstanding day for Elam and Rachel for more reasons than one: *At 8 a.m. became heir to an 11½ lb. boy* [Elbert]. *At 11 went down to neighbor C. C. Foote's with Dr. H. F. Albright of Smith Center and Rev. Theo. Bracken of Phillipsburg who had called to see why I had failed to attend a duly called meeting at the Foote home for the purpose of organizing a Presbyterian church. When they learned the circumstances*

*causing my failure to show up I was duly excused. We then went on with
the services and proceeded to organize the Bow Creek Presbyterian
church with five charter members, as follows: Mr. Sam'l Hebrew, Sr.,
Mrs. Jane Hebrew, Mrs. Kittie E. Hebrew, Mrs. Rachel Bartholomew, the
latter joining by letter from the Farmington, Ill., Presbyterian church, and
myself. To complete the organization I was duly elected, ordained and
installed ruling elder!*

Two days later, on the 20th: *At 11 a.m. attended the first Sabbath meeting of our new church at the home of neighbor C. C. Foote where services
will be held for the present. Heard a good sermon by Mr. Bracken.* Bad
weather for several weeks of early winter kept Rev. Bracken and most others from attending, so the future of this fledgling congregation was indeed
tenuous.

1879

Every winter there was a special event called a "necktie party," which
included singing and games. The community was invited, and the clergy
were recognized for their dedicated service. (This is not to be confused
with the other kind of "necktie party" — execution by hanging.) On January 14, 1879: *Went to Mr. Samuel Hebrew's to attend a necktie festival
given for the benefit of Rev. Bracken, our minister, and Rev. A. B. Conwell,
the Methodist minister having charge of the Bow Creek Methodist church.
Neckties were sold at 25¢ per piece, thirty seven numbers being sold,
yielding a revenue of $9.25, which was equally divided between the two
above named reverend gentlemen. About 80 persons were present and a
general good time was indulged in by all hands.*

Because he was an elder in the church, Elam sometimes had to take
over when a minister could not be present. On March 1: *Went over north
about a mile and a half to Mr. Ed Roberts to attend the funeral of his little
three year old daughter who died with the diptheria, at 11 a.m. yesterday,
and the minister failing to come, assisted in conducting a short service
after which we repaired to the Hebrew cemetery where the remains were
consigned to their everlasting place about 2 p.m.*

On September 25, Elam was a delegate to a Presbyterian conference.
This was the first of many such trips, and he felt honored. The details
are meticulous and precise: *Having been selected as a representative, by
the Bow Creek Pres. Church, to the Presbytery of Solomon and also to the
Synod of Kan., to be held at Salina, the former Sep. 30th and the latter*

Oct. 2nd, and having made all due preparations had brother Geo. start with me at 6 a.m. for Kirwin where we arrived at 10 oclock, and meeting there our minister, Rev. Theo. Bracken, according to previous arrangements, (he being accompanied by his wife and three little boys) we set out on our journey for Salina, a distance of about 135 miles from Kirwin, travelling in Mr. Bracken's democrat buggy.

We stopped about 2 miles west of Cedarville, after passing over into Smith Co., and while our team was feeding, partook of a dinner lunch and starting on again passed through Cedarville at 1:30 p.m. and going on about 2 miles further came to where the workmen on the Cen. Branch U.P.R.R. were busily engaged in laying track on the previously constructed road bed.

How odd indeed it seemed to see the iron horse attached to the construction train, standing at the very end of the track, with his head pointing toward the land of the setting sun, seemingly eager to plunge farther and farther into the trackless wilds of the untrodden west! How odd I say it seemed when I took into consideration the fact that in Oct. 1875 when I last travelled over this same valley the western terminus of the railroad was at Waterville, 150 miles east of Kirwin.

The trip continued through Gaylord, Harlan, Bethany, Downs, Cawker City, Glen Elder, Beloit, Asherville, Glasco, Delphos, and Minneapolis before reaching Salina. At Asherville they met another railroad crew *working on the Solomon valley branch of the Kan. Pacific R.R. which is to reach Beloit sometime this fall.*

While in Delphos they saw results of a June 10 tornado that had destroyed half of the village's 60 buildings. *We found rather an odd but perhaps a very advisable practice in vogue among the citizens of the town which was that they had made little dugouts or caves near their houses that they might fly thither in case of the appearance of another tornado; we were told that many of the people, during the latter part of the season, would fly to their little dugouts whenever a little thundershower came up.*

Passing over into Saline Co. we crossed the Saline river shortly after 4 p.m. and arrived in Salina at 5. Going to the Pres. church we met Rev. W. A. Simkins, the pastor, who gave Dr. Albright and I an introductory card to Mr. Thos. White who resides on the outskirts of town at the N.E. side, his house being built on the bank of the Smoky Hill river. Mr. Bracken and his father were given quarters in another part of town.

The next morning Elam got his first look at the largest town in northwest Kansas: *Passing through the business part of town on our way to the church this morning we found it to be a well laid out and finely located town, being a large, prosperous and thrifty business centre of about 3500 inhabitants.*

Proceedings of the presbytery, followed by the synod, were mostly routine, with two items worthy of note. *The advisability of locating a Presbyterian College for the Synod of Kansas was discussed and after a long, hot, spirited and somewhat acrimonious debate it was decided that the question was premature and as Salina, Emporia, Marion Centre and Peabody had each offered the sum of $20,000 for its location, no decision was arrived at and the question of location was put off until next year.* (Emporia was the site later chosen.)

On Sunday all the Protestant churches of Salina opened their pulpits to the Presbyterian clergymen who were in town. One of the evening services included this presentation: *Dr. Hill of Kansas City gave a short sketch of the history of Presbyterianism west of the Mississippi river and quite a full account of its progress in Kan. from its two small churches in 1856 to its 271 in 1879.*

1880

Beginning in 1880 Elam started the practice of faithfully recording every Sunday the biblical text from which the sermon was taken, and the theme of the message. On January 4: *Attended church at 11 a.m. and listened to an instructive sermon by Mr. Bracken on the subject of "The Fullness of Christ's Salvation" from Col. 2:10, "And ye are complete in him".*

The next day a business trip to Stockton found him on one of his frequent visits to a favorite clergyman friend: *Went to Stockton on official and other business, spending several hours during the day at the residence of the Rev. F. E. Sherman, the Congregational minister, who invited me to dinner and supper with him at his boarding place, Mrs. M. J. Patterson's. After supper accompanied him to prayer meeting and still later returned to his house where I remained all night, passing a very pleasant evening in social chat and examining many of the books of his library. Mr. Sherman has a residence of his own, but being an unmarried man gets his meals at Mrs. Patterson's.* Elam needed this fellowship with one who could be his spiritual mentor, and his inquiring mind and limited budget relished the opportunity to borrow religious and other books.

1881

Charles Darwin (1809-1882) had caused much consternation in religious circles with his books *The Origin of Species*, in 1859, and *The Descent of Man*, in 1871. Without a doubt Elam's scientific mind was stimulated thereby, and his religious convictions challenged. But there is no evidence that he entirely repudiated these concepts. He did, however, take offense at some of the presentations being made on the subject. For example, on June 11, 1881, he recorded: *In the evening went over to the school house and listened to a very weak, disconnected and illogical discourse on the subject of "The creation as it was, as it is and as it will be" by one Daniel Fike of Greenfield Tp., this county.*

And on the next day, a Sunday: *Attended S.S. at 10 a.m. and after the exercises closed, the above Mr. Fike was on hand again and "inflicted" on us another of his unorthodox, soul-sleeping discourses.*

Elam began looking around to see how things were going with Sunday schools elsewhere in the county, for he was concerned that they be conducted in a responsible and respectable fashion. Thus on July 31: *Attended the Rockport Sab. school at 10 a.m. as vice president of Farmington Tp. for the county Sunday school Association. Found the attendance small, about 12 or 15, and rather poorly managed, principally on account of the school being held in a very small and poorly arranged room.* But he sensed there might be something else wrong besides the room situation, and that turned out to be true. On August 28: *Went up to Rockport to attend Sab. school at 10 a.m. but the Supt. being the subject of a scandal originating last week and he not being present and the school all having refused to come out, no services were held so I came home at noon.* (The nature of the scandal was not revealed.)

1882

July 2, 1882: *On account of the unsafe condition of our sod school house* [from heavy rains] *we moved our school fixtures down to Mrs. Foote's house where Sab. school and church will hereafter be held. Listened to a fair sermon by Rev. Joseph Patterson, our new minister, from Deut. 32:47. Got home at sunset, preaching being at about 4:30 oclock.*

Near the end of the year, on December 17, Elam wrote an impassioned obituary for something he held dear: *Attended Sab. school at the usual hour of 11 a.m. or rather <u>went</u> to attend but only about a half dozen per-*

sons being present, no school was held, and the school will be suspended for the winter. At church last Sab. it was announced that on today the question of whether we <u>could</u> or <u>should</u> continue through the winter would be brought up and as a large congregation was present all knew what the result of their absence today would bring. But we also have to succumb to the inevitable, and at last our dear old Mt. Lebanon Sab. school has had to lay down its life work, the value of which can only be brought to light on the resurrection morn. We have run uninterruptedly in peace and prosperity since Feb. 23, 1879, a period of nearly four years. And now let us inquire into the causes of suspension. We can trace our failure to only two causes. The first can be attributed to the fact of a large number of persons who were formerly very regular in attendance removing from the neighborhood and none coming in to take their places, and the second cause is one for deep regret and heartfelt anxiety! It is simply this: Lukewarmness, Laziness, Soul-leanness, Worldly-mindedness and Indifference to the cause of Christ and the upbuilding of the Redeemer's Kingdom by those who profess to be Christ's children, branches of the Living Vine and heirs of Salvation! How true indeed are the lines:

> *"The sword may be burnished, the armor bright,*
> *For Satan appears as an angel of light;*
> *Yet darkly the bosom may treachery hide*
> *While lips are professing, I'm on the Lord's side."*

Of my own work or faithfulness in attendance at the sabbath school I have nothing whatever to say but will simply let this diary and the Great Judge mark the record.

1883

The neighborhood began to feel the loss of having no Sunday school four months later. On April 22, 1883, Elam wrote: *In company with Rachel and the children went to the school house* [which had been repaired] *at 11 a.m. where a goodly number of persons had met and we then and there proceeded to reorganize the Mt. Lebanon Sab. school which so ignominiously suspended the 17th of last December. Much against my will I was again chosen Supt. Mrs. Mary Lovell Assist. Supt. and Myrtle Southard Secy. & Treas.*

1885

Elam recorded a significant baptism on May 3, 1885: *Attended Sab. school at 10 a.m. and at 11 heard a fair sermon by Mr. Bracken from John 6:28&29. Afterward participated in the celebration of the Lord's supper. Just before the sermon we had our two youngest children — Jesse & Earl — baptized.* Jesse was three years old and Earl eight months.

1886

On July 29, 1886, Elam was greatly encouraged by the success of Sunday school efforts in the area: *Convention met at 4 p.m. in the Methodist church of Stockton and a large audience was present which is an unusual thing at the opening exercises. After a short devotional Rev. J. C. Walker, "Chalk Talker of Cawker"* [Cawker City, Kansas] *gave an exceedingly interesting blackboard talk on "Four of the devil's traps" as follows:*

> *1. No harm in it*
> *2. Just this once*
> *3. Nobody knows it*
> *4. Everybody does so*

Session closed about 5:30 oclock.

Things continued to go well the next day: *At 10 oclock p.m. the meeting adjourned having been the most successful S. S. convention ever held in this county.*

Infant son Hubert was baptized at age five months on November 7. He died on January 15, 1887.

1888

Then on April 1, 1888, there was an event of outstanding significance for Elam: *Attended Sab. school at 10 a.m. and church an hour later listening to a good sermon by Mr. Bracken from 2nd Cor. 5:18-21. Between Sab. school and church, the church session held a meeting and Mother came forward presenting herself a candidate for examination and admission into the church which proving satisfactory she was received by baptism. After the sermon the sacrament of the Lord's supper was administered.*

Elam's father had died seven years earlier without having been baptized or received into church membership, so this event was of importance to him beyond measure.

Rachel began to get involved with Sunday school work, giving Elam great pleasure. On June 14: *Fifteenth Wedding Anniversary! A combined Children's Day exercise consisting of the Bow Creek M.E. school and our school met in the Bailey grove at 10 a.m. and after the opening song a good address was made by Rev. M. J. Bailey and shortly thereafter an intermission was taken until after dinner when singing and various exercises were held until about 3 p.m. when the meeting closed with an address to the children by <u>wife</u>! Spent remainder of the day miscelaneously.*

1891

At the annual meeting of the Farmington Township Sunday School Association on November 11, 1891, two keynote speakers failed to show up and things went poorly. Elam's critique gave some insight into the friction between religious leaders and a populist political faction. He blamed the low attendance on the weather and on "old Nick's agents" from the Farmers' Alliance, who seemed to oppose all religious efforts.

1892

On February 3, 1892, Elam attended an impressive midweek worship service: *After supper wife and I in company with A. B. Wilson and family and the Hackmaster Bros. went up west four miles to the Marshall school house to attend church. A Mrs. Watkins, a colored lady, preached a very good sermon from Acts 3:19. She proved to be a very well educated and fluent speaker. She was neat appearing, well dressed, and her features when speaking were certainly very graceful. Her voice was as strong and powerful as that of most any minister and even more so than many. A most striking fact was noticeable whether in singing, at prayer or when making her address was that her voice registered an octave lower than that of the female voice in soprano or alto. This is a thing which I have heard before but never until tonight has it come under my own observation. She was tall, fair faced, robust and apparently about 35 to 38 years old.*

In mid-April 1892 Elam again attended the semi-annual meeting of the presbytery, this time in Hill City. It was a routine meeting, but the trip home involved stopping at a unique town: *Saddled my horse and at 9 oclock a.m. bade good bye to Hill City and its hospitable people and in a sort of foggy rain began the journey homeward, passing through the "darkie" town of Nicodemus at 11 oclock and stopped for dinner and to feed my horse at John Humphries. Was quite wet by this time so I stopped about 1¾ hours, when I again resumed my journey, stopping about 1¼ hours at John Gartrell's in Sugar Loaf township to dry again and warm myself. Mr. Gartrell lives on the place formerly occupied by the Mont-gomery boys* [Rachel's brothers]. *Arrived home at 6 oclock.*

Elam can scarcely contain his joy and pride in an event on June 18: *In the p.m. attended preparatory communion services at the school house at 3 oclock and listened to a good sermon by Mr. Bracken from Matt 5:6. Immediately after the sermon the Session met (to receive members.) The consummation of our prayers and the effort to bring up in the nurture and admonition of the Lord, our children whose births are noted in this diary under dates of May 1st, 1877, Oct 18, 1878 and Jan 3rd 1881 resulted today, by the grace of God, in calling them to present themselves to the Lord and before the Session, and passing a satisfactory examination were <u>each</u> received into the church, and thus this day has passed over onto the Lord's side one half of our little flock — George, Elbert and Lizzie!*

1893

Then on March 30, 1893, Elam eloquently recalls his own religious journey: *In looking over this diary I find that just 20 years ago today I made a public profession of faith in the saving power of Jesus Christ as the savior of mankind by uniting with the 1st Presbyterian church of Farm-ington, Ill., and this evening, as I look back over the many important events embraced in this score of years I rejoice greatly at the wisdom man-ifest in the step that day taken and God being my helper I shall ever delight to walk in the King's highway of Holiness.*

The presbytery met at Hays in April, and again Elam was a delegate. He recorded some items worthy of note: *Considerable time was devoted to a discussion of a revision of the confession of faith but all of the 28 overtures sent down by the General Assembly were answered in the negative.* The next day: *After dinner drove out south east of town about five miles to the little Russian village of Munjor and crossing Big Creek returned to town across the old Ft. Hays military reservation and among the buildings of the post which has not been occupied as a garrison for several years.* And on the final day: *Shortly before the adjournment of Presbytery the matter of electing Commissioners to the General Assembly which meets in Washington D.C. the 18th of May, was taken up and resulted in the choice of Rev. Bracken and myself as such Commissioners.*

Each presbytery was allowed two delegates to the annual meeting of the Presbyterian General Assembly: one minister and one layman. This was an honor of highest respect and responsibility, for the selection process took recognition of one's spiritual grounding and moral standing, one who would with highest integrity represent the membership back home in all matters coming under consideration. The Assembly of 1893 was going to deal with a most extraordinary matter, which meant the delegates carried a larger than normal burden of responsibility. They would hear charges of heretical teachings by a seminary professor.

Elam was well aware of this and relished the challenge. So were the members of the presbytery who selected him as the most qualified layman of the area to deal with this concern. He was also thrilled at the opportunity to visit the nation's Capitol. While there, he could visit the Department of Agriculture, with special attention to his botanical pursuits. And while en route, he could visit his former home in Illinois, with stops in Chicago going and coming to see the World's Columbian Exposition at Chicago.

On May 18: *At 7:30 p.m. arrived in Washington and I went at once to my lodging place previously assigned, 716 14th St. N.W. as the guest of Mr. Ridenour. After a hasty meal I went at once to the place of the meeting of the General Assembly, the New York Ave. Pres. Ch. and participated in the Assembly communion service.*

On the next day: *At 4 oclock the Assembly adjourned to attend a reception given at the White House by President and Mrs. Cleveland. At the appointed hour the Assembly, headed by Moderator Willis G. Craig of Chicago and the various other officers of the Assembly, marched in solid column about four abreast to the White House where the head of the column was ushered into the great East room which was soon packed as full as sardines in a box. Soon as the room was full Moderator Craig made a little speech to the President who responded in a few well chosen words after which every member of the Assembly was given a personal introduction to Mr. and Mrs. Cleveland who responded with a hearty handshake. I believe that Mrs. C. had a smile for everyone with whom she shook hands. Ex Justice Strong of the U.S. Supreme Court and Rev. Dr. Sunderland (the President's pastor) stood in line and also shook hands with every member of the Assembly. The presentations were made by Rev. Dr. Bartlett, pastor of the New York Ave. Ch., and an army officer whose name I did not get. We then passed through into the Red, Blue and Green Rooms where we spent some time strolling forth and back or sampling the easy chairs and settees. On going out onto the north porch whom should I meet but my old friend I. C. McMillan, formerly of Rooks County, Kansas, but now an employe in the P.O. Department. I had a very pleasant chat with him and promised to go out to visit him soon at his home in the little suburban town of Brightwood.*

Actions of the General Assembly were mostly routine — committee reports, presentations by foreign and home missionaries, and so on — which, though informative and edifying, were not particularly noteworthy. Then on the 24th the excitement began with the opening of the trial of Professor Briggs.

At 2:30 p.m. when the Assembly met it first disposed of overtures on miscellaneous subjects and then proceeded in real earnest to a preliminary hearing in the Briggs case in the matter of entertaining the appeal made by the prosecuting committee, from the finding of the New York presbytery last winter.

May 29: *The celebrated trial of Dr. Chas. II. Briggs of New York on the charges of heretical teaching and preaching as professor of Biblical Theology in Union Seminary came on at 10 oclock and the arguments for the prosecution were introduced by Col. J. J. McCook in a preliminary speech of considerable length which was followed by Dr. J. J. Lampe also in behalf of the prosecution. This occupied the time until 4 p.m. when Dr. Briggs took the floor in his own behalf continuing his address through the evening session until 10 oclock when the Assembly adjourned to meet as a Judicial body at 9:30 a.m. tomorrow.*

May 30: *At 9:30 I went to the church and listened to a continuation of*

Dr. Briggs address until noon. The Assembly met again at 2:30 p.m. and listened to the remainder of Dr. Briggs plea until 3:40 at which time he closed, apparently completely exhausted. The closing arguments of the prosecution were then begun by Col. McCook who occupied a little less than an hour after which a recess was taken until after supper. At the evening session a two hour's pro and con discussion was allowed to the members present from the Presbytery of New York, speeches being made by 9 or 10 ministers and elders, whereupon the Assembly adjourned.

May 31: *The Assembly met as a judicial body at 9:30 a.m. and spent the whole day in listening to three-minute speeches by various members of the Assembly both for and against Dr. Briggs. This continued with the usual recess until 8:45 p.m. when voting on the 34 specifications covering the several charges began and was continued until 10:30 oclock when the Assembly adjourned, having sustained the various charges formulated by the prosecuting committee by the very decisive vote of 379 to 116!*

And thus has ended the most important trial that the General Assembly of the Pres. Ch. in the U.S.A. has ever had come before it. Its effect and general bearing on the church as a whole cannot as yet be safely predicted yet it is thought generally that it will go a long way toward ridding the church of that class of obnoxious higher critics who have been making themselves so loud during the past two or three years.

June 1: *Spent the a.m. at the Assembly in the transaction of miscellaneous business. At 2:30 p.m. when the Assembly met the report of the committee on the rendering of judgement in the Briggs case was heard and the report being adopted Dr. Briggs stands suspended from the ministry of the Presbyterian church.*

Elam's closing statement for this journal entry looked at his total experience in Washington, D.C.: *And thus endeth one of the most important events in the life history of the writer of this diary, either morally, socially, politically or religiously!*

1894

Elam and Rachel both went to the meeting of the presbytery on April 12, 1894, at Wakeeney. This conference became a significant milestone — both for Elam personally and for the church as a whole. *At 7:30 oclock attended the opening meeting of the Presbytery and listened to a good sermon by Rev. S. S. Wallen from Jer. 6:16. The election of moderator next ensued and a thing never before done in Kansas took place, viz: the*

*placing of a layman in the moderator's chair and the mantle of authority
fell on my shoulders, much against my protestations.*

Elam was more tolerant than many of his day when it came to issues
of gender and race in religion and politics. On August 16: *Attended a
religious and patriotic concert at the Mellon grove given under the direction of the famous colored lady preacher Mrs. Watkins. The musical recita-
tions and addresses were very good.*

1895

Irrigation ponds can be used for more than watering crops. On April 28,
1895: *After services (at the Pleasant Valley school house 4 miles west) we
all went a half mile north to an irrigation pond where 7 persons were baptized by pouring.*

For several years Elam had been doing what he could to organize and
nourish Sunday schools in communities near his home. He had been president of the Rooks County organization since 1893. By 1895 his aspira-
tions included wider horizons. Thus, on August 20 that year: *Frank Kizer,
missionary for the American Sunday School Union, drove in at our
place last night while we were at the school house and proceeded to make
himself at home until our arrival. At 7 oclock this morning Mr. Kizer and
I started out on a Sunday school convention trip to be gone a week or
more.*

*Our first point was 20 miles S.W. at McCroskey's grove in Alcona town-
ship where we participated in the exercizes of their convention which was
rather poorly attended. At the close of the meeting I organized a township
S.S. association.* The next nine days were consumed by this kind of activity until all of Rooks County had been covered.

On the last night they arrived at the residence of L. B. Flint, 3½ miles
southeast of Stockton. Then the next morning: *Mr. Kizer got up at 5 a.m.
and walked over to Stockton to take the morning train for his home in
Downs and at 8 oclock I took his team, the famous "Dan and Beersheba"
and started for home, arriving here at 10:30 oclock. Thus endeth our ten*

days convention trip in which we travelled about 165 miles. (The Kizer team was picked up at a later date on another trip.)

Those engaged in religious work have utilized modern visual aids as rapidly as they became available. At the end of the county Sunday school convention on November 19: *To raise money for county and state work we had the use of the Congregational church stereoptican and gave an entertainment at the opera house on "The Life of Christ".*

1896

During June 1896 Elam traveled around the county, attending each of the township's annual Sunday school conventions. Most seemed to be thriving, not only in numbers but in spiritual formation as well. Not so back home. He was embarrassed and disgusted with the one near his own township despite the large attendance: *At 8 a.m. set out for the Bow creek township S.S. convention and got to Webster's grove where it was to be held at 11 oclock.*

The attendance was large — 175, but it was the slimmest convention that I have ever attended. It seemed to be a huge baseball and swinging party with ice cream and lemonade attachments including the sale of cigars for the benefit of the Sunday school!!! A veritable disgrace indeed! A complete failure as a convention! Miss Tillie Reed was president. Wm. Edwards was elected to the presidency for the ensuing year. Elam was not opposed to having fun at the right time, including Sunday school picnics and parties, but when the appropriate time came for something inspirational and nothing was offered, he found it intolerable.

One of the tenets Elam and Rachel held from their Judeo-Christian heritage was that the firstborn son was dedicated to life in a religious vocation. This George accepted, and it was understood from his early years that he would become an ordained minister. Thus he entered a Presbyterian college in the autumn of 1896, choosing one that had been established in 1882: the College of Emporia at Emporia, Kansas — not to be confused with the state teachers' college (Normal) in the same town.

A Sunday school was organized on November 22 at the "Red" school house four miles south, with Elam as superintendent. Later this group was named "Mt. Nebo."

1898

Two more family members joined the church on February 27, 1898: *At 3 oclock we all attended church at Mt. Lebanon and heard another good sermon on the subject of baptism. There were four additions to the church today, Jesse [15] and Earl [13] being among them. The rite of baptism was administered to 11 subjects.*

Then on May 22 the last child — Lee — joined, and Elam was exuberant in his pride, yet humble in thanksgiving: *After the sermon we held communion services at which time our baby boy, Lee, 10 years old, united with the church and now in God's dear providence all of our six children have been gathered into the fold by a public acknowledgement of the Redeemer's saving power for which we praise his most gracious and adorable name.*

1902

The full-time Sunday school missionary was a disappointment. On October 6, 1902, Elam wrote: *In company with daughter Lizzie went to Phillipsburg to Dr. Bracken's where we took dinner and a conference of Presbytery's committee on Sab. School Work having been called to meet there, Rev. J. C. Everett of Norton, Dr. Bracken and I went into a conference on the question of the re-commission of Mr. L. J. Allen (who, by the way, also drove over in our company) as S.S. missionary after March 1st, 1903, but we decided not to ask for his re-appointment unless more and better work was immediately manifest, and calling him before the committee we so informed him.*

1903

This issue was resolved in a surprising way on March 2, 1903: *In this morning's mail I received a commission from the Presbyterian Board of Publications and Sabbath School Work as S.S. Missionary for the Presbytery of Osborne at a salary of $800 per annum with an additional allowance of $160 for expenses. Mr. L. J. Allen resigned his position here and I have been chosen to fill the vacancy.*

The matter has been pushed and carried through by my friends chief of whom was Dr. Theo. Bracken of Phillipsburg, and I look upon the appointment as a very gratifying compliment, but I have misgivings in regard to my ability to fill an office of this character, but if I may be an instrument in the Lord's house to do some good I will rejoice!

Work began on Wednesday, March 18: *At noon went out on my first actual missionary tour in the interests of the Board in organizing Sabbath schools.* He had done this before within Rooks County, but now all of northwest Kansas was his field of work. *Drove N.W. into Plainview township, Phillips county, where I canvassed the S.E. quarter of the precinct and making some 7 calls arranged to put in a school at the Brittain school house next Sab. at 2:30 oclock p.m.*

Then on Sunday the 22nd: *At one oclock p.m. in company with Jesse drove up N.W. to the Brittain school house when at 3 oclock I met the company of 34 persons and proceeded to duly organize a Sab. school with J. W. Delay, Supt.*

It was deemed necessary to purchase an additional team of horses to provide transportation in the performance of Sunday school missionary duties, so on April 20: *In the p.m. with Earl drove over S.E. about 7 miles to C. C. Hopkins' to look at a driving team which I desire to purchase.* On the following day: *With Lee went to Stockton on business and returning by way of Hopkins' purchased and brought home the team for which I paid $110.*

An excursion was enjoyed on August 4: *With wife boarded the 5:35 a.m. train for Lincoln Park, 46 miles east of Stockton, to attend the Chautauqua now being held there. The speech of Capt. Hobson, the hero of the Merimac, was a thrilling effort from start to finish! At 7:30 p.m. we took the train and with several members of the Nash family went down to Glen Elder, 9 miles, where we passed the night.*

Mary Nash was the fiancée of son George when he died in 1900. Following his death, Elam and Rachel desired that one of their remaining four sons become a minister. The next in line, Elbert, felt his destiny was in horticulture, which made Elam very proud — he would not discourage the idea. So the question of "Who will take George's place?" was put to the three younger boys. The next in line, Jesse, had definitely shown an interest, though he loved farming, as did Earl and Lee.

Finally Jesse made the affirmative decision and accompanied his father to the meeting of the presbytery at Natoma, where on October 7, 1903, the act became officially sanctioned: *At the afternoon meeting Jesse was called before Presbytery and examined touching his Christian experience, etc. and passing a satisfactory examination was taken under care of Presbytery as a candidate for the ministry and will expect to enter Emporia College in a few days as did his brother George 7 years ago.*

Jesse's first two years at the College of Emporia were spent completing his secondary schooling in preparation for college work, for the Stockton Academy had closed in 1896 and the fledgling public high school was not considered adequate for that purpose.

On October 12: *At 4 a.m. took Jesse to Stockton to catch the 5:35 train east on his way to Emporia. Three of the children will now be at Emporia — Elbert in the State Normal and Lizzie and Jesse at the College of Emporia!*

On December 20 Elam enumerated ten Sunday schools that were established in 1903 under his guidance: *This rounds out ten schools for the year as follows:*

Rockwell	*March 22nd*
High Prairie	*March 29th*
Fairview	*April 5th*
Harmony	*April 19th*
N. Twin Mound	*April 26th*
Sunny Slope	*May 10th*
Box Elder	*May 24th*
Truesdale	*July 5th*
Elm Creek	*Oct. 4th*
Elm Grove	*Dec. 20th*

When Elam traveled about the 22 counties of northwest Kansas establishing new Sunday schools and then returning to give them guidance, he amply described his trips, but most were without incident. Occasionally, though, some hazards were encountered — he described the hotel in Rexford, Thomas County, as *a fine resort of bed-bugs.*

1905

Elam encountered racial segregation when attending a regional Sunday school convention in St. Louis on December 9, 1905: *We were all, with the exception of Rev. W. D. Feaster a colored missionary from Arkansas, assigned lodging at the Edison Hotel, a block and a half from the Union depot on 18th street.* He made no other comment about the situation. Seemingly no one protested.

Rachel became an increasingly important part of the Sunday school ministry. With the children growing older, she was no longer confined to the home scene, so she accompanied Elam on many of these trips, often making presentations as well.

1907

During one of the trips, Elam encountered a serious problem. On July 7, 1907, traveling from Hill City to Morland and back that evening with Reverend Keeler: *At 9:45 oclock we started on our return drive to Hill City hoping to escape somewhat the intense heat of the day. When our journey was about half completed one end of the neck yoke came loose and dropped down which frightened the horses and in spite of our most strenuous exertions the team ran off at a most frightful speed!*

After running ¾ of a mile and doing much damage to the harness and buggy, as well as cutting one horse in the wire fence and injuring the other very badly by her getting her hind legs fast in the buggy by kicking, we finally got them stopped and after getting a lantern at a neighboring house we patched things up in a way and drove on into Hill City at 2 oclock and put up for the remainder of the night at Mr. Keeler's. Our experience was a most thrilling one indeed and only God's grace and protecting care saved us from violent injury or death.

The next day, after getting the buggy repaired, Elam returned home. *The badly injured horse stood the trip fairly well but showed signs of very great distress when I reached here.* But on the following day: *From the muscular tension of the run-away Sunday night I was so sore this morning in my arms, legs and hips that I could scarcely stand to dress myself. Horse scarcely able to move out of her tracks — legs swollen very badly!* But they both recovered, with no more mention of the incident.

Then on the next day, July 10, a decision was made, not related to events of the previous days: *Since March of 1903 I have been constantly employed in the work of Sab. school missionary but today, owing to advancing age and for other reasons, I sent to the Board my resignation to take effect at the expiration of my present commission September 1st, 1907.* One of the reasons was that his botanical work was suffering from lack of attention.

Before that termination Elam had the joy of seeing a son become involved in leadership of a Sunday school. On July 21: *At 3 p.m. with Jesse and Lee went up west 1½ miles to the Rockport school house where, after an address, I proceeded to organize a Sab. school with son Earl for Supt.*

1909

Jesse graduated from the College of Emporia in 1909. On September 13 he departed for three years' study in the McCormick Theological Seminary at Chicago. What a thrill for Elam, because a dream once anticipated for George was now to be realized in another son!

1910

Elam was again selected for a leadership role on April 12, 1910: *At 8 p.m. attended the opening meeting of the Presbytery of Osborne at the new Presbyterian church in Plainville and heard a good sermon by the retiring moderator, Rev. J. C. Everett of Phillipsburg, from Isa. 62:10, after which Presbytery was duly organized for business by the election of myself as moderator and Rev. T. C. Everitt for temp. clerk.*

During May of that year Elam attended the World Sunday School Convention in Washington, D.C., a highlight in his work in this field. After that event he made a stop in Philadelphia, where on Sunday the 29th he experienced something truly impressive: *Attended the Men's Conference at 9 a.m. at the Bethany Presbyterian church which was presided over by the world famed merchant prince, John Wanamaker. Mr. Wanamaker is the Supt. of the S.S. and the membership is 3500!*

Mr. Wanamaker's class of men and women numbers about 800! I was in his class today. I staid for the after-meeting, which is a practice that has been kept up for over 50 years, and heard many interesting comments and experiences.

1911

On February 15, 1911, a new church building was planned: *In the p.m. at 2 oclock, with wife, drove over to W. H. Hale's where at that hour we participated in a congregational church meeting called for the purpose of taking steps looking toward the building of a church structure in the vicinity of Mt. Nebo* [school].

After a full discussion of the matter it was decided to go forward and build. The site chosen being one-half mile north of the Mt. Nebo school house. As a board of trustees, which was also made the building committee, the following persons were chosen, viz: E. Bartholomew, president, W. H. Hale, secy., Henry Marshall, treasurer and E. R. Allen and Chas. Hamit.

Work began on the 27th: *At 2 p.m. went over south with Earl to the site of the proposed new church where we met with E. R. Allen and W. H. Hale and proceeded to stake off a square acre of land on the S.W. corner of the N.W. gr. of Sec. 27 of this (Farmington) township.* The next day: *With Earl at 8 a.m. drove over south 3½ miles to the site of the new church, where, with several others worked all day at excavating for the basement.*

Materials were purchased on April 22: *Made a trip to Stockton and while there met with the church trustees at the Stockton Nat. Bank and let the contract for lumber, cement and lime to the Chicago Lumber Co. and the carpenter work to J.W. Pickens for the new church at Mt. Nebo.*

Cement work began on the 27th: *With J. F. Jerby who came down this morning went over to the church site where, with some others worked all day at starting the cement work on the basement of the new church.* This was completed on May 11.

Jesse had completed two years of seminary by this time, and while he was home for the summer he got experience working in two parishes in the area. On May 19: *Lee took Jesse to Stockton this afternoon on his way by train to Alton and thence by private conveyance to Kill Creek, about 9 miles south, where he goes to preach day after tomorrow, he having taken up a 4-month's service there and at Pleasant Hill, N.E. of Logan. He will preach every other week at each place until the 11th of Sept. shortly after which he expects to return to his school work at Chicago.*

Elam was not heavily involved in the church construction, because of other obligations, but there were days such as July 6 when he *with Jesse went over to the church to do some work about the windows.* That summer he made a botanical trip, which took much of his time.

Then on November 4: *To Stockton to help get out of the cars and load onto wagons the pews for our new church.*

First services were held at the new building on the 12th: *Attended S.S. at 10:30 a.m. in the basement of the new church which was the first service held in the building and in the future our religious services will all be held at the church instead of at the old school house where we have been meeting for the past 15 years.*

On Thanksgiving Day, November 30, a box supper was held to raise money for an organ for the new church. A total of $32 was given.

1912

Weather interfered with dedication of the new building on April 14, 1912: *With wife, Earl and Lee drove over to Mt. Nebo at 10 a.m. and held Sab. school and at 11 oclock Dr. Bracken of Phillipsburg having arrived he conducted what was to have been the dedicatory sermon taking for his text Psalm 145:11-13, preaching a most excellent sermon. Following this came the ordination of Chas. Hamit as an additional ruling elder in the congregation. Then came a good dinner in the basement and at 2 oclock p.m. Rev. J. C. Everett having come in an auto from Phillipsburg preached another most excellent sermon from Mark 9:10.*

The weather being exceedingly disagreeable with a most terrific west wind and dense clouds of dust filling the air the attendance was cut down to such an extent that it was deemed best to postpone the dedication until another date and June 2nd was selected as such date.

The exercizes all were excellent, but less than 75 people were present and in consideration of the many who desired to be present and could not be on account of the inclement weather the dedication was postponed.

Jesse returned from Chicago on April 30: *At 7 p.m., Lee, who had gone to Stockton to meet him, drove in with Jesse on his return from Chicago where he graduated last week in his three-years course as a student at the McCormick Theological Seminary, fitting himself for the gospel ministry. He has made application to be sent to the foreign field but will most probably not go for perhaps a year.*

The next phase of action for the new minister was on May 8: *With Jesse left home in the buggy at 7 a.m. and drove to Phillipsburg to attend an adjourned meeting of Presbytery set for the purpose of examining Jesse and licensing him to preach. Reached Phillipsburg at 9:30 oclock and at 10 went to the Presbyterian church where the meeting was held. The examination came on shortly after 11 oclock and continued, including a short sermon, until 4 p.m., the examination being sustained by a unanimous vote, after which the act of licensure was carried out.*

It was a proud day on the 12th: *With the whole family we went to the church at 7:45 p.m. when Jesse preached his first sermon to the home folks, taking for his text Acts 4:12. His discourse was well received indeed.*

Finally, the official dedication of the Mt. Nebo church building took place on June 2, 1912, with an added feature: *In the p.m. at 2 oclock we all attended the dedicatory services at the Mt. Nebo church. The sermon was preached by Rev. Dr. Bracken of Phillipsburg from 2nd Chron. 6:7-8. Then came the raising of $375 deficit which was soon done after which the closing dedicatory services were conducted by Rev. Clay Bobbitt which continued until 5 oclock at which time the strains of the wedding march floated up from the organ presided over by Miss Ruby White of Franklin, Neb. and Lee and Miss Lillian White, preceeded by Rev. J. E. Bartholomew and the little flower girls, Ilah Foster and Helma Dahlgren, marched down the center aisle to the altar where the Rev. J. E.* [Jesse Elam] *conducted a fitting service uniting in marriage the young couple just mentioned. This closed the exercises of the day and we came home at 6 oclock.*

And thus ended the triumphant building and dedication of a house of worship in our community, in the face of much bitter opposition from both within and without by those who said "you never can do it", showing their faith by their works in laying every possible hindering cause in the way of the work by trying to prevent subscriptions being made and later trying to prevent the collection of subscriptions already made.

On the next day: *Sometime before noon a goodly number of invited guests assembled for the remainder of the day to participate in the infair reception of Lee and Lily who will make their home with us.*

In the evening about 10 oclock pandemonium and a few other choice noises broke out when about 50 young men, boys and a few girls gave a hilarious chaviari party to the newly married. Being invited in they all partook of refreshments and went away apparently happy and satisfied.

The Mt. Nebo Presbyterian Church, 1911. *Moses viewed the Promised Land from Mt. Nebo* (Deuteronomy 34:1-4).

Jesse left on June 28 for his first full-time position: *Wife with Lee and Lily drove to Stockton in the p.m. in the surrey and took Jesse along to take the evening train for Glasco where he has taken up work in the Presbyterian church for the present.*

1914

Elam had been unimpressed with the revival preacher Billy Sunday when hearing him in Galesburg, Illinois, some years earlier, but he formed a better opinion while in Denver on September 6, 1914: *I went up to the great Billy Sunday tabernacle on 11th St. where fully 10,000 people were comfortably seated with about 2000 more who could not get in. The great choir, under the leadership of the great Rodeheaver did some great singing. Mr. Sunday took for his text Luke 6:46 and the sermon was of the thunder and lightning type characteristic of the man and his methods!*

1915

On October 8, 1915, Elam was pressed into accepting a responsibility he no longer wanted: *Was re-elected today to my old post of Secy. of the County S.S. Association which position I laid down Oct. 30th 1903 — 12 years ago. The Association seems to be at the lowest ebb and the most inefficient at any period in the past 30 years!* He was especially pleased, therefore, when the convention on October 4, 1916, went so well: *The meeting was one of the largest and most enthusiastic conventions ever held in the county and cannot help but do great good in the Master's cause.*

1917

After the minister had served the Mt. Nebo church for just five years, it was decided that he should be replaced. On March 25, 1917: *Heard a rather flat and wandering sermon by Rev. Bobbit from Luke 8:11 which winds up his work on this field with many peculiar slips in conduct and speech that were not to his credit!*

Then just two weeks later: *In the a.m. time was spent with W. Baylor of Lawrence and our ex-preacher, Rev. Clay Bobbit of Stockton who called on me for the purpose of persuading me to take stock in a Colorado gold, silver, copper and lead mining project — 1000 shares for $150! But I didn't bite!*

1919

Elam was elated with news on January 18, 1919: *Learned today of the ratification, by more than three-fourths of the states of the Union, of National Prohibition of the nefarious liquor traffic! Amen and Amen!!!*

Elam was a delegate to the Presbyterian General Assembly at St. Louis. On May 15: *At 10:30 the meeting was duly opened by the retiring moderator, J. Frank Smith, in the grandest sermon I have ever heard! His text was John 3:7. The theme was reconstruction and reorganization following the material and spiritual devastation wrought by the great world war. It was a sermon never to be forgotten. It burned with beautiful patriotism and thrilled with spiritual fervor. It was filled with pathetic incident to the tear-breaking point yet often contained flashes of pleasing humor. A sermon of matchless eloquence and dramatic force!*

We met again at 3 p.m. at which time we proceeded to the election of a moderator. On the first ballot Elder John Willis Baer of Pasadena, Calif. was chosen. This was the first ruling Elder ever elected to this high office.

1920

Rachel retired from Sunday school teaching on January 11, 1920: *Wife, who has been an active primary teacher for the past 40-odd years laid down her active work today and Daughter-in-law Alice was chosen to take her place and hard indeed it will be to measure up to the consecrated efficiency of the one who gives up her class.*

Elam was excited about the importance of January 16: *A red letter day for the United States of America as this is the day on which National Prohibition goes into effect!*

On March 30, a negative element in the church was turned into something positive: *In the p.m. with wife and Lee attended our annual church meeting at Mt. Nebo where we all sat down gracefully on one member's everlasting pessimism regarding the <u>positive</u> <u>inability</u> of the Mt. Nebo church to continue its life without his say-so!*

The steam roller was brought out and set at work in such a delightfully squelching way that he was so flattened out that every part of the program was carried out with a promise of increased financial support and profitable work in the church for the ensuing year!

On April 15, Jesse received a high honor: *Learned this afternoon of son Jesse's election, yesterday, as ministerial commissioner to the Presbyterian General Assembly which meets at Philadelphia next month.*

On June 9, Elam expressed pleasure with the annual Sunday school picnic in his grove: *Birth-Day: Age 68! Through the a.m. continued preparations for the picnic and in the p.m. participated in the festivities thereof. Fine weather and a fine time! Good program! Good music! Good crowd! Good supper and good bye at 7 oclock! It was one of the most pleasant of pleasant affairs!*

A series of evangelistic services at the Mt. Nebo church was well received by Elam. On November 14: *Rev. Nance took for his text Mat. 27:22 — "What shall I do then with Jesus which is called Christ?" and preached what I consider the most powerful, dramatic and soul stirring sermon that has ever been heard in this region. The church was full and this marks an era in the work long to be remembered by those who were so fortunate as to be present.*

The last service was on the 21st: *In all there were 10 additions to the* *church. For Rev. Nance's services we raised $140. We also voted to purchase a $450 piano with a $114 commission thrown off making it $336. Its real purchase and payment therefore are matters yet to be worked out and perhaps fought over!* By December 28: *We wound up the canvass with $5.00 more than the amount required to purchase the new piano.*

1921

A best friend and spiritual mentor died on March 10, 1921: *We learned with genuine sorrow today, of the death this week, at Junction City, of our dear old-time friend, Rev. F. E. Sherman. A prince has fallen in Israel indeed! A man of pure Christian character, gentle demeanor and as true as steel. A friend once, a friend always! Our hearts are filled with deep sadness when we think that never more on time's side of eternity shall we see his dear face and feel his warm hand clasp!*

On April 20, 1921, a significant honor was bestowed on Rachel at the presbytery meeting in Wakeeney: *In the Woman's Presbyterial Missionary Society today wife was elected as an honorary member of the Board of Foreign Missions of New York. In like manner Mrs. Lucy G. Bracken, our good friend of Phillipsburg, was elected as an honorary member of the Board of Home Missions. These two are the first in the history of the Presbytery to receive this distinctive honor.*

Mt. Nebo church was the site of the autumn meeting of the presbytery in September 1921. Elam was proud to be a host. One of the side features was a tour for delegates to see his laboratory.

1922

A new Presbyterian church was built in Phillipsburg in 1922, so on December 25: *We drove over to the Burg where we called on Rev. L. A. Kerr who showed us through the new church which is nearing completion. It is a fine structure and will cost about $50,000.*

1923

From the frequent critiques about the sermons, it is obvious that Elam was growing uncomfortable with the way the minister at Mt. Nebo conducted services, though there were numerous times when the Moores and Bartholomews visited back and forth and shared rides. Finally on March 1, 1923, Elam lost his temper: *Kicked S. J. S. Moore out of the laboratory for slanderous remarks about the family!*

1926

At the presbytery meeting at Hoxie on April 13, 1926, Jesse completed his term as moderator, with Reverend Apel of Colby replacing him. A note of dissension appeared on the next day: *In the p.m. made a speech denouncing the teaching of Prof. J. S. Corvett, Bible instructor at the College of Emporia. The Presbytery seemed to be <u>unanimously</u> against him!* Of course the presbytery had no jurisdiction in the matter, but their voice would be heard by those in authority.

1929

Elam was again selected as a delegate to the General Assembly of the Presbyterian church, this time at St. Paul, commencing May 21, 1929. A special honor came his way on the 25th: *On account of having served 50 years or more, as an elder in the church, I with 8 other ministers and elders from various parts of the U.S. were called to seats on the platform by the Moderator!*

Concern surfaced on the 27th over a shift in theological instruction: *Wonderful debate from 3:30 to 5:30 p.m. on the Princeton Seminary resulting, I fear, in a complete overthrow of the time-honored policy in the government of that great institution of religious training. For my part I consider it a rotten deal all the way through as it virtually puts the modernistic bunch in supreme control! "What shall the harvest be" is a mooted question. We can only hope and pray that things may turn out better than it now seems possible. Poor humiliated Princeton!*

In August of 1929, Elam and Rachel moved to Hays, but they had not yet transferred their church membership when they returned to visit Mt. Nebo. It was a sad day on September 24 of that year: *With wife, Lee and Lily drove to the Mt. Nebo church where we attended a regularly called congregational meeting and after full discussion of the matter it was unanimously decided to ask Presbytery to dissolve the church organization and to dispose of the church property! Thus comes to a sad and regretful end a work launched in this community 51 years ago! A sad historic day!*

Elam must have felt that since he had moved away he was somehow responsible for the church's demise. But he was just too old to have held it together much longer, even if he had stayed. With increasing mobility as people acquired autos, and as roads improved, it was no longer practical to have so many rural churches scattered across the countryside.

1930

After moving to Hays, Elam and Rachel and Lee's family transferred their church membership to the Hays Presbyterian church. They appreciated the preaching of Reverend David McCleave, but took exception to certain aspects of church life. On March 10, 1930: *In the evening attended the wind-up subscription campaign at the church when the fund was reported at $17,580 which is $2420 short of the goal and <u>my prediction is that the $17,580 will not be realized by a long shot, with the present management and methods to be pursued in making collections</u>!* The campaign was conducted to pay off the debt on the recently erected building.

More discontent surfaced on the 26th: *At 7:30 oclock attended the annual congregational meeting at the church. The Presbyterian church of Hays appears to be a very close corporation, indeed, <u>under the dictatorship of Rev. McCleave</u>. The thought seems to be manifest that all those who are in, officially, should be retained and those who are <u>out should be kept out</u>! This leaves a carbon dioxide scent in the air and a dark brown taste in the mouth!*

Likewise Elam grew impatient with the leadership of the adult Sunday school program. On September 7: *Elected teacher of the adult men's Bible class which really should have come a year ago!*

1932

Elam could not continue teaching very long, however, because of failing health, so on January 10, 1932, he wrote: *Closed out my career as a Sab. school teacher which continued almost constantly since the summer of 1873 at Farmington, Ill.*

The baccalaureate program on the Sunday prior to the 1932 class graduation at Fort Hays State was satisfying to Elam: *Sermon by Dr. John H. Gross of Philadelphia, Pa. Brilliant assembly! Finest downright gospel sermon, without frills, that I have heard in many years!* It is interesting to note that this was on the campus of a state college!

Elam was the designated representative of the presbytery for the disposal of the Mt. Nebo property, so on October 5: *With Lily in the car left Hays about 1:30 p.m. for Stockton where we arrived in due time and I went at once to the business of seeing to the release of the mortgage which was put on the Mt. Nebo Presbyterian church property in Farmington township, Rooks Co., Kansas in the year 1911.*

They had two instruments drawn by lawyer Skinner transferring the church building, first to the trustees of Osborne Presbytery, and second, to the trustees of the Fairport Presbyterian church to have and to hold forever. All papers signed or in process of signing.

Then on the 27th Elam had to make one last pilgrimage to the Mt. Nebo site, a painful experience: *At 1 p.m. with Lily in our auto left for Stockton where we arrived in due time and after attending to some business there drove out to the site of the dear old Mt. Nebo church which has recently been dismantled and moved to Fairport, Russell County.*

1934

A colleague and good friend of Jesse came to Hays as a guest preacher on April 4, 1934: *In the evening attended a special service at the Presbyterian church and heard a good sermon by Rev. Orlo Choguill of Ellsworth, Kan.* He later went to Topeka to become minister of the First Presbyterian church.

It seems appropriate that the last entry in Elam's diary — September 21, 1934 — was of a religious nature: *Great Rodeheaver temperance meeting at Presbyterian church. Great crowd and magnificent meeting.*

Elam died at his home in Hays on November 18, 1934, at the age of 82. (Rachel lived until 1941, age 86.) Two funeral services were held: one at Hays, where he had become a respected member of the community in the few years he had lived there, and one at Stockton. At Elam's funeral the President of Fort Hays Kansas State College, Dr. C. E. Rarick, paid the following tribute:

Dr. Bartholomew's Funeral

(10:00 a.m., Wed. Nov. 21, 1934 at
Hays, Ks. and at 3:00 p.m. at Stockton, Ks.)

Words are often futile in expressing sentiments and experiences that have been many years in developing. However, I shall attempt to relate a few of the impressions which the life of Doctor Elam Bartholomew has made upon me, both before he came to the campus of our college and since that time.

My acquaintance with Doctor Bartholomew began many years ago. I had known him by reputation before I had had the opportunity to meet him personally, sometime during the year 1903. From the time of our first acquaintance until his departure, I have known quite definitely of his activities, of his purposes in life, and of the underlying philosophy that guided him. These qualities have challenged my admiration. I not only admired the way in which he attacked the problems of life, but respected greatly his manner of thinking. Also, I loved him because of the fineness of character, which years of study, close application and strict adherence to lofty ideals had brought him. He was both a scholar and a gentleman.

Doctor Bartholomew was a man of energy. Scholarship requires energy. He knew what it was to toil long hours and to enjoy the satisfaction that comes from rest after arduous labor. He not only worked consistently and persistently, but he worked intelligently, also. He had high regard for the scientific approach to tasks in life, and he used this approach in attacking his problems. No wonder that institutions of learning throughout the world respected his thinking and had confidence in the results which he announced. He merited all this because of his ways of thinking and his loyalty to truth.

Doctor Bartholomew was not alone an efficient scholar, but he was a man of remarkable gentility of character. Such a quality must have a secure foundation. Through the years of his life he had accumulated a wise, but a potent philosophy of life. He was a man of great faith both in his fellows and in his God. This faith, to him, became one of the underlying elements of his existence. He believed in the fatherhood of God and, therefore, in the brotherhood of man, and his life's activities and purposes were shaped strictly in accordance with that belief. He loved men and he utterly disliked every condition or element in life that was contrary to the welfare of his fellow-men. He contributed constantly to their well being. Therefore, he had a secure foundation for gentility of character.

Since coming to the campus of the Fort Hays Kansas State College, Doctor Bartholomew has endeared himself to the faculty and students of this institution. Although comparatively few of them had the privilege of knowing Doctor Bartholomew personally and closely, the impact of his scholarship and of his character was felt by all, and all held him in high esteem. His attentiveness to duty, his regularity of living, his dignity of bearing, and his unquenchable desire for truth, have left an impress upon this institution that can never be lost.

Others, better qualified to do so than I, will speak of personal traits in the life of Doctor Bartholomew but, in closing, I wish to pay this tribute to him. During the years of my acquaintance with him, his life has been to me an inspiration. The evident steadfastness of his purposes in life was a constant and worthy example. The integrity of his thinking and of his character appealed constantly to me as worthy of highest consideration and emulation. Thus has my faith in the intangible values in human experiences been continuously strengthened, and my hold upon eternal verities, even upon immortality itself, has become more potent — all because of the contacts and associations with this friend.

C. E. Rarick
President, Fort Hays Kansas State College

Afterword

*E*LAM BARTHOLOMEW'S WORK and influence live on. In fact, they have become even more significant with the passage of time. From the vantage point of more than 60 years after his death, and over 100 years since his botanical work got into full swing, one can see that the usefulness of what he did will never end. Present-day botanists and mycologists attest to that.

When Elam began his work, the "germ theory of disease" was a new concept. At the very end of his career came the discovery of antibiotics. He knew intuitively that among the fungi there could be some that were pathologically beneficial. The real breakthrough came in 1928, with the discovery of medicinal properties derived from a fungus mold called penicillin.

In laboratory testing, research scientists need to know what there is in nature that might be useful. But they need to know more than that. It is essential for them to learn where these things grow, both geographically and environmentally, and if they are identical to those found in other parts of the country and the world.

This is the function of mycologists — indeed, of all areas of the natural sciences. Elam perceived the need and he did his work well. His attention to meticulous detail and his perfectionism are still viewed with respect and awe by those specializing in the field.

In a paper entitled "A History of Mycology in Kansas," Dr. Charles L. Kramer, curator of mycological collections for the herbarium of Kansas State University, now *emeritus*, states:

> Although Bartholomew had no formal college education, he was honored in 1898 when Kansas State University conferred upon him the honorary degree of Master of Science. The following year he published *The Kansas Uredineae* in recognition of that degree. In 1927, the same institution conferred upon him the honorary degree of Doctor of Science, a distinction which may be unique in the field of science for a person having had no formal college education. Also in that year, he published *The Fungus Flora of Kansas* as contribution no. 268 of Kansas State University. This publication listed 1,829 species as occurring in Kansas. Until that time only about 465 species were reported from the state.

Identification of fungi can be subject to different interpretations; it is largely microscopic work. Most of the correspondence file kept by Elam (nearly 4,000 letters) concerned identity interpretations. Possibly much of that resulted from slight variations depending upon where the samples were collected.

Some of the significance of the work done by Elam and the skillful dedication he had in doing it is revealed in correspondence in 1993 from Barbara M. Thiers, Administrative Curator of the Cryptogamic Herbarium at the New York Botanical Garden:

> As far as the practical importance of Bartholomew's specimens, I do not know what might have motivated Bartholomew to do this work, but his legacy is exceedingly important to the study of fungi today, both from the academic point of view of

understanding the full range of diversity of the fungi, and from the point of view of agriculture, and understanding the diseases of plants that are important to humans. Of course I am sure you know about the severe pathogenic properties of the rusts — wheat rust is an excellent example of a rust that had devastating consequences on agriculture in this country. The most common use of a reference collection of specimens, such as North American Uredinales is for comparison with a rust that is encountered in a crop field. Another use is to document the parasites in a given area at a particular time, to try to understand how rusts migrate and evolve. For example, it is useful to know what rust fungi Bartholomew found around his home in Kansas, and compare that flora to what occurs in the region now. We still understand very little about the evolution of rust fungi, their life cycles and their migration around the world.

I can give a specific example of how useful Bartholomew's specimens can be. A few years ago, The New York Botanical Garden purchased the herbarium of DePauw University, which had a complete set of Bartholomew's North American Uredinales. Because we already had two sets, I wanted to give the DePauw set to an institution that could use it. I learned that there was a very active plant pathology herbarium in Brazil where there were several rust specialists, so I wrote to them and asked if they would like to have the DePauw set as a gift. I received an immediate, and ecstatic response — the Brazilians were delighted to receive the set, because the ability to consult a set of Bartholomew's specimens would help them identify the rust parasites that they encountered in their own country. Because the institution did not have a large library, they were frequently not sure what name to use for a given rust, and without knowing the name, they did not know how to control the infection.

After Elam's death, his original herbarium of about 40,000 specimens was acquired by the Farlow Herbarium at Harvard University. Dr. Donald H. Pfister, Asa Gray Professor of Systematic Botany, wrote to this author:

Collections in the Farlow Herbarium are used by investigators all over the world for varifying concepts of species, for establishing geographic ranges of species, and to study the ecology of species. Although your grandfather's collections are old, it is still possible in some cases to extract DNA samples from such specimens. Modern mycological systematics use DNA studies to help elucidate relationships of taxa (taxonomic categories or groups). Collections in general are very much a part of our work even today.

Conversations in 1995 with Dr. Joe Hennen, of the Arthur Herbarium at Purdue University, now retired and working at the Botanical Research Institute of Texas (BRIT) in Fort Worth, brought out these points of interest:

Bio-diversity has recently become a popular concept in ecological conservation. Elam Bartholomew was a pioneer in learning about the bio-diversity of plant rusts. The specimens he collected and identified serve as a basis for knowledge of the location where found and their specific identity as of those dates and locations. Moreover, by comparing his specimens with those collected today, from the same location, we can determine what evolution has taken place, if any. His work serves to either confirm old ideas about these matters, or cause us to change newer ideas.

We do not know how widely distributed individual rusts are, so those who collect specimens help define that. Moreover, we can secure new knowledge from even old specimens, such as those collected by Elam, as we now have better microscopes than he had, and we can put them through DNA tests, etc.

There are now about 7,000 known species of rusts. The work continues. There may be as many as 21,000, three times that number.

We should not think of rust fungi as all being bad. To me rusts are wonderful. Some can be useful in the bio-control of weeds, for example, eliminating or cutting down on the use of petro-chemicals for certain weed species with their many deleterious effects.

The number of rust species that cause serious problems in economically important plants is relatively small. In nature, an almost symbiotic relationship exists between the rust and its host plant. From a strictly scientific point of view, rusts are extremely complex and variable, and thus are very interesting and important in teaching us about basic biology, and helping us to understand some other types of fungi, etc.

Peter H. Raven, Director of the Missouri Botanical Garden at St. Louis, wrote in the January/February 1994 issue of *Nature Conservancy* magazine in an excellent article called "Defining Biodiversity":

> We have named only about 69,000 kinds of fungi, a group of incredible ecological and economic importance, but as many as 1.5 million may actually exist!

At the time of Elam's death, in 1934, he had 40,000 identified, though some of them may have been duplicates.

Some practical uses of mycological collections are explained in a 1995 letter from Dr. Amy Y. Rossman, Research Leader of the Systematic Botany and Mycology Laboratory of the Agricultural Research Service, U.S. Department of Agriculture at Beltsville, Maryland:

> I can assure you that these specimens (such as those collected by your grandfather) have been of great importance to the scientific community over the past decades and may become even more important as techniques are perfected for extracting DNA from dried organic material. Even now, I have been contacted by a plant pathologist attempting to determine the distribution of the fungus that causes late blight of potatoes, the fungus that also caused the Irish potato famine. As you may know, this fungus is threatening potato crops in the United States because of a newly discovered strain. We have specimens in the U.S. National Fungus Collections dating back to the mid-1800's that may shed light on the origin of the fungus and its introduction into this country. Nowadays techniques have been

developed that allow scientists to extract nucleic acids from these old specimens and determine if the fungus in the potato fields today is the same as the one from one-hundred years ago.

Here at the U.S. National Fungus Collections we house about one-million specimens of fungi, most of which are from the United States. The documentation of the fungi that occur within our borders is extremely important for many reasons ranging from monitoring changes that may occur in fungal species as a result of global climate changes and habitat destruction to whether or not shipments of citrus from Mexico should be allowed into the country. Allowing the import of agricultural commodities is directly related to which fungal diseases already occur within the country and which fungi we must guard against accidentally introducing.

In order to obtain information about these fungi, we have entered all the data from most of the specimens into a computer. Over the past years, we have entered data on over 600,000 specimens and can now extract that data. This includes 7,872 specimens collected by Bartholomew.*

And so the work goes on. Elam Bartholomew's enthusiasm and dedication to his religious and political beliefs, as well as to his botanical vocation, carried him through many arduous times. Were he living today, he would be ecstatic over the ways his work is still in use, and the potential for things even greater as new technologies are developed.

---

* *Via Internet: Telnet fungi.ars-grin.gov. For log-in, type 'user.' For password, also type 'user.'*

Bibliography

Barkley, Theodore M. Letter to the author. June 13, 1993.

Bartholomew, David M. "Government Commodity Support Programs in Cash and Futures Markets." *Journal of the American Oil Chemists' Society* 45 (June 1968): 322A-359A.

Bartholomew, Elam. Botanical correspondence. Kansas State Historical Society, Topeka.

_____. "Chasing the Illusive Fungus." *The Aerend.* 1.3. Hays: Kansas State Teachers College, 1930.

_____. Diaries and Correspondence. Archives of Kansas State Historical Society, Topeka. 1871-1934.

_____. "Edible Mushrooms of Kansas." *Kansas Academy of Science.* Topeka: Kansas Academy of Science, 1919, 174-179.

_____. *Fungus Flora of Kansas.* Agricultural Experiment Station Bulletin. Manhattan, KS: Kansas State Agricultural College, 1827.

_____. *Handbook of the North American Uredinales.* Morland, Kansas: A. R. Spurrier, 1933.

_____. *Index to Fungi Columbiani — Centuries I to XXX.* Stockton, KS: Record Print, 1910.

_____. "Some Enemies to Plant Life — An Unseen World." *Kansas State Board of Agriculture Report.* Topeka: Kansas State Board of Agriculture, 1925.

_____. "Why Study Botany?" *The Aerend.* 5.2. Hays: Ft. Hays Kansas State College, 1934.

Bartholomew, Elbert T. "Elam Bartholomew." *Mycologia.* 27.2 (Mar.-Apr. 1935): 91-95.

Bartholomew, George Wells, Jr. *Record of the Bartholomew Family.* Salem, MA: Salem Press, 1885.

Breining, Greg. "Back Home on the Range." *Nature Conservancy Magazine* (Nov./Dec. 1992): 13.

"Cereal Diseases Work." *Yearbook of the Department of Agriculture — 1910.* Washington, D.C.: U.S. Government Printing Office, 67.

Cummins, George B. Letter to the author. July 14, 1993.

DeQuattro, Jim. "Whitefly Fungus on Its Way to Growers." *Agricultural Research Magazine.* (May 1995): 16-17.

_____. "The Whitely Plan — 5-year Update." *Agricultural Research.* (Feb. 1997): 4-12.

"Extension of Cotton Culture in the United States." *Yearbook of the Department of Agriculture — 1910.* Washington, D.C.: U.S. Government Printing Office, 58.

Government's Experiment in Wheat. Kansas City Board of Trade. Ca. 1932.

Hall, Larry. "The Fungus Among Us." *Arbor Topics* (Hendersen Tree Service, Wheeling, IL) (Spring/Summer 1997).

Hennen, Joe. Letter to the author. Jan. 18, 1996.

Johnson, Allen. "Briggs, Charles Augustus." *Dictionary of American Biography.* Vol. 3. New York: Charles Scribner's Sons, 1929.

Kansas State Board of Agriculture — Excerpts from Biennial and Other Reports 1864 to 1877. Reprinted in 44th Report, 1960-1961.

Kirwin Chief. Kirwin, KS. Mar. 21, 1874.

Kramer, C. L. "A History of Mycology in Kansas." Unpublished manuscript. Manhattan, KS: Kansas State University. Ca. 1965.

"Laire Plum." *Yearbook of the Department of Agriculture — 1911.* Washington, D.C.: U.S. Government Printing Office, 430.

Lest We Forget. Rooks County Historical Society. *Osborne County Farmer*, publisher. 1980.

Lyons-Johnson, Dawn. "Fungus, Corn Plants Team Up to Stymie Borer Pest." *Agricultural Research.* (Nov. 1997): 12.

McDonald, Dale. "Biological Breakout." *Farm Journal.* (Feb. 1995): N-1 to N-4.

Morison, Samuel Eliot. *Oxford History of the American People.* New York: Oxford University Press, 1965.

Norris, Kathleen. *Dakota—A Spiritual Geography.* Boston: Ticknor & Fields, Houghton Mifflin, 1993.

Pfister, Donald H. Letter to the author. April 24, 1995.

Pickett, A. G. "Anthrax." *Kansas State Board of Agriculture Report.* Topeka: Kansas State Board of Agriculture, 1957-1958.

Raven, Peter H. "Defining Biodiversity." *Nature Conservancy Magazine.* (Jan.-Feb. 1994): 11-15.

Rooks County newspapers. Topeka: Kansas State Historical Society archives. 1876-1927.

Rossman, Amy Y. Letter to the author. May 23, 1995.

Suszkiw, Jan. "Fungal Rivalry Protects Tomatoes." *Agricultural Research.* (Aug. 1997): 20-21.

Thiers, Barbara M. Letter to the author. July 6, 1993.

Tinker, E. F. "Here Is a Man Whose Hobby Has Made Him Famous." *The American Magazine.* (Nov. 1919).

World Book Encyclopedia. Chicago: Field Enterprises Educational Corp. 1964.

Index

by Lori L. Daniel

— A —

Abbott, John, 3, 9
Abrams, L. R. (Dr.), 260
Adams, J. Q., 131
Adelphian Literary Association, 189
Africa, 264
African-American, 216
Agnew, Dean, 187
A Handbook of the North American Uredi-
  nales including Citations and Synonyms,
  268-270
ailanthus tree, 51
Alabama
  Auburn, 244-245
  Tuskegee Institute, 266
Albertson, F. W. (Professor), 187, 264, 271-
  273
Albright, H. F. (Dr.), 281, 283
Aldrich, W. W., 49
alfalfa, 52, 56-57, 84, 86, 88
Alleghaney Mountains, 130
Allen
  E. R., 300
  Henry, 225
  L. J., 295
  Theodore J., 38, 41, 231

Allies, 226
Allis, W. E., 147
Allison, S. L., 160
America, xvi, xx, 251
  East, 11, 16, 20, 26, 31, 149
  Great Plains, xx, 33
  North, xix
  Pacific Coast, 83, 223
  Pacific Northwest, 158
  South, xx
  West, 11
  West Coast, 163, 259
American, xix, 227, 252, 266
American Association for the Advancement
  of Science (A.A.A.S.), 260
American Bible Society, 279
American Magazine, 227
American Phytopathological Association,
  260
American Sunday School Union, 281, 293
Amish, 276
Anthony
  George T., 215
  Susan B., 216
Apel, Henry (Reverend), 307
appendicitis, 149

Archer, William, 280
Arctic Ocean, 268
Arizona, 57
Arkansas, 11, 152, 252, 265, 298
  Batesville, 252
  Electric Springs, 252
  Rogers, 252
Armstrong, James, 3
Arnhold, Fred, 187
Arthur
  Chester A., 204 (Vice President)
  Joseph Charles (Dr.), 248, 251, 256
  R. (Reverend), 53, 79, 144, 150
Arthur and Holway publishers, 245
ash tree, 41-42, 51
Asia, 262, 264
Atkinson, George F. (Professor), 244
Austria, 226
autocratic government, 227
automobile, 160

— B —

Babbit, C. H., 49
Bacchus, King, 112
Backus, E. M., 234
Baer, John Willis, 304
Bailey
  J. A., 36, 107, 109, 201-202
  M. J. (Reverend), 288
  Reverend, 124
Bains, Bessie, 117
Baker
  C. F. (Professor), 263
  Reverend, 109
  William, 215, 216
Baldwin, J. W., 30
Ballentine and Buchman, 38
Baptist, 204
barbed wire, 2, 44
Barnes, W. H., 207
Bartholomew, xv-xvi, 22, 58, 62, 104, 146,
  153, 187, 278, 281, 306
Bartholomew Family, Elam (son of George E.)
  Ben (cousin), 155
  David H. (cousin), 155
  Earl Robert (son), 8, 25, 54, 56-57, 60, 64,
    67, 80-81, 119, 123, 143-144, 146, 149-
    153, 159-160, 162-165, 168-171, 173,
    175-176, 185, 214, 222, 225-226, 245,
    247-248, 256-257, 287, 295-296, 299-301
  Alice Fern Hale (wife), 8, 160, 162-163,
    165, 168, 225, 305
    see also Hale, Alice
  Earl Robert, Jr. "Bobby" (son), 8, 168, 175
  Elizabeth Alice (daughter), 8, 160, 163
  Ethel Roberta (daughter), 8, 176
  Marie Fern (daughter), 8, 171
  Elam (husband), xi-xii, xvi-xxii, 1-3, 5, 8-
    11, 14, 16-18, 20, 23-24, 26-27, 30-32,

Bartholomew Family, Elam (continued)
  Elam (husband) (continued), 34-39, 41-55,
    57, 59-61, 63-66, 69, 73-76, 81, 83-84,
    86-87, 89-92, 94-104, 107-110, 112-113,
    117, 119-121, 123-125, 128-137, 141-
    148, 150-155, 157-171, 173-185, 187-
    194, 200, 202-203, 205-206, 208, 210,
    212, 214, 216-217, 221-222, 224-228,
    230, 232-233, 235-237, 239-290, 292-
    295, 298-300, 303-304, 306-311
  Census Enumerator, 224
  Clerk of District Court, 195, 198
  congressional delegate, 209, 224
  expense account, 126-127
  Justice of the Peace, 211-212
  Kansas Legislature candidate, 222
  moral code, 275
  township trustee, 195-196, 198, 200
  weather log, 71-72, 79
  Elbert Thomas (son), 8, 20, 25-26, 30, 44,
    52, 109, 118-119, 123, 133-135, 138-142,
    144, 146, 149, 151, 156, 159, 162, 165-
    166, 168, 185, 205, 239-240, 242, 248,
    252, 256, 261, 271, 281, 289, 296-297
  Lois Jeanne (daughter), 8
  Martha Lucille (daughter), 8
  Mary Lucille Keen (wife), 8, 165-166,
    168
  Elizabeth Fanny ("Lizzie," "Beth") (daugh-
    ter), 8, 25, 52, 80, 115, 118, 123, 135, 138,
    141, 144, 147, 149-151, 153, 159-160,
    162, 174, 185, 214, 289, 295, 297
    see also Ingle, Elizabeth
  Chester (son)
    see also Ingle, Chester, Jr.
  Floyd (cousin), 163
  George Edgar (son), 8, 29-30, 44-46, 49-51,
    108, 111-112, 115-116, 118-119, 123-
    124, 131-132, 135, 138-140, 143-144,
    149, 197, 205, 209, 222-223, 231, 235,
    281, 289, 294, 296-297, 299
  Hubert David (son), 8, 119, 121, 123-124,
    287
  Jennie (cousin), 155
  Jesse Elam (son), 8, 52, 54, 57, 64, 67, 81,
    118, 123, 135, 138, 140-141, 143, 145-
    146, 153, 156-159, 163, 165-166, 168,
    170, 174-177, 179, 181, 185, 187, 248-
    249, 252, 257, 262, 268, 271, 287, 295-
    297, 299-300, 302-303, 305, 307, 309
  David Morris (son), 8
  Florence Cook (wife), 8, 174, 176, 262,
    268
    see also Cook, Florence
  Robert Daniel (son), 8, 67, 174, 179
  Lee Montgomery (son), 8, 54, 56-57, 60-61,
    63-67, 85, 88, 124, 140, 144, 147, 152-
    153, 156, 158-160, 162-166, 168-170,
    172-173, 175, 180-188, 227, 248, 252,

Bartholomew Family, Elam *(continued)*
  Lee Montgomery (son) *(continued)*, 256-257, 269-270, 273, 295-296, 299-303, 305, 307-308
    Elam Albert (son), 8, 169, 182, 184, 186
    Emma Lillian White "Lily" (wife), 8, 64, 67, 159-160, 162-166, 169, 172-173, 175, 180-181, 184-185, 187-188, 227, 269-271, 302-303, 307, 309
      see also White, Emma Lillian
    Margaret May (daughter), 8, 166, 182, 185, 188
    Rachel Caroline (daughter), 8, 64, 165, 170, 185-186
  Rachel (wife), 7-8, 11, 18, 20, 22, 29-30, 37-38, 52, 54, 66, 106-112, 117-119, 121-124, 128, 131-133, 135-136, 139-140, 142-147, 149, 150-151, 154, 158-160, 163, 165, 168-170, 175-179, 181-183, 185-188, 196-197, 205, 214, 225, 227, 259-260, 262-264, 268-269, 278-282, 286, 288-289, 292, 294, 296, 298, 305-309
    see also Montgomery, Rachel
Bartholomew Family, George E.
  Amos (son), xvi, xix, 20, 154
  Ann (daughter), xvi
  David (son), xvi, xix, 159, 171
  Edmund "Ed" (son), xvi, 20-21, 26, 31-32, 37-38, 42-43, 97, 110, 113, 115-116, 120, 123, 131, 135, 145, 150, 161-162, 168, 180, 188, 257
    Floyd (son), 162, 226
    Mabel (daughter), 131
    Marion (son), 162, 168
    Myrtle (wife), 188
  Elam (son)
    see Bartholomew Family, Elam
  Elias "Eli" (son), xvi, xx, 10-11, 14-15, 19, 27, 30, 34-35, 57, 95, 103, 111, 116-117, 142, 180, 195, 237
    Bessie, 27, 180
    Etheleen, 27
  Emma "Em" (daughter), xvi, 20, 26-27, 31, 97, 110, 116, 120-121
    see also Hebrew, Emma
  Fanny (wife), xvii, 20, 26-27, 31, 43, 110, 115-118, 120-121, 150, 157, 168
    see also Bowman, Fanny
  Franklin "Frank" (son), xvi, 20, 31, 43-44, 75, 110, 115-116, 120, 163, 231, 233
  George (son), xvi, 4, 20-22, 26, 31, 37, 39, 97, 110, 116, 180, 246, 283
  George E. (husband), xvi-xvii, 20-22, 31, 35, 38, 103-105, 110, 113-117, 123, 141, 150, 157
  John (son), xvi, 4-5, 20, 22, 31, 39, 97, 116-117, 128, 168, 174
    Mary (wife), 22, 117, 168

Bartholomew, George W., 164
Bartholomew, Henry, xvi
Bartlett, Reverend Dr., 291
Barton, Dr., 272
Battle of the Argonne Forest, 227
Baxter, Mr., 238
Baylor, W., 304
Bennington, Lieutenant, 219
Benton
  County Superintendent, 99
  Otis, 224
Bethel
  Alice, 265
  Ellsworth (Professor), 151, 260, 262, 265
  Dorothy, 265
Bieber, C. D., 53
Bigge, George, 176
Bird, Chester, 227
Blake
  C. D. (Dr.), 182
  Michale, xx
Bland-Allison Act, 192
Blasdale, W. C., 242
Board of
  Foreign Missions, 306
  Home Missions, 306
Bobbitt, Clay (Reverend), 302, 304
Bollman, W. J. (Reverend), 278
Bolters ticket, 200
Book, Dr., 149, 153, 170
Borglum, Gutson, 175
Boss, Dr., 268
botany, xxii, 47, 63, 83, 129, 132, 141, 151-152, 155-156, 163, 167, 169-171, 174, 184, 217, 225, 231-237, 239-242, 244, 247, 249, 251-252, 254-255, 257-259, 261-262, 265-266, 268-269, 272-273, 299
Bow Creek Cemetery Association, 209
Bow Creek Telephone Association, 145
Bowen, Alma, 183
Bowman, Fanny, xvi
  see also Bartholomew, Fanny
box elder tree, 41, 51
Bracken
  Charles A., 54
  Mrs. Lucy G., 223, 306
  Newton, 132
  Theodore (Reverend Dr.), 111, 115, 121-122, 132, 140, 146, 160, 205, 234, 239, 245, 281-284, 287, 289-290, 295-296, 301-302
Brand
  Charles P. (Professor), 83
  C. J., 56
Breese, Assistant, 239
Bremgardt, Pauline, 183
Brenckle, J. F. (Dr.), 270
Brewer, Dr., 187
Briggs, Charles H., 255, 291-292

Brimmer, Jake, 128
Britton
  Mrs. N. L., 254
  N. L. (Dr.), 254-255
Brodbeck, Mr., 135
Broughton, William, 211
Brown
  Carl, 227
  Edgar, 56
  Ernest, 156-157
  W. B., 160
Bruce, B. K., 217
Bryan, William Jennings, 52, 192
Buchan, W. J., 216
Buckeye twin binder, 43
buckwheat, 3-4
Budd
  D. H., 47, 210
  John, 278
  Mrs., 278
buffalo, xii, xx, 15-17
Bulgaria, 226
Bulis, Tunis, 195
"Bull Moose" Party, 224
Bumpers brothers, 3, 104
  Irvin, 97
  Silas, 97
Burbridge farm, 1
Burchard, Reverend, 206
Burlingame, L. L. (Dr.), 260
Burt, E. A. (Dr.), 261
Burton
  J. R., 216
  J. W., 227
Buschman
  C. H., 203
  Chas. H., 203, 207

— C —
Cadorett, W. H., 144
Cain, Adah, 182-183
Caissman, Shirley, 183
California, 56-57, 65, 260
  Berkeley, 242, 260
  Fresno, 174
  Long Beach, 163
  Mill Valley, 260
  Mt. Tamalpais, 260
  Muir Woods, 260
  Pasadena, 304
  Riverside, 263
    Citrus Experiment Station, 263
  San Francisco, 163, 228, 260, 268, 270
    Golden Gate, 260
    World's Fair, 163, 260
  Sausilito, 260
  Stanford University, 168
    Hearst Memorial Hall, 260
    University Club, 260

Callender
  Dr. 149
  J. W., 207
Callendar and Dewey, 43
Calvin, John, xv
Canada, 244
  Ontario, 262
  Toronto, 146-147, 262
Capper, Arthur (Governor), 225
Carleton, Professor, 255
Carver, George Washington, 266
Catholic, xvi, 228
Catt, Carrie Chapman, 221
cattle, 45, 52-54, 91
  Holstein, 50
Central States Telephone and Power Co., 180
cherry orchard, 32, 51, 55, 59-62, 64, 77
Chambers, W. L., 133
Chautauqua, 147, 162, 296
Chicago Fire of 1871, 68
Choguill, Orlo (Reverend), 309
Christian, xv, 204, 216, 278, 280, 306
Civil War, xvi, xix, 2, 11, 105, 159, 181, 190-192, 194
Clark, Emerson, 129
Cleveland
  Grover, 205-206, 290-291
  Mrs., 290-291
Clift and Lewis attorneys, 20
Clothier, George L. (Professor), 244
coal, 1-2, 4, 35, 43-44, 261
Cobb, Benjamin, 233, 235
Cockerell, Dr., 270
Cody, W. F. "Buffalo Bill" (Colonel), xx-xxi, 174
Collins
  G. N. (Professor), 56, 254
  William, 25
Colorado, 151, 182, 223, 245-247, 252, 270, 304
  Boulder, 182, 247
    Protestant Hospital, 182
  Burlington, 166
  Colorado Springs, 245-246
  Colorado University, 270
    Hale Hall, 270
  Denver, 151, 163, 166-167, 182, 225, 245-246, 265, 303
    City Park, 151
    Congregational Church, 265
    Crown Hill Cemetery, 265
    Park Hotel, 245
    Union Station, 151, 245
  Gold Dirt Mine, 167
  Gunnison, 2465
  Iron Mountain Springs, 245-246
  Limon Junction, 166, 245
  Manitou, 245
  Marshall Pass, 246

Colorado *(continued)*
　　Moffat Road, 166
　　Penobscot Mining & Milling Co., 166-167
　　Pike's Peak, 245-246
　　Pueblo, 246
　　Rollinsville, 166-167
　　Salida, 246
Colorado Portland Cement Company, 164
Columbus, Christopher, 125
Confederate, 11
Congregational Church, 284, 294
Congressional Convention, 209, 224
Connally, William E., 268
Conwell, A. B. (Reverend), 123, 282
Cook
　　D. P. (Dr.), 145, 168
　　Ella Webber, 145
　　Florence, 145, 157, 169
　　　see also Bartholomew, Florence
　　Mrs. D. P., 176
　　O. F. (Professor), 255
　　R. R. (Professor), 170
Coolbaugh, M. J., 172
Coolidge, Calvin (President), 227
Cooper
　　Carl, 61
　　Harvey, 226
corn, 2-5, 8-9, 25, 35, 37, 41, 45-46, 48-49, 51,
　　54, 73, 76-77, 80, 87, 89-90, 95, 98, 101,
　　114, 188
　　Central American, 56
Corvett, J. S. (Professor), 307
cotton, 57
cottonwood tree, 15, 18, 36, 41, 44, 48, 51, 91,
　　134, 136
Coulter, J. M. (Dr.), 260
County Sunday School Association, 303-304
Coville, F. V., 241
Coy
　　Mrs. O. P., 122
　　O. P., 38, 207
Craig, Willis G., 290-291
Culbertson, G., 53
Cumbour, A. F. (Reverend), 209
Cummings Bros., 39
　　Den., 41
Cummins, George B. (Dr.), 248
Cunningham, Thomas, 45
Curtis, Charles, 216, 228
Custer, George (General), xx, 158
Custer's Last Stand, 17
Czechoslovakia
　　Weisskirchen, 269

— D —

Dahlgren, Helma, 302
Dakota: A Spiritual Geography, 33
Damon. W. E. (Dr.), 244
Dances with Wolves, xx

dark horse, 210
Darwin, Charles, 285
Davis
　　_____, 20
　　Loren L., 269
Dawes, F. C., 216
Dawson, John, 227
Day
　　Addie, 129
　　Charlie, 95, 100, 276
　　George, 3, 14, 94
　　Howard, 94-95, 97, 128, 276
Delay
　　J. W., 296
　　R., 211
Delta Epsilon, 273
de Médicis, Catherine, xv
Demo-Alliance, 217
democracy, 200
Democrat, 191, 205-206, 224, 227-228
Denney, J. C., 210
Denver-Kansas City commercial airplanes, 182
DeObert, Dr., 219
Department of Agriculture, 55
Devenney
　　Helen, 156
　　Sam, 156
DeVries, Mr., 163
Dewey, C. H., 23
diabetes, 181
diphtheria, xx
Dikeman
　　Lanta (Dunn), 129
　　Steve, 128
　　Will, 128
Dimler, Fred J., 269
Dirty Thirties, 92
Disler, J. H., 210
Dodge, Richard (Colonel), 16
Donnell
　　E. J. (Dr.), 199, 203-204
　　W. T., 204
Dorsett, P. H., 241
drought, 39, 51, 54, 70, 80, 86, 88-89, 123, 241
dry farming, 57
Duff
　　D. A., 15, 39, 181, 280
　　D.H., 101, 107
Duggar, B. M. (Dr.), 261
Dunn
　　Chas. N., 99
　　J. T., 99, 106
　　J. Y., 129
DuPree, Alma, 183
dust storm, 51, 73-74, 76-78, 80-82, 84, 86, 89-
　　93

— E —

Earle, F. S. (Professor), 245, 260

Earp, Wyatt, xx
earthquake, 70, 77
Eastern Establishment, 191
Eclipse generator, 172
Edwards, W. C., 217, 294
Egypt, 270
    Cairo, 269
        Egyptian Department of Agriculture, 269-
        270
electricity, 145
11th Kansas Volunteer Cavalry, 11
Elliott, John, 45
Ellis
    Cora, 254
    J. B. (Professor), 242, 245, 247-248, 251,
    254
England, xvi
Esbenshade
    Ben, 155
    John, 155
Eurasia, 89
Europe, 63, 225-226, 239, 249, 264
European, 247
Evans, C. J., 213
Everhart, Mr., 247-248
Everett, J. C. (Reverend), 160, 165, 295, 299,
    301
Ewing, R. H., 173
Extension Service, 44

— F —
Failyer, George H. (Professor), 232, 238
Fair Association, 55
Fairchild, George T., 46-47, 238
Fairman, C. E. (Dr.), 254
Farm Bureau, 55, 64
Farmer's Alliance, 212-216, 288
Farmer's Institute, 46-50, 236, 264
Farmers State Bank, 187
Farmer's Union, 55
Farnsworth, John, 203
Farr, George, 46, 133
Farrell
    F. D., 184, 266-268
    Mrs., 268
Fawcett, H. S. (Professor), 260
Feaster, W. D. (Reverend), 298
Ferguson, _____, 4
Fesler, C. A., 234
Fike
    Daniel, 285
    J. M., 208
Fink
    Celia, 67, 169
        see also Montgomery, Celia
    John D., 147, 169, 222
Fleming, Will, 22, 25
Flint, L. B., 293
flooding, 44, 55, 75, 81-83, 86, 92, 144

Flora of Kansas, 232, 235
Foote, 281
    Charles C., 14-16, 18, 20, 34-35, 103, 107-
    109, 117-118, 195, 281-282
    Kitty, 14, 18, 103, 109
    Mrs. Susan, 18, 43, 152, 154, 285
Forrey, Bert, 82
Foster
    A. S., 226
    Ilah, 302
    J. Ellen, 221
    W. E., 281
France, xv, 168, 227
    Arnas, 247
Free Silverites, 52, 192
free state, 190
French, Mim A., 195, 210
French's mill, 75, 208
Fuller, H. J. (Dr.), 113, 117, 203
fungi, 230, 235, 237, 241-242, 244-247, 249,
    252, 254-255, 257, 259, 261-266, 269, 272
    Diplodina Bartholomi, 236
    Kansas, 242, 244
    parasitic, 236, 238, 240
    specimen labels, 243
Fungi Columbiani, 85, 247-250, 252-253, 259,
    261, 264, 269-272
Fungi Malayana, 263

— G —
Galloway, B. T. (Professor), 241
Galvin, _____, 207
Garber, R. M., 56
Gardner, M. H., 280
Garfield, James A. (President), 204-205
Garlow, Mr., 172
Garrett, A. O. (Professor), 259-260
Garrison
    Dwight, 182
    Loyd, 182
Gartrell, John, 289
Garver, T. F., 217
Gates, F. C. (Dr.), 273
geology, 233
Geology, 233
George E. Bartholomew Scholarship, 164
Georgeson, C. C. (Professor), 46-47, 51, 237-
    238
Georgia, xix-xx
    Atlanta, 171, 175
    East Point, 159, 171
    Marietta, 170
        National Military Cemetery, 170
    Stone Mountain, 175
German, 225, 236
Germany, xvi, 225-226, 247
    Berlin, 266
germ theory, 47, 236-237, 240
Gibson, _____, 14

Gillenwaters, Miss, 170
Gilliland, I., 67
Glick, _____, 206
Glidden, Joseph F., 2
Goff, M. J., 182
gold, 50, 52
Gold Bonds, 180
Graham, Professor, 238
Granger, G. T., 211
Grant
    J. M., 270
    Ulysses S., 192, 194
grasshopper, 11, 37, 81
Green, John S., 1, 129
Greenback Party, 192, 206, 215
Greenbacks-Democratic Fusion ticket, 203
Griffen, W. R., 162, 257
Gross, John H. (Dr.), 308
Gulf of Mexico, 144
Gundogers, Michel (Dr.), 247
Guthrie, S. R., 118, 200, 202-203

— H —

Haberly, Reverend, 225
hackberry tree, 41
Hackmaster Bros., 288
Hackney, W. P., 216
Hale
    Alice, 153, 159
        see also Bartholomew, Alice
    W. H., 153, 159, 299-300
Hall, William, 211
Halley's Comet, 84
Hallowell, J. R., 216
Hamble, P. J., 167
Hamilton, _____, 213
Hamit, Chas., 300-301
Hampton, Frank, 246
Hanback, _____, 213
Harding, Warren G. (President), 227-228
"Hard-times" Social, 154
Haring, H. W. (Reverend), 155
Harkness
    _____, 3
    F. P., 144
Harper's Ferry, 130
Harrington, M. T. (Dr.), 14, 100
Harshbarger, W. A., 220
Hart, H. A., 204, 207
Haskin sisters, 129
Hastings, John, 36
Hawkes, S. N., 133
Hayes, President, 192
Hays, R. R., 133
header, 38-40
header box (header barge), 38-40
Hebrew, 26
    Alice, 159

Hebrew *(continued)*
    Emma, 31, 125, 159
        see also Bartholomew, Emma
    Evan, 26, 141
    James A., 21, 25-26, 36, 38-39, 109, 111-
        112, 208
    Jane, 282
    Jas, Sr., 41
    Kittie E., 282
    Mary E., 101, 111
    Mr., 26, 41
    Mrs. S. A., 121, 132, 205
    Samuel, 17, 38-39, 41-42, 107-109, 132,
        147, 203, 205, 282
    Samuel, Sr., 101, 111, 116, 280, 282
    William, 26-27, 39, 111-112, 132, 211
    W. J., 31, 159
Heiner, Glenn, 162
Henderson
    Professor, 270
    Mrs., 280
Herbarium
    cryptogamic, 272
    Elam Bartholomew's, 239, 257, 262-264,
        266, 270
    Stockton Academy, 239
herbarium specimen, 236
Herron, _____, 3
Hickok, "Wild Bill," xx
Higley, Brewster (Dr.), xxi
Hill
    F. P, 140, 211-212, 284
    H. M., 14
Hobson, Captain, 296
Hodgkin's Disease, 184-185
hogs, 4, 26-27, 36, 45-46, 48-52, 54, 91
Holland, xvi
Hollingsworth, _____, 147
Holt, Mr., 53, 222
Holway, E. W. D., 247, 255
"Home on the Range," xxi
Homestead Act, xvii, 11, 19
Homestead Certificate, 24
Hood, Professor, 238
Hoover, Herbert, 216, 228
Hopkin, Reverend, 265
Hopkins
    C. C., 296
    Winnie, 152
Horne, W. T. (Professor), 260
Howe, M. A. (Dr.), 254
Hubble, J. B., 211
Hughes
    Chas. E., 225
    D. W., 4
    J. W. F. (Colonel), 217
Huguenot, xv-xvi
Hulse, County Commissioner, 61
Humphries, John, 289

Hunter
  Henry, 3-4
  Jas. H., 129

— I —

Illinois, xiii-xix, 9, 11, 17, 20, 22, 25, 31-32,
  34-35, 44, 101, 125, 151, 156, 194, 198, 231,
  262, 265, 277, 280, 290
  Bushnell, 125
  Canton, 128
  Chicago, 50, 65, 68, 92, 125, 129-131, 146,
    153, 156-157, 160, 167, 210, 224-225,
    290, 300-301
    Board of Trade Building, 146
    Chicago Art Institute, 167
    Jackson Park, 129
    Lincoln Park, 146
    Marine training camp, 167
    McCormick Theological Seminary, 153,
      299, 301
    Montgomery Ward, 146
    Polk St. Depot, 147
    Presbyterian Hospital, 160
    Sears Roebuck, 146
    World's Fair, 50, 129, 131, 146
      Columbian Exposition, 125, 290
  Cuba, 128
  DeKalb, 44
  DeKalb County, 2
  Elmwood, 95
  Farmington, xvii-xviii, xx, 1-6, 9, 14, 20, 22,
    31, 47, 68-69, 89, 94-96, 98-100, 103,
    105-106, 110-112, 118-119, 128-129,
    132, 143, 169, 194, 198, 201, 203, 209,
    215, 251, 276, 278-281, 285, 289, 300,
    308
    Congregational Church, 279
    Methodist Church, 276-277, 279
    Presbyterian Church, 97, 100, 104, 128-
      129, 277-279, 282, 289
  Fulton County, 1, 11
  Galena, 194
  Galesburg, 14, 103, 106, 151, 303
  Good Hope, 125, 128
  Jacksonville, 149
  Lewistown, 99
  Liberty, 100, 103
  Littler's Creek, 1, 9
  Macon, 25
  Maquon, 99
  McDonough County, 31
  McLean County, 31
  Middlegrove, 176
  Monmouth, xx
  Mt. Pisgah, 99
  Peoria, xvii, 1, 4, 99
  Quincy, 14, 103, 106, 125
  Springfield, 194
  Troy Grove, xx

Illinois (continued)
  Williamsville, 244
  Yates City, 95, 98
Independent ticket, 195
Indian, xx, 11, 16-17, 19, 108, 158, 189
  Cheyenne, 19
  Commanche, xxi
  Crow Agency, 158
  Dakota, 158
    Sitting Bull (Chief), 158
  Kaw, 216
  Kiowa, xxi
  Omaha, 17
Indiana
  Garrett, 130
  Lafayette, 256, 259
  Michigan City, 167, 261
  North Baltimore, 130
  Purdue University, 248, 251, 259
Indian Territory, 19, 149
Industrial Revolution, xi, 93
influenza, 169
Ingle
  Chester, Jr. "Chettie," 8, 157, 160, 162
  Chester R., 8, 149-150, 153, 157, 159
  Elizabeth
    see also Bartholomew, Elizabeth
International Sunday School Convention, 146
Interurban train, 167
Iowa, xx, 133, 142
  Bedford, 22, 30, 133, 142
  Decorah, 247
irrigation system, 48, 51-52
Israel, 306
Isthmus of Panama, 268
Ives, Frank, 64

— J —

Jack
  Matthew, 129
  Samuel, 129
Jackson, H. S., 260
Jansen hot water treatment, 50
Jardine, Professor, 255
Jayhawks, xxi
Jenkins, Theresa, 221
Jerby, 118
  J. F., 300
  Mary C., 108
  N., 36
Jerold, Reverend, 108
Johnson, M. H., 210, 255
Johnston
  C. O. (Professor), 266
  Cora, 152
  Irene, 152
Jones
  _____, 147
  Frank, 156

Jones *(continued)*
  Isaac, 52
  John A. "Bub," 156
  Sarah, 156
Judeo-Christian, 294
Judd, C. P, 48

— K —

Kansas, xiii-xiv, xvii-xxi, 5, 9-13, 16-18, 20,
  22, 29, 31-34, 36, 44, 53, 55, 64, 70, 73, 76,
  78, 82, 85, 88, 93, 95, 100, 103-104, 106,
  114, 117, 128, 130-131, 144, 154, 167-168,
  176, 190, 192, 195, 198, 205-206, 208, 214-
  215, 217, 223, 225, 228, 231-234, 277, 279,
  284, 292, 297
  Abilene, xx
  Adamson, 48
  Alcona, 293
  Almena, 53
  Alton, 163, 207, 300
  Amboy, 234
  Armourdale, 47
  Asherville, 283
  Beloit, 232, 283
  Bethany, 283
  Bethel
    Bethel School, 152
  Big Creek, 92, 272, 290
  Blue Rapids, 53
  Bogue, 66-67
  Bow Creek, 15, 17, 35-36, 51, 69, 75, 81-82,
    85, 86-87, 136, 181, 263
  Bow Creek (township), 10, 14, 25, 60, 67,
    101, 107, 131, 161, 182, 195, 197-198,
    200, 288, 294
    Methodist Church, 282
    Presbyterian Church, 282
  Bow Creek Cemetery, 122-123, 125, 143,
    154, 172, 175, 188, 209
  Box Elder Creek, 50
  Brightwood, 291
  Brittain school house, 296
  Bull's City, 207
  Burlingame, 11
  Calvert, 53
  Cawker City, 22-23, 283, 287
  Cedarville, 283
  Circleville, 10
  Clay Center, 144, 156, 168-169, 176
  Clinton, 61
  Clyde, 166, 168, 175
  Colby, 212, 214, 307
    Opelt House, 212
  Collyer, 183
  Concordia, 209
  Covert, 183
  Cuba, 260
  Decatur County, 19, 213
  Deer Creek, 280

Kansas *(continued)*
  Delphos, 283
  Dibble Creek, 132
  Dodge City, xx
  Downs, 283
  Ellis, 234
  Ellis County, 208, 234
  Ellsworth, 309
  Ellsworth County, 212-213
  Emporia, 132, 143-146, 149, 153, 164, 222,
    252, 284, 297
    College of Emporia, 132, 144, 153, 164,
      273, 294, 297, 299, 307
    State Normal School, 143-144, 151, 156,
      252, 294, 297
  Fairport, 309
    Presbyterian Church, 309
  Farmington, 223, 288
    Sunday School Association, 288
    Township Board, 61
  Fort Hays, xx, 152, 290
  Fort Hays Kansas State College, 270, 308-
    309, 311
  Fort Riley, 226
    Camp Funston, 226
    Cantonment, 226
  Gaylord, 283
  Glade, 57, 164, 182
    Taylor Hotel, 57
  Glasco, 159, 283, 303
    Presbyterian Church, 303
  Glen Elder, 22, 140, 283, 296
  Gove County, 213
  Graham County, 67
  Greenfield, 285
  Halstead, 184
    Hirschler Hospital, 184
  Hamilton, 234
  Harlan, 283
  Harvey County, 184
  Hays City, xx, 14, 16, 18, 20-21, 66-67, 91-
    92, 103, 106, 113, 132, 144, 152, 181-183,
    185, 269-273, 290, 307-309
    Agricultural Experiment Station, 152
    Boot Hill, 152
    First National Bank, 183
    Presbyterian Church, 308-309
    Reeder's Addition, 182
    Sheridan Coliseum, 184
    State Normal School, 152
    State Teachers College, 182, 264, 272
  Hebrew Cemetery, 116, 122, 282
  Hiawatha, 138-140
    Hiawatha Academy, 138
  Hill City, 83-84, 289, 298
  Holton, 10
  Howard, 168, 174
  Hoxie, 307
  Independence, 232

Kansas (continued)
  Iowa Township, 223
  Jewell County, 31, 213
  Junction City, 144, 226, 306
  Kansas City, 26, 82, 222, 236, 284
  Kill Creek, 300
  Kirwin, 20-22, 24, 44, 54, 75, 78, 101-102,
    108, 112-113, 202, 205-206, 208, 210,
    280, 283
    Chicago Lumber Yards, 208, 300
  Lanark Township, 138, 141, 223
    Trasher-Lambert School, 138
  Lansing, 176
  Lawrence, 132, 304
    Kansas University, 235
  Leavenworth, xx, 195
  Lenora, 210
  Liberal, 150-151, 153
  Liberty, 277
  Lincoln County, 52
  Lincoln Park, 296
  Logan, 25, 53, 144, 300
  Logan County, 213
  Long Island, 53
  Lost Creek, 234
  Louisville, 14, 19, 26-27, 31, 111, 117, 124-
    125, 142, 150, 168, 180, 237
  Manhattan, 26-27, 46, 51, 57, 64, 236-238,
    244, 261, 266-267, 269-270
    Kansas Academy of Science, 261
    Kansas State College, 237
    Kansas State University, 230, 233, 240
      Herbarium, 230
    Shamrock Inn, 266
    State Agricultural College, 27, 46, 57,
      173, 232, 237, 244, 266-267, 269
      Botanical Department, 173
      Horticultural Department, 46, 238, 266-
      267
  Marion Centre, 284
  Marshall, 288
  Martin, 18, 107
  Marvin, 42, 44-46, 54, 76-77, 83, 139-140,
    142, 153-154, 209, 211, 232
  Medicine Creek, 280
  Medicine Lodge, xxi
  Minneapolis, 159, 283
  Mitchell County, 22, 213
  Morland, 298
  Mt. Lebanon, 286, 295
    school, 140
  Mt. Nebo, 86, 89, 153, 225, 295, 300-303,
    305, 307, 309
    Mt. Nebo Church, 158, 304-306
    Presbyterian Church, 303
  Munjor, 290
  Natoma, 297
  Nicodemus, 276, 289
  Norton, 295

Kansas (continued)
  Norton County, 53
  Oakley, 51
  Oberlin, 175-176, 179-181, 187, 209-210,
    224, 268
  Oronoque, 210
  Osage County, 11, 216
  Osborne, 48, 165, 210, 281, 295, 299, 309
  Osborne County, 208
  Palco, 63
  Paola, 237
  Peabody, 284
  Phillipsburg, 11, 26, 53, 56, 63, 83, 124, 132,
    140, 146, 153, 160, 162, 164-165, 182,
    185, 188, 239, 245, 252, 256, 263, 281,
    295-296, 299, 301, 302, 306
    Presbyterian Church, 160, 165, 281, 302,
    306
  Phillips County, 53, 69, 103, 208, 296
  Plainview, 296
  Plainville, 20-21, 135, 144, 153, 204, 207,
    210, 212, 234-234, 299
    Clark Hotel, 135
    Presbyterian Church, 299
  Pleasant Hill, 278, 300
  Pleasant Valley, 293
  Pottawatomie County, 14, 26, 31, 111, 132,
    142
  Prairie Dog Creek, 53
  Rawlins County, 19
  Reno County, 216
  Rexford, 297
  Rockport, 39, 107, 113, 118, 142, 195, 198,
    221-222, 281, 285, 299
    Rockport Post Office, 147
  Rooks County, xiv, 10-11, 25, 29-31, 47-48,
    50, 52, 79, 84, 100, 107, 174, 180, 195-
    197, 199, 203-204, 208, 210, 212-213,
    215, 222-223, 234-235, 239, 264, 266,
    291, 293, 296, 309
    Rooks County Fair, 131
  Royal Neighbor camp, 140
  Rush, 141
  Russell, 51, 183-184
  Russell County, 309
  Salina, 180, 183, 273, 283-284
    Hassler Book Bindery, 273
    Presbyterian Church, 283
    Synod of Kansas, 282, 284
  Saline County, 283
  Sand Creek, 234
  Sayler, 102-103, 107, 279, 281
  Sharon Springs, 223
  Sheridan County, 19, 209
  Sherman County, 213
  Smith Center, 226, 281
  Smith County, xxi, 214, 283
  Solomon, 159, 166, 282
    North, 109

Kansas *(continued)*
  Solomon *(continued)*
    Valley, 283
  Stockton, xviii, 10, 14-15, 17-18, 20-21, 25, 28-30, 38-39, 41-47, 50, 52, 54-56, 60-61, 63-65, 75, 80, 85, 88, 90, 100-103, 107, 112, 118-120, 123-124, 131-133, 135-136, 140, 143-145, 147, 149-150, 152, 180-182, 188, 195, 198, 200, 202-205, 207-212, 214, 221-223, 225, 227-228, 231, 233-237, 239-242, 248, 252, 257, 259, 265, 269, 271, 284, 287, 293, 296-297, 300-301, 303-304, 309
    Christian Church, 153
    Commercial House, 25, 233-234
    Congregational Church, 133, 233-234, 242
    Coolbaugh Banking Institution, 180
    Coolbaugh Motor Co., 173
    Griffen and Beckley, 166
    Griffen Garage, 160
    Hotel Hicks, 46
    Kay and Snyder, 60
    Maxwell Auto, 160
    Methodist Church, 287
    Robinson and Smith, 64
    Stockton Academy, 132-134, 293, 241
      see also Herbarium
    Stockton High School, 151
    Stockton National Bank, 66, 172, 180, 300
    Stockton Telephone Exchange, 161
  Sugar Loaf, 23, 25, 47-48, 236, 289
  Thomas County, 297
  Topeka, xii, 27, 52, 55, 159, 169-170, 181, 187, 195, 216-217, 224-226, 264, 266, 268, 272, 309
    First Presbyterian Church, 309
    Grand Opera House, 225
    Kansas Academy of Science, 217
    North, 170
      Topeka High School, 170
    Second Presbyterian Church, 187
    State Board of Agriculture, 52, 55
    Third Presbyterian Church, 187
    Throop Hotel, 268
    Washburn College, 218
    Washburn University, 224
      Benton Hall, 224
  Twin Mound, 204
  Wabaunsee, 26-27
  Wabaunsee County, 26
  Wakarusa, 187
  Wakeeney, 292, 306
  Waldo, 183
  Wallace County, 213
  Walton, 234
  Wamego, 27, 237
  Waterville, 283

Kansas *(continued)*
  Webster, 67, 119, 143, 234
    Commercial House, 119
  western, 31, 38, 49, 55, 57, 69-71, 73, 76, 80, 93, 100, 120, 158, 204
  Wichita, xx, 31, 67, 120, 236
    Federal Land Bank Corporation, 67
    Wichita Acetylene Light Company, 163
  Woodman camp, 140
  Wyandotte, 222, 235
Kansas
  Academy of Science, 64, 266
  Compiled Laws of 1879, 202
  General Statutes of Kansas, 202
  Legislature, 222
  Revised Statutes of 1879, 200-202
  State Board of Agriculture, 12
  State Historical Society, xiii-xiv, 266, 268
  Statutes of 1868, 202
Kay, _____, 147
Kedzie, Mrs. 238
Keeler, Reverend, 298
Kellerman
  Mrs., 237, 239
  Wm. A. (Professor), 232-233, 235-239, 255
Kelley
  Dan, xxi
  J. B., 49
Kent, Professor, 152
Kentucky, xxi, 174, 255, 265
Kerr, L. A. (Reverend), 306
Killam
  Lizzie, 167
  Nelson, 167
King
  Mr., 221
  Mrs., 221
King Charles IX, xv
Kirkpatrick, Mr., 66
Kirwin Chief, xxi
Kizer, Frank, 293-294
Kling
  D. G (Reverend), 280
  John, 15, 101, 108, 280
Knaus, Dr., 268
Knouse, Elizabeth
  see also Montgomery, Elizabeth
Koch, Robert, 236-237

— L —

Laird, Dan, 153
Laire, Abram, 60
Lake Michigan, 167, 261
Lambert
  B. G., 139
  Fred, 160
Lampe, J. J. (Dr.), 291
Landreth, _____, 211
Lantz, Professor, 238

LaRue, H., 52
Lease, Mary E., 221
LeConte, _____, 233
Lee
    Dean, 184
    F. B., 187
Leeper
    Isaac, 5
    John, 5, 103
Leigh, W. A. (Dr.), 120-121, 123, 211
Lewis, W. A. (Dr.), 187, 184
Liberty Loan Bonds, 172, 180
Lincoln, Abraham, xx, 191, 194, 217
Lindsay, Hank, 218-219
Lloyd, C. G., 244, 255
Lloyd's Mycological Notes, 255
Locke, J. T., 211-212
locust tree, 51
Loggan, Mr., 280
Long, C. I., 216, 255
Lovells
    _____, 43, 74
    Mary, 286
Low, Walter, 266
Lynch, J. B., 217

— M —

Manners, J. W., 139
Marconi, Guglielmo, 199
marker, 2
Marshall
    Henry, 300
    John, 15, 129
    J. R., 195
    L. L., 226
    Luther, 45
    Mack, 39
Martin, Frank L., 216
Maryland
    Anacostia, 255
    Cabin John Bridge, 255
    Cumberland, 130
    Georgetown, 255
    Lanham, 254-255
    Potomac Valley, 130
Mason, S. C., 46, 56, 237-238, 255
Mason & Dickson line, 228
Massachusetts
    Wellesley, 269
        Wellesley College, 269
Masterson, Bat, xx
Mathes, A. R. (Reverend), 104, 106, 128, 280-
    281
May
    Mrs. T. R., 271
    T. R., 160
Mayhew, Frank, 246
McAfee, J. B. (Lieutenant), 11
McBreen, T. C., 203

McCabe, F. S. (Reverend), 216
McCauley, J. W., 182
McCleave
    David (Reverend), 186, 308
    Mrs., 186
McCollum, U.S., 210
McComb
    Lizzie, 26, 31
        see also Montgomery, Lizzie
    Millard M., 25-26, 31
McCook, J. J. (Colonel), 291-292
McCroskey, Jas., 84
McCue, Thomas, 57
McEndaffer
    Jas., 211
    Mrs., 211
McKeighan, Alex, 104
McKenzie, Wyatt, 227
McKinley, William, 52, 143, 192, 223
McLennan, _____, 213
McMillan
    E. N., 211
    I. C., 210
    Lee, 46
McMillen, Pearl, 17
McNall, Webb, 213-214
McNulty
    _____, 101
    grove, 162, 214
McNutt
    N. R., 47
    W. R., 47-48, 210-212
Mead
    Chas., 140
    Mrs., 149
Meade, Dr., 182
Meinecke, E. P. (Dr.), 260, 270
Melchers, L. E. (Professor), 173, 266, 270
Mellon, 293
    J. M., 21, 39, 44, 49, 140, 198
    Mrs. J. M., 115, 117
Merimac, 296
Merrill
    Cap, 128
    Henry, 9
Messinger, Mary, 108, 196
Metcalf, Haven, 260
Methodist, 282
Michigan, 261
Mickel, G. N., 211
microscope, Spencer Lens Co., 259
Millburn, Andy, 156
Miller
    Charles H., 201, 203
    E. C. (Professor), 266-267, 269
    J. H., 57
    John C. (Reverend), 160
    Mrs. W. F., 121, 124
    W. F., 46, 91, 120, 140, 145

mimeograph, 244
Minnesota, 256
　Rochester, 184-185
　　Mayo Brothers, 184
　St. Paul, 307
Missouri
　Columbia, 166
　Hannibal, 14
　Hopkins, 167
　Kansas City, 14, 106, 184, 272
　Maryville, 167
　Parnell, 147
　Savannah, 147
　St. Joseph, xx, 14
　St. Louis, 145, 244, 249, 251, 261, 298, 304
　　Edison Hotel, 298
　　Missouri Botanical Garden, 244, 249,
　　　251, 261
　　Union Depot, 298
　　World's Fair, 145, 249
　　　Louisiana Purchase Exposition, 145
Mohler, Martin, 214
Montana, 158-159, 264
　Billings, 159
Montgomery, 29-30, 104, 278, 289
　A. B., 203-204
　Celia (daughter), 147
　　see also Fink Celia
　Ed (nephew), 129, 170, 257
　　Raymond (son), 257
　Elizabeth (wife), 6, 128, 132, 142, 149
　　see aslo Knouse, Elizabeth
　Fannie, 167
　　see also Sparks, Fannie
　Frank (nephew), 128
　George K. (son), 47, 129, 176
　　Hattie (wife), 176
　Jim (son), 129
　Lizzie (daughter), 25, 99, 167
　　see also McComb, Lizzie
　Rachel I. (daughter), 5-6, 14, 97-100, 104-
　　105
　　see also Bartholomew, Rachel
　Robert "Rob" (son), 22-23, 25, 30-31, 48,
　　121, 123, 133, 142, 147, 167
　　Addie, 167
　　Beryl, 167
　　Garland, 167
　　Tom (son), 31
　　Will (son), 31
　Thomas (husband), 3, 6, 98-100, 103-105,
　　112-113, 128-129, 142-143, 277-279
　Thomas "Tommy, Tom" (son), 22-23, 25,
　　31, 122, 129, 142, 147
　Tillie (niece), 225
　Will (son), 22-23, 25, 30-31, 47, 133
　　Addie (wife), 30
　　Fanny (daughter), 30
　　Lizzie (daughter), 30

Moore, 306
　D. J., 200
　R. F., 217
　S. J. S., 306
Morgan
　A. P. (Professor), 240
　Olney, 129
　W. Y., 268
Morrill, _____, 216
Morris, Dr., 187
Movie (moving pictures), 151
　talkie show, 182
Mugwumps, 206
Muir
　A. G., 198, 200-202
　A. J., 200
Mullen, John, 210
Murdock, Victor, 216, 225
Murrill, W. A. (Dr.), 254
Mycological Index, 257
mycology, 235, 237, 244, 247-248, 250-251,
　255, 270-271, 313

— N —

Nance, Reverend, 305-306
Nash, Mary, 140-141, 296
Nation
　Carry A., xxi
　David, xxi
National American Woman Suffrage Associa-
　tion, 221
National Food Co., 147
National League of Women Voters, 221
National Tire, 183
Nebraska, 17, 56, 158, 187
　Alma, 165
　　Moore Garage, 165
　Bertrand, 165
　Custer County, 211
　Franklin, 302
　Lexington, 165
　Lincoln Highway, 165-166
　Omaha, 166
　necktie party, 282
Nevada, 259
New Champion grain binder, 55
New England, 262
New Hampshire
　Dartmouth College, 204
New Jersey, 247
　Camden, 2545
　New Brunswick, 269
　　Rutgers College, 269
　Newfield, 242, 245, 251, 254
　Vineland, 254
New York, 45, 206, 221, 223, 238, 244, 262,
　271, 291
　Alcove, 242
　Brooklyn, 269

New York *(continued)*
  Buffalo, 223, 259
  Ithaca, 244
  Lyndonville, 254
  New York City, 155, 254
    Brooklyn Bridge, 155
    Bronx Park, 254
    New York Botanical Garden, 254-255,
      259, 270
    Wall Street, 155, 176, 271
    Westfield subway station, 255
    Zoological Park, 255
  Niagra Falls, 147
  Tammany Hall, 228
New Zealand
  Nelson, 270-271
    Cawthron Institute, 270-271
Nicodemus, A., 207
Nield, J. A. (Reverend), 133
Noonan, Jimmy, 41
Norris, Kathleen, 33
North America, 16, 264, 268
North American Fungi, 247
North American Uredinales (NAU), 256, 259,
  262-264, 269, 272
North Carolina
  Asheville, 259
  Biltmore, 259
    Biltmore Estate, 259
  West Raleigh, 259
    Agricultural Experiment Station, 259
Noyce, John W., 274

— O —

O'Connor, Jas., 63
Ohio, xix, 10, 130, 174, 194, 231, 244, 255
  Cincinnati, 242, 244, 255, 262
    Lloyd Bros. Chemical laboratory, 255
    Lloyd Bros. Wholesale Druggists, 242
  Columbus, xvii
  Delaware County, 156
  Granville, xvii-xviii, 1, 155, 159
  Johnstown, 156
  Licking County, xvii
  Newark, 130, 155
  New-way, 156
  Preston, 240
oil belt, 130
Oklahoma, 140, 149, 264
  Chickasha, 149
  Tulsa, 180
Oldfield, Nelson, 4
Oregon
  Portland, 163, 261
    Alberta Street car, 163
    Scribner Bros., 163
Osage Orange shrub, 44
Osborne
  Edith, 163

Osborne *(continued)*
  Nate, 163
  Oxford Teachers Bible, 125
  Oyster, J. H. (Dr.), 237

— P —

Parker, John H. (Professor), 269
Pasteur, Louis, 236-237
Patchin, A. L., 201, 204
Patterson
  G. W., 14, 35, 195
  Joseph (Reverend), 285
  Mrs. M. J., 284
peach orchid, 64, 83
Pennell, F. W. (Dr.), 259
Pennsylvania, xix
  Bingham Center, 11
  Conestoga Creek, 155
  Lampeter Square, 155
  Lancaster, 155, 254
    James Buchanan Monument, 155
    Memorial Presbyterian Church, 155
  Lancaster County, xvi, 276
  Philadelphia, xvi, 154, 254, 281, 299, 305,
    308
    Bethany Presbyterian Church, 299
    Independence Hall, 154
    Witherspoon building, 154
  Pittsburgh, 130
    Monongahela House, 130
  Potter County, 11
  Strasburg, xviii, 155, 276
Pennsylvania Dutch, xvi, 276
Petrak, F. (Dr.), 269
petroleum industry, 43, 65
Philippines, 262-263
phonograph, 151-152
  Edison, 172
Picken, Superintendent, 152
Pickens, J. W., 300
Pickle, R. M. (Judge), 133
Pierce, Superintendent, 170
Plank, E. N. (Professor), 232-236
plum tree, 18, 51, 54, 65, 83
  Laire plum, 60
  Layer plum, 56
Polyhymnian art, 110
Pony Express, xx
Poponoe, E. A. (Professor), 238
poplar tree, 51
Populist, 217
potato, 3, 9, 35, 54, 76
  sweet, 44, 50-51, 54, 78
Potter, John, 211
prairie fire, 11, 15, 17, 35, 69-70, 73-77, 83
prairie hay, 52
Prather, Van B., 214
Presbyterian, 106, 164, 175, 282, 284, 292,
  299, 309

Presbyterian *(continued)*
  Church, 145, 292
  College, 284, 294
  General Assembly, 130, 180, 241, 261, 268, 290-292, 304-305, 307
Presbyterian Board of Publications and Sabbath School Work, 295
Price, Professor, 266
Princeton Seminary, 307
Privett
  Mrs. Willis, 135, 152
  Sarah, 41, 108, 151-152
  W. C., 41
  Willis, 107, 152
Progressive Party, 224-225
prohibition, xxi, 192, 205-206, 228-229
  National, 304-305
Prohibition Party, 205-206
Protestant, xv-xvi, 277, 284
Public Utilities Bond, 180
Puerto Rico
  Mayaguez, 257

— R —

racial segregation, 298
radio, 180, 199
Railroad, 44
  B & O, 130, 154
  C. B. & Q., 103, 128
  Central Iowa, 128
  D. & R. G., 245-246
  Kansas Pacific, 14, 106, 283
  Missouri Pacific, 208
  Narrow Gauge, 128
  Pennsylvania, 155
  Rock Island, 151, 239
  T. P. & W., 125, 128
  U. P., 268, 283
Ramaley, Dr., 270
Ramey
  Alice, 156
  Elizabeth, 156
  Gifford, 156
Ramsey, Sheriff, 102
Randall, E. F., 212
Rankin, Roy, 187
Rarick, C. E. (Dr.), 187, 309, 311
Red Cross, 226
Reddish, Josh, 252
Reed
  County Commissioner, 174
  Tillie, 294
Reeder, W. A., 224
Republican, 194-195, 200, 203-204, 206, 210-212, 214-217, 223-225, 227-228
Republican National Convention, 224
Reville, M. C., 207
Richards
  Ed, 41

Richards *(continued)*
  John, 41
Richardson, Jim, 207
Richmond, F. E. (Dr.), 181
Ridenour, Mr., 290
Ritchie, Ora, 53, 222
River
  Kansas, 27
  Mississippi, 14, 284
  Monongahela, 130
  Paradise, 18
  Platte, 165
  Potomac, 255
  Saline, 18, 20-21, 103, 107, 144, 234, 283
  Smoky Hill, 283
  Solomon, 18, 41, 75, 124
    North Fork, 18
  Spoon, 99, 105
  Yohoghany, 130
Robbins
  C. R., 78
  Raymond, 225
Roberts, Ed, 282
Robinson
  County Commissioner, 174
  John, 30
Rocky Mountains, 245
Rodeheaver, Homer, 303, 309
Rooks, John Calvin, 11
Rooks County Farmers Institute, 57
Rooks County Record, 102, 211
Roosevelt
  Franklin D., 229
  Theodore "Teddy," 223-224
Rose
  E. M., 129
  Emma (Dunn), 129
Rowland, F. M., 20
rural mail delivery, 147
Rusler
  H. B., 156
  Mrs. H. B., 156
Russian, 290
Russian thistle, 89
rust, prevention of, 239-241, 245, 248, 255, 271
Ryan, Nat, 155
Rydberg, P. A. (Dr.), 254
rye, 3-4, 36-37, 43-44, 50, 52, 55, 76, 120

— S —

Sanford, W. C., 200, 202
Sayler, B. F., 103
Schiesser, Reverend, 280
Schneider, A. G., 227
Schueler, Claire, 272
Scofield, C. S. (Professor), 254
Scott, Professor, 64
Seaver
  Fred J. (Professor), 254, 270

Seaver *(continued)*
  Mrs., 270
self-binder, 3
7th Regiment Band of New York, 131
76th Ohio Volunteer Infantry, 159, 171
  Company B, 171
Sharp
  Aldus, 222
  W. D., 10, 53
Shaw
  Dan, 82
  Jack, 140, 173
  Tom, 226
Shear, C. L. (Professor), 242, 247, 254, 260
Sheibley, John, 75
Sheldon, Chas. M., 216
Shell
  Hiram, 21
  Jacob, 70, 196
  Mrs. Jacob, 115, 118-119, 124
  Sam, 19, 120
  S. T., 121
shelterbelt, 73
Shepard, Deputy, 102
Sherman
  Eli, 46-47, 49
  F. E. (Reverend), 231, 233, 240, 284, 306
  William T. (General), xix, 159, 171
Sherman Silver Purchase Act, 192
Shirley, J. P., 200
Shockley, Reverend, 245
Shope, Paul F. (Professor), 270
silver, 50
Simkins, W. A. (Reverend), 283
Simms, Harry, 54
Simpson, John, 129
Singapore Island, 262-263
  Malay Peninsula, 263
Skinner, Mr., 309
slave state, 190
slavery, 276
  anti, xxi
Small, J. K. (Dr.), 254
Smith
  Al, 228
  A. W., 216-217
  C. O. (Professor), 260
  C. W., 199
  D. C., 160
  E. E., 222
  Erwin F. (Professor), 241
  G. A., 204
  I. C., 30
  J. Frank, 304
  J. G., 210
  Judge, 80
  Laf. C., 19, 199, 201-203
  O. L., 215
  R. E., 260

Smyth, B. B., 217
Snow, F. H. (Professor), 240
Snyder
  Grace, 103
  Mr., 47
Sorehead ticket, 199-202
Sousa, John Phillip, 131
South America, 264
Southard, 43
  J. A., 103, 201-202
  Mrs. J. A., 18
  Myrtle, 123, 286
  Summer, 18, 26, 121
  W. S., 226
South Dakota, 17
  Black Hills, 174
  Edgemont, 158
  Northville, 270
Southern Confederacy, 175
Spalding, Reverend, 188
Sparks
  Alva, 167
  Fannie
    see also Montgomery, Fannie
  Judge, 176
Spears, Mrs., 167
Speer, Dr., 180
Stahl, William, 241
Stalwarts, 206
State Institute Association, 57
Steck, Mr., 129
Stephen
  B. D., 66-67
  Mrs., 66
Stevens, F. L. (Dr.), 257
Stevenson, Thomas (Reverend), 277
Steward, Charles, 15
Still, Fred, 43
St. John, John P. (Governor), 205-206
Stockman, Bill, 190
Stockton Educational Association, 133
Stockton News, 199
Stoddard, Elijah, 211
Streeter, F. D., 187
Strong, Justice, 291
Stroup, 159
  Elmer S., 111-112
  Jas., 147
  J. T., 113
Sunday, Billy, 151, 303
Sunday school, 277, 279-281, 286-288, 293-
  299, 305, 308
Sunday School Association, 285
Sunderland, Reverend Dr., 291
sunflowers, 34
Sutor, H. T., 63
Sutton, W. B., 51
Sweden
  Stockholm, 249

Swingle, W. T. (Professor), 238-239, 252, 254-255
Switzerland, xvi
Sydow
　　H., 266
　　P. (Professor), 247

— T —

Taft, President, 224
tame grasses, 44
Tax Payer's League, 227
Taylor, George P., 160
Teachers Examining Board, 198
telegraph, 199
telephone, 144-145
television, 145
temperance, 279, 309
　　Blue Ribbon, 281
Tenley, Jas., 129
Tennessee, 259, 265
Texas, 264
　　Austin, 164
Thayer, Caleb, 234
The Bartholomew Family, 164
The Descent of Man, 285
The Home Visitor (Farmington, IL), 251
The Origin of Species, 285
The Stockton News, 199
The Stockton Record, 23, 130
The Timber-Culture Act, 73
Thomas
　　County Commissioner, 61, 174
　　Mr., 115-116
　　W. S., 190, 201
Thompson, Mr., 238
Thrasher, R. D., 139
threshing, 9, 37, 39, 41, 50, 55, 70, 120
　　machine, 3, 39-40, 42
　　　　Elliott and Potter, 50
Tillotson, T. T., 204
Tilton, W. S., 48
Tinker, Professor, 64
Titus, William F., 200, 202, 211
Toepffer, Mr. H. V., 47, 50
Topeka State Journal, 169
tornado, 91
Torrens, Jas., 129
Totten, C. W., 172
Townsley, Phil, 53
Travis, J. S., 209
Trelease, William (Dr.), 244, 249, 251
Turner, E. J., 209, 213-214
typewriter, Royal, 180

— U —

Underwood, L. M. (Dr.), 244
Uniformed State Guards, 226
Union, xix-xx, 171, 191, 259, 267, 304
　　Army, xix-xx, 154-155

Union Labor Party, 215
United Brethren, 280
United States, xix-xx, 74, 87, 225, 228, 239, 244, 305
　　Army, 16
　　Cavalry, xx, 16-17
　　Congress, 74, 191-192, 209, 215, 221, 229, 276
　　　　House of Representatives, 74
　　　　Senate, 74
　　Constitution, 191, 229
　　　　17th Amendment, 191
　　　　18th Amendment, 229
　　　　19th Amendment, 276
　　Department of Agriculture, 56-57, 60, 83, 130, 239-241, 254-255, 261, 290
　　　　Division of Vegetable Pathology, 240
　　　　Experiment Station, 238
　　Supreme Court, 227, 291
United Telephone Co., 173
University of Illinois, 64
University of Wisconsin, 162
Utah
　　Ogden, 259

— V —

Vanderbilt, George W., 259
Van Horn, John, 241
Vestergran, Tycho (Professor), 249
Victorian era, xiii
Viers, Harley, 147
Virginia, 254

— W —

Walker
　　B. P., 268, 271
　　J. C. (Reverend), 287
Wallace
　　County Commissioner, 61
　　Florence, 176
Wallen, S. S. (Reverend), 292
walnut tree, 42, 51
Wanamaker, John, 299
War Bond, 226
Ward
　　H. B. (Dr.), 64
　　S. J. (Reverend), 160
Washington
　　Bremerton, 157, 159
　　Marysville, 270
　　Pullman, 264
　　　　State College of Washington, 264
　　Seattle, 153
Washington, D.C., 56, 60, 83, 125, 130, 154, 224, 241, 252-253, 255, 261-262, 290, 292, 299
　　Department of Agriculture
　　　　see United States
　　New York Ave. Presbyterian Church, 290-291

Washington, D.C. *(continued)*
  White House, 290-291
watermelon, 64
Watkins, Mrs., 288, 293
Watson
  Bros., 234
  Ed, 234-234
  Thos., 101
  W. W., 210
Webbert, C. R., 212
Webster, F. S. (Dr.), 131
Wells, T. W. (Professor), 272
"Western Home", xxi
West Indies, 268
West Virginia, 174
  Grafton, 262
  Parkersburg, 262
  Wheeling, 130
Wetherilt, William, 101
wheat, 2-3, 9, 37, 40-44, 50-51, 54-55, 61, 63-
  65, 70, 75, 93, 114, 208, 232, 239-241
  fall, 39
  winter, 9, 87
Wherrey, Mr., 167
Whitaker, Frank, 128
White
  Albert, 144, 146, 165
  E. F., 200
  Emma Lillian (Lily), 147, 158, 302
  Howard, 57
  R. P. (Professor), 173, 238, 266
  Ruby, 302
  Thomas, 283
  William Allen, 225
Whitsett
  Carl, 182
  Mrs., 182
Wichita acetylene gas generator, 172
Wight, W. F., 60
Wilcoxen, _____, 281
Wilkerson, Sheriff, 220
Wilkin, Stephen, 44, 75, 207
Willard, J. T. (Dean), 267
Williams
  H. E., 18-19, 102, 107, 202
  Hugh, 102
  Mrs. H. E., 102-103

Wilson
  A. B., 48, 121, 124, 147, 211, 214, 221, 288
  A. D., 99, 106
  A. S., 164
  H. B., 240
  Henry, 194
  Mrs. A. B., 121-122, 124, 214, 221
  Woodrow, 224
Wilsonism, 227
wind break, 81
wind erosion, 93
windmill, 64, 87, 91
Wisconsin
  Madison, 156, 168, 261-263
  Ripon, 221
  State University, 156
Woman's Presbyterial Missionary Society, 306
woman suffrage, 221, 276
Wood, Colonel, 171
Woods
  Doc, 45
  Ralph, 47
Wooster, L. D. (Professor), 264, 273
World Sunday School Convention, 154, 224,
  253, 299
World War I, 87, 227
woven wire, 2
Wright, _____, 216
Wright's nursery, 129
Wyoming, 64, 158, 164-165, 174, 221
  Burns, 61, 166
  Carpenter, 166
  Casper, 180
  Cheyenne, 166
  Cody, 174
  Ogallala, 166
  Thermopolis, 174

— Y —

Yeager, Tressie, 183
Young
  Bradley, 180
  F. E., 182
  J. E. (Reverend), 281

— Z —

Zollers, John, 54